The Red Rooster Scare

The Red Rooster Scare

Making Cinema American, 1900–1910

Richard Abel

UNIVERSITY OF CALIFORNIA PRESS

Berkeley   Los Angeles   London

University of California Press
Berkeley and Los Angeles, California

University of California Press, Ltd.
London, England

© 1999 by the Regents of the University of California

Library of Congress Cataloging-in-Publication Data

Abel, Richard, 1941–
    The red rooster scare : making cinema American, 1900–1910/Richard Abel.
      p. cm.
    Includes bibliographic references and index
    ISBN 0–520–21203–7 (cloth : alk. paper).—ISBN 0–520–21478–1 (pbk. : alk. paper)
    1. Motion pictures—United States—History.   2. Pathé Frères (U.S.)—History.   3. Motion
pictures, French—United States.   I. Title.
  PN1993.5.U6A68   1999
  791.43'0973—dc 21   97–52074

Printed in the United States of America
9 8 7 6 5 4 3 2 1

One fine winter's day when Piglet was brushing away the snow in front of his house, he happened to look up, and there was Winnie-the-Pooh. Pooh was walking round and round in a circle, thinking of something else, and when Piglet called to him, he just went on walking.

"Hallo!" said Piglet, "what are you *doing?"*

"Hunting," said Pooh.

"Hunting what?"

"Tracking something," said Winnie-the-Pooh very mysteriously.

"Tracking what?" said Piglet, coming closer.

"That's just what I ask myself. I ask myself, What?"

"What do you think you'll answer?"

A.A.MILNE, WINNIE-THE-POOH, 1926

CONTENTS

ILLUSTRATIONS

PREFACE

During this summer Clarence took his own defeat indoors, deserting the sunny harsh streets of door-to-door rejection for the shadowy interiors of those moving-picture houses that, like museums of tawdry curiosities, opened their doors during the day. . . . Some of the original nickelodeons had already passed into history: the Paterson Show, on Market, and the Nicolet, at Main and Van Houten, which had displayed the latest pictures from France in the era when Georges Méliès and the Pathé and Lumière brothers had led the fledgling industry.

JOHN UPDIKE, *IN THE BEAUTY OF THE LILIES*

No one writing about the silent cinema in France after World War I can ignore the fact that American films so dominated the French market that they determined, in part, what constituted a "French" cinema. Certainly the French writers and filmmakers of *les années folles* could not do so, whatever accommodation or resistance they chose to advocate. But is the converse true for the period prior to that war? Can anyone writing about the cinema's emergence in the United States, especially before 1910, ignore the fact that French films dominated the American market and so determined, in part, what would become an "American" cinema? Apparently American historians can, or at least they can avoid dealing with French films all that seriously. Even Charles Musser's *Emergence of Cinema* pushes French films to the margins (in sections appended to chapters), following the long-held, probably unconscious tendency of film historians to assume, as common sense, a teleological model of early American cinema's development as a national cinema.[1] But what if one challenges this tendency, with its attendant amnesia, a tendency that all too blindly reappropriates the "Americanizing" process of those prewar years, and rethinks the period's significance as a unique moment (never since repeated) when "foreign films" were both more numerous and more popular than those of domestic manufacture? What if one recognizes the "structuring absence" around which the early American cinema was constituted and foregrounds the "alien bodies" of French films so prominent in its midst? That is what I propose to do in this book, focusing on the decade from 1900 to 1910, the years of the cinema's emergence as an increasingly popular form of mass culture in the United States. For it was then that the films of Pathé-Frères in particular had such a profound impact, so that, by the summer of 1905, the French company had become the leading supplier of moving pictures on the American market.

Rethinking the history of early American cinema requires a further reframing, however, through the contexts of modernity (or modern consumer society) and what Homi Bhabha has called "the ideological ambivalence" of the "nation-space."[2]

xi

For it was during this period that the cinema as a specific instance of modernity—a new technology of perception, reproduction, and representation; a new cultural commodity of mass production and consumption; a new space of social congregation within the public sphere—was inscribed within the discursive fields of imperialism and nationalism and their conflicted claims, respectively, of economic and cultural supremacy. Here imperialism can be understood, following Eric Hobsbawm, as the aggregate of rival capitalist economies, divided into national blocs in Western Europe and North America, which, fueled by the demand for profitable investments and markets for products, had embarked on a binge of global expansion by the turn of the last century.[3] A national economy depended on a "nation-state," as Hobsbawm puts it, a macrostructure of interconnected social institutions in which those of education and culture (that of the mass market) had assumed particular importance in constructing a national sense of collective identity.[4] Such institutions were the principal locus for a discursive conception of the nation "as a system of cultural signification . . . [or] representation of social life," to again cite Bhabha, whose ideological parameters increasingly were being defined not only in terms of language and ethnicity but also in terms of the foreign "other."[5] In this, the United States was somewhat unique, Richard Ohmann argues, for even before its people could think of themselves as "a nation politically," they were being gathered "into a nation organized around markets, money relations, and commodified culture."[6]

Indeed, the United States provides a compelling instance of early cinema's inscription within the discursive field of nationalism.[7] Here, the foreign "other" was Pathé, the French firm (headquartered in Paris) that led the way in industrializing the cinema worldwide, pioneering a system of mass production and mass distribution (with dozens of agencies selling its products across the globe), all instituted between 1904 and 1906.[8] This country rapidly became Pathé's largest market for the products that, in both quantity and quality, would prove crucial to the nickelodeon's emergence, a new venue of exhibition devoted exclusively to moving pictures (and songs) that soon claimed a mass audience of weekly "moviegoers." By 1907, as *New York Clipper* kept repeating, "Pathé films [were] features on all moving picture programs."[9] The nickelodeon especially attracted the disenfranchised, chief among them recent immigrants from eastern and southern Europe, whose record numbers coincided with, and included many Jews who would become so active in, the cinema's transformation.[10] As these diverse peoples came to be seen as a major target audience for cheap amusements, some feared (and others hoped) the nickelodeon would turn into an oppositional or alternative public sphere at odds with the industrial-commercial public sphere of mass consumer culture and its assimilationist operations.[11] This produced, I would argue, a crisis of anxiety over the American "experience of modernity" in terms of how the cultural and social power of the cinema would be defined and controlled.[12] At issue was whether or not Pathé, as a foreign company selling foreign commodities—specifically, its trademark "red rooster" films—could be assimilated within the new cinema industry, and whether or not it could participate in circulating ever more significant representations of social life and behavior.[13] With an "alien" body like Pathé at its center, how could an American cinema be truly American? How could it inculcate what so many Americans wanted to claim, however dubiously, as a distinctive, "morally superior" national identity?

The Red Rooster Scare, then, is not simply a history of the Pathé company in the United States, nor is it an economic history of the American cinema between 1900 and 1910.[14] Instead, by telling a more or less "new" story about early American cinema, with French Pathé films at the center, it offers something more like a cultural history of our own cinema's nationalization. Writing such a history, as Barbara Klinger rightly insists, means "mobiliz[ing] a number of different extrafilmic fields to interrogate cinema's relation to its historical context," especially those having to do with the exhibition of moving pictures and the discursive conditions of their reception, from promotional materials to representations of the moviegoing experience.[15] In this story, Pathé films played an absolutely crucial role in expanding and legitimating the American cinema well into 1907 or 1908. Thereafter, they were repeatedly stigmatized and/or marginalized, especially in the trade press, as foreign or alien to (in a sense "not white enough" for) American culture. In the United States, in other words, where the institutionalization of the cinema constituted a defining moment of modernity, the debate over Americanization acted as a significant framing, even determining, discourse.

This book extends the previous research I have done on silent cinema, but with several important differences. Once again, I pose a riddle in order to investigate, excavate, and recover material long considered lost, forgotten, even absent. This time, however, I reconceive the problematic of analysis, drawing on recent historical work dealing with turn-of-the century American culture, as well as recent theoretical work on social and discursive formations and reception (who went to the movies, where and when, according to what social categories, and for what reasons).[16] Consequently, my primary sources are not, as they have been previously, surviving archive film prints, although having done extensive research on many of the French films that were familiar to American spectators during this period does give me a unique perspective from which to reconceptualize the history of early American cinema. Here, instead, I turn to written texts (many of them almost as rare as the films, accessible only on microfilm or in special collections), principally those that, through selective representation, discursively constructed early cinema in the United States.[17] Whatever their position of self-interest (and however that fluctuated), trade journals obviously are a crucial resource, from those like *New York Clipper* or *New York Dramatic Mirror*, which covered a variety of staged performances, to those like *Views and Films Index* or *Moving Picture World*, which concentrated on moving pictures. Equally crucial sometimes are daily newspapers serving not only metropolitan areas but also small cities and towns, national mass-circulation magazines, and even a few books; so, too, are certain collections of private documents devoted to film exhibition (Keith's vaudeville circuit), film rental and distribution (George Kleine), and film manufacturing (the Edison Company).[18] Moreover, given the cultural arena within which the cinema emerged, and the fervent, anxiety-ridden nationalism dominating that arena, my sources also include a range of writing within (or about) mass-market culture at the time, as well as texts that were especially influential in the turn-of-the-century debate over the Americanization process.

This time, too, I offer a textual experiment in how one "does history." That is, this book can be read as an extended argument or narrative, but it also can be viewed somewhat like a vaudeville program and can even be explored like a "wonder cabinet."[19] The principal trajectory of my argument runs through the book's six chapters, charting the emergence of American cinema in terms of Pathé's position of relative power and dominance. Organized chronologically at first, these chapters increasingly overlap as the unfolding narrative simultaneously separates and connects the various arenas—material and discursive—within which Pathé's films circulated. The last two chapters climax in parallel studies of Americanization at work in our country's early cinema, offering an analysis of how that process excluded the Pathé red rooster, especially through the development of early westerns, only to include it once again, within the strictures dictated by assimilation. As sequential, interrelated acts in a program, however, these chapters also are interrupted by short entr'actes that present issues and subjects relatively neglected so far in research on early cinema: trademarks, the trade press, color, and sound. Initially defined in relation to Pathé's strutting red rooster, these, too, were reconfigured and then wrapped in the mantle of Americanization. Finally, as a series of deliberately arranged yet disparate displays, including documents, graphic illustrations, and even notes, this book is analogous to a museum space or wonder cabinet. Its rooms continually open onto discrete alcoves and curiosity cases that invite the inquisitive visitor to puzzle further over such riddles as what really is foreign, what is not, and why.

In the end, this book is a bit more personal than others I have written.[20] *The Red Rooster Scare* is different not only for the way it focuses on American history and culture but also for the way it engages with the historical construction of American subjectivity. Here, I must confess, family history has sharpened my awareness of my own paradoxical situatedness as a writer of cultural history. At the turn of the last century, my ancestors were second-generation white immigrants (English and Welsh, German and Swiss), living for the most part around Canton, Ohio. They were farmers, factory workers, and white-collar workers, devout or not-so-devout Protestants, the lower end of that vast population that was being transformed into a new middle class of consumers. Perhaps because he was a professional, it was Clyde Wolfe, my grandfather on my mother's side of the family, whom I remember admiring most as a child. In some sense, he haunts this book as its displaced subject. Adept at creating visual displays, he began work as a clothing store window dresser in 1911, an early recruit to the new profession so deftly promoted by L. Frank Baum.[21] In short, he was caught up in the regime of the visual that so defined American mass culture at the turn of the last century; eventually, he would earn the title "dean of Canton's display specialists."[22] Family rumor has it, however, that as a young man my grandfather also was a member (for how long remains unclear) of a local vigilante group, although not the notorious Ku Klux Klan. If so, he probably was a willing proponent of the racist ideology that so powerfully shaped the "reconstruction" of American identity, of what it meant to be an American at the turn of the last century. In other words, he may well have been a model spectator for what Robert Rydell has called the "white supremacist entertainments" (which also included the cinema) of our emerging mass culture.[23]

I write this book, then, not only to recover and disentangle the conditions and forces that irrevocably enmeshed early American cinema within the process of Americanization but also to recover and deconstruct my own "origins" as a social subject, a lower-middle-class "white boy" whose first wages came from caddying at a Jewish-owned country club and then from stocking and sacking groceries at one of a chain of Jewish grocery stores in northeastern Ohio, a suburban kid in the 1950s industrial heartland who fell under the century-old spell of the western wilderness (and once imagined he would be the next best thing to a mountain man, an expert in forestry or wildlife management). I write, in other words, to uncover the paradoxical bases of my own fascinations.

ACKNOWLEDGMENTS

Over the past four years, many colleagues and institutions have been generous in their support of my research and writing on *The Red Rooster Scare*. The book began as an open-ended project, with the aim of redirecting my research on early cinema; it was funded by an invaluable 1993–1994 John Simon Guggenheim Memorial Foundation Fellowship, in conjunction with a sabbatical leave from Drake University. That project gathered direction and force (despite the 1993 Des Moines flood and the 1994 Los Angeles earthquake), coalescing into a sketchy argument worked out in a dozen papers and essays, and finally in a manuscript, with the help of a half dozen grants (for travel to archives, microfilm purchases, and course load reductions) from the Center for the Humanities, the College of Arts and Sciences, and the Provost Office's Faculty Research Program, all at Drake University.

The following archives were crucial in offering access to a wide range of documents: the Academy of Motion Picture Arts and Sciences Library, Los Angeles; the Bobst Library, New York University, New York; the Lincoln Center Branch of the New York City Library, New York; the Motion Picture and Manuscript Divisions of the Library of Congress, Washington, D.C.; the Harold Washington Public Library, Chicago; the Edison National Historical Site, West Orange, New Jersey; Special Collections in the University of Iowa Library, Iowa City; the State Historical Society of Iowa Library, Des Moines; the Southern Oregon University Library, Ashland; the Des Moines Public Library; and Cowles Library at Drake University.

Numerous conferences and colloquiums allowed me to try out various conceptual frameworks for this historical research and rethink my arguments in response to comments and questions: International Domitor Conferences (Lausanne, 1992; New York, 1994; Paris, 1996); Society for Cinema Studies Conferences (New Orleans, 1993; New York, 1995; Dallas, 1996; Ottawa, 1997); a Drake University Cultural Studies Colloquium (1994); a University of Utrecht Lecture Series (1994); a Chicago Film Seminar (1994); a Symposium on Early Cinema at the University of

Iowa (1994); a session of Seminaire: Histoire et représentations: L'Image au XXème siècle (Paris, 1995); an early cinema panel at the Modern Language Association Convention (Chicago, 1995); the Amsterdam Workshop on Color (Nederlands Filmmuseum, 1995); the Celebrating 1895 Conference (Bradford, 1995); the Udine Conferences on Color and Authorship before the Auteur (1995, 1996); and the Back in the Saddle Again Conference (Utrecht, 1997).

I am indebted to Tom Gunning for an enthusiastic reader's report, which enabled me to sharpen the main arguments, consult several new sources, and correct specific points of information. Although much less complimentary, a second reader's report made me more aware of what the book's subject was not, prompted me to seek out a number of old and new sources, and led me to take up directly several debates concerning early cinema in the United States.

The following colleagues provided research sources, as well as ideas, for the book: Paolo Cherchi Usai, Scott Curtis, Steven Higgins, Antonia Lant, J. A. Lindstrom, Laurent Mannoni, Charles Musser, Roberta Pearson, Lauren Rabinovitz, Vanessa Schwartz, Ben Singer, Judith Thissen, William Uricchio, and Gregory Waller. Others who helped at one time or another include Rick Altman, Ben Brewster, Edward Buscombe, Leo Charney, Ian Christie, Donald Crafton, Monica Dall'Asta, Christian Delage, Thomas Elsaesser, John Fullerton, André Gaudreault, Sam Gill, Alison Griffiths, Miriam Hansen, Daan Hertogs, Nicholas Hiley, Lea Jacobs, Charlie Keil, Nico de Klerk, Ron Magliozzi, Rosanna Maule, Guglielmo Pescatore, Leonardo Quaresima, Catherine Russell, Mark Sandberg, Matthew Solomon, Peter Stanfield, and John Zeller.

At Drake University, I want to thank the 1993–1996 Cultural Studies faculty (especially Andrew Herman, Deborah Jacobs, Nancy Reincke, Joseph Schneider, John Sloop, and Jody Swilky), who offered intellectual support; the Center for the Humanities Board, Ron Troyer (Dean, College of Arts and Sciences), Michael Cheney (Associate Provost for Research), and Joe Lenz (Chair, Department of English), all of whom provided financial support; the undergraduate students in my course The Emergence of Mass Culture (especially two in its first semester, Samantha Thorpe and Rachel Lesky), who contributed to the research and asked good questions; the Cowles Library staff (especially Jim Leonardo, Susan McIlheran, and Karl Schaefer), who facilitated access to a variety of research materials, and the Media Services staff (especially Denise Wicker and Anje Gray), who prepared some of the illustrations.

At the University of California Press, I am grateful to have had Edward Dimendberg's consistent, strong encouragement for a second, much shorter manuscript. I also am pleased to have had Erika Büky handle the book's production so graciously and efficiently, Susan Ecklund perform a marvelously meticulous job of copyediting, and Mimi Kusch and Jan Johnson neatly resolve several late problems.

Encore une fois, my deepest debt is to an extraordinary writer and scholar in her own right, my partner, best reader, and collaborator, Barbara Hodgdon. Working together on this book and on her book *The Shakespeare Trade* was especially delightful because our trajectories of research and inquiry intersected in such surprising and productive ways.

Permission has been granted to reprint portions of this book, which originally appeared in different formats in Leo Charney and Vanessa Schwartz, eds., *Cinema and the Invention of Modern Life* (California, 1995), *Cinema Journal* 35 (Fall 1995), and *Fotogenia* 1 (1995), as well as *Il Colore nel cinema muto* (Bologna, 1996).

The following individuals and institutions provided illustrations: Antonia Lant and Bill Ford / Olin Library, Cornell University (figures 27, 54); Chicago Historical Society (figure 12); Curt Teich Postcard Archives, Lake County Museum, Wauconda, Illinois (figure 25); Marnan Collection, Margaret and Nancy Bergh, Minneapolis (figure 36); Museum of Modern Art (figure 46); Paolo Cherchi Usai (figure 32); private collector, Paris (figures 30, 33); State Historical Society of Iowa (figures 1, 17). All other illustrations are drawn from original or microfilm copies of newspapers and magazines from the turn of the century.

CHAPTER ONE

Trick or Treat
What "Commercial Crisis," 1900–1903?

All what I see wit' me own eyes I knows an' unnerstan's
When I see movin' pitchers of de far off, furrin' lans
Where de Hunks an' Ginnes come from—yer can betcher life I knows
Dat of all de lans' an' countries, 'taint no matter where yer goes
Dis here country's got 'em beaten—take my oat dat ain't no kid—
'Cause we learned it from de movin' pitchers, me an' Maggie did.
MOVING PICTURE WORLD (5 MARCH 1910), 333

A commonplace of early American cinema history has it that the years 1900–1903 were a "period of commercial crisis," that moving pictures verged on not becoming a viable form of cheap amusement.[1] This was the result, Charles Musser argues, of "problems with technological standardization, patent and copyright problems, audience boredom with predictable subject matter, stagnant demand, and cutthroat competition." Its immediate effect was a decline in American film production, a falloff in traveling exhibitor tours, and the failure of several early storefront theaters devoted exclusively to films. Without denying at least some of these problems and their effects, I want to look at these years from a different perspective, one more in line with that of Robert Allen, who has argued that, at least in vaudeville during this period, moving pictures did find "a stable market [and] a large audience of middle-class theatre-goers."[2] For if one focuses on exhibition rather than production, and on the most prominent sites of consumption, where films were shown frequently and regularly, in vaudeville houses and summer amusement parks, one sees not a "commercial crisis" but rather a more or less steadily expanding market.[3] The "common cry" that motion pictures "were losing their hold upon the public," George Kleine later wrote, may have circulated widely (if misleadingly) in 1900, but not thereafter.[4] Moreover, according to the trade press on stage performance—that is, *Billboard* and *New York Clipper*—as well as selected local papers, the trick films and *féeries* or "fairy plays" of Georges Méliès and Pathé-Frères from France, whether purchased outright or circulated in duped or pirated prints, were crucial to that expansion.

My argument begins with a *New York Clipper* report on the vaudeville program at Tony Pastor's, in New York, for the second week in January 1900:

> The American Vitagraph presented a series of moving pictures illustrating the story of *Cinderella* as the feature of its display on Monday, January 8, and scored one of the most distinct successes within our knowledge of animated views. The costumes are colored to match the originals, and the reproduction of the pantomime detailed with exactness. The dear old story, thus pictured, should remain for many weeks the delight of the little ones and a charm for the elders.[5]

"Attendance," the trade weekly added, "tested the [theater's] full capacity" and led Pastor's to make sure that *Cinderella* was on the bill for another three weeks.[6] By 1900, as Allen, Musser, and others have written, moving pictures had become a familiar, relatively reliable act on vaudeville programs, known principally by the name of the projecting apparatus or exhibition service supplying the films.[7] So the *Clipper*'s reference to a single film's popularity, over the course of a month at one location, was quite unusual. But there are other noteworthy points in this brief text that lay out the trajectories I want to pursue. One is that Vitagraph's exhibition service provided a guarantee of quality performance at Pastor's: at the time, no other company operated weekly in more vaudeville houses in the United States. Another is that the presence of children made, or could make, vaudeville houses into family entertainment centers, and that films like *Cinderella* especially appealed to them.[8] *Cinderella* could even serve as a featured act or "headliner" because it seemed to achieve such a high standard of "reproduction" (which included hand-colored costumes) and ran four hundred feet in length (six or seven minutes). Finally, its maker, although unacknowledged at the time, was not American but French, the Paris magician Georges Méliès.

GUARANTEEING THE QUALITY OF EARLY MOVING PICTURES: FROM APPARATUSES TO EXHIBITION SERVICES

Before 1900, the moving pictures that audiences viewed in vaudeville houses, dime museums, summer amusement parks, tent shows, church halls, and legitimate theaters were "authorized" in several ways.[9] In the beginning, the apparatus itself did the performing, through its uncanny power to animate pictures as a new kind of attraction, within what Neil Harris once called the "operational aesthetic."[10] In vaudeville houses and theaters across the country, it either shared the bill with more familiar attractions or starred as the principal feature. As late as April 1897, for instance, the American Biograph machine was in its fifth month at Keith's New Union Square house in New York; nearby, the Lumière Cinematograph was still being featured at Proctor's and the Pleasure Palace.[11] A month later, the Grand Opera House in Des Moines was advertising Edison's Projecting Kinetoscope as the sole attraction on a three-day program.[12] By then, as Musser has shown, the locus of authority for moving pictures was shifting to traveling exhibitors, many of whom already had made a name for themselves as illustrated lecturers, using magic lantern slides and phonographs.[13] The most successful of these undoubtedly was Lyman Howe, who soon built up a circuit of annual concert tours for the so-called cultural elite throughout the Northeast—in local opera houses, theaters, churches, and town halls. In his advertising, Howe's name became the stable, reliable guarantee of quality entertainment as his tours changed from "Animotiscope" and "War-Graph" exhibitions to "High-Class Moving Pictures."[14] The trajectory was the same for others like Burton Holmes, whose career as an illustrated lecturer began at the Brooklyn Institute, or even D. W. Robertson, who, although operating out of New York with Edison projectors, chiefly toured summer Chautauquas and other church groups in the Midwest.[15] In sum, as the moving picture apparatus grew familiar, the chief performer on many stages once again became human, in the shape of the traveling showman.

By 1900, however, a third locus of authority was on the ascendant. This was the exhibition service that could furnish a projector and projectionist, along with a series of moving pictures (renewed each week, often by means of railway transport), to a vaudeville house not just for special occasions but throughout its annual season.[16] American Biograph, for instance, negotiated an exclusive contract with the Keith circuit of "high-class" vaudeville houses (in the Northeast) to exhibit its special 68mm films. But most of the exhibition services supplied 35mm films, and to a more widely distributed clientele. Some followed Biograph's example and had an exclusive contract with a major vaudeville circuit: from headquarters in Chicago, George Spoor supplied a "kinodrome" service to Orpheum houses throughout the Midwest.[17] Others aligned themselves with a single vaudeville entrepreneur: William Paley's Kalatechnoscope served all four Proctor's houses in New York. Still others developed their own network of contracts: starting at Huber's Museum in New York, Percival Waters's Kinetograph Company (allied with Edison) reached out to vaudeville houses from Worcester to Toronto.[18] It was American Vitagraph, however, that established the most extensive service, beginning with an exclusive contract at Tony Pastor's in New York.[19] Soon the company had projection units, linked by railway arteries, in unaffiliated houses from Boston to Atlantic City, from Pittsburgh to Detroit. Based on its experience at West End Park in New Orleans, it also may have been the first to recognize the summer amusement park as a profitable vaudeville venue. If, indeed, motion pictures were a "great boon" to vaudeville managers, as *Billboard* claimed in December 1900,[20] it was due in large part to exhibition services like the American Vitagraph or the kinodrome, which guaranteed that the film show would consistently please their regular clientele.

EXPANDING THE CINEMA MARKET THROUGH VAUDEVILLE

Over the next three years, the growing market for moving pictures was closely tied to the expansion of vaudeville.[21] By January 1901, according to *Billboard*, there were at least seventy major vaudeville houses in the United States and Canada, predominantly in the Northeast and Midwest.[22] Most of these theaters offered "high-class" vaudeville, that is, long programs of "respectable" variety acts that could attract middle-class patrons, "with special provision made," as a Keith's ad in *The Club Woman* discreetly put it, "for the accommodation and comfort of ladies and children."[23] Such a program might include as many as fifteen acts (common on the Keith circuit of houses) or as few as eight or nine (on the Orpheum circuit). Moving pictures usually occupied the last act on a vaudeville bill, although certain subjects such as *Cinderella* could be positioned as headliners. According to sources that long dominated histories of early American cinema, this put moving pictures in the category of the "chaser," a final act so poor that it served to trick an audience into leaving the theater and making room for a fresh one.[24] Allen's research has shown, however, that the term was hardly derogatory, at least for the Keith and Orpheum circuits, and usually meant an inexpensive or "medium" act (often silent, one not based on dialogue or monologue) that signaled the end of a show or filled the slack time in "continuous" shows (allowing people to move in and out of houses at their leisure).[25] For some, this even meant that moving pictures could serve as the "big flash" that closed a performance, "filling all spectators with the memory of a show that had been action-packed to the last moment."[26] Whatever function the chaser served—and distinctions may have depended on the quality of film subjects shown in any particular week—moving pictures remained a reliably popular vaudeville act.

Significantly, a new venue for moving pictures opened up during this period in what soon was called "cheap" vaudeville or "family" vaudeville. These theaters tended to be smaller and ran shorter programs of just five or six acts, and their lower ticket costs also made them more accessible to working-class and, perhaps more significant, white-collar audiences.[27] Allen first called attention to cheap vaudeville's rapid development but mistakenly claimed that moving pictures were not shown there before 1906.[28] He also followed other historians who located its origins on the West Coast (particularly in the Northwest), but cheap vaudeville also emerged in the Northeast and Midwest.[29] In the fall of 1901, for instance, in the textile factory town of Lowell, Massachusetts, both the Boston and People's showed "bioscope" moving pictures as the last of five or six acts.[30] So did the Gem and Mechanic's Hall in nearby Lynn, whose principal audience was the families of shoe factory workers.[31] But such houses also were a feature attraction in summer amusement parks (now growing in number following the success of Steeplechase on Coney Island and the Chutes and Sans Souci in Chicago).[32] Ingersoll Park, which opened on the west side of Des Moines in June 1901, offers a good example of this cheap vaudeville: its weekly bill comprised five or six acts, and its ads targeted the working-class population of the city's east side—encouraging them to use the crosstown trolley cars of the company that built the park.[33] And the closing act, in both 1901 and 1902, was Selig's Polyscope (another exhibition service headquartered in Chicago). Most likely, these were the "small

Figure 1. Postcard of Ingersoll Park Entrance (Des Moines), ca. 1902.

exhibitors" that, in the *Clipper*'s words, served "the general mass of the public" throughout the country.[34]

Summer parks, those "laboratories of the new mass culture," in John Kasson's insightful phrase, seem to have become an established venue for moving pictures by the summer of 1902.[35] Vitagraph exploited them with some regularity, perhaps drawing on its long experience at West End Park in New Orleans. That summer, for instance, the company's films were found on vaudeville programs in parks from Atlantic City and Baltimore to Toronto. But Spoor's kinodrome matched its advance with park bookings from Sandusky and Toledo, Ohio, to Evansville, Indiana. Once having fended off Edison's patent suit, in March 1902, Biograph also began to target the "managers of summer parks" for "standard size sprocket films" (35mm prints) of its catalog titles. Its "biographet" projector (and films) began showing up in parks from Birmingham, Alabama, to London, Ontario. Through *Billboard* specifically, Lubin, too, began advertising its "cineograph" projector (and films) to "park managers and street fair men." Small businessmen also started up local exhibition services. W. A. Reed, for instance, operated his "komograph" in several parks in Boston, as well as at Sea View, near Portland, Maine; Prof. Atwood, who had been showing moving pictures in Lynn vaudeville houses, now was projecting them for vacationers at the Seaside Theatre, Marblehead.[36] As a further sign of their importance, for the first time, a major poster printer, Hennegan and Company (Cincinnati), now offered a "new line" of "moving picture paper" to its clients.[37]

By the end of that summer, moving pictures were "coining" so much money in the parks, as both Edison and Lubin ads put it, that they helped fuel a further boom in both cheap and high-class vaudeville houses. In Evansville, for instance, the kinodrome simply shifted from Oak Summit Park to the new Park Theatre. Atwood moved from Seaside to the new Grover's Garden Theatre in Lynn; Reed's komograph took up new quarters at the Boulevard Theatre in Boston. Vitagraph added several new houses to its service: S. Z. Poli's two big theaters in New Haven and Bridgeport, the smaller Bon Ton in Jersey City, and (at least briefly) Dixie's Orpheum in Scranton.[38] On the opposite coast, it was that summer that cheap vaudeville (with moving pictures) really established itself in the Northwest. One of the first houses to make an impact was A. S. Rohrer's La Petite Theatre in Seattle, which may have used an Edison kinetograph to show its moving pictures; but the model was soon followed by the Edison Theatre (with its "projectoscope"). And the *Clipper* described La Petite's initial bills that June as "high class vaudeville, catering to lady audiences."[39] This phrase would be picked up and repeated over the course of the next year, as cheap vaudeville houses throughout the country (in and out of the summer parks) promoted moving pictures as part of what one Council Bluffs ad described as a "cultured rendezvous for ladies and children."[40]

MÉLIÈS WORKS HIS MAGIC ON THE NEW WORLD

Assuming there was indeed some basis for *Billboard*'s claim, made as early as December 1900, that motion pictures were a "great boon to the vaudeville manager," there still is the question of whether French films were an unstated referent in that claim. Was a film like *Cinderella*, for instance, an anomaly or something closer to the norm? Some years ago, Tom Gunning and André Gaudreault coined the still useful term *cinema of attractions* to describe the first ten years of cinema history, a period in which moving pictures served as one of a variety of attractions within a wide range of public amusements, especially vaudeville.[41] The films, too, came in such variety in order to fulfill the sense of novelty, change, and "shocking" juxtaposition that many sought in weekly vaudeville programs.

From 1900 through 1902, all kinds of films were advertised in the trade press and occasionally even cited in specific exhibition venues. Lubin, Selig, and Edison continued to promote boxing matches, for instance, but these usually were shown in burlesque houses, such as the Court Street or Lafayette in Buffalo. *Actualités*, or current events, such as Edison's films of President McKinley's funeral, remained timely attractions, watched with "deep interest" at Proctor's and Pastor's in New York, Méliès's *Coronation of King Edward VII*, or French views of Mount Pelée's volcanic eruption on Martinique.[42] The latter two films were shown widely across the continent, including park venues in Kansas City and Des Moines, and were featured for two weeks at the annual International Exhibition, in Saint Johns, Nova Scotia.[43] Local *faits divers* sometimes also caught the trade press's attention, but more rarely now; although advertised by both Edison and Lubin, comic subjects, similarly, received scant notice.[44] What did excite consistent interest, however, were "magical subjects" or "mysterious films,"[45] especially the longer spectacle plays like *Cinderella*, nearly all of them French. These were the real boon to vaudeville.

One way to gauge this interest is to track the French films that gained notices, in the trade press and local papers, between 1900 and 1902. *Cinderella*, for instance, not only played for at least a month at Tony Pastor's in New York; the following summer it played for three weeks without losing any "of its extraordinary popularity" at the West End in New Orleans, and that Christmas it was the "most notable feature of the week" at Heck's Wonder World in Cincinnati.[46] In May 1901, Méliès's long spectacle film, *Joan of Arc*, was "warmly applauded," again at Pastor's; in June, Vitagraph made it "one of the regular features" of the West End's weekly summer programs.[47] Six months later, another Méliès *féerie*, *Little Red Riding Hood*, was singled out at the Orpheum in Brooklyn; and when Vitagraph began exhibiting at the Avenue in Detroit, in February 1902, *Little Red Riding Hood* was the first film it put up on the screen. Later that spring, a new Méliès *féerie*, *Bluebeard*, not only turned up at the Avenue and at Shea's Garden in Buffalo[48] but also was held over for an extra week at Huber's Museum in New York. That summer, along with views of Mount Pelée's eruption, the Polyscope presented Pathé's long fairy play, *Aladdin and His Lamp*, at Ingersoll Park in Des Moines.[49] All this would culminate, in the fall and winter of 1902–1903, with the enthusiastic reception given to Méliès's *A Trip to the Moon*, which Kleine would later recall as the first important story film on the American market.[50]

The level of attention this film garnered in the trade press was unprecedented. In their weekly listing of vaudeville programs that season, both the *Clipper* and *Billboard* cited at least fifty houses showing moving pictures on a regular basis. These citations only once mentioned a boxing film, Lubin's *Jeffries-Fitzsimmons Fight*, playing at the Crystal, a burlesque house in Lowell. They referred perhaps ten times to specific travel views, such as *A Trip through Algiers*, at the Orpheum in Brooklyn, or *A Trip through Europe*, at the Empire in Cleveland, most of them unacknowledged Pathé subjects.[51] But the majority referred to just one film, *A Trip to the Moon*. There were seven alone in November: from the Avenue in Detroit and Chase's in Washington to Poli's in New Haven and Hurtig & Seamons in Harlem (all using Vitagraph's exhibition service). At the Orpheum in Kansas City, *A Trip to the Moon* was a "decided feature" of the kinodrome; at the Empire in Cleveland and then at the St. Charles Orpheum in New Orleans, it was "the best [film] ever seen."[52] The film's popularity extended to cheap vaudeville as well: in early December it proved "one of the hits" at Grover's Garden in Lynn. When Keith's Union Square Theatre in New York switched its exhibition service from Biograph to Vitagraph in early April 1903, one of the first programs included *A Trip to the Moon*—"the best moving picture film which I have ever seen," manager S. K. Hodgdon reported, "it held the audience to the finish and was received with a hearty round of applause."[53] Finally, in Los Angeles, when T. L. Talley reopened his "vaudeville of moving pictures," the Electric Theater, in January 1903, he often featured the film during its first two months of operation, identified

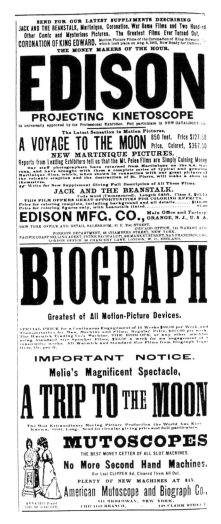

Figure 2. Edison and Biograph ads, *New York Clipper* (4 October 1902), 712.

Méliès (from Paris) as its creator, and called it "the most wonderful subject ever attempted in moving pictures."[54]

Another, more indirect way to gauge exhibitor interest is to look at the ads that Edison, Lubin, Selig, and Biograph placed in the trade press, particularly in the *Clipper*. For two years after the opening of *Cinderella* at Pastor's, only one subject was promoted more often than Méliès's spectacle films: the *Passion Play of Oberammergau*.[55] In March 1902, when Biograph won a temporary legal decision in the patents war initiated by Edison,[56] none of the American companies felt secure

Figure 3. Vitagraph ad, *New York Clipper* (21 March 1903), 108.

enough to rush into producing more films; instead they opted to buy and/or dupe "foreign" subjects from Europe. Biograph, for instance, sold itself as the "sole agent" for "original" Warwick Films and Méliès "Star" Films. Edison and Lubin offered dupes of Méliès subjects for summer amusement parks and then vied with one another in promoting films of the Martinique disaster (made by either Méliès or Pathé) as products of their own photographers.[57] Selig said it was making "a speciality of mysterious films," among them Pathé's biblical subject, *The Prodigal Son*.[58] That fall, every company had its own version of *A Trip to the Moon*, but only Biograph identified the film as "Méliès's Magnificent Spectacle"—in one of the earliest references to Méliès's cultural capital in the United States.[59] For the first time, also, both Biograph and Edison began to advertise Pathé films (without identifying their maker, of course): "a new series sensation," *The Downward Path*, and a "new . . . spectacular production," *Ali Baba and the Forty Thieves*.[60] By January 1903, Edison and Lubin were listing the titles of short French "mysterious" films such as *Magical Egg, Wonderful Suspension and Evolution*, and *The Resourceful Waiter*. The following spring, when Vitagraph replaced Biograph on the Keith vaudeville circuit and began promoting itself as the leading exhibition service for theaters and summer parks (although that honor equally may have gone to the kinodrome), at least half the films the company featured as "spectaculars" or headliners came from Méliès and Pathé.

MARKETING FRENCH FILMS FOR VAUDEVILLE

These trade press notices and ads give some sense of how significant the French "spectaculars" were in generating interest in moving pictures on vaudeville programs. The way they were marketed, however, suggests another reason for their importance. Perhaps the first instance of this approach comes in a December 1900 Edison ad that featured three titles as especially apt for the Christmas season (a recently invented, commercial tradition), with two of them by Méliès: *Cinderella* and *Astronomer's Dream*.[61] A year later, Edison promoted Méliès's *Little Red Riding Hood* for "the holiday season" but again included *Cinderella* as a suitable subject.[62] The following summer, Lubin listed both films in its ads for *Bluebeard, Martinique Disaster,* and *Jack and the Beanstalk* (all dupes, of course), the last of which was an Edison attempt to imitate Méliès. And Edison itself advertised the same Méliès titles once again as "Christmas pictures" in late 1902.[63] What this meant was that, unlike *actualités*, Méliès's spectacle films could have a relatively long shelf life; like the best live acts in vaudeville, they offered repeated performances, from one season to the next. In other words, once acquired and as long as the print held up, a Méliès moving picture could be a continuing source of profitable exploitation. D. F. Grauman of San Francisco testified retrospectively to this advantage in calling *A Trip to the Moon* "one of the funniest subjects ever shown at the Unique," his vaudeville house: it created such a sensation that he "showed it a great many times."[64]

That it was French films, not just "European imports," that fueled what Musser concludes was, by 1902–1903, "a growing demand for story films" on the American market probably should come as no surprise.[65] By then, Méliès and Pathé were perhaps the world's biggest producers of films (especially long spectacle films), so they could more or less guarantee a supply of product in quantity. Moreover, the French films meshed smoothly with certain practices that were already well established in American vaudeville. One was the large number of "foreign" acts on "high-class" programs, acts that could be exploited for their "artistic" and/or "exotic" appeal. This had been the case when the Lumière Cinematograph premiered at Keith's Union Square Theatre in 1896 and went on, briefly, to become a regular feature at Proctor's, as well as at Koster & Bial's (which specifically advertised "great foreign stars" like Yvette Guilbert or "the latest sensation from Paris").[66] It was still the case five years later, particularly on the Keith circuit, then still a model for vaudeville programs. When Méliès had his brother Gaston open a sales office and printing laboratory in New York in May 1903, he was seeking not only to curtail the circulation of "bad and fraudulent copies" of "genuine and original 'Star' Films" but also to promote himself as a Paris inventor and theater proprietor who could supply, on a consistent basis, quality foreign acts for American vaudeville.[67]

Figure 4. Edison ad, *New York Clipper* (15 November 1902), 712.

Another practice was program bookings that could appeal specifically to women and children. This was something, Musser recently suggested, that American producers seemed slow to recognize, or at least plan for, as an investment opportunity.[68] The reason could be a lingering assumption that the cheap amusements for which they made and sold both apparatuses and films were primarily masculine spaces of leisure. With its boxing films, for instance, Lubin consistently targeted burlesque houses and other venues catering to a working-class male audience. Edison, it should be remembered, first tried to exploit moving pictures in kinetoscope or peep-show parlors (a variation on the phonograph parlor), a move that Biograph then imitated.[69] However important the parlors briefly may have been as "drop-in" centers "offering entertainment in compact packages" for a diverse clientele in downtown business districts, David Nasaw argues, by 1900 they were being transformed into penny arcades that cultivated a male-only crowd.[70] In Indianapolis, for instance, arcades first "were patronized liberally by the tougher element of the city"; in New York, they could raise the ire of middle-class reformers when, as on Coney Island, the "disgusting photographs" of their peep-show machines inadvertently attracted women and children.[71] Some observers flatly linked the arcade and the saloon, which was anything but a "family resort."[72] Herbert Mills, an early arcade entrepreneur, claimed that when he entered the business in 1901, "it was essential that the operator be a man of extreme sporting proclivities."[73] The clientele of the arcades would shift and expand within a few years, but that would come as a delayed response to the feminization of cheap amusements generally, especially to vaudeville and its unusual growth and popularity.

If Edison, Lubin, and Biograph seemed unable to adapt quickly to this change, perhaps they acted prudently in the short term, as manufacturers, in buying and selling "foreign" products. Whatever the case, they seemed slow to realize that vaudeville, whether of the high-class or cheap family variety, inhabited the larger emergent space of mass consumption (encompassing both the middle class and working class, but perhaps most crucially the aspiring class of white-collar families), where women, according to *Printer's Ink*, already did "75 to 90 per cent" of the shopping.[74] Indeed, as "The Matinee Girl," a lighthearted 1897 article in *Munsey's* had to admit, "woman is the mainstay of the amusement business."[75] This, then, was a feminized cultural space of leisure largely defined by the presence of women and children.[76] For children, who tended to be afternoon customers, may well have been important as regulars, especially on the Keith circuit, if only to incite the rest of the family to attend the evening program.[77] The "dear old stories" of the Méliès and Pathé spectacle films turned out to be perfectly suited "treats" for such "regulars," as Vitagraph had claimed at least as early as 1900, with its first "hit," *Cinderella*.[78] Throughout 1902 and 1903, Pathé added more and more such story films to its catalog of available titles, from *Spring Fairy* and *Fairy of the Black Rocks* to *Sleeping Beauty* and *Puss-in-Boots*. In the fall of 1903, Méliès's latest "spectacular," *Fairyland* (which, according to the company's publicity, "took three months" to make, using "the leading pantomimists of Paris"), was an even bigger hit than *A Trip to the Moon* in Keith houses from New York to Cleveland, playing three weeks straight, for instance, in the New Theatre in Philadelphia.[79] In Providence, the local newspapers pointedly reported that the "weird and gorgeous moving pictures" called *Fairyland* "made quite a stir" at Keith's, most notably "among the little people."[80]

Trick or treat? The French, unlike their American competitors, cannily elided the difference. Within the expanding markets of mass consumption in the United States, both Méliès and Pathé turned the tricks and transformations of their new trade into magically renewable treats.

DOCUMENT 1

"Clever Moving Pictures," *Los Angeles Times* (11 October 1903), 6.2

A set of moving pictures called "Fairyland," shown at the Lyric Theatre in this city now, is an interesting exhibit of the limits to which moving picture-making can be carried in the hands of experts equipped with time and money to carry out their devices.

In brief, "Fairyland" relates an old fairy story—of how the prince and the princess are betrothed, of the wiles of a witch, of spells thrown over both prince and princess by her, and then a long series of impossible and supernatural happenings supposed to come to these parties.

The series was made on a large Paris stage, with an infinite variety of mechanical and scenic accessories. According to statements of the manager, people from seventeen Parisian theaters were engaged in the photographic production, and rehearsals have been going on since March. It is said that the same set was produced simultaneously in London, Paris, and New York in the month of September. T. L. Talley, manager of the Lyric, claims to have the only film of its kind in the West.

The action and the various scenic enchantments, of course impossible before an audience, who would have to see the mechanical makeshifts, is an easy thing for the biograph. There are no curtains or changes of scene. Although there are numerous sets, all fade into each other, just as the fairy-land scene is supposed to do.

Perhaps the best one is that representing the sinking of a ship, with the aftermath that comes to the sailors. These are rescued by a mermaid queen, who comes with a chariot drawn by great crabs to release them from the spell of the water. By some interposition of an aquarium before the films, when these were exposed, pictures of real fish, swimming around in real water, are given. There is also a huge devil-fish, constantly waving its arms about the drowning mariners.

Various submarine scenes are afterward shown, always with the same live fish photographically exhibited. Some of the sets are evidently of careful and painstaking design, and show considerable cleverness.

Another pretty picture is that of a castle interior, with all its woodwork in flames, and the hero coming to rescue the princess, "just in time." Through smoke and flame, with red fire flashing around them, they pass unscathed, although the woodwork is seen to fall on all sides. By double exposures such a thing, of course impossible of accomplishment on a real stage, is made pictorially picturesque in this way. . . .

ENTR'ACTE 1

Marketing Films as a Product Category

Brand Names and Trademarks

What's in a name, a brand, a mark, especially one that seems to be everywhere and available to everyone? That is something often ignored yet crucial to the American cinema's emergence. Here, again, the point is to turn
our attention from production (and the litigation over patents and copyrights that sought to protect it) to consumption and the efforts to both stimulate and control that consumption through marketing.[1] What we ignore is
what Susan Strasser calls national "product education," an essential component of the new system of mass marketing being put in place at the turn
of the last century.[2] Talking about his success with Quaker Oats, Henry
Crowell said simply that his aim "was to do educational and constructive
work so as to awaken an interest in and create a demand for cereals where
none existed."[3] Much like packaged cereals, soups, and soaps, in other
words, moving pictures had to be promoted as a new "product category"
worthy of being accepted as a regularly repeated cultural experience in
cheap amusements everywhere.

Exhibition services such as American Vitagraph and the kinodrome
had done this so successfully, with just enough support from manufacturers, that, as vaudeville steadily expanded, so did the market for moving pictures. By 1903, a new and improved means of promoting and marketing
was taking shape. This, of course, was advertising, whose success in stimulating "new needs and new desires through visual fascination" now made it
a major institution of cultural hegemony.[4] Only recently had advertising
in mass magazines and on billboards "educated" Americans, through a
process of "*incremental* repetition," writes Ohmann, to connect their
expectations about a product with recurring symbols or brands.[5] "Once
we skipped [ads] unless some want compelled us," quipped a writer in
Harper's Weekly (1897), "while now we read [them] to find out what we really want."[6] The very foundation of American business, a later treatise asserted, was "built upon the significance and guaranty conveyed to the purchasing public through the medium of those particular marks, names, and
symbols."[7] The "good will value" of the brand name and trademark now
assumed an increasing importance for moving pictures, particularly as the
new industry began to concentrate on the commerce of story films. Yet
striking differences developed between American and French manufacturers in how they used a brand for the purposes of exploitation.[8]

Surprisingly, at first American companies exploited the "name on the
label" in a rather limited fashion. The names of Edison, Biograph, and

Lubin, for instance, appeared in trade press ads in the *Clipper* and *Billboard*, which circulated to a wide range of exhibitors and showmen. These served to guarantee, more or less, the quality of the film reel(s) offered for sale that week or month. This use of brand names may have stemmed from Edison's general prominence on the market. Through such new products as electric lightbulbs and phonographs, the Edison name had become a mark as familiar as that of Ivory Soap, Quaker Oats, or Kodak.[9] Edison's strategy for films as a product category, however, was not so much to "brand" each commodity sold (or even copyright its materiality) but rather to monopolize the commerce in films through exclusive patents on apparatuses involved in their production and exhibition.[10] Because films were consumed in cheap amusements, and not in the home, supposedly only those who managed that public space needed to be assured, by the Edison name, of product quality.

Yet Edison films did appeal directly to audiences in at least two ways. Musser has shown that the company tended to manufacture films with stories that were already familiar—and thus "readable"—to American audiences.[11] In other words, Edison assumed a cinema market that marginalized or even excluded recent immigrants. Many of these films were based on stage plays, from *Uncle Tom's Cabin* and *The Great Train Robbery* (1903) to *The Miller's Daughter* (1905), or were adapted from vaudeville sketches, such as *The Ex-Convict* (1904). Some, however, exploited the trademarks of well-known advertising campaigns: *A Romance of the Rail* (1903), for instance, sent a white-gowned Phoebe Snow, the chief promotional figure of the Lackawanna Railroad (a major carrier of anthracite coal), through a whirlwind courtship, spoofing the romance associated with train travel.[12] Perhaps the most intriguing example of this exploitation came in *The Great Train Robbery*, specifically in the emblematic shot of a robber firing point-blank at the spectator that has long been an icon of early cinema history. This famous shot, which Edison even reproduced in its ads, actually was an unacknowledged "dupe" of a widely circulated poster at the time.[13] The poster was Sam Hoke's "Highwayman" for Gold Dust Powder (a packaged cleanser), which *Billboard* hailed as unusually compelling: one "weak-minded" seamstress in Des Moines, forced to look at it for hours out her apartment window, supposedly was "driven to the verge of insanity."[14] *The Great Train Robbery* impressed itself so deeply on audiences, then, partly because it re-created the shock value of a notorious poster brand.

French film manufacturers, by contrast, put more stock in the "authorizing" power of trademarks. Georges Méliès, for instance, came up with the brand name "Star" Films," for which he could substitute an easily identifiable logo. When Gaston Méliès set up facilities in New York to print and sell "Star" Films, in May 1903, his *Clipper* ads promoted the trademark star as much as the Méliès name in order to authorize the

Figure 5. Gold Dust "Highwayman" poster, *Billboard*
(18 May 1901), 3.

company's products.[15] That star appeared in black in all "Star" Films
ads, and its "negative" (a white cutout) was punched into, and later em-
bossed on, the opening frames of every film reel the company sold.
Méliès adopted this trademark strategy for several reasons. One, of
course, was to counteract Edison's and Lubin's extensive practice of duping and selling his films as their own, which reached a crisis point with
the phenomenal success of *A Trip to the Moon.* The trademark proved
ineffectual for Méliès as a means of asserting ownership (as did copyright), but it did assure the quality of his "original" film subjects in contrast to that of the dupes.[16] Another reason, perhaps, was that Méliès saw
his films as artistic creations. The trademark star, Paolo Cherchi Usai argues, was an extension of his signature, allowing him to sign each film

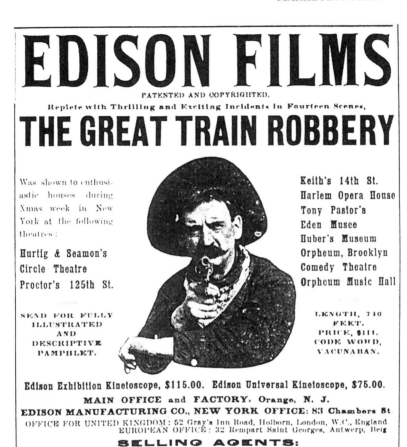

EDISON FILMS

PATENTED AND COPYRIGHTED.

Replete with Thrilling and Exciting Incidents in Fourteen Scenes,

THE GREAT TRAIN ROBBERY

Was shown to enthusiastic houses during Xmas week in New York at the following theatres :

Hurtig & Seamon's
Circle Theatre
Proctor's 125th St.

Keith's 14th St.
Harlem Opera House
Tony Pastor's
Eden Musee
Huber's Museum
Orpheum, Brooklyn
Comedy Theatre
Orpheum Music Hall

SEND FOR FULLY
ILLUSTRATED
AND
DESCRIPTIVE
PAMPHLET.

LENGTH, 740
FEET.
PRICE, $111.
CODE WORD,
VACUNABAN.

Edison Exhibition Kinetoscope, $115.00.   Edison Universal Kinetoscope, $75.00.

MAIN OFFICE and FACTORY, Orange, N. J.
EDISON MANUFACTURING CO., NEW YORK OFFICE: 83 Chambers St

OFFICE FOR UNITED KINGDOM: 52 Gray's Inn Road, Holborn, London, W.C., England.
EUROPEAN OFFICE : 32 Rempart Saint Georges, Antwerp, Belg

SELLING AGENTS:

THE KINETOGRAPH CO.....................................41 E. 21st St., New York
KLEINE OPTICAL CO..52 State St., Chicago, Ill
PETER BACIGALUPI..933 Market St., San Francisco, Cal.

Figure 6. Edison ad, *New York Clipper* (9 January 1904), 1113.

print much as an artist would sign a painting or, perhaps more pertinent, a lithograph poster.[17] As a sign of "authorship," then, this could be read as a literal mark of Méliès's unique anti-industrial position during the early cinema period.

At the same time, Pathé-Frères adopted a similar strategy of quality guarantee, but for quite different reasons.[18] At least as early as 1903, the French company's catalogs began to carry an announcement that claimed its own trademark, the Gallic cock or rooster.[19] More important, each film subject bore that trademark (a rooster drawn in profile) on an opening title

Figure 7. Méliès "Star" Film ad, *New York Clipper* (6 June 1903), 368.

Figure 8. Pathé ad, *New York Clipper* (4 February 1905), 1172.

card, and in a red tint matching the title's large block letters on a black background.[20] Soon Pathé's longer story films, such as *Don Quixote, Napoleon,* and *Puss-in-Boots,* also were including intertitle cards (a company innovation), with terse phrases in the same red block letters, accompanied by the red rooster trademark. For Pathé, as for Méliès, the trademark served (not all that effectively) as a deterrent against forgery (Pathé never even bothered to seek the protection of copyright). But the trademark did much more. Unlike its American competitors, whose products circulated chiefly within the North American continent (the border limits of their "readability"), Pathé quickly began marketing its films across the globe (which also meant translating its titles and intertitles into other major languages). Because of its high visibility, the Pathé red rooster traveled as a kind of supersalesman, promoting the excellence and dependability of the company's films to audiences anywhere in the world.[21] Pathé became perhaps the first film manufacturer to use the trademark much like the American companies selling packaged soaps or cereals: it forged a direct link to consumers.[22] The red rooster gave the French company a singular, fixed identity, distinguishing it from most other companies; and it circulated as a recurring symbol of goodwill that, in guaranteeing the quality of its products' performance on any stage or screen, incited increasing consumer demand.[23]

CHAPTER TWO

"Pathé Goes to Town"
French Films Create a Market for the
Nickelodeon, 1903–1906

THE MOVING PICTURE SHOW

The phonograph is a marvel sure,
With a charm that's all its own;
And it's hard to overrate the lure
Of the mystic telephone.
The telegraph, with its mighty range,
Is a wonder, as we know,
But nothing yet is half as strange
As the Moving Picture Show.

Full of surprises all the time
And only its patrons know
The pleasures exchanged for half a dime
At the Moving Picture Show.

JAMES D. LAW, *SHOW WORLD* (16 MAY 1908), 24

For Charles Musser, the "key preconditions for the nickelodeon era" were the development of story films and rental exchanges between 1903 and 1905.[1] For Robert Allen, however mistaken his reference points, it was "the rapid development of a type of inexpensive vaudeville, variously called 'ten-cent,' 'nickel,' or 'family' vaudeville."[2] These preconditions obviously were important, but a crucial component of all three has long been overlooked: the quantity and quality of Pathé films on the American market. Pathé's well-crafted, well-packaged films, I would argue, promoted the new product category of moving pictures in the United States to a degree unmatched by any others. During the years leading up to the nickelodeon boom, and even during its initial months, the trademark spectators associated over and over with moving pictures was the Pathé red rooster. Indeed, the Pathé trademark became almost synonymous with the movies and the ever-renewed satisfaction of "going to the show." Put simply, Pathé's presence on the American market provided the single most significant condition of emergence for the nickelodeon.[3]

In order to reconstruct the stages (or exhibition sites) on which French films played during this period, and to gauge their impact, I draw not only on the extensive research of Musser, Allen, and others but also on several strands of public and private discourse then in circulation. First, there are catalogs and trade press ads of production companies (from Edison and Biograph to Méliès and Pathé), as well as exhibition services, sales agents, and rental exchanges (from Vitagraph and Kleine Optical to National Film Renting), all of them promoting films (and various apparatuses) on the American market.[4] Second, in the trade press, notably *Billboard* and *New York Clipper* (both long committed to promoting live performance), and in certain daily newspapers, there are scattered reports, expressing varying degrees of enthusiasm, about different exhibition sites throughout the country. Third, and most specifically, there are privately circulated managers' reports on weekly programs presented in a half dozen "high-class" vaudeville houses operated by the Keith circuit, from Boston and Washington in the East to Detroit and Cleveland in the Midwest.[5] These strands of discourse turn out to be unusually heterogeneous. Accordingly, I want to examine the disjunctions within this discourse on how French films were figured at the same time that I use that figuring to recover their shifting significance, season by season, from 1903 to 1906. These were the years (modifying Musser's schema slightly) of the cinema's "transition to story films," its "saturation" of a wide range of exhibition venues—with vaudeville houses, according to Fred C. Aiken, easily being the most important—and the initial "proliferation of specialized storefront moving-picture theaters."[6]

THE PATHÉ "RED ROOSTER" AS A
VAUDEVILLE FEATURE ATTRACTION

It might seem poetic justice to argue that *A Trip to the Moon* single-handedly created a stable market for cinema exhibition and for the "staged" story film in this country. Unfortunately, the argument simply won't fly, even if Méliès's film clearly enjoyed an unusual popularity with vaudeville audiences for at least a year.[7] Along with his earlier fairy plays, *A Trip to the Moon* provided a potential, if expensive, model for the staged story film, although it still used the story primarily as a pretext for spectacle attractions. It also emblematized the difference between one kind of travel views in time and space and another, as if projecting the cinema itself into the future. Indeed, as Musser discovered, Edwin S. Porter studied Méliès's film in order to make his own *Life of an American Fireman*, which Edison released in January 1903.[8] What one can argue is that *A Trip to the Moon* fueled the transition to story films and the concomitant expansion of the American cinema market that accelerated during the 1903–1904 season. Yet, by then, Méliès's films offered just one of several models for the story films that would soon be popular. Others came from manufacturers like Edison, Biograph, Warwick, Hepworth,

Haggar & Sons, British Gaumont, and especially from the largest French producer, Pathé-Frères. Recovering Pathé's role, compared to American and English
producers in this period of transition and expansion, however, is not easy. For
there are discrepancies in the trajectory of cinema's emergence as a viable form of
mass culture, depending on which strands of public and private discourse one
chooses to privilege.

The evidence for a continually expanding cinema market between the summers of 1903 and 1904 is compelling. According to trade press reports, exhibition
increased only moderately that fall—most notably in Denver, where no less than
four vaudeville houses now included moving pictures in their programs.[9] Over the
winter and spring, however, another forty houses began listing them, with the
biggest increases occurring in the Northeast (in and around Boston, for instance),
throughout the upper Midwest, and along the West Coast; everywhere family
vaudeville houses, with their shorter, more frequent programs, were competing
with larger high-class vaudeville theaters.[10] It was then, too, that Archie Shepard
went from doing "black top" shows to booking circuit tours of commercial theaters throughout New England, presenting two-hour shows (with Sunday concerts) that were especially popular with working-class audiences.[11] By the summer
of 1904, the number of exhibition sites was double what it had been the year before, with moving pictures firmly established not only in amusement parks
throughout the Northeast and Midwest but also in vaudeville houses from San Antonio to Oakland.[12] In late 1903, Percival Waters (New York) and Miles Brothers
(San Francisco) initiated a system of renting films to their customers.[13] Within
months, ads for new selling agents and rental exchanges suddenly appeared, most
of them based in Chicago, like Eugene Cline & Co. or George Spoor's new Film
Rental Bureau—already suggesting the significance of the Midwest market.[14]
Other ads promoted Kleine Optical's supply of Edison films and apparatuses
(again, from Chicago) for two dozen vaudeville houses in the Great Western circuit.[15] During May and June, Vitagraph's exhibition service took over several
houses in the East altogether—closing out the final week of the Empire Theatre
in Holyoke, for instance, and running for one month at the Steeplechase Pier in
Atlantic City.[16]

That many more new film subjects were available is clear from the trade press
and newspapers, but which ones contributed most to the market's expansion? All
kinds of films still attracted notices. Throughout the year, travel views and *actualités* (or fictional reenactments) could be found as headliners—from the "moving
pictures of India" at the Lyric Theater in Los Angeles to views of catastrophes like
the "Baltimore Fire" at the Orpheum in Brooklyn or the "Iroquois Theater Fire"
at the Gem Theatre in Sioux City.[17] The outbreak of war between Russia and
Japan certainly sustained this interest—witness Biograph's *Battle of Yalu*, featured
at Keith's in Boston in early April, and the scattered references to battle scenes on
land and sea throughout the summer. Méliès's *féerie* films also continued to serve as

special attractions, especially, but not exclusively, for children. That fall, for instance, Talley screened *Fairyland* for over a month at the Lyric Theater in Los Angeles, while the Keith Theatre in Providence placed it prominently in the middle of its bill.[18] The next spring, the Bijou Theatre in Duluth used *The Damnation of Faust* as one of its first features; the Lyric Theater in Portland did likewise with *Robinson Crusoe;* and several houses offered reprises of earlier films.[19] But Méliès-like fairy plays, such as Hepworth's *Alice in Wonderland* (shown in Boston and Buffalo during the Christmas season), received nearly as much attention. The newest story films were the "sensational chase pictures" from England, such as British Gaumont's *The Poachers,* cited at Keith's in Providence in early January.[20] But there were others from Edison and Biograph, ranging from condensed versions of melodramas like *Uncle Tom's Cabin,* cited at the Orpheum in Brooklyn, to traditional comic sketches like *Rube and Mandy at Coney Island* or "episodes" in the life of *Kit Carson,* cited at Keith's in Boston, and later at Keith's in Providence, as well as at Cleveland's Theatre in Chicago.[21]

The most famous of these new subjects, of course, was *The Great Train Robbery,* released by Edison in December 1903.[22] Our assumption of its popularity in some twenty vaudeville houses from New York to Chicago in late December, however, comes not from trade press reports but from two ads run by Edison and Kleine Optical in the *Clipper.*[23] Otherwise, the trade press itself mentioned the film rarely: once in December, at the Orpheum in Brooklyn, once in February, at the Park Theatre in Youngstown, and once again two months later at Keeney's Theatre in Brooklyn. The earliest newspaper citations also appeared in February, when, according to Musser, Edison's film "reportedly scored the biggest moving picture hit ever made in Rochester."[24] More frequent references to *The Great Train Robbery* occurred that summer, not only in amusement parks but also in vaudeville houses from Detroit to Duluth. Repeated ads by Edison, Kleine Optical, Lubin, and others throughout the spring and summer also testified to the film's impact; and in June, Kleine Optical claimed that the film was "the most popular subject" it had ever sold.[25] Yet *The Great Train Robbery* alone cannot account for the cinema market's expansion any more than *A Trip to the Moon* could the year before.[26] Many more new subjects, and subjects of sufficient quality and variety, had to be available for purchase, rental, and exhibition. And that, I would argue, is what Pathé was able to supply, given its relatively high production capacity. The problem is that not once during this entire year did trade press reports on exhibition refer to a Pathé title, even though Pathé films were known to be in circulation as early as the summer of 1902 (and as deep into the provinces as Des Moines).[27] The initial silence over *The Great Train Robbery*'s popularity—due perhaps to the *Clipper*'s and *Billboard*'s investment in live performance—was even greater over Pathé's films.

When one looks at the catalogs and trade press ads of American producers, rental exchanges, and exhibition services, however, Pathé story films suddenly become quite visible, whether in "original" or duped versions. Certain Pathé titles

already had been cropping up (their maker unidentified, of course) the year before. Both Edison and Lubin, for instance, offered copies of Pathé's fairy play, *Ali
Baba and the Forty Thieves,* while Edison also sold copies of *The Story of a Crime* and
The Gambler's Crime.[28] By spring 1903, when Vitagraph began advertising its exhibition service in earnest, it too was offering Pathé films, and not only travel views
of Algiers and the Alps.[29] Within six months, and with the addition of *Sleeping
Beauty,* as well as a new comic fantasy, *Don Quixote,* Pathé story films constituted
nearly a quarter of the titles the company featured as "spectaculars" in its new
catalog addressed to vaudeville managers.[30] All of them "headliners" running
fifteen to twenty minutes in length, they now equaled the Méliès titles in number,
making French films, arguably, the most important on Vitagraph's programs. Further evidence of Pathé's growing presence appears in weekly *Clipper* ads, in which
Edison, Biograph, and even Méliès substantially increased the number of new
subjects they were offering for sale. Although some of that increase resulted from
Edison's and Biograph's own slightly higher levels of production, even more was
the result of imports from English producers, most of them short comic subjects
or chase films sold during the summer and fall.[31] In the winter and spring, however, it was the longer Pathé films (still not identified as such) that came to the fore,
especially in Edison's ads. In early November, for instance, Edison offered Pathé's
Life of Napoleon (in its full two-reel format, as well as in separate scenes) along with
The Great Train Robbery.[32] In January, its featured films were Pathé's *William Tell* and
the "spectacular" *Puss-in-Boots;* in February, the principal new subject was Pathé's
Marie Antoinette.[33]

All the titles released by Edison, of course, were dupes. Yet Pathé's own prints,
with their red block-letter titles and red rooster trademark, seem to have been not
only in circulation but highly valued.[34] One indication was an April 1904 ad from
Harbach & Co. (in New York), the first firm to single out "original 'Pathé-Frères'
films" for sale.[35] The most telling sign, however, comes from the weekly managers' reports of the Keith vaudeville theaters,[36] all of which attest to the popularity of *Fairyland* (which played three weeks at one theater in Philadelphia), *The
Poachers* (which played two theaters, consecutively, also in Philadelphia), and *The
Great Train Robbery.* But they also call attention to and highly praise Pathé's longer
films. In September, for instance, *Sleeping Beauty* played on one of the first programs at the Empire in Cleveland. In October, *The Rise and Fall of Napoleon* was
featured at Chase's Theatre in Washington; a month later the same two-reel film
scored a hit in Cleveland. And it was this particular Pathé historical series, as
Musser has shown, that both Lyman Howe and Edwin Hadley made the "featured subject" of their "high-class moving pictures" tours that fall and winter,
capping a decade-long American fascination with Napoleon as the epitome of
the heroic individual.[37] Meanwhile, on the Keith circuit, in December, *Don
Quixote* was being given a "very good" notice in Washington; in February, *Marie
Antoinette* was described as "excellent" in Boston, "decidedly of historic and ed-
ucative value." That spring, *Marie Antoinette* was a feature attraction of Shepard's

Moving Pictures; and in April, it was being shown in Providence for the "special benefit of the school children."[38] Yet it was not until August 1904, when Kleine Optical confirmed that such "feature films were in great demand," that Pathé, along with Edison and Biograph, at last was acknowledged publicly as a leader in their production.[39]

PATHÉ STAKES A CLAIM OF DOMINANCE

Recognizing the demand for its films on the American market, the French company finally opened a sales office in New York late that summer. The initial ads placed by Pathé Cinematograph, like those of Méliès the year before, drew attention to the "worldwide reputation" of its films, "which have been copied and duped by unscrupulous concerns"—an unmistakable indictment of Edison and Lubin.[40] Not only did Pathé promise to sell only "original films," but it offered most of them at a lower price than the dupes then on the market.[41] Moreover, its September list of two dozen titles still available, along with eight new "novelties," covered every kind of story film then being produced and included many already featured by its American competitors.[42] The earliest surviving Kleine Optical catalog, from October 1904, also called attention to the popularity of Pathé films over the course of the previous year, in a warning to exhibitors about the inferior quality of duped films. Explicitly naming "Pathé-Frères, of Paris" as "victims of this practice to a greater extent than any other manufacturer," Kleine Optical listed ten Pathé story films (as well as three from Méliès) "among the [most] successful films . . . duplicated in America"—from older titles such as *Napoleon* and *Marie Antoinette* to new ones such as *Indians and Cowboys* and *The Strike*.[43] Now, Kleine Optical recently had broken with Edison (whose catalogs continued to promote duped Pathé titles) and become Pathé's and Biograph's principal sales agent in Chicago, which problematizes its own catalog's language as evidence.[44] Yet in a brief history of how "the long subjects called 'Feature Films'" had won such "great popularity," the company refused to ignore Edison's contribution and placed its films between those of Méliès and Pathé in a chronological list of recent "hits": "*Trip to the Moon, Jack and the Beanstalk, Great Train Robbery, Uncle Tom's Cabin, Christopher Columbus, Life of an American Fireman, Napoleon, Marie Antoinette, Gambler's Crime*, etc."[45] And in advising exhibitors to purchase at least one feature film per program, Kleine Optical gave as examples Pathé's *Christopher Columbus* and Edison's *Great Train Robbery*.[46]

Firmly established in New York and Chicago, through its sales agent Kleine Optical, Pathé Cinematograph was well positioned to take advantage of the continuing upsurge in exhibition during the 1904–1905 vaudeville season, especially as "ten-cent" or "family" houses continued to proliferate.[47] That fall, the trade press reported that moving pictures for the first time had become a regular vaudeville feature in several major cities—for instance, the Maryland Theatre (now part of Keith's circuit) in Baltimore, the Star Theatre in Atlanta, the new Hopkins

718	THE NEW YORK CLIPPER.		SEPTEMBER 24.

PATHÉ FILMS.

LATEST NOVELTIES:

Our Best Known "Original Films" Which Have Been Copied and Duped by Unscrupulous Concerns.

THE STRIKE (¹⁄₄ Series)	435 Feet	ANNIE'S LOVE STORY	FALLS OF RHINE	SLEEPING BEAUTY
INDIANS and COWBOYS (Or Attack)	585 Feet	BUTTERFLY	PUSS IN BOOTS	ALI BABA and THE 40 THIEVES
JOSEPH SOLD BY HIS BROTHERS (Biblical Subject)	610 Feet	NEST ROBBERS	MARIE ANTOINETTE	QUO VADIS
ICE CREAM EATER	80 Feet	TOUR IN ITALY	WILLIAM TELL	MAGIC PICTURE HANGING
DRAMA IN THE AIR	195 Feet	JAPANESE AMBUSH	NAPOLEON'S LIFE	JAPONAISERIE
FOX and RABBITS	65 Feet	BARNUM'S TRUNK	A GOOD STORY	THE LIFE OF A GAMESTER
GAMBLER'S QUARREL	65 Feet	CHRISTOPHER COLUMBUS	PRODIGAL SON	THE FAIRY OF THE SPRING
A BOAR HUNT	320 Feet	SCENES AT EVERY FLOOR	SAMSON AND DELILAH	THE DEVIL'S 7 CASTLES

We Sell Only Our Original Films. **PATHÉ CINEMATOGRAPH CO.,** 42 E. 23d Street, New York.

Figure 9. Pathé ad, *New York Clipper* (24 September 1904), 718.

Theatre (seating twenty-two hundred people) in Louisville, the Grand and Crystal Theatres in Milwaukee, and a new Orpheum in Minneapolis.[48] They became part of even more vaudeville houses in New York City and the region around Boston; it was in the latter area that Vitagraph again took over complete programs for several days in October and, along with Shepard's Moving Pictures, became a fixture on the "Sunday concerts" in certain "legitimate" theaters.[49] That winter, George Spoor's Film Rental Bureau and kinodrome service (featuring "foreign and American" films) expanded northward into family vaudeville houses in Duluth and Winnipeg, westward into others in Des Moines and Dubuque, and southward into several in Saint Joseph and Evansville.[50] In the New York area, the Colonial, Alhambra, Amphion, and Atlantic Garden theaters all introduced moving pictures onto their vaudeville programs. At the same time, on the West Coast, several new family vaudeville houses began showing films in Seattle and Portland, and others reported screening them in Vancouver and Fresno. By February 1905, at least three family houses were offering moving pictures in Peoria, Illinois. That spring, with Miles Brothers now regularly renting the films of "Pathé-Frères, Biograph, Crescent, and other[s]" from its home office in San Francisco, new vaudeville venues opened up not only there and in nearby cities such as Oakland, Sacramento, San Jose, Stockton, and Santa Rosa, but also as far north as Eureka and as far south as Santa Cruz.[51] Finally, four new venues suddenly opened up in Los Angeles, and for the first time moving pictures were reported in San Diego.[52]

Yet again, trade press reports provided little evidence that specific Pathé films spurred the cinema market's expansion. Instead, they continued to celebrate *The Great Train Robbery*, which served to kick off moving picture shows in new family vaudeville houses like the Star in Pittsburgh and the Bijou in Des Moines.[53] In terms of new subjects, they quickly picked up on the popularity of Biograph's comic chase film, *Personal!*, which played for four weeks that August at Keith's in New York and then was followed by others such as *The Lost Child, The Chicken Thief, The Suburbanite,* and *Tom, Tom, the Piper's Son,* as well as Edison variants like *The Escaped Lunatic.* The trade press also took notice of the crime films trying to imitate *The Great Train Robbery*'s success—from Lubin's *Bold Bank Robbery* and *The Counterfeiters* to Biograph's *The Moonshiners* and Edison's own *Capture of the "Yegg" Bank Bur-*

Figure 10. Grand Theater ad, *Sunday Oregonian* (5 March 1905), 19.

glars.[54] Otherwise, the only new Méliès film to receive attention was *The Impossible Voyage,* whose citings were scattered from Milwaukee, Des Moines, and Forth Worth to Lowell, Massachusetts.[55] The references to Pathé films were just as slim: *The Strike* at the Crown Theatre in Fort Worth, *The Passion Play* at the Opera House in Lowell, *A Drama in the Air* at the Star Theatre in Saint Louis, and *The Incendiary* at the Des Moines Bijou (all but one of them family houses). In other words, according to trade press reports, the American films of Biograph, Edison, and even Lubin would seem to have been far more popular than the French films of either Méliès or Pathé.

Yet the local newspapers in at least two widely separate cities suggest something very different. From June through November, in Cedar Rapids (Iowa), Selig Polyscope supplied French films almost exclusively to the Auditorium (a family house), including *Faust and Marguerite* and *Fairyland* (each twice), as well as Pathé's *Forsaken* or *Annie's Love Story,* a rare reference to this allegedly popular title.[56] In December the Polyscope service shifted to another family house, the new People's Theatre, and its opening attraction, Pathé's *Passion Play,* ran for nearly a month.[57] In Portland (Oregon), French films were even more prominent. During the summer of 1904, the Lyric "specialized" in Pathé films from *Sleeping Beauty* and *Christopher Columbus* to *Annie's Love Story,* the only film to be held over for an extra week.[58] The following December, the Bijou Theater drew special attention to Pathé's *The Strike* during its Christmas week program.[59] At the same time, the Grand Theater advertised *The Impossible Voyage* as "the latest Parisian film" and then rebooked the Méliès film in January for a repeat performance.[60] At the end of December, it promoted Pathé's *Life of Louis XIV* exactly the same way; six months later, this "Parisian film story" returned to the Star Theater, which only once before had advertised its concluding act as an "imported film."[61] Throughout the winter and spring of 1905, along with Biograph's comic chase films, the

Grand consistently booked Pathé titles from *From Christiana to North Cape* and *Hop o' My Thumb* to *The Bewitched Lover* and *The Incendiary*.[62] In Portland, billing a closing act as "the latest Parisian film" seems to have meant more to family vaudeville audiences than simply calling it the "latest Biograph film" or "latest Edison film."[63]

That difference is no less telling when one looks at the Keith managers' reports.[64] As before, these reports parallel the trade press in noting the popularity of American comic chase films and crime subjects, and they initially give greater attention to Biograph titles: *The Lost Child*, for instance, ran for four weeks in New York, and *The Moonshiners* played for two weeks in Pittsburgh (at the Grand Opera House, now part of Keith's circuit).[65] They also indicate that English titles (even if no longer new) sometimes served to fill out (but never headline) the film programs. Méliès's *The Impossible Voyage* came in for high praise: it was held over for an extra week at Christmas in Boston (and later in Philadelphia) as "one of the laughing hits of the show," and it was described as the "best picture of that kind" in Providence.[66] References to Pathé films, however, are extensive and cover a wide range of genres. In January 1905, for instance, the Providence manager called the fairy play *Puss-in-Boots* "very good for children," as did those in Pittsburgh, New York, Philadelphia, and Boston three months later, referring to *Hop o' My Thumb*. Throughout the previous fall, one of the first titles Pathé advertised, *Nest Robbers*, was judged a "very good" comedy in Pittsburgh, Cleveland, and Boston; another early title, *A Drama in the Air*, first called a "good novelty" in New York and Cleveland, later ran as "the principal picture" in Pittsburgh.[67] In Boston, in January, audiences watched the "beautiful" historical film *Life of Louis XIV* "with deep interest"; in May, they gave the "well carried out" chase film *The Incendiary* "considerable applause at the finish."[68] There, too, in December, the "melodramatic" feature *The Strike* (one of the few films representing labor unrest) was "watched with deep interest," ending in applause.[69] And the words "watched with deep interest" were used for no other films shown on the Keith circuit throughout the 1904–1905 season.[70]

Production company catalogs and trade press ads, as well as rental exchange ads, also suggest that, through Pathé Cinematograph, the French company was becoming the principal supplier of new subjects on the American market. In September 1904 both Edison and Eugene Cline, for instance, featured either new Pathé dupes or "originals," with the latter promoting *The Strike* as a "sensational film," one of the "greatest headliners since *The Train Robbery*."[71] In October a Lubin ad in the *Clipper* listed a half dozen Pathé titles, including *Puss-in-Boots*, as his company's own product.[72] This duping was so extensive that, in a December *Billboard* ad, J. A. Berst, the company's New York manager, could turn the practice to Pathé's advantage, declaring that "the best advertising for our films is the fact that so many concerns dupe them."[73] Meanwhile, Lubin kept exploiting the French company, publishing a catalog the next spring that not only listed seventy-five

Figure 11. Pathé ad, *New York Clipper* (6 May 1905), 290.

Pathé titles (out of a total of ninety) as its own but also actually reproduced the page layout of Pathé's new English-language catalog.[74] In May, Pathé finally sought to discredit the publicity from this "well known house in Philadelphia," and protect itself further, by printing "Pathé Frères Paris 1905" along the perforation edge of each copy it sold.[75] More important, the New York office now claimed to be able to offer its sales agents (Kleine Optical and the Miles Brothers), exchanges like National Film Renting or the newly organized Chicago Film Exchange, and exhibitors like Vitagraph and Spoor's kinodrome service "something new every week."[76] If the public, in *Billboard*'s words, now had "grown to expect a wonderful creation each week,"[77] Pathé's ads promised to fulfill that expectation, with every possible kind of story film.

Clearly, no American company could make such a claim in 1905. Edison had thwarted Biograph's production surge by raiding some of its key personnel that spring, yet its own production schedule actually decreased slightly (Porter made only fifteen story films over the course of the next year) as the company invested its resources instead in the manufacture of projectors and other related equipment.[78] Vitagraph also began producing its own films that summer in order to fill a projected fall schedule of biweekly releases, but its output (along with the increases at Lubin) did little more than compensate for the production declines at Biograph and Edison, as well as Crescent and Selig.[79] Besides, none of the American companies had more than a single studio available for shooting interior scenes; both Edison and Vitagraph started construction on new studios in late 1905, but neither would be ready until the following summer or fall. By contrast, Pathé had three studio facilities on the outskirts of Paris (two of which had double stages), where "director units" headed by Ferdinand Zecca, Lucien Nonguet, Gaston Velle, Georges Hatot, and Albert Capellani all would be able to work more or less simultaneously.[80] As the French company shifted into a factory system of production, its extensive laboratories geared up to print an average of forty thousand feet of positive film stock per day (primarily story subjects), a good percentage of which now was being shipped to the United States.[81]

PATHÉ FUELS THE EARLY NICKELODEON BOOM

That summer in Pittsburgh, a real estate developer and impresario named Harry Davis opened the Nickelodeon, a storefront theater with a continuous program of moving pictures.[82] The idea for such a theater was hardly new, and many of those who had experimented with the venue were associated with the amusement parlor or penny arcade.[83] The association was apt, as David Nasaw writes, for, by 1903–1904, "visiting an arcade was almost like window shopping."[84] One of the best known was T. L. Talley in Los Angeles, with his Electric Theatre, in 1902 and again in 1903.[85] Some later would even become major figures in the industry. Adolph Zukor, for instance, claimed to have converted the second floor over his Fourteenth Street Arcade (on Union Square, New York) into the Crystal Hall, in 1904.[86] Marcus Loew always said that he appropriated the idea for his People's Vaudeville arcades (also in New York)—and first tried it out in Cincinnati—from a Covington, Kentucky, arcade show sometime in 1905.[87] Others who had experimented with storefront theaters, however, were traveling showmen, like J. W. Wilson, who operated one in Houston, between February and April 1905, and Frank Montgomery, who briefly opened an "Edison's Family Theatre" in Fort Worth.[88] The Nickelodeon also originated in an amusement arcade (attached to the Avenue Theatre), part of which Davis used to project moving pictures to standing spectators.[89] When a fire destroyed both the theater and the arcade that June, Musser writes, Davis simply "moved his motion-picture show to a larger storefront," one of his commercial properties nearby: within weeks, it was "an instant hit."

Throughout the fall, Davis and other entrepreneurs opened more storefront theaters in Pittsburgh (one report, undoubtedly exaggerated, claimed there were twenty by December), and similar theaters began appearing in Philadelphia—at least one of which, the Bijou Dream, was financed by Davis.[90] By November, either Davis or his associate John Harris had entered the Chicago market, where Eugene Cline may have been operating a "promotional" storefront adjacent to the New American Theatre; by Christmas, on State Street, Aaron Jones was turning one of his downtown arcades into a moving picture show, and Gustav Hollenberg was about to open the Chicago Theatre.[91] About the same time, in New York, Loew was converting his Twenty-third Street arcade into a People's nickelodeon; he was soon followed by Zukor (after a short investment in Hale's Tours), J. Austin Fynes with his first Nicolet "miniature playhouse" on West 125th Street, and William Fox with a "nickelette" in Brooklyn.[92] It was then, too, perhaps as early as November 1905, that William Bullock caught the "fever," opening his first nickelodeon in Cleveland for the American Amusement Company.[93] In parallel with this trend, Miles Brothers announced that its offices would offer film program changes not just weekly, which had long been standard in vaudeville houses, but semiweekly—probably to service the small theaters in or near such amusement parks as Coney Island's Steeplechase or Luna Park and Chicago's White City, some of which already were featuring only films.[94] That the first nickelodeons

Figure 12. Chicago Theatre, on State Street between Harrison and Polk (Chicago), January 1906.

emerged in the region of the country from Pittsburgh and Philadelphia west to Chicago strangely coincides with a relative lack of prior trade press reports on moving picture programs in vaudeville houses there, almost as if there had been an attempt to suppress or deny their growing appeal.

By the opening of the 1905–1906 vaudeville season, according to Kleine Optical and National Film Renting ads in both *Billboard* and the *Clipper*, nearly every theater in the country (in hundreds of downtown shopping districts), from Keith's "high-class" house in Boston (seating twenty-seven hundred) to the Bijou "family" house in Des Moines (seating five hundred), was showing moving pictures.[95] Moreover, many of those in eastern urban centers were presenting regular Sunday concerts exclusively given over to films: in New York alone, Shepard now was supplying nearly two dozen theaters.[96] Anticipating the "exceptional" demand for features or "headliners"[97] in vaudeville houses, amusement parks, and now nickelodeons, Kleine Optical substantially upped its orders from Pathé Cinematograph, from June through September, making the French company the principal supplier of the films it sold on the American market—among them the 1903–1904 *Passion Play*, which it strongly recommended over all others.[98] And on the strength of Pathé's unusual production capacity, Kleine Optical now claimed to be the industry's largest sales agent, not only in the Midwest but across the country as a whole.[99]

Throughout the summer and fall, Pathé titles became more and more prominent on the Keith vaudeville circuit and elsewhere.[100] *The Moon Lover,* the comic fantasy of a drunk's "trip to the moon," first played at Keith's New York house in late May and was still circulating as a "very good comedy" at the Providence house in early November. *The Life of a Miner,* or *The Great Mine Disaster,* a loose adaptation of Zola's *Germinal,* was a major hit from June through August. In New York it was described as "rather serious" but "very good"; in Boston it "won considerable applause from the balconies" (that is, from working-class audiences); and in Des Moines it was one of only five titles singled out in ads that summer and concluded the season at Ingersoll Park.[101] In July the Philadelphia house found *Two Young Tramps* an excellent color film; six weeks later, it was an opening feature at the Boston Theatre in Lowell.[102] In August, the New York house called the sports feature *The Great Steeplechase* "the greatest racing picture . . . ever"; two months later, the Temple Theatre in Detroit found it "beautiful, exciting, a masterpiece."[103] And managers everywhere agreed that the industrial "feature" *Scenes at Creusot's Steel Foundry* was "excellent." Throughout August and September, Pathé titles clearly dominated programs on the Keith circuit. Over the Labor Day weekend, for instance, the Boston house showed nothing but Pathé films; for consecutive weeks, both the New York and the Philadelphia houses made Pathé titles their principal features, among them, *The Wonderful Album,* which served as an apt and timely advertisement.

That Pathé films maintained their prominence within the Keith vaudeville circuit throughout the 1905–1906 season is clear from the weekly managers' reports, especially from New York and Boston.[104] That they enjoyed a similar prominence on family vaudeville and nickelodeon programs is less obvious. One reason is that, during this period, the trade press offered fewer and fewer references to individual film titles playing at specific exhibition sites. In the *Clipper,* for instance, only the Boston and People's Theatres in Lowell now consistently listed the films on their weekly programs—and People's kept Pathé's *The Deserter* for a rare second week in February 1906.[105] Instead, what interested the trade press—and that interest seemed grudging, given its long-standing commitment to live performance—was the phenomenal growth of moving pictures and moviegoing generally within the entertainment industry. For nickelodeons represented a different kind of amusement: they catered to a drop-in audience through programs of films and illustrated songs that could last anywhere from fifteen to thirty minutes each but run continuously from noon (or even earlier) to late at night.[106] In the spring of 1906, for instance, *Billboard* may have been the first to acknowledge the nickelodeon's phenomenal growth, as well as its potential value, in a regular column entitled "Moving Picture Shows." Still, the Cincinnati-based weekly continued to stress the alleged dangers of moving picture fires at the same time it reported on the increasing number of new and profitable storefront theaters, in both big cities and small towns.[107]

For references to specific film titles, again one can turn to certain local newspapers. Here, ads for the Bijou Theater in Des Moines provide some measure of the French company's continuing penetration of the family vaudeville market. Two weekly programs in December 1905, for instance, were composed almost exclusively of Pathé films, and at least one Pathé title was included on nearly every program for the next five months.[108] In Portland, Pathé's dominance now extended to the Star as well as the Grand, leaving few program slots open for the films of Edison and Vitagraph or for Méliès *féeries* such as *Arabian Nights*.[109] The Grand singled out Pathé's *French Coal Miners* as a "Great Film" but attributed it to Edison (which indicates the company still was duping its competitor's films), and it described *Christian Martyrs* as "special," "sensational."[110] Repeatedly, Pathé titles such as *French Coal Miners, The Moon Lover,* and *Young Tramps* would appear at the Grand one week and then return months later at the Star.[111] Yet, by the end of the year, there were enough Pathé subjects available that the Star could feature such films as *Modern Brigandage, The Hen with the Golden Eggs,* and *The Deserter*.[112] Whether or not similar references can be gleaned from local newspaper ads in other cities during this period ought to be the subject of further research.

The question of Pathé's prominence on family vaudeville and nickelodeon programs is crucial, however, because those were the sites of the cinema's real expansion. As early as December 1905, *Billboard* suggested that the "great impetus" for the new industry's "remarkable leaps and bounds" over the previous year came from the "popular [or 'ten-cent'] vaudeville circuits."[113] For the first time, circuits for such houses appeared beyond the West Coast, as in the Consolidated Vaudeville Managers Association, whose theaters were named Bijou or Crystal.[114] *Variety* seems to have taken a special interest in the growth of family vaudeville (and generally ignored moving pictures); by March 1906, it was predicting that the country would be "thoroughly vaudevillized very soon."[115] By that time, however, the nickelodeon had become a fad (especially for a mixed class of shoppers, off-work employees, and neighborhood residents, many of them women and children) and was beginning to compete with family vaudeville.[116] At least two dozen storefront theaters were operating in Pittsburgh; there were another dozen or more in Philadelphia.[117] Others were cropping up in New York (on the Bowery, lower Sixth Avenue, 14th Street, and 125th Street) and in Chicago (on State and North Clark Streets, as well as on Halstead and Milwaukee Avenues, with Carl Laemmle's White Front Theatre among them).[118] Partly fueled by Harry Davis—whose Bijou Dreams now stretched from New York and Buffalo to Cleveland and Detroit—nickelodeons, theatoriums, and electric theaters now could be found from cities like Birmingham, Louisville, and Des Moines (where the Bijou turned into the Nickeldom) to small towns like Charleroi, Pennsylvania, and Pine Bluff, Arkansas.[119] As Shepard, with the financial backing of Philadelphia developer Felix Isman, began leasing theaters for permanent picture shows, Keith opened nickelodeons near several of his Rhode Island theaters.[120] By the summer of 1906, there were ten nickelodeons around the boardwalk area of Atlantic City and at least thirty on Coney Island.[121]

That Pathé could and did supply a major portion of the films used on family vaudeville and nickelodeon programs admittedly has to be inferred, but the cumulative weight of inferences, I think, is persuasive. For one thing, along with "biograph," "vitagraph," and "kinetograph," the term "cinematograph" (now associated with Pathé's American offices) was appearing more frequently as a generic label for the film programs shown in vaudeville houses and amusement parks.[122] For another, rental exchanges like Miles Brothers and Eugene Cline, as well as sales agents like Kleine Optical, all of whom drew attention to their distribution of Pathé films (Eugene Cline, for instance, had an extensive list of the company's titles), generally were linked to the family vaudeville circuits and earliest nickelodeons.[123] In fact, in late December 1905, Pathé itself became the first to address ads specifically to these new "moving picture men."[124] By then, of course, there was a sufficient backlog of older films, both American and foreign, so that storefront theaters could fill their programs, at least initially, with already popular titles, especially for spectators who may not have seen them before. Yet once they began to compete with one another (and with vaudeville houses) for customers—a moment which George Kleine later dated as December 1905—the nickelodeons too had to have a ready supply of new subjects.[125] And Pathé clearly was the principal supplier of new subjects throughout 1905–1906. Moreover, while Edison, Vitagraph, and Biograph tended to produce a limited number of relatively lengthy "headliner" films, Pathé could offer a wide range of film lengths, from one hundred to more than one thousand feet, and in a variety of genres.[126] Such a production strategy was perfectly suited to nickelodeons, which demanded variety, novelty, and increasingly frequent changes in their programs. And it was endorsed by the Mueller Brothers, who were running four moving picture shows on Coney Island in May 1906: their clientele, who loved melodramas and comedies, clearly preferred Pathé films.[127]

Finally, there is evidence that Pathé itself developed several strategies to solidify its dominant position on the American market, especially among the new storefront theaters. In early September 1905, it established a second sales agency in Chicago, which *Billboard* now claimed as "the leading film market in the world."[128] That fall, Pathé's ads began stressing the superior quality of its films: not only were they "photographically finer . . . and steadier than any other films," but because they were "imported from Paris" they were all "good subjects" simply because the company could not "afford to pay heavy duty on doubtful sellers."[129] By November, Pathé Cinematograph was so entrenched on the American market that, along with Kleine Optical, Vitagraph, Biograph, and Méliès (but, significantly, not Edison), it would participate in the first attempt to organize "the leading manufacturers of films," the Moving Picture Protective League of America.[130] By March, well before a court decision seemed to further weaken Edison's control

Figure 13. Pathé ad, *New York Clipper* (30 December 1905), 1156.

over moving picture patents, Pathé was selling its own projector, the "New 1906 Model Exposition Machine," shipped direct from its Paris factories (which now had a production capacity of two hundred projectors, cameras, and other apparatuses per month).[131] Within another month, now in partnership with Vitagraph, the French company would finance the first trade weekly devoted almost exclusively to exhibitors in the new moving picture industry, *Views and Films Index* (whose readers allegedly reached several thousand within weeks).[132] And it was then that the Grand Theater, in Portland, began advising audiences they could always find "the latest Pathé films" on its weekly programs.[133] By the summer of 1906, "the air [was] full of moving picture exhibitions,"[134] largely because Pathé was releasing from three to six subjects per week, its production of positive film stock having doubled over the previous nine months to eighty thousand feet per

Figure 14. Grand Theater ad, *Sunday Oregonian* (8 April 1906), 29.

day.[135] According to *Billboard,* the French company was close to having advance orders, on average, of seventy-five prints of each new film title it placed on the American market.[136]

If, as Musser writes, echoing the words of Fred Aiken, the "nickelodeon boom" in the United States constituted a "radical change" or "revolution in exhibition on an unprecedented scale," [137] it was due in no small part to Pathé-Frères and its capacity, by 1905–1906, to produce and deliver a variety of films of high quality, en masse and on a regular, relatively predictable basis. By fulfilling the basic economic imperatives of standardization and differentiation, by orchestrating both "the *effect* of stability and the *effect* of novelty," the French company almost single-handedly assured the viability of a new kind of cheap amusement.[138] It assured nickelodeons of precisely what Edward Bok, the editor of *Ladies' Home Journal,* considered essential to the success of the new mass magazine or modern store: "wares [that are] constantly fresh and varied to attract the eye and hold the patronage of its customers."[139] In other words, the "foreign bodies" of Pathé films, which American film historians so long have overlooked, once played perhaps the determining role in the emergence of our own cinema.

DOCUMENT 2

"An Unexploited Field and Its Possibilities: A Chance for Good Exhibitions," *Views and Films Index* (6 October 1906), 3–4

In the course of the progress of the motion picture business as a means for affording enjoyment to the great masses, the question has many times arisen as to whether it would be wise to cater to the public by establishing in a purely residential district. As yet little experiment has been made in this direction, but a discussion of the question and a few points from the experiences of different cities may help toward determining the value of the field for exhibiting purposes. New York probably contains more shows than any city in this country. It is the most cosmopolitan city and contains the most various forms of settlement. Beginning at the lower end of Manhattan it is found that motion picture shows flourish on the Bowery, Fourteenth street, Sixth avenue, Eighth avenue, and One Hundred and Twenty-fifth street. An analyzation of the character of business which these places do and a comparison of this with some conditions now existing throughout the country certainly tells decisively how much money there is for motion picture shows in residential districts.

On Park Row and the Bowery, which are really one street about a mile in length, there are at least two dozen moving picture shows and as many more slot machine arcades. They all do business. This is evident at any hour during the day and up to 12 o'clock at night. Places are continually opening. East of the Bowery lies the great East Side section of New York, with its great tenements and the countless humanity living in it. The character of the people who use the Bowery as a thoroughfare and who may be classed as transient is not of such a nature that they would attend these shows; therefore the logical conclusion, and what is now the established fact, is that these moving picture shows and arcades are supported by the residents of the vicinity, the great Italian settlement on one side and the greater Jewish settlement on the other. Proof of this is that on Saturdays, which is the Jewish Sabbath, great holiday crowds from the East Side throng the Bowery, peeking into the slot machines, looking at the pictures and testing their powers on other devices, and this is the best day of the week.

In view of these facts it has been difficult to understand why these business men stick to the Bowery instead of branching out on thoroughfares like Grand and Canal streets. Presumably they do not care to take the risk, but at the beginning of the past summer two slot machine arcades established on Grand street, and having done business, one moving picture man determined to take the chance. He built a very attractive little theatre and advertised that motion pictures could be seen for five cents. The result was gratifying. The place commenced to do a rushing business, and is doing it yet. The films are changed frequently and the East Siders are willing to be kept interested. This knocked to pieces the theory that the Bowery is the only place where moving pictures would pay, yet exhibitors seem to be slow about taking the hint.

A study of the motion picture showing business, as conducted further uptown, seems to point in the same direction. On Fourteenth street the audiences are purely transient. One particularly attractive theatre on the street may be taken as an example for the character of audiences which patronize. They are for the most part shoppers from the neighboring department stores. The same may be said of the theatres on Sixth avenue, which is also a shopping district. It is important to note that the women who buy from the stores in the neighborhood are mostly flat dwellers from the upper section, who may not have the facilities near their homes, which Fourteenth street affords; and when these people visit the lower section of the city it is usually for the purpose of buying their necessities and going home again. Therefore the fact that they do stop in to see motion pictures, paying the price and using their time, shows very clearly that if the motion picture theatre were established nearer to their homes they would patronize it more often. Transient or not transient, it has been demonstrated that the general New York public approves of moving picture shows. The box office receipts of exhibitors and the growth of the business makes this more than a mere theory—an established fact.

In the face of this we find that from Ninety-first street to One Hundred and Sixteenth street, extending from Fifth avenue for four long blocks east, there is not one place where cheap amusement can be gotten. This section is thickly populated by a uniform class of people. The general character of the residents is good; they are of the middle class and intelligent people. It is they who journey to One Hundred and Twenty-fifth street nightly and pay their money to the many theatres on that thoroughfare. But even there only one or two moving picture theatres exist. As a rule, when people travel that far, they want to see something good. Anything which is not particularly high class they do not deem worth while traveling that distance for. And for this reason the vaudeville theatres and other play houses along that street do good business. Still there are many people who attend the theatre only very rarely, for the reason that it means more elaborate arrangements for doing so than it would if the theatre were nearer to the home. While these people will go to One Hundred and Twenty-fifth street for the sole purpose of attending a regular theatrical performance they will not make the trip for the sole purpose of attending a motion picture show. Still, when they are in the neighborhood of one, as they are when they go shopping to Fourteenth street, they will stop in. This gives us, on one hand, a public willing to see the shows, and, on the other, shows too far away from the public for them to attend conveniently. Now the question is, "Will it pay to bring them together?"

This must be judged by precedent. Besides the instance quoted of the Grand Street theatre, it is known that Chicago has tried the experiment successfully. The number of people attending the shows there is a great deal larger than in New York for the reason that exhibitors cater to resident audiences. They establish right next to one another, but the fact that they do not have the same films insures all good business; for when people know that they can attend two shows in an evening for ten cents and that they will see different pictures at each place, they seize the opportunity. The result is that some people have been observed to pass out of one theatre and into another, visiting perhaps three or four in one evening. This in itself should be proof for those inclined to doubt the practicability of doing business on the same plan in other cities.

There is a demand for cheap amusement in the residential sections of New York City, also elsewhere, and as soon as a man can take his family down a short distance from their home and afford them an hour's enjoyment without the inconvenience of dressing for a longer trip to the theatrical section, the exhibitor who will bring about this condition will find his enterprise duly rewarded. The fact that it is cheap to witness a motion picture show is no reason why it should not be a first-class one. There must be music during the performance and full attention must be given to mechanical effects; the films must be interesting, topical and well shown; there must be frequent change of programme and general preparations made for catering to an intelligent class of people. This is the only kind of show for which there is a big field in a section of this character in New York and corresponding ones in other cities.

ENTR'ACTE 2

The Color of Nitrate

Pathé's "Heavenly Billboards"

Imagine yourself a young woman, specifically a sales clerk, in October 1905, seated in Keith's vaudeville house in Boston or, four months later, a textile factory worker at the People's Theatre in Lowell. What might have struck you as so distinctive about Pathé's *The Wonderful Album* or *The Deserter* that you would watch either film "with deep interest"? One thing would have been "the peculiar form of coloring," which set many of the French company's films apart from those of its competitors during the first decade of this century. Only recently have historians begun to reexamine the significance of color in early cinema, to pose certain questions about its function in the cinema's emergence.[1] Several are especially germane here. Given their broad distribution at this crucial historical moment, what role did Pathé color films play in the cinema's development as an American public amusement? More generally, how was cinema's emergence situated within the larger transformation to a "modern consumer society" in the United States? For, central to that transformation, if we follow William Leach, was a "commercial aesthetic" in which "color . . . and light" functioned as the principal "visual materials of desire" in a new mass culture.[2] To the extent that early cinema in the United States incorporated this commercial aesthetic, why was it that French manufacturers like Pathé seem to have exploited its attraction so much more than did their American competitors?

At least as early as 1873, the French writer Villiers de l'Isle-Adam had envisioned such a commercial aesthetic in a satiric short story, "The Heavenly Billboard." There, the "magic of electricity" made possible a new "celestial" medium of projected advertising, capable of generating "an absolute Publicity." "Wouldn't it be something," he mused, "to surprise the Great Bear himself, if, suddenly, between his sublime paws, this disturbing message were to appear: *Are corsets necessary, yes or no.*"[3] Today, of course, the Great Bear has become a clan of polar bears, the commodity a Coke, and questions seem irrelevant. Electricity would turn out to be one of the principal technological marvels powering this aesthetic of visual display, creating what, in France, Rosalind Williams has called "dream worlds" for a new mass public of spectators/consumers.[4] Yet, in the United States, other technological innovations that first involved and then superseded chromolithography were nearly as important, especially in facilitating the production and distribution of color images en masse for promotional purposes.[5] Indeed, during the last decades of the nineteenth century, color "chromos" circulated so widely—in trading cards, mail-order catalogs, posters, book covers, magazine ads, Sunday comic strips, cheap reproductions of paintings, and other kinds of illustrations—that the United States, writes Peter Marzio, came to be dubbed the "chromo-civilization."[6] Whatever the technology involved, however, these bright displays and images with their add-on color, "testifying," Neil Harris notes, "to the greater wealth, ambition, or taste of [their] subject or purchasers," proliferated according to explicit commercial demands.[7]

The chief dilemma of late-nineteenth-century capitalism, Ohmann argues, was that its tremendous productive system could not sufficiently be controlled.[8] The challenge was to find a way to move and sell new commodities in volume, predictably, regularly; what businessmen hit on was the idea of exercising control through sales—that is, through mass marketing and, by extension, through national advertising campaigns that, in the words of Emily Fogg Mead (in 1901), could create and diffuse desire throughout an entire population.[9] Perhaps because of the rapid pace at which commodity production accelerated in relation to the country's geographic size, this challenge was especially acute in the United States. By the turn of the century, a "new set of [color] commercial enticements" shaping the desire to consume was well in place; and a New York lithographer could write, "People in these days seem to have gone picture-crazy. There never has been such a demand as there is now. They do not care so much for black-and-white as they used to—they want color."[10] One could find such enticements in full-page color ads in all kinds of mass-circulation magazines, from *Munsey's* and *McMclure's* to *Ladies' Home Journal* and the *Saturday Evening Post*.[11] One could also find them in dazzling visual displays, not only in interior showrooms (as in the Bon Marché in Paris) but also in street-level show windows of department stores like Wanamaker's (Philadelphia), Macy's (New York), and Marshall Field's (Chicago).[12] And one could find them in the "fairyland" of billboards and electrical signs that transformed metropolitan shopping and entertainment districts at night into "Great White Ways," lorded over by "phantasms" like the forty-five-foot Heinz pickle in green bulbs on New York's Madison Square.[13]

In the United States, moving pictures cannot be extricated from this context of commercial enticements, whatever their venue of exhibition, from vaudeville houses to nickelodeons. Nor can their spectators be extricated from the primary group of consumers for whom such enticements were seen, in the words of Elizabeth Wilson, as "an Aladdin's cave of riches."[14] For those consumers were largely women (and children), the women either single or married, ranging across a stereotypical spectrum, according to *Views and Films Index,* from middle-class shoppers on Union Square or (Jewish and Italian) immigrant workers on the Bowery in New York to white-collar sales clerks in downtown Chicago.[15] Assuming such an

audience of spectators/consumers, why was it Pathé rather than one or
more of its American rivals that seems to have produced, promoted, and
circulated the vast majority of color moving pictures?

That American companies did circulate color films is clear as early as
the summer of 1902. From advertisements in the *Clipper,* one can gather
that film prints normally were sold in black and white or, at extra cost, with
one or more colors applied by hand ("colored," at the time, was a code
word for hand-painted). Edison, for instance, repeatedly recommended
coloring "EVERYTHING . . . including the Sky, Water, Flames and
Smoke" in *The Martinique Calamity*.[16] Edison story films like *Jack and the
Beanstalk* also were promoted as "great opportunities for coloring effects,"
whether that meant the "figures only" or the "background and all details"
as well.[17] When Selig began recording its own travel views of Colorado
and Arizona that fall, it too sold them as "colored films."[18] Over the course
of the next year and a half, however, no American company drew attention to color in its advertisements, even though at least two kinds of color
films now were in circulation. Many of these probably were available
tinted throughout in one color by means of a chemical process that used
aniline dye. In May 1904, Lubin already was criticizing this process for its
"monotony of one colored moving pictures."[19] Others were still hand-
colored: Biograph's *Kit Carson* received high praise on the Keith vaudeville
circuit, in early 1904, as a "beautifully colored" film.[20] Yet Biograph never
advertised its films as being available in color (of whatever kind). And
Lubin's purpose in attacking those "one colored moving pictures"
was to announce his own "new discovery," one that characteristically
turned out to be someone else's—namely, Méliès's or Pathé's.[21]

When the Méliès sales office first opened in New York, in May 1903, its
ads rarely insisted on the "coloring effects" of its films.[22] That fall, however, brought a change. Méliès offered *Fairyland*, for instance, in three versions: "plain," or black-and-white; "polytint" (for 300 of the film's 1,040
feet); and "colored" (or hand-painted).[23] This hand-colored version was
featured at Talley's Lyric Theatre in Los Angeles throughout the month of
October 1903.[24] At the same time, other color prints were scoring hits on
Keith's vaudeville circuit in the Northeast and Midwest: the Philadelphia
house, for instance, held *Fairyland* over for three weeks, and the Providence
house placed it prominently in the middle of its program.[25] Close on the
heels of the Méliès film came a hand-colored version of Pathé's two-reel
Life of Napoleon in Keith's theaters: according to the Cleveland manager, it
"held the audience [and] received considerable applause."[26] That fall and
winter, color prints of the same film, writes Musser, also served as the "featured subject" on Lyman Howe's "high-class moving picture" tours (one
company covered "legitimate" theaters in the Northeast, a second, those in
the Midwest).[27] Likewise, Edwin Hadley used a color print of Pathé's

Napoleon to anchor his own exhibitions now competing with Howe's in the Northeast.[28] Although not specifically described as such, other Pathé titles such as *Don Quixote, Puss-in-Boots,* and *Marie Antoinette* probably circulated in hand-colored versions; and they were equally popular not only in Keith theaters but also on Shephard's much more varied touring programs for working-class audiences in the Northeast.[29]

These French color films were so popular among audiences in the United States that by the spring of 1904 American manufacturers and sales agents such as Lubin and Harbach seized on them as a promotional device.[30] By summer's end, just as the vaudeville season was to open, not only was Kleine Optical (headquartered in Chicago) claiming that "feature films" (including Pathé's) were in "great demand," but both George Spoor's Film Rental Bureau and Eugene Cline (also located in Chicago) were promoting "foreign" color films (again, all Méliès and Pathé titles).[31] Yet, if French films were being lauded for their finely crafted color effects, differences between Méliès and Pathé also were emerging. Both companies seem to have shifted around this time to a unique stencil process, similar to that used in chromolithography,[32] by which "colorists" (all women) could apply up to three different colors within a single film frame, with greater precision and uniformity.[33] Unlike Méliès, however, Pathé used stencil color on a much wider range of films; moreover, the company already had introduced the practice of adding tinted titles and intertitles to all its films (whether colored or not), titles bearing large red block letters, as well as the red rooster logo in each bottom corner of the frame.[34] In other words, a full range of color effects, with stencil color the most celebrated, was fast becoming a distinctive Pathé trademark.

When the French company finally opened its own sales office in New York, in late August 1904, it also arranged for Kleine Optical to serve as its principal sales agent in Chicago.[35] Taking advantage of these parallel moves, Pathé ads in the *Clipper* offered stencil-color films in a wide variety of genres and complemented them with 47-by-63-inch "imported color posters."[36] Much like Méliès, the company also continued to describe these films as "hand-colored," in a marketing strategy that invested its mass-produced commodities with the cultural capital of "individual artistry."[37] Short trick films like *A Butterfly's Metamorphosis* and *Fireworks* were "hand-colored" throughout, whereas a biblical film like *Joseph and His Brethren* culminated in a final multicolor scene.[38] Such Pathé titles continued to be well received on the Keith circuit: in Boston, audiences watched stencil-color versions of the sensational melodrama *The Strike* (in December), as well as the "beautiful" historical film *Louis XIV* (in January), "with deep interest."[39] But the company's stencil-color prints also drew "big crowds" elsewhere: witness its *Passion Play,* which closed the 1904 summer season at a Kansas City amusement park and played for several weeks at the People's

Theatre in Cedar Rapids during Christmas and New Year's.[40] With only one Méliès title, *The Impossible Voyage,* gathering comparable notices during this period,[41] Pathé seems to have enjoyed something close to a monopoly in supplying stencil-color films on the American market.

The summer and fall of 1905 was a crucial moment for the American cinema, marked by a sudden expansion in the exhibition market. Although that expansion occurred in amusement parks and the growing circuits of family vaudeville houses, it was most notable in the new venue of permanent storefront theaters or nickelodeons emerging in large cities from New York and Philadelphia to Cleveland and Chicago (a venue also marked by richly colored slides illustrating popular songs). If, by this time, Pathé had become the principal supplier of moving pictures for this expanding market, one cannot insist enough on a crucial reason: its stencil-color films. Throughout August and September, for instance, many Keith theaters showed almost nothing but Pathé films on their programs. The company's color films were unusually prominent: they ranged from trick films like *The Language of Flowers* and *A Stunning Creation* (in Boston) to comic chases like *Two Young Tramps* and industrials like *Scenes at Creusot's Steel Foundry* (in Philadelphia).[42] The most remarked on throughout the circuit, however, was *The Wonderful Album,* in which a magician produces a half dozen life-size figures, each in a differently colored costume, out of an enormous album of illustrations for an appreciative spectator.[43] Emblazoned on the album cover, suggesting the real source of its magic, was Pathé-Frères' own name in shimmering gold letters. In other words, this film was nothing less than a "heavenly billboard" advertisement for the French company. And its release was perfectly timed to help fix Pathé's trademark as the best possible guarantee of fine film product, for the "high-class" vaudeville theaters on Keith's circuit now began to serve chiefly as a venue to promote Pathé titles, which could then circulate more widely in the growing number of family vaudeville houses and nickelodeons.

Throughout the 1905–1906 season, Pathé itself gave special attention in trade press ads to its distinctive color films. Some of these, like the "anthropological" fashion series *Different Hairdresses,* the trick film *Fire Cascades,* and the comic *féerie Tit for Tat,* were stencil-colored throughout.[44] The *grand guignol* melodrama *The Deserter,* however, was offered in a special tinted print (later this was revealed to be toning).[45] And *The Hen with the Golden Eggs* included both tinted and stencil-colored scenes.[46] Moreover, Pathé received additional support from Kleine Optical (now perhaps the largest sales agent in the country) when its November 1905 catalog strongly recommended the company's stencil-color *Passion Play* as the best version on the American market.[47] By spring 1906, when Pathé was addressing its ads directly to "moving picture men" and releasing no fewer than three and sometimes as

Figure 15. Pathé ad, *Views and Films Index* (3 November 1906), 2.

many as six film titles per week, at least one always was singled out for its stencil color.[48] In one of the initial issues of *Views and Films Index*, J. A. Berst claimed that his company not only "had made a specialty of color films" (employing at least three hundred women to produce stencil-color prints in Paris) but also "had made a great success of it."[49] Several weeks later, the trade weekly singled out Pathé's new "chemical process . . . called mono-tinting" (that is, toning), noting its expense and praising the effects it created as far better than those of what it called the "cheap method" of "aniline dye tinting."[50] Based on the evident popularity of its color films, particularly on the American market, Pathé set about developing a mechanized

Figure 16. Pathé ad, *Views and Films Index* (4 January 1908), 16.

system for the stencil-color process in order to reduce its costs further and achieve an even greater degree of efficiency and standardization.[51]

And what were American manufacturers doing to counter Pathé's use of color to sway the American market? Very little, it seems. In April 1905, for instance, Edison made a rare reference to color when it described *The Seven Ages* as having "two beautifully tinted scenes."[52] Over the next year, during the initial nickelodeon boom, only three other American titles were advertised in color: an early Vitagraph title, *Raffles*, with many scenes tinted at no extra charge; Edison's *Dream of a Rarebit Fiend,* available in a "beauti-fully mono-tinted" version; and Edison's "hand-colored" *Three American Beauties.*[53] Now, according to most popular reports, moving pictures gener-ally were "ordinary black and white" or "tinted," except for Pathé's more costly stencil-color films.[54] Yet it is clear from a September 1908 *Moving Pic-ture World* editorial that American companies such as Edison and Selig did use color (but not stencil color) admirably, and perhaps even extensively.[55] Still, archivists like Paolo Cherchi Usai have found only limited traces of such color in archive prints of early American films: if some survive with tinting, scarcely any do with toning.[56] Even if, by the time of the nick-elodeon boom, they did produce and circulate color films (of whatever kind), however, why did they not promote them? How could American film companies hope to prosper on their own market, given the "commercial aesthetic" that so defined modern consumer society, if they did not exploit "color and light" as the principal "visual materials of desire"? The answer, we will see, would come in the creation and exploitation of a desire for dis-tinctly American subjects.

CHAPTER THREE

The French Rooster Rules
the Roost, 1905–1908

"WHY THE 'NICKELS' ARE POPULAR"

The other day a Mirror *reporter had reached the corner of Hanover and Elm streets, when two matronly women rushed at each other and embraced as effusively as an armful of bundles would permit. They had been shopping and were evidently tired, though smiling.*
  "Let's go up to the Nickel and see the show," said one.
  "What is it?" said the other.
  "Moving pictures. Come on. It's only a nickel."
  "But I have to get home and get John's dinner."
  "Come ahead and get rested. You will get him all the better supper after resting there half an hour," and off they trotted.

MANCHESTER, N.H. *MIRROR, IN MOVING PICTURE WORLD* (26 OCTOBER 1908), 541

For nearly three years, from the fall of 1905 through at least the summer of 1908, Pathé dominated, and defined, the nickelodeon as a "cheap amusement." Pathé's name was prominent in *Views and Films Index*, of course, but also in *Moving Picture World*, which soon after its initial publication, in March 1907, acknowledged how crucial the "Red Rooster" films were in spurring the American market's growth.[1] Even Edison, Pathé's chief competitor/partner, and the only American firm determined to assert a measure of control over the industry, accepted the French company's dominant position. The testimony given by Frank Dyer, Edison's former vice president, for instance, in the famous antitrust case against the Motion Picture Patents Company (MPPC) contains the following exchange:

> Q. At that time, what was the most popular brand of film being exhibited in this country? In January and February, 1908?
> A. I think the Pathé pictures were the most popular of them, although the Biograph pictures came into vogue shortly afterwards, and have always been popular.
> Q. Then, had Pathé at that time established, so to speak, a standard of good quality?
> A. Yes, sir. The Pathé pictures were the highest standard known in the art at that time. They were pre-eminent.[2]

At another point in his testimony, Dyer even claimed that, in 1908, Pathé films constituted 60 percent of the total film product then in circulation in the United

States.[3] Several years later, Pathé itself asserted that, among its many accomplishments, no other firm had done as much "to boom [or build up] the film business" in the United States.[4] That assertion has considerable validity, as the previous chapter has shown, for the period leading up to the nickelodeon's emergence. This chapter demonstrates its continuing validity and offers several explanations for that, during the boom years of the "nickelodeon era," between 1906 and 1908.

As before, my argument, while drawing on previous research, singles out and contextualizes several strands of public and private discourse from those years. Again, there are catalogs and trade press ads from the manufacturers and a proliferating number of rental exchanges. Also, there are essays on moving pictures in several national magazines, investigative surveys by metropolitan agencies and moral reform groups, and articles and exhibitor ads in local daily newspapers from New York and Chicago to Des Moines. Less important are weekly managers' reports from the Keith circuit, now that high-class vaudeville houses, as the Detroit theater manager complained, made up an increasingly marginal portion of the market.[5] Of growing significance, by contrast, are editorials, commentaries, reports, and gossip published by the trade press itself. *Views and Films Index,* for a full year the only weekly devoted almost exclusively to the new industry, suddenly had rivals in 1907: specifically, *Moving Picture World* (also published in New York) and *Show World* (first published in Chicago that summer). And, in 1908, two other trade weeklies concerned with "arts and entertainment," the more recent *Variety* and the much older *New York Dramatic Mirror* (both published in New York), joined *Billboard* and the *Clipper* in reporting on moving pictures. Within each of these discursive strands (as the next chapters reveal even more fully), the Pathé company and its films once again were figured quite differently.

"THE MOST PERFECT FILMS ON EARTH"

The number of nickelodeons, electric theaters, or theatoriums that opened across the country between the summers of 1906 and 1907 is impossible to determine, given their sometimes ephemeral existence and limited newspaper advertising, but undoubtedly it was phenomenal.[6] If in June, *Billboard* was still surprised by "the vogue for moving picture shows," by September it had accepted the fact that "in every town of sufficient size to support it there exists a theatre where moving picture shows are given exclusively [and] dozens of new ones are being installed every week."[7] According to scattered reports, there were at least forty in Philadelphia and Pittsburgh, many more in Chicago and New York, and more than a dozen in Cleveland.[8] Some of these new places were either unusually spacious or elegant. In Worcester, for instance, The Nickel seated nearly a thousand and was often filled with the same "lively and demanding crowds" it had once served as a burlesque house.[9] In Boston, by contrast, the Theatre Comique, built by Mitchell Mark, was treated by the *Clipper* as one of several legitimate theaters located on Scollay Square.[10] By December, *Billboard* had compiled a list of more than three hundred "electric theatres" in thirty-five states and three Canadian provinces, with short programs that ran anywhere from four or five to fifty or more times per day.[11] Yet this list was far from comprehensive: none at all were mentioned, for instance, in New York, Boston, Toledo, or San Francisco, and only seven in Chicago. Moreover, in a good number of cities in the Northeast, vaudeville houses (many of them still supplied by Shepard) continued to exploit the "boom" with special Sunday moving picture shows.[12] That same month, in a report on Chicago, the *Index* estimated there were nearly 100 storefront shows in the city; three months later, *Billboard* itself claimed there were more than 150.[13]

By spring 1907, the moving picture business had reached a "record of prosperity."[14] The *Mirror* put the number of storefront shows and arcades in the New York City area at five hundred (Police Commissioner Bingham counted four hundred in June); at the same time, at least twenty were reported in cities from Youngstown and Atlanta to Saint Louis, Dallas, and Houston.[15] If Harry Davis's circuit of Bijou Dreams included "twenty-five of the largest and most successful picture shows in America," Archie Shepard now had at least thirty, stretching from Atlantic City to Maine.[16] In Boston, the Theatre Comique expanded into the building next door and then was taken over by Automatic Vaudeville, which soon added the Theatre Premier (also in Boston) to its exclusive circuit; as for the original owner, Mark opened another Theatre Comique in Lynn, where a half dozen nickelodeons were doing "big business."[17] By May 1907, the *World* estimated the total number of "5-cent theaters" in the United States at between twenty-five hundred and three thousand.[18] That figure probably was more accurate than the five thousand "electric theatres" that the *Index* had guessed in January, but the latter's comment that "Pennsylvania [was] in the lead and Ohio a close second" may well have been on target.[19] Whatever the case, "the work of upbuilding" the new industry was seen as complete, "the confidence, indulgence and approval of the public [had] been won."[20] In Chicago, where as many as one hundred thousand people patronized them each day, especially in "residential portions of the city," the "cheap amusement" of the "5-cent theaters," wrote the *Chicago Record-Herald*, was fast becoming "a permanent feature of municipal life."[21] In smaller towns, the *Index* added, they were a boon to downtown stores, converting an ordinary street "into a bright, gay avenue, where the residents flock nightly to 'see what is new.'"[22]

As impressive as the 1906–1907 boom in nickelodeons clearly was, the parallel boom in rental exchanges that supplied them with films was no less astounding.[23] The rapid incorporation of new companies during the spring of 1906, especially in Chicago (where Inter-Ocean Film Exchange, United States Film Exchange, and Temple Film all entered the business between April and June), resumed at an even higher rate the following fall and winter.[24] In Chicago alone, the newcomers included Royal Film Service, American Film, Globe Film Service, New Era Film Exchange, Grand Film Rental Bureau, Peerless Film Exchange, and Theatre Film Service (managed by Fred Aiken and Samuel Hutchinson).[25] Most important of

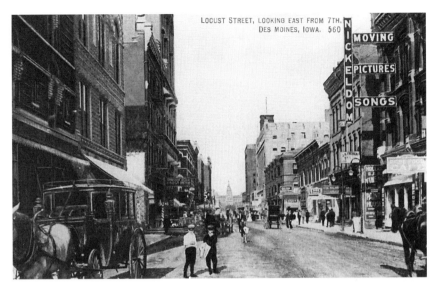

Figure 17. Nickeldom Theater, on Locust Street between Seventh and Fifth (Des Moines), 1907.

all, perhaps, there was William H. Swanson & Co. (run by a former circus owner-manager) and Laemmle's Film Service, whose ads were marked by a distinctive style of direct address full of "streetwise" "straight talk."[26] Joining those with central or branch offices already in New York that winter or spring were Acme Film Exchange, Eberhard Schneider, Lou Hetz, and, finally, William Fox's Greater New York Film Rental, whose success partly depended on its well-designed "Film Rental Facts" booklets.[27] Joining the American Film Service in Pittsburgh were Pittsburgh Calcium Light and Film, Fort Pitt Film Service, Columbia Film Exchange, Duquesne Amusement Supply (owned by Harry Warner), and even Harry Davis.[28] Others cropped up in areas especially dense in exhibition sites: Detroit Film Exchange, Indianapolis Calcium Light, F.J. Howard (Boston), Western Film Exchange (Milwaukee), Yale Film Exchange (Kansas City), O.T. Crawford (Saint Louis), Novelty Moving Pictures (Oakland), and Consolidated Film (Birmingham).[29] As the rental field expanded, "older" companies had to open branch offices and also to specialize in certain brands of films: Kleine Optical, for instance, became the exclusive American agent for French films from Gaumont and Urban-Eclipse, while Miles Brothers tried to corner the market on English films.[30] And, by the summer of 1907, companies like Chicago Film Exchange were offering as many as seven film program changes per week, in order to meet the voracious demand of nickelodeon managers, driven by incessant competition, for different "novelties" almost daily.[31]

Given this astonishing increase in exhibition venues and rental services, and the reciprocal shortening "shelf life" of individual film titles, the growth of film production was surprisingly slow.[32] Although the monthly volume of film subjects released on the market almost tripled from ten thousand to twenty-eight thousand feet between November 1906 and March 1907, most of that increase came from just a few companies.[33] Neither Biograph nor Edison, for instance, contributed to the increase. Biograph had difficulty maintaining its production level of two films per month after its chief director, Frank Marion, left the company in early 1907; Edison continued to invest most of its resources, quite profitably, in the manufacture of projectors and other apparatuses. After G. M. Anderson was hired as an actor/director, Selig's output slowly rose to one film per month. The only substantial increases from American companies were at Lubin and Vitagraph. Expanding into the rental business as well as exhibition, Lubin also was able to produce at least one film per week by May 1907.[34] With its new studio in Brooklyn and its three production units (headed by J. Stuart Blackton, Albert Smith, and James Bernard French), Vitagraph was able to match Lubin's level of production, but with films of better quality; and it became the only American company to open sales offices overseas, in London and Paris, in early 1907.

A significant portion of the increase in film subjects on the American market, of course, came from foreign imports such as the French and English titles supplied by Kleine Optical, Miles Brothers, and Williams, Brown, & Earle. But by far the greatest number of films still came from Pathé's studios and factories in Paris. By September 1906, the French company regularly was releasing no less than six films per week; within another month, its production of positive film stock had reached one hundred thousand feet per day, and its New York office had advance orders for seventy-five prints of each title shipped to the United States.[35] By the following April, Pathé again raised its output to "one novelty for each day in the week," which meant that nickelodeon managers could count on a steady supply of the company's red rooster films however often they chose to change their programs.[36] In other words, the Pathé trademark assured them of a relatively "predictable and controllable market."[37] As a result, Kleine admitted in a letter to Marion, the company's sales now were enormous.[38]

If Pathé did not have the American market for moving pictures entirely to itself during this period, it certainly came close. Its films continued to monopolize the Keith vaudeville houses. Throughout the summer, one of the circuit's biggest hits was *Dog Smugglers,* a violent chase picture that exploited all the latest techniques of alternation in editing.[39] That fall and winter, some of the best notices were given to the company's comic films and travel scenes, such as *The River Ozu, Japan,* as well as the ingenious comic fairy tale *Mephisto's Son* and the more conventional *Aladdin's Lamp.*[40] In February, *The Policeman's Little Run* was held over for a second week in Philadelphia; in April, *Cinderella* won praise as a "spectacular series" for children.[41] As the "nickel craze" erupted into the wider discourse of the daily newspapers, scattered ads, articles, and letters indicated that most of the

Figure 18. Pathé ad, *Views and Films Index* (20 April 1907), 2.

films shown in the nickelodeons were French (almost always Pathé's) and that they were preferred to all others.[42] From its opening in September 1906, for instance, the Theatre Comique in Boston consistently showed one or two Pathé subjects on its weekly two-reel programs; from December through February, it used Pathé titles almost to the exclusion of any others.[43] The same was true of the Nickeldom in Des Moines, which alternated Pathé and Vitagraph films throughout the 1906–1907 season.[44] When the Colonial Theatre opened in the

COLONIAL THEATRE
Moving Pictures
UNTIL THURSDAY

Picturesque Canada
The Female Spy
Distress
Mrs. Brown's Bad Luck
Hello Grinder

706 Walnut Street
ADMISSION 10 CENTS

Figure 19. Colonial Theatre ad, *Des Moines Register and Leader* (30 April 1907), 5.

city that spring, it, too, featured such Pathé titles as the *grand guignol Female Spy,* the domestic melodrama *Distress,* and the comic *Hello Grinder.*[45] At the same time, in its first general survey of the nickelodeon boom, the *World* assumed film subjects were "for the most part manufactured abroad," with most coming from Paris.[46] More specifically, the *Clipper* asserted that Pathé titles were imported in such numbers that they could be found on programs everywhere.[47] Two of Chicago's largest rental exchanges, Swanson and Laemmle, agreed in letters that Pathé itself used as testimonials in its ads, for they attributed the success of their business to the quality of the red rooster films they bought and rented in such volume.[48] In fact, Laemmle claimed that many of his customers (mostly nickelodeon managers) wanted "Pathé films or none" at all.

As some moving picture shows closed down for the summer of 1907, there were fears that the "nickel craze" might have peaked, just as Hale's Tours had the summer before. Yet there were plenty of optimistic signs for the entertainment William Bullock aptly called "a veritable Chautauqua for the masses."[49] Two important Chicago businessmen incorporated new production companies, Kalem in New York (Kleine, together with Marion and Samuel Long) and Essanay in Chicago (Spoor, along with G. M. Anderson), each of which soon was releasing

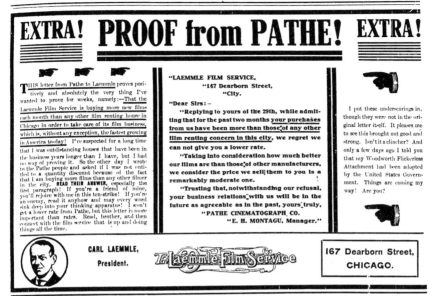

Figure 20. Laemmle ad, *Billboard* (13 April 1907), 33.

one "headliner" per week.[50] *Show World,* a third trade weekly devoted chiefly to moving pictures, appeared in Chicago and promptly praised the city's 158 moving picture theaters for leading the industry to "a higher plane."[51] It was there, too, that Laemmle first announced "snappy, eye-catching" posters "free to [his] film customers."[52] In perhaps the first widely circulated survey of the "nickel madness," in *Harper's Weekly,* Barton Currie reported that in Manhattan alone within the past year two hundred licenses had been issued for "nickelets" and perhaps a half million people were being "thrilled daily" throughout the New York City area.[53] Moving picture houses also continued to proliferate in other parts of the country. A good example was Des Moines, where at least five new nickelodeons and vaudeville houses (showing pictures) opened to compete with the Nickeldom between April and August: the Colonial, the Jewel, the Radium ("the brightest spot in town"), the Dreamland, and the Lyric.[54] By summer's end, Aaron J. Jones, the "Napoleon" of Chicago's amusements, who operated six downtown nickelodeons and arcades (as well as nearly fifty concessions in White City), boasted that the Bijou Dream, on State Street, could draw forty-eight hundred people per day and had a clientele "as regular as a milkman's" because they could always count on seeing "a fresh picture."[55]

    Given its regular release schedule of seven film subjects per week, Pathé's position within the American market seemed quite secure throughout the summer of

Figure 21. Laemmle ad, *Show World* (6 July 1907), 2.

1907. In *Show World,* Eugene Cline claimed that as much as 80 percent of the film footage released weekly was foreign, most of that coming from Pathé, the remainder from Gaumont and Urban-Eclipse (through Kleine Optical).[56] Another "Chicago film man" made that claim more precise—whereas American production rarely reached two thousand feet per week, European production usually ran between seven and eight thousand feet—and frankly admitted that "Pathé is universally acknowledged as the finest moving photographer and his subjects are world famous."[57] In Des Moines, specifically, the Radium and the Dreamland used Pathé films like *Two Sisters* (a domestic melodrama) and *Police Dogs* (a comic chase) to kick off their initial programs; for its first three weeks, the Dreamland showed Pathé titles only.[58] Similarly, the new Lyric (which replicated Harry Davis's showcase theater in Pittsburgh) advertised as attractions the latest French films "right off the reel from foreign shores."[59] At the Nickeldom, where Pathé's *Carnival at Nice* played one week, a man was overheard saying, "As good as a foreign trip and for only ten cents."[60] In *Harper's Weekly,* Currie concluded that "the French seemed to be the masters in this new field" of "innocent entertainment," noting that "thousands of dwellers along the Bowery [were] learning to roar at French buffoonery."[61] Currie also singled out Pathé's *Pirates* as a perfect example of the fast-paced, "hair-raising" melodramas one could find on the Bowery and elsewhere in New York.[62] Finally, some moving picture houses apparently gave substance to Laemmle's claim that summer by showing nothing but the French company's red rooster films, at least if the names of the "Home of Pathé" in Chicago's Riverside Park and the "Pathé" in Cairo, Illinois, as well as Tampa, Florida, are any indication.[63]

Although an economic recession in 1907, culminating in a brief stock market collapse in October, exacerbated fears that the "nickel craze" had been "too sudden and too energetic to last," its effect was minimal, perhaps even advantageous.[64] Late that summer, the *Index* predicted that orders for new film subjects would double or even triple for the 1907–1908 season, and apparently they did.[65] In his Thanksgiving article in the *Saturday Evening Post,* Joseph Medill Patterson accepted an estimate of four to five thousand nickelodeons now "running and solvent" across the country, with the number "still increasing rapidly."[66] If New York and Chicago had by far the most, other cities could match them in ratio to population: Lynn now had ten, Grand Rapids had eleven, Dayton had twenty-two, Saint Louis had more than sixty, and Cincinnati was said to be "dotted" with them.[67] The circuits that Davis (Pittsburgh), Jones (Chicago), Bullock (Cleveland), Lubin (Philadelphia), Fox and Loew (New York), and Shepard had built up during the previous year became models for others. They included Keith's Nickel Theater Circuit (with the Albee brothers and J. E. Moore), which operated twenty-one houses in New England and Canada, Casino Amusement Enterprises (Detroit), Montgomery Amusement Company (Memphis), and O. T. Crawford (Saint Louis): by late November, Crawford controlled a chain of fifty houses "reaching from Chicago to El Paso, Texas."[68] In Philadelphia, the *World* reported, some of

Figure 22. Lyric Theatre ad, *Des Moines Register and Leader* (21 July 1907), 3.7.

the dozen or more theaters lining several blocks of Market Street (the largest being one of Lubin's, near Wanamaker's department store) now had reached the point of changing their pictures twice daily.[69]

In order to supply all these venues, as well as the vaudeville houses that still showed the "latest pictures," between September and November no less than ten or twelve film rental exchanges opened each month across the United States and Canada.[70] In Ohio alone, there were eight new ones based in Cleveland, Cincinnati, Toledo, Columbus, and Canton.[71] Four months after its founding in September 1907, the Toledo Film Exchange already was supplying three hundred nickelodeons, the same number Eugene Cline had mentioned as clients the previous summer.[72] In New York, after "many exhibitors . . . requested [his] services,"

Marcus Loew entered the film rental business with People's Film Exchange.[73] In order to compete with these newcomers, the established exchanges kept opening more and more regional branches. Cline, for instance, now had branch offices in Kansas City, Saint Louis, Salt Lake City, Minneapolis, Cleveland, and Atlanta; Kleine Optical had them in Montreal, Seattle, Denver, and Indianapolis; Laemmle had expanded into Evansville, Memphis, and Omaha; Swanson, into Saint Louis and New Orleans.[74] In fact, by October, Kleine Optical and Pittsburgh Calcium Light and Film both were opening rental exchange offices in Des Moines.[75] If, as George Spoor suggested, "the renting business [was] becoming more localized every year," Chicago still served, in the words of R. G. Bachman (20th Century Optiscope), as "the great, natural distributing center of the North American continent."[76]

In its predictions for a record-breaking 1907–1908 season, the *Index* wrote of "a scramble" among agencies to book foreign productions. Even if this has the ring of a promotional tactic, it seems borne out by Pathé's experience that fall. In October, J. A. Berst told *Billboard* that the company's volume of business had doubled over the past four months.[77] Within weeks, the New York office was publishing a "Weekly Bulletin" of information on its new releases and offering this directly to nickelodeon managers.[78] By December, Pathé's ads were boasting that its six Paris factories were turning out an incredible "230,000 feet of film daily," more than double that of the previous year.[79] That same month, in the *Index*, the company reproduced a letter from Eastman Kodak to Charles Pathé, confirming that, in order to print such a high volume of product, he had placed an order, in October, for fifty million feet of positive film stock.[80] There were other signs, however, of the broad circulation of red rooster films. The *World*, for instance, reported that most of the Chicago rental exchanges "contract[ed] with French manufacturers for their films," and the newly established Standard Film Exchange supported this claim, specifically recommending the Pathé films it purchased each week.[81] In December, Pathé moved more directly into the South, making the Bailey Film Service, in Birmingham, its third sales office.[82] At least one new exchange, Imported Film & Supply (New Orleans), even advertised itself as an "All Pathé Films Service," adding the quips "Explanations and Arguments Not Necessary" and "You Know the QUALITY."[83] And Laemmle's new office in Memphis "did a cracking good business . . . completely supplied with Pathé films."[84] According to scattered ads in the *Des Moines Register and Leader*, throughout the fall Pathé films were the most frequently listed on the city's half dozen moving picture shows; in December, the Lyric even took the unusual step of describing its screening of *Bluebeard* as "the last word from the studios of Pathé, the world's most wonderful filmmakers."[85]

As E. H. Montague (the company's Chicago manager) first suggested in August, Pathé's biggest seller throughout the 1907–1908 season turned out to be a new stencil-color version of the *Passion Play*, whose four reels took a full hour to project.[86] In preparation for the fall season, Pathé issued a special "booklet of

Figure 23. Lyric Theatre ad, *Des Moines Register and Leader* (29 September 1907), 7.

forty-four pages" describing the film for exhibitors, and later offered a large poster with "photographs of the most impressive scenes in the course of the film."[87] Both promotional strategies came in response to, and then accentuated, the film's phenomenal popularity. In September, for instance, the Des Moines Lyric held the film over for an extra second week, and estimated that it was seen by thirteen thousand people.[88] In November, the Wonderland (New Orleans) reported that the Pathé film had been running for six weeks (with fifteen shows per day); in December, it even gave several benefit performances for the city's public school teachers.[89] At the same time, the Theatre Royale (Detroit), which had opened with the *Passion Play* in August, revealed that over the course of thirteen weeks "nearly 250,000" had seen it.[90] Throughout the winter and into the spring, the Pathé film remained a favorite of all kinds of exhibitors and their customers. An Oskaloosa manager rented an extra print to open an "electric theatre" in the black mining camp of Buxton, Iowa (twenty-five hundred attended the first week); another entrepreneur used the film to establish the Electric Theatre in Eugene, Oregon; and

Keith's Fifth Avenue Theatre presented special screenings to Christmas shoppers in New York.[91] Rental exchanges consistently called attention to the *Passion Play* in their ads during this period, and the People's Film Exchange claimed it was the only film "always on hand" (the exchange disposed of all others after a month).[92] During Easter week, according to the *World*, "the demand for it was so great that not a renter in the country could secure enough prints."[93] There can be little doubt that in the United States, between 1907 and 1908, more people saw Pathé's *Passion Play* (and many probably more than once) than any other single film.

FIRST-CLASS SERVICE AND HIGH-PRICED THEATERS

Several events in late 1907 were to have a considerable effect on the development of the American cinema industry. The formation of the United Film Service Protective Association and the Moving Picture Exhibitors Association, which signaled a change in Pathé's position on the market, is better left for the next chapter. The emergence of larger, "high-class" cinemas, however, can be dealt with here, for they actually helped sustain the circulation of red rooster films. This transformation of moving picture exhibition, which the *Index* promoted with its new cover design in early 1907,[94] initially involved some of the best melodrama theaters and vaudeville houses in the country.[95] One of the first was the old Manhattan Theater on Broadway (near Herald Square) in New York, which Felix Isman leased for Archie Shepard, in late April 1907, to run as a moving picture house for the summer.[96] Shepard's programs were so successful, even with "evening dress audiences," that the building's scheduled demolition was delayed, and he continued "giving moving picture entertainments exclusively" into the fall and winter.[97] The real impetus may have come from Aaron Jones's Orpheum, a new Chicago vaudeville house on State Street, which in late November changed exclusively to moving pictures.[98] Within another month, perhaps spurred by the legal defense of Sunday performances in New York, William Brady turned the twelve-hundred-seat Alhambra, on Fourteenth Street (just opposite Pastor's), into the Unique.[99] Weeks later, Fynes persuaded Keith & Proctor's to reopen its Twenty-third Street house as the "flagship" theater in a circuit of Bijou Dreams; according to *Variety*, it soon was grossing twenty-eight hundred dollars a week.[100] It was then, too, that Isman finally renovated the Manhattan, and William Ganes, who succeeded Shepard, confirmed the "money-making qualities of 'pictures'" to the tune of six-hundred-dollar weekly profits.[101]

Given such a quick return on investment, Fyne soon was supervising similar changes as, one by one, Keith & Proctor's big houses turned into Bijou Dreams: Union Square (in February), Fourteenth Street (in March), Fifty-eighth Street (in May).[102] Others soon joined the transformation in New York City: Pastor's (opposite the Unique), the Third Avenue Theatre (taken over by Charles Blaney), the Dewey (acquired by Fox), and the Novelty, Unique, Park, and Royal (all in Brooklyn).[103] The trend quickly took hold in other cities as well: the Hopkins in Saint

Figure 24. Swanson's Theatre (Chicago), *Nickelodeon* (March 1909), 65.

Louis; the Nelson in Springfield, Massachusetts (leased by S. Z. Poli); the Olympic in Lynn (controlled by the men who operated the Dreamland); the Haymarket and the Olympic houses in Chicago; and the Bijou Dream in Boston.[104] The move to diversify and expand into this new form of exhibition, represented most boldly perhaps by Fox in New York and Lubin in Philadelphia, also spread into the Midwest. O. T. Crawford, for instance, took up leases on the Garrick Theatre in Saint Louis and the Shubert in New Orleans.[105] Now that his rental business had grown to the point of being divided into four departments, Swanson, too, took the plunge into exhibition by constructing a new "luxury" cinema on Thirty-ninth Street and Cottage Grove in Chicago.[106] At the same time, the Keith circuit continued to expand with new theaters like the Star, in Pawtucket, which the *Mirror* singled out as a model "modern moving picture theatre."[107]

The size of these new "cinemas," with their minimum admission cost of ten cents, placed them in the same category as established theaters with respect to licensing fees.[108] This change, along with their location on downtown commercial

Figure 25. Lubin and Bijou Theaters (Richmond, Virginia), ca. 1908.

streets with the highest rents (the Orpheum, for instance, was opposite the new Palmer House hotel in Chicago),[109] was a good indication of the industry's prosperity and presumed permanence, even in the face of recession. The programs they offered, which usually ran three reels or forty-five to fifty minutes in length, benefited from two projectors operating in alternation—a practice made standard by the Orpheum and the Unique, as well as by smaller theaters like the Princess, in South Framingham.[110] Other standard practices included hiring dozens of uniformed attendants to provide courteous, efficient service and assembling small orchestras for musical accompaniment, most notably at the Olympic and Swanson theaters. The construction of such "large and elaborate moving picture theatres" continued into the fall, with many of them now reported in states "west of the Mississippi and the Middle Atlantic states."[111] Again, the *Mirror* gave its blessing to this phenomenon by describing it as an "evolution . . . from the cheap store show to the neat and permanent theatre."[112]

Despite their significance, however, these large houses represented only a fraction of the venues for moving pictures in the United States, which the nickelodeons would continue to dominate for another several years. By the spring of 1908, *Show World* estimated that the number of nickelodeons across the country had reached eight thousand; Sears Roebuck was even offering a prepackaged nickelodeon kit in its 1908 catalog.[113] Although figures varied from month to month and from source to source, there were anywhere from 400 to 800 or more nickelodeons in metropolitan New York, at least 320 (and probably more) in the

Chicago area, from 200 to 250 in Philadelphia, perhaps 100 in Boston, more than 80 in Saint Louis, and 40 already in Washington, D.C.[114] By May, "every theatre" in Toledo had "moving pictures as the entertainment"; one month later, motion picture theaters in Los Angeles were so popular they were "lined three or four a block."[115] In their four-month survey of the greater New York area alone, the Woman's Municipal League and People's Institute reported that the city's nick-elodeons now "entertained from three to four hundred thousand people daily"— confirming Fynes's earlier estimate of three million a week.[116] Yet, as John Bradlet would later remind the *World*'s readers, "the combined show places of New York, Chicago, and Philadelphia represent[ed] only 10 per cent of the shows scattered all over the country."[117]

The seemingly boundless demand for Pathé films continued unabated into 1908, as if to confirm the *Index*'s claim that the "success of your show depends exclusively on the number of Pathé-Frères films you receive."[118] In February, Globe Film Service ads began promoting the release dates of the French company's titles, implying that it enjoyed a privileged position as a supplier.[119] At the same time, Swanson and Laemmle ads were stressing the large size of their orders of new Pathé films.[120] According to Fox, Greater New York Film Rental also "bought a good many thousand dollars of film from Pathé Frères" and "always . . . show[ed] preference to [the] company."[121] The trademark red rooster was nearly omnipresent, now that the company was "issuing from eight to twelve new films every week," which amounted to five reels in all, and selling, on average, two hundred copies of each title released in the United States.[122] Despite this volume, from New York, where Keith's first Bijou Dream often featured Pathé films, to small towns like Spencer, Indiana, exhibitors could never "get enough . . . 'Rooster' film[s]," so much did audiences appreciate them.[123] Stoking what seemed an obvious demand, Pathé now introduced a new ad that was striking in its simplicity: enframed in a design drawn from its own films' titles and intertitles, it read simply "OUR FILMS LEAD ALL OTHERS."[124] *Show World* concurred, concluding its survey of film manufacturers with this paean of praise: "The popularity of the Pathé product is so great that no moving picture show is considered complete without Pathé pictures."[125] Looking back at his youth, around 1907–1908, the cinema historian Edward Wagenknecht recalled that "all the films shown" at Brown's Family Electric Theatre, his neighborhood theater in Chicago, "were French Pathé" (among them *Geneviève Brabant* and the *Passion Play*) and described how he "loved the titles and subtitles . . . always tinted red, with enormous lettering, and the famous Pathé roosters at the bottom of each."[126]

During the spring of 1908, specific references to Pathé films could be found throughout the spectrum of moving picture venues. Beginning in February, *Variety* offered summary reviews of the headliner attractions at several of the new cinemas in New York; many turned out to be Pathé subjects, which the trade weekly clearly identified as such. In March and April, for instance, both the Manhattan and the Unique featured the French company's films almost exclusively—from *Ali Baba* and *A Poor Man's Romance* to *The Little Cripple* and *Christmas Eve Tragedy*.[127] A

Figure 26. Pathé ad, *Show World* (23 May 1908), 33.

month later, in a detailed description of Keith's Fourteenth Street Theater program, the *New York Sun*'s Walter Eaton described *Christmas Eve Tragedy* as "a touching domestic tragedy," made all the more effective by a ballad that followed, "about a forsaken maiden 'in a village by the sea.'"[128] All that spring, according to the *Clipper*, the special Sunday shows of the Brooklyn vaudeville houses also were usually full of Pathé films. Throughout April, for instance, the Majestic, the Star, and the Gaytey offered predominantly Pathé programs, with the Star making a rare reference to *A Narrow Escape*, whose story D. W. Griffith would later remake as *The Lonely Villa*.[129] Meanwhile, in Keith's vaudeville houses, from Providence and Philadelphia to Detroit, Pathé's *Runaway Horse* was being called "one of the best comedy films ever shown."[130] Moreover, the French company's films continued to flourish in nickelodeons from Galveston and Des Moines to Lexington and even New York, as Joseph McCoy discovered in a June 1908 survey for the Edison Company of the films projected in the latter city.[131] Of the 515 film titles that he viewed over the course of a month, more than a third (177) came from Pathé.[132] In an interview that same month in *Variety*, even Thomas Edison had to admit—without uttering the company's name—"that the French [were] somewhat in advance," and not only in "artistic merit."[133]

By 1908, Pathé had achieved the remarkable feat not only of mass marketing the largest number and greatest variety of film subjects for an ever-expanding exhibition market but also of producing the one subject, the *Passion Play*, with the longest "shelf life."[134]

"A STRANGE, MAGNETIC FASCINATION"

There are at least two questions to consider further. The first may seem relatively obvious: Why did nickelodeons become so successful, so quickly, between 1905 and 1908? But that question presupposes another, which has usually gone unasked: Why were Pathé films so popular, for so long, with nickelodeon audiences as well as those in other venues? How could the French rooster "rule the roost" on the American market at least through 1908?

The first question preoccupied many writers at the time, and not only within the trade press. The *World*, for instance, found moving pictures' appeal similar to vaudeville's: nickelodeons presented standardized programs of "short, complete acts" that ran continuously, changed frequently, and could be enjoyed at a small cost.[135] In conjunction with that, *Billboard* pointed to the relatively low cost of operating a storefront theater, at least initially,[136] as well as the profits that accrued in every sector of the new industry. A study by the National Federation of Settlements, titled *Young Working Girls*, provided a more general context for these appeals by focusing on "the widespread commercialization of every form of recreation," one of four crucial areas of urban social life (the others were the family, neighborhood, and workrooms and stores) that modern industry had invaded and thoroughly reorganized.[137] Within that category, along with the dance hall and amusement park, the inexpensive moving picture show was of particular importance. It alone promised to fill, by repeatedly selling, the empty time created as a residue by modern industrialization, especially the "time between" (analogous to the "space between") those ever more regimented periods of working and shopping.[138] Young John Collier, of the People's Institute in New York, was one of the first to recognize "this great mechanical device [as] a new social force, perhaps the beginnings of a true theatre of the people."[139] The *Index* was more specific: as a "family resort," the nickel theater "seems destined to fill the place . . . now occupied by the ten cent magazine."[140] As Kathy Peiss and other historians have argued, the nickelodeon, more than vaudeville, perhaps more than the mass magazine or even the department store (that "cathedral of modern commerce," as Zola called it), came to epitomize "the rapid expansion and commercialization of leisure" that radically altered who could enter, move through, participate in, and exercise some measure of control within the public sphere of urban American society at the turn of the century.[141]

If the nickelodeon appealed to a mass audience, writers were nearly unanimous about its constituency. Moral reformers, journalists, and trade press staff repeatedly described audiences as being composed predominantly of families, from the lower through the middle classes. The Chicago Relief and Aid Society claimed, for instance, that the city's residential theaters, which catered chiefly to families, "answer[ed], imperfectly to be sure, a real need of the community."[142] If *family* often served as a consumer code word for *respectable*,[143] it referred more specifically to children (both girls and boys) and women (not only married women but also young, single working women who would soon be married). As early as

May 1907, the *Index* attributed the boom in moving pictures over the course of the previous year principally to "the patronage [of] women and children."[144] The *World* concurred, reporting that young people were the most frequent viewers, that nickelodeons everywhere were "great places for the foot-sore shopper," and that "mothers . . . take the children and spend many restful hours there at small expense."[145] At the same time, the *Chicago Daily Tribune* observed that the early evening audiences on Chicago's lower State Street "were composed largely of girls [sales clerks and others] from the big department stores."[146] Of the "people who will go to a picture show every day and night if the programme is changed accordingly," the *Index* concluded, most were women and children.[147] Such "repeaters" were observed frequently, but not always kindly, well into 1908.[148] In March, for instance, the *Birmingham Herald* seemed stunned to find that nickelodeons were "largely, almost exclusively, patronized by school girls and young women."[149] In June, a reporter for the *Washington Post* spent an afternoon and evening visiting a dozen picture shows, all "comfortably filled with audiences consisting for the most part of women and children."[150] Perhaps the *Indianapolis News* sums up this litany best: "Certainly the old family album never was to be compared with this one that 5 cents opens and puts into motion."[151]

The widespread existence of these accounts provides evidence for Hansen's argument that cinema, at least during the nickelodeon years, "functioned as a particularly female heterotopia."[152] It provided, in her felicitous phrase, "a space apart and a space between," an alternative social site where different kinds of women, but especially single working women, could engage imaginatively in negotiating the newly opened "gaps between family, school, and workplace." Mary Carbine and Gregory Waller have argued that cheap amusements could function similarly for blacks, if severely circumscribed by Jim Crow laws.[153] Excluded from many places (from a Topeka vaudeville house, for instance, to the Atlantic City boardwalk) and considered by many whites unable "to grasp the idea of moving pictures,"[154] some blacks set up their own cheap amusements, on the model of the Pekin Theatre in Chicago or the Frolic in Lexington.[155] White-owned venues also sometimes catered to blacks: in Iowa alone, the Electric Theatre in Ottumwa once featured a "colored quartette," well before the nearby Oskaloosa manager introduced a show into the Buxton mining camp.[156] From the standpoint of the industry, however, women (especially those of the lower middle or even middle class) represented the most valued category of consumers, and persistently appealing to them became a commercial strategy of legitimation. As early as the fall of 1906, Zukor's Comedy Theatre was presenting special "souvenir matinees" for women shoppers.[157] In the summer of 1907, nickelodeons from Boston to Des Moines catered in their ads to both: when the Lyric opened in downtown Des Moines, one of its promises was to be a "ladies and children's resort in earnest."[158] In an interview for *Show World,* the Chicago manager for Eugene Cline generalized that "better business in the long run" came only to theaters patronized by "ladies and children."[159] One of his competitors even advised exhibitors to use children as

Figure 27. Wladyslaw T. Benda, "The Line at the Ticket Office," in Mary Heaton Vorse, "Some Picture Show Audiences," *Outlook* (24 June 1911), 442–443.

promoters: when they attended matinees, they often got their parents to attend evening performances.[160] Fred Aiken, too, took up the litany in Chicago, encouraging "the patronage of women and children" well into the summer of 1908.[161]

If one effect of this discourse was to position the nickelodeon ever more securely within a middle-class space of consumption (one writer even recommended running them like efficient, well-stocked neighborhood grocery stores),[162] the corollary was its construction as an antidote to the saloon. By the turn of the century, in most American industrial cities, the saloon served as a crucial institution of leisure for working-class men.[163] A distinctive social site for cultivating an ethos of working-class masculinity (also often distinctly ethnic), this "poor man's club" could be seen as a residual alternative to the emerging society of consumption.[164] For moral reformers (and others), however, such clubs just as often were assumed to be dens of dissipation and "breeders of violent crime," for keepers and clients alike.[165] As the nickelodeon competed with and often replaced the saloon, the trade press echoed the reformers and police inspectors in celebrating its new status as the principal social center in many working-class residential areas.[166] "The 5-cent theater," Chicago's police chief, George Shippy, concluded, "if rightly conducted is an

Figure 27. (*continued*)

admirable institution." [167] That status was buttressed by psychological studies like those of Hugo Münsterberg, who supported "everything which strengthens family life and works against its dissolution . . . everything which . . . helps toward the prevention of crime." [168] In effect, by reconfiguring women and children everywhere as part of a generic middle-class family, this discourse helped to pull working-class men, women, and children into not a "true theater of the people" (much less a "female heterotopia"), but a new social space of commercialized leisure. [169]

Still, why were the most popular films in the nickelodeons Pathé's, just as they had been earlier in vaudeville houses? Why, as W. L. Larned asked, in early 1908, were "foreign films so eminently successful? Why [was] there such a demand for them? Why [did] the announced titles of these films hold a strange, magnetic fascination?" [170] The quantity and quality of the French company's films had a good deal to do with that success: the "foreign stamp" of the red rooster and Pathé's "peculiar form of coloring" usually "promise[d] sure returns." Larned himself explained their continuing fascination in terms of several features that distinguished French story films from their American counterparts and still have validity. First, he pointed to the elaboration of decors, down to the smallest details, so that "a room on film became a REAL room," something that assumed the kind of studio

Figure 28. "Empty Baby-Buggies at the Entrance," in Asa Steele, "The Moving-Picture Show," *World's Work* (February 1911), 14024.

facilities and personnel only Pathé, and perhaps Vitagraph or Gaumont, could offer before 1908. Second, he insisted that in a film "the story must be connected, obvious, and self-evident. . . . through the eye alone must come every heartache, every laugh, every gasp of admiration or amazement." Unlike Edison and Biograph, for instance, Pathé did not often exploit familiar subjects drawn from popular American culture (which required prior knowledge on the part of the spectator to be understood); instead, Pathé's subjects could often be unfamiliar, at least to American audiences: good examples would be *Dog Smugglers, Two Sisters,* and *Christmas Eve Tragedy.* There was great pressure, consequently, on the company to develop techniques of representation and narration so that its films could be understood and enjoyed across social and cultural boundaries, throughout Pathé's global sales market but especially in the United States.[171] Moreover, that demand for "self-evident" understanding points to another, crucial segment of the new moviegoers who frequented the nickelodeons.

Of all those who constituted the nickelodeon's mass audience, the one group that most attracted attention in the press was the disproportionally large number of recent immigrants, concentrated in metropolitan centers throughout the Northeast and the Midwest, from New York and Philadelphia to Cleveland and Chicago.[172] Not only was turn-of-the-century immigration perceived as a tidal wave, peaking at nearly one million in 1907, but most of the new arrivals, unlike those who came earlier, were from eastern and southern Europe (Russia, Poland,

Austria-Hungary, and Italy).[173] Reminiscing about his early days as a New York exhibitor, William Fox claimed that "the motion picture appealed mainly to the foreign born . . . a Pole, a Russian, a Slav or of some other foreign nationality."[174] Many accounts from the period bear him out. In October 1906, for instance, in one of the earliest descriptions of moving picture shows in Manhattan, the *Index* noted that there were dozens already on the Bowery and Park Row, drawing their clientele from the nearby Jewish and Italian immigrant working-class wards.[175] The following spring, the Chicago newspapers were alarmed at how popular the nickelodeons along Milwaukee and South Halsted were among the "foreigners" of this "slum population."[176] That summer, both Currie's survey of New York nickelodeons, in *Harper's Weekly*, and a *Chicago Daily News* letter from a "practical man" with long experience in the business singled out "the popularity of these cheap amusement-places with . . . newly arrived immigrants."[177] That November, in the *Saturday Evening Post*, Patterson reported that in "cosmopolitan city districts the foreigners attend in larger proportions than the English speakers."[178] In February 1908, a Philadelphia journalist wrote that in "cities where a new foreign population swells the census rolls an astonishingly large percentage of the audience in the nickelodeon is drawn from the Latin races who cannot speak English."[179] In other words, nickelodeons functioned like adjunct "schools" or, in Judith Mayne's apt turn of phrase, "back rooms of the Statue of Liberty."[180]

The precise relationship between newly arrived immigrants and the nickelodeon boom still needs to be explored, but specific studies like Ben Singer's on Manhattan (1907–1909)[181] suggest that many of the first moving picture shows were located not only in the shopping and entertainment districts (along Fourteenth Street near Union Square and around Sixth Avenue–Broadway in New York City, on State Street in Chicago, and on Market Street in Philadelphia), but also within or near immigrant ghettos. In 1902, for instance, according to data compiled by Walter Laidlaw, the Lower East Side (encompassing the Jewish ghetto and Little Italy) already had the highest concentration of the "foreign-born" in Manhattan, with smaller concentrations in Jewish Harlem (mostly white-collar workers) and Uptown Little Italy.[182] For 1910, according to maps drawn from data compiled by Laidlaw at a later date, Singer plots a similar concentration, with the most densely populated areas closely paralleling those of the foreign-born (now 47.9 percent of the overall population).[183] As the *Index* reported in the fall of 1906, and as Singer's study shows, it was precisely in those areas that nickelodeons flourished most.[184] And a specific sign of that flourishing was the fact that, between the summers of 1907 and 1908, nickelodeons had replaced nearly all the vaudeville houses (one of the principal forms of entertainment) in the Jewish ghetto and could be "found on every other street."[185] A similar situation may have existed in Chicago, where one of the earliest concentrations of nickelodeons, on South Halsted, bisected the "Chicago Ghetto" of the city's West Side and where the "younger element" of Jewish residents in particular was drawn to "the play-houses" on the surrounding streets as well as downtown.[186] Indeed, it may well be that the nickelodeon boom, which originated in the upper Midwest and the Northeast, depended far more than has been acknowledged on the concentration of immigrants, which reached 30 percent or more of the urban population not only in New York, Philadelphia, and Chicago but also in cities such as Boston, Providence, Cleveland, and Detroit.[187]

Little evidence survives of what film titles were shown, or even what trademarks circulated, in the nickelodeons located in or around the immigrant areas of New York, Chicago, and elsewhere. Because most catered to a nearby residential clientele, and may have operated on minimal budgets, their managers had little need to advertise beyond posting the day's bill outside the theater or sending circulars around the neighborhood.[188] Among those few specific references to Pathé films are several already mentioned: the *Chicago Tribune*'s attack on *From Jealousy to Madness* at a nickelodeon on South Halsted; Currie's comment on the French comic films, along with *The Pirates,* playing on the Bowery; and Wagenknecht's childhood memory of the famous Paris roosters at his neighborhood theater in Chicago. But there also was Jane Addams's complaint about the "highly colored lithographs" promoting films like *The Pirates* and *The Carman's Danger* in the nickel theaters around Hull House.[189] By contrast, there was pianist Arthur Barrow's praise of the Pathé trademark at Harry Altman's theater (on 108th Street and Madison) in the "thickly populated" center of Jewish Harlem (with its "appreciative class [of] Russian, Roumanian, and Hungarian Jews").[190] And there was the *World*'s contention, some years later, that, because "they mostly tell their stories without the aid of sub-titles," Pathé films were popular in Chicago's Jewish ghetto, as well as in its Polish and Slavic neighborhoods (near Milwaukee Avenue).[191] Still, one thing is certain: although Pathé did not make anti-Semitic films like Vitagraph's *Humorous Phases of Funny Faces* (1906) or Edison's *Cohen's Fire Sale* (1907), it rarely chose subjects catering specifically to these audiences, whether those might be "pogrom films" such as Lubin's *Hebrew Fugitive* (1908) or "ghetto films" such as Biograph's *Romance of a Jewess* (1908).[192]

Yet there is every reason to believe that the regular roster of Pathé films was a staple of such theaters, that they may have had a special attraction, especially for the most recent immigrants. That is because those arriving from Russia, Poland, Austria-Hungary, and Italy would, if they had attended a moving picture show between 1904 and 1907, already have seen Pathé films (but none or few from the United States). For it was during that period, through branch offices or sales agents, that the French company secured a dominant or at least significant position within each of those regions and sometimes, as in Russia, actually created the cinema market it then profitably exploited.[193] Adult Jewish immigrants especially could have viewed the Pathé trademark as a familiar icon with links to Europe, making it that much easier to turn the public space of the nickelodeon into the safe haven of a neighborhood center, a "space apart," with its own distinctive ethnic community identity.[194] If their children struggled to disengage from that community and mix with "the people," as Hutchins Hapgood described so well as early as 1902, they could have viewed the omnipresent red rooster instead as a recurring icon of popular

American culture.[195] By repeatedly abetting the desire for moviegoing, the Pathé trademark made of the nickelodeon a significant "space in between," an anonymous haven of commercialized leisure that eased assimilation into the new "modern" society of their adopted country. In 1906, *Munsey's* claimed that "Jews make good raw material for citizenship, because they are the only immigrants who come to us without a country. . . . America is their home, and their only home."[196] And Jewish youth, Andrew Heinze recently argued, took to the "intense acculturation" of Americanization "more quickly and thoroughly than other groups of newcomers," partly because of organizations such as the Jewish Immigration Society and Educational Alliance (in New York) whose very reason for existence was "rapid assimilation."[197] Could this kind of immigrant audience have played a significant role in sustaining Pathé's dominant position on the American market?

However speculative these last few sentences may seem, they do raise questions about the increasingly widespread circulation of Pathé red rooster films on the American market between 1906 and 1908, questions that the next chapters will address. Could the products of a foreign company be so widely accepted, become so dominant in such a competitive market, and not incite some kind of opposition? Where would that opposition come from, and where might it be muted, among the various sectors of the new industry—the manufacturers, the rental exchanges, the exhibitors—since their vested interests did not always mesh? And how would the French company respond to such opposition? How would the issue of acceptance, even promotion, versus opposition have played out in the trade press—another contested territory, given its shifting alliances with the industry—and in that of the national media? What use value could the Pathé films have for different moving picture audiences, however those might be differentiated by class, gender, race or ethnicity, generation, or region? And how would that use value, especially for the disenfranchised, be circumscribed within the discourse of moral uplift and the debate over "Americanization," a particular historical nexus marked by racist overtones of invasion and contamination, which increasingly imposed themselves on the new public sphere of the cinema?

DOCUMENT 3

John Collier, "Cheap Amusements,"
Charities and Commons (11 April 1908), 73–76

For four months a joint committee of the Woman's Municipal League and the People's Institute has been engaged in an investigation of the cheap amusements of Manhattan island. The committee has been composed as follows: Michael M. Davis, Jr., secretary of the People's Institute, chairman;

Mrs. Josephine Redding, secretary of the Woman's Municipal League, secretary; Mrs. R. H. McKelvey, Miss Henrietta B. Rodman, Miss Alice Lewisohn, Mrs. F. R. Swift, Michael H. Cardoza, Charles H. Ayres, Jr., John Collier, and W. Frank Persons. The investigation has been made financially possible through the Spuyten Duyvil branch of the Woman's Municipal League. The writer has acted as field investigator.

Attempt has been made to cover all phases of the cheap amusement problem, excluding from the detailed investigation dance-halls and skating-rinks on the one hand and high-priced theaters on the other. Legal and business aspects have been studied as well as educational and sanitary. The subject-matter has been fourfold: melodrama, vaudeville and burlesque; nickelodeons, or moving picture variety shows; penny arcades; and miscellany. The miscellany are anatomical museums, fake beauty-shows, etc., which are confined to a limited area of the city where they maintain a difficult existence. They can be passed over in the present brief report. What follows sums up the results of the investigation.

The whole topography of the cheap amusement problem has changed within the last six years. To illustrate: the old-time crass melodrama has been in large measure dethroned, crowded out by the cheap vaudeville and the nickelodeon. The cheap vaudeville has spread widely and has become a problem in itself; it plays a fairly constructive role in a few instances, and in several is about the vilest and most brutalizing form of entertainment in New York. Withal, it generally keeps within the bounds of the laws protecting public decency, which are largely matters of interpretation, but only through agitation, hard fighting and a constantly aroused public sentiment can it be kept within bounds. But even the cheap vaudeville has been eclipsed by the tremendously expansive nickelodeon, the number of which in Greater New York has grown in a few years from nothing to more than six hundred. The nickelodeon is now the core of the cheap amusement problem. Considered numerically it is four times more important than all the standard theaters of the city combined. It entertains from three to four hundred thousand people daily, and between seventy-five and a hundred thousand children. And finally, the penny arcade has sprung into mushroom existence, has proved itself to be irredeemable on the educational side and without the elements of permanent growth in popular favor and has worn out its public. It is now being driven from the field by the nickelodeon.

Not only the superficial aspect, but the essential nature of the cheap amusement problem has changed—and changed for the better. Constructive elements have entered and triumphantly made good with the public, so that now the cheap-amusement situation offers an immediate opportunity and a rousing challenge to the social worker. The nickelodeon's the thing, and the story of its development is instructive.

Five years ago the nickelodeon was neither better nor worse than many other cheap amusements are at present. It was often a carnival of vulgarity, suggestiveness and violence, the fit subject for police regulation. It gained a deservedly bad name, and although no longer deserved, that name still clings to it. During the present investigation a visit to more than two hundred nickelodeons has not detected one immoral or indecent picture, or one indecent feature of any sort, much as there has been in other respects to call for improvement. But more than this: in the nickelodeon one sees history, travel, the reproduction of industries. He sees farce-comedy which at worst is relaxing, innocuous, rather monotonously confined to horseplay, and at best is distinctly humanizing, laughing with and not at the subject. Some real drama: delightful curtain-raisers, in perfect pantomime, from France, and in the judgment of most people rather an excess of mere melodrama, and in rare cases even of sheer murderous violence. At one show or another a growing number of classic legends, like Jack and the Beanstalk or Ali Baba and the Forty Thieves, can be seen any night. The moving picture repertoire amounts to tens of thousands, and is amazingly varied. One firm alone in the city has two million feet of "film" stored away until it can be used again as fresh material, after the public has forgotten it. In addition to the moving-picture, the nickelodeon as a rule has singing, and almost invariably the audience joins in the chorus with a good will. Thus has the moving-picture show elevated itself. But the penny arcade has not elevated itself, and the cheap vaudeville, if anything, has grown worse.

The nickelodeon is a family theater, and is almost the creation of the child, and it has discovered a new and healthy cheap-amusement public. The penny arcade is a selfish and costly form of amusement, a penny buying only a half-minute's excitement for one person. Its shooting-gallery and similar features are likewise costly. In the short-lived pictures there is no time for the development of human interest, but the gist of a murder or of a salacious situation can be conveyed. So the penny arcade has resembled the saloon, from which the family has stayed away; and everything artificial has been mustered in to draw the floating crowd. As for the cheap theater, it has had a false tradition behind it, and managers have taken for granted that a low-priced performance could be given only by an inferior cast. So when the cheap theater has departed from the crudest melodrama it has gone over into inferior vaudeville and has depended on illegitimate methods for its success. This is the rule, although there are exceptions, and vaudeville at best has only a limited interest for the great, basic, public of the working and immigrant classes in New York.

But the nickelodeon started with a free field and a marvelous labor-saving device in the moving-picture, and it began above all as a neighborhood institution, offering an evening of the most varied interest to the entire family for a quarter. Thus the nickelodeon grew as solidly as it grew swiftly, and developed a new amusement seeking public, the public that has made the nickelodeon what it is. Right here is found the most significant aspect of the present amusement situation. All the settlements and churches combined do not reach daily a tithe of the simple and impressionable fold that the nickelodeons reach and vitally impress every day. Here is a new social force, perhaps the beginning of a true theater of the people, and an instrument whose power can only be realized when social workers begin to use it.

The investigation led almost immediately to constructive opportunities. On the legal side, an anomalous situation was found. In no existing law, state or municipal, was penny arcade or moving picture mentioned. These theaters were grouped by construction as common shows, along with ferris wheels and bicycle carrousels, and were put under the authority of the license bureau. But where the standard theater is regulated in the minutest detail as regards its building requirements, by written law, there is no law and no printed specification for the moving-picture show, which plays with fire. The theaters are controlled by the police, in whom responsibility is centered, and who co-operate with the proper department. But the nickelodeon is controlled by the license bureau, a clerical department, and up to ten months ago it went to all intents and purposes unsupervised. Then popular agitation, and the initiative of a hard working official in the fire department, set the city's machinery at work, and a good deal has been done. The moving picture show is reasonably safe from fire now; it is not yet safe from contagious disease, and the air is often very bad.

As a first step toward adjusting the legal situation, the investigation committee framed a bill, which has been introduced by Assemblyman Samuel A. Gluck at Albany, which has passed the Assembly by a large majority. Barring unforeseen obstacles it will pass the Senate at the present session. This bill provides for the raising of license fees on nickelodeons from $25 to $150 a year, for the placing of this license under the direct control of the police, along with the license for standard theaters, and for the exclusion of school children from nickelodeons during school hours, and after eight o'clock at night, except when accompanied by guardians. This bill went to Albany with the endorsement of various civic organizations, the Board of Education, and the Moving Picture Association itself which has shown every desire to co-operate in the improvement of moving picture standards.

On the side of co-operation with the moving-picture business looking toward more elevated performances, and even the improvement of the artistic and educational quality and of sanitary conditions through direct competition on a commercial basis, the opportunity is immediate and large. In this field it is probable that the drama machinery of the People's Institute will be turned to use in some co-operative plan, giving endorsement to the best of the shows and receiving in return the right to regulate their programs. Settlements on their own initiative could do valuable work in this way. The investigation committee, which is to be perpetuated as a sub-committee of the People's Institute, will in all probability start one or more model nickelodeons, with the object of forcing up the standard through direct competition, of proving that an unprecedentedly high class of performance can be made to pay, and perhaps, in the event of success, of founding a people's theater of the future.

DOCUMENT 4

David Hulfish, "A Store-Front Theater Building,"
Cyclopedia of Motion-Picture Work (1911), 114–117

A Store-Front City Theater Building

A vacant business house having been selected both for location and for size, the process of converting it into a motion-picture theater is to remove the glass front and framing for the door and window, to replace it with a closed front a few feet back from the sidewalk line into which are built the ticket seller's booth and the entrance and exit doors and on the inside of which is built the projection operator's booth. At the inner end of the room a muslin screen about 3 by 4 yards is stretched. The room is filled with rows of chairs, either kitchen chairs or opera chairs, as the expense justified by the location will permit, and a piano is placed near the picture screen.

FLOOR PLAN

A few general rules which may be followed in floor-plan construction are given herewith; aside from these a large variation in floor plan is possible.

The projecting machine should be at one end of the room and the picture screen at the other end, both being so high above the floor that the rays of light from the projecting machine to the lower edge of the screen will not be interrupted by patrons passing down the aisle.

The front of the room must be closed against the lights of the street, even when a patron is entering.

The operator's room must be laid out with reference to comfort and convenience, 6 feet square is a desirable smaller limit.

The floor space, if limited, must be laid out to seat as many people as possible, up to the number which the traffic study will require.

The operator's booth must be lined with sheet iron, top, bottom, and sides, with a door having a latch, and with two look-out holes, one for the beam of light from the

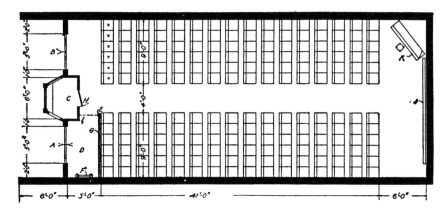

Fig. 1. Floor Plan for a Small Store-Front Theater

lenses and another at least a foot square and with the center at the height of the operator's eye, through which the operator may look to see his picture on the screen; these require-ments are for protection against fire.

A floor plan which is adaptable to the general requirements of any store-front theater is given in Fig. 1. This shows an arrangement for the maximum seating capacity for a store room 22 feet by 58 feet inside the walls. The seating capacity shown is 192. The front partition of the theater is placed 6 feet back from the sidewalk. The ticket booth extends forward from this partition. A still deeper front is desirable if the floor space can be spared; it gives advertising space; it gives opportunity for decorative efforts without the expense of decorating the entire front of the business house; it suggests refinement in the theater, and when the prospective patron steps off the sidewalk he feels that he is already within the theater, even before he has purchased his admission ticket.

The entrance and exit doors in the partition should be double doors. The entrance doors at *A* should swing both ways, while the exit doors at *B* should swing outward but not inward.

The ticket booth in Fig. 1 is 6 feet by 5 feet inside, with a shelf 1 foot wide across the front for making change. The three glass windows should be made with removable sash in order that screen wire or grille may be substituted in the warm weather.

The operating booth occupying the upper part of the space *D* is built over the ticket booth upon an elevated platform about 5 by 9 feet in size. As the patrons of the theater are required to pass under this platform it should be built upon a platform about 7 feet from the floor. A stanchion is set from floor to ceiling at *E*, about 9 feet from the side wall and 5 feet from the partition, and with this stanchion as a corner post a platform is built to cover the space D, then closed in with walls from the platform to the ceiling to form the operating room. Windows for projection and look-out are left in the wall toward the screen J, and another window may be left in the end for ventilation and over the doors A in the partition. Entrance to the operating room is obtained by means of the ladder at F, which extends upward along the wall and through a hole about 30 inches square in the floor of the operating room.

Below the operating-room platform, extending from the stanchion E to the wall, a screen G should be placed to prevent the light of the street from reaching the screen when the doors A are open; this may be a curtain hung from the edge of the operator's booth. The doorkeeper stands at the post marked H. A movable chain or bar is provided to extend from the stanchion E to the wall of the ticket booth to close the passage at the dotted line I. This enables the doorkeeper to hold back patrons who come so near the close of a picture or act that they would be interfered with by patrons passing out, or by patrons for whom there is no seat.

The piano may be at K, either automatic or manual. The screen J is shown at one side of the center; this has two advantages in the floor plan as shown. It gives more room for the piano and singer at the side of the screen, and it brings the center of the screen nearer to the direct line from the projection machine at the end I of the operating room at D.

Another method of building an operating room is to build it over the cashier's booth, extending through the partition and projecting into the theater room as far as the stanchion E. Set two stanchions like E and build the platform to the ceiling, placing the ladder F beside the short wall of the cashier ticket seller's booth, just inside the entrance door. The projecting machine will stand against the wall of the operating room at the exit-door side, and the projection and look-out windows should be placed in the front wall accordingly.

A space of 6 or 8 feet between the front chairs and the picture screen should be allowed, as the pictures cannot be viewed at a very close range. If the seats marked X are left out, the added convenience to patrons in passing out of the theater may more than compensate for the decreased seating capacity.

ENTR'ACTE 3

A Trade Press for the "World's Greatest Show"

Put yourself in the position of J. A. Getchell and B. F. Elbert, who, in early
May 1906, were about to turn Fred Buchanan's Bijou, a family vaudeville
house in Des Moines, into a moving picture show, the Nickeldom. Where
would you get information on what films to select for your programs? You
could, of course, always let a Chicago exchange like Kleine Optical or
National Film Renting (run by Spoor, whose kinodrome service had
shown a weekly reel of pictures at the Bijou) make the decision for you. If
you subscribed to *New York Clipper* or *Billboard*, you could also glean from
the manufacturers' ads each week some sense of what new films were
being released or what others were still available. Or, if you chanced upon
the first issue of *Views and Films Index* (25 April 1906), you would read the
following:

> Exhibitors and showmen have sought for years and still seek for their trade news in
> the theatrical papers. . . . We step into the breach and offer them all the news and not
> only the news, but all the novelties of the profession. We intend to make a specialty
> of the trade and not mix it up with a thousand theatrical details which have nothing
> to do with our business. . . . We are your trade paper.[1]

Here was a trade weekly that addressed you directly as a moving picture
exhibitor, a trade paper that promised news and information you could use
to advantage in running your business and, in particular, in negotiating
with rental exchanges. There can be little doubt that Getchell and Elbert
followed the *Index* closely—throughout the year, the Nickeldom showed
Pathé and Vitagraph subjects almost exclusively—and many other exhibitors (the numbers were rising exponentially) must have done likewise.
    The *Index* arrived at a crucial moment. Until then, the only consistent
sources of information were the *Clipper* (New York) and *Billboard* (Cincinnati), the most widely circulated trade weeklies dealing with stage performances and cheap amusements.[2] Yet much of that information was promotional, coming as it did from the ads of manufacturers and rental
exchanges. Of the two, the *Clipper* more readily accepted moving pictures
as a viable act in vaudeville (both Méliès and Pathé placed their first ads
there), and its reports on vaudeville programs across the country gave considerable attention to moving picture exhibition. By the summer of 1905,
Billboard was showing an equal interest, chiefly because Warren Patrick, its
Chicago correspondent, recognized the city's growing business in selling
and renting films. The nickelodeon phenomenon of 1905–1906, however,
caught the two weeklies by surprise. George Kleine later singled out

Figure 29. *Views and Films Index* (12 May 1906), cover.

December 1905 as a turning point, when nickelodeons began competing with vaudeville houses as the primary venue for moving pictures, and it was precisely then that *Billboard*'s interest fell off sharply.[3] The *Clipper*'s interest did not wane, but its February anniversary issue had a revealing photo page promoting "prominent manufacturers" that pushed both Edison and Vitagraph to the margins and excluded Pathé altogether.[4] By April 1906, again according to Kleine, nickelodeons had become so numerous that no one from manufacturers to exhibitors could be satisfied with either the *Clipper* or *Billboard*. The time was ripe for a new trade paper devoted principally to moving pictures.

The *Index*'s position within the new industry was clear from the beginning. Several editors may have succeeded one another rapidly within the first nine months: E. Mitchell, Ellis Cohen, and Alfred H. Saunders, the latter an experienced British projectionist and former editor of *Optical Lantern Weekly*.[5] But Pathé and Vitagraph remained the principal advertisers (if not the outright owners), providing the revenues that financed the paper's weekly publication out of New York.[6] The two companies undoubtedly influenced its editorial direction, especially in creating a forum that bypassed the rental exchanges and linked manufacturers directly to moving picture exhibitors and, it was hoped, the "general public."[7] To do so, its "Trade Notes" column adopted a familiar, even breezy, language of direct address, the kind of "simple, straightforward talk" of a man talking to his neighbor that Frank Munsey believed to be "the very essence" of good advertising, and that Laemmle soon honed to perfection in his own ads.[8] Initially, the *Index* also sought to imagine an integrated cultural arena within which to balance its French and American interests. Equal space was given alongside Pathé and Vitagraph ads to reproductions of contemporary French and American paintings (a strong sign of "uplift" and "high seriousness"),[9] to each country's contribution to moving picture history, and to interviews with French and American industry leaders (if any were slighted, it was Edison and Biograph). The editors paid close attention to and encouraged the nickelodeon boom, in New York especially, but in Philadelphia, Pittsburgh, and Chicago as well. They also called repeatedly for the formation of a protective association in Chicago in order to counteract "dishonest customers" (that is, renters and exhibitors).[10] When rental exchanges suddenly began advertising in the *Index* that fall, they probably did so partly to claim a position of honesty and integrity. For nearly a year, this trade weekly (with its "classic" black-and-white covers) offered exhibitors exclusive listings of the titles, lengths, and plot synopses of most current films, listings that consistently backed Pathé's claim as the most dependable supplier.

Early in 1907, Saunders's name disappeared from the *Index* (the reason remains a mystery) and, in March, he turned up as editor of "an independent weekly," *Moving Picture World* (also published in New York).[11] The new trade paper had a more readable design—a larger typeface, a two-column format (instead of four), and a length of sixteen pages (instead of twelve)—and it charged both advertisers and subscribers far less, forcing the *Index* to cut its subscription rate in half.[12] The *World* promoted every sector of the new industry but, like its rival, gave particular attention to exhibition. In May 1907, it published a survey of the "nickelodeon" that served as a model for national magazines like *Harper's Weekly* and the *Saturday Evening Post;* by June, it was claiming to be "the official organ of the Moving Picture Exhibitors' Association" of New York.[13] From the beginning, the *World*'s discourse closely aligned with that of the Progressive moral reformers.[14] Yet its pitch was broader than its predecessor's, more focused on the "nuts and bolts" of running a show: "no item of interest to the profession at large" was excluded (which meant everything from electrical equipment to practical tips for all kinds of projection). No one company or cluster of companies "controlled" the *World* as Pathé and Vitagraph did the *Index*, but its "independent" position was hardly unbiased. Pathé did not place ads there for more than a year, and it did not always receive favorable treatment: its 1907 version of *The Passion Play,* for instance, was first labeled a "French . . . faked-up copy."[15] Saunders and his publishers also depended on ad revenues from a wider range of manufacturers (including two new companies, Kalem and Essanay) and, more important, from a growing number of rental exchanges and their interests in the American market. They especially favored Kleine Optical, whose large shipments of imported Gaumont and Urban-Eclipse films, according to a *Billboard* survey, made it "the only rival of the Pathé people in this country."[16]

That summer, the nickel craze spawned a third new trade paper, *Show World,* a "twentieth-century amusement weekly" edited in Chicago by Warren Patrick, formerly of *Billboard.* With its colorful circus poster covers, large folio size, and thirty to forty pages, *Show World* had a unique look and heft that set it apart.[17] During its first month of publication, Patrick devoted most of those pages to moving pictures; but that bold move must have proved costly, for thereafter it reverted to a format closer to *Billboard*'s, which covered a wide range of entertainments. Despite that change, however, *Show World* continued to serve as a promotional vehicle for Chicago's "great film industry" (as did *Billboard*) and for the major rental exchanges and exhibitors there.[18] Special interview articles focused, for instance, on Laemmle, Cline, Spoor, Robert Bachman (20th-Century Optiscope), Max Lewis (Chicago Film Exchange), W. N. Barlow (Inter-Ocean Film Exchange), Fred C. Aiken (Theatre Film Service), and Aaron Jones (the "Napoleon of Chicago Amusements"). Although Pathé films were admired in these articles (after all, they were crucial to these men's businesses), respect sometimes was granted grudgingly. In one editorial, Patrick even tried to rewrite the cinema's development, claiming that "the American film renters and exhibitors have made Pathé-Frères in this country," rather than vice versa.[19] Time and again, there were calls for more and better product from American manufacturers to counterbalance the powerful position Pathé seemed to occupy on the American market, a position *Show World* feared could be used as a threat, perhaps similar to the one that troubled the French market when the company diversified into renting and exhibiting films.[20]

By the fall of 1907, the *Index* no longer fully satisfied Pathé's interests, for the *World* had overtaken the pioneering weekly to become the most influential trade paper in the industry. Although Pathé continued to advertise in the *Index* and in *Billboard* (but not in the *Clipper*), the company, newly incorporated in New York, now tried another strategy. In November, the New York office began to print and distribute the industry's first weekly bulletin providing the title, plot synopsis, length, and specific release date of every new Pathé film.[21] More than likely, this was another effort to bypass the rental exchanges, as well as the influence of the *World*, and once again address exhibitors directly.[22] The strategy worked, at least to the extent that Pathé films continued to dominate the American market for one more year, and the company kept publishing the bulletin, with its blatantly boosterish cover illustrations, for another four years. Still, with business booming everywhere, the trade press could not afford not to expand. The *Clipper* and *Billboard* began giving more attention to films; both now had relatively regular "Moving Pictures" columns, and *Billboard* occasionally ran special features, such as a directory of "electric theatres" throughout the country (December 1906) and semiannual reviews of the business in Chicago and New York.[23] Two other trade weeklies based in New York, *Variety* (first published in 1905) and *New York Dramatic Mirror* (which had been published nearly as long as the *Clipper*), also "discovered" moving pictures. In September 1907, *Variety* began introducing film subjects into its weekly review of "New Acts"; by January 1908, it was devoting a full page to "Moving Picture News and Reviews."[24] Shortly thereafter, the *Mirror* announced its interest in the industry's "amazing growth"; by May, Frank Woods was writing a new page entitled "The Moving Picture Field."[25]

By late 1908, an American trade press for moving pictures was fully constituted and spread across a spectrum of industry interests. At one end was the *Index*, closely associated with the Film Service Association or FSA, and the "licensed" manufacturers aligned with Edison.[26] At the other were *Variety, Billboard, Show World,* and *Moving Picture News* (another New York weekly founded by Saunders), all of which supported the "Independents" led by Biograph and Kleine.[27] Under editor J. P. Chalmers, the

ANOTHER STATUE FOR THE HALL OF FAME.
No. 13.   January 27th, 1908.

Figure 30. *Pathé-Frères Weekly Bulletin* (27 January 1908), cover.

World secured its dominant position by staking out a middle ground between these factions.[28] Each issue now ran twenty-four pages, twice the
length of the *Index*, which remained little changed, even after being reti-
tled *Film Index* in September.[29] Chalmers also attracted writers such as
W. Stephen Bush, James D. Law, and Rollin Summers as special correspondents and initiated new columns offering expert advice to projectionists and evaluating theaters and audiences in greater New York (and later
Chicago).[30] At the *Mirror*, Woods adopted a similar strategy that sought
to encompass the entire industry, first by extending *Variety*'s practice of selectively reviewing films at one or more New York theaters with a systematic weekly "Reviews of Late Films," in which "dramatic criticism" was

brought to bear on a potentially new art form, and then by writing a
"Spectator's" column of commentary in order to "elevate the quality and
character of [all] moving picture subjects." [31] In deference to this innovation, the *World* "yield[ed] to the requests of many of [its] readers," and invited reporters and theater managers to send in their comments on specific
films, which it then compiled as its own "criticism." [32]

Within this discursive arena, Pathé found itself increasingly challenged
and contested, most crucially within the middle ground staked out by the
World and the *Mirror.* The significance of that position was evident, in January 1909, when *Nickelodeon* appeared in Chicago (published by the Electricity Magazine Corporation), the first relatively deluxe monthly devoted to
moving pictures. [33] Running to thirty pages, with relatively few ads (and
none initially from Pathé), *Nickelodeon* aimed to be a constantly updated
"text book" on "motography" as a means of entertainment (*Motography*
was its name within two years). [34] That meant "cultivat[ing] closest harmony with the user of films," either those just entering the business or
those wanting to further upgrade their shows. [35] In other words, *Nickelodeon*
represented a "tasteful" guide for moving picture theaters like Getchell and
Elbert's Unique in Des Moines (the result of renovations at the Nickeldom
in 1908), [36] and a clear sign that "the world's greatest show" was in the
process of being transformed into something else.

CHAPTER FOUR

Reclaiming the Market, Cleaning Up the Barnyard, 1907–1909

Meet me down at the picture show,
That's the place where the crowds do go.
Old and young and short and tall,
Happy and "sassy," one and all.

Only a dime or a nickel a seat,
To list to songs by singers sweet,
See good pictures and vaudeville,
Forget all your troubles and "laugh to kill."

Don't you know that song is a New York "hit"?
And the moving pictures are really IT.
The picture makers are up to snuff,
They are putting out some "candy-stuff."
Off they go, with an encore loud,
While the curtain drops to a well-pleased crowd.

JACK SANDS, ROSEVILLE, OHIO, *MOVING PICTURE WORLD* (11 APRIL 1908), 320

By stimulating and then exploiting the nickelodeon boom in the United States, Pathé sharply defined the issue of who would exercise control over the cinema market, and how. Once that struggle for control is framed in terms of American interests versus perceived foreign interests, as it was during the period from 1907 to 1909, the threatening "foreign body" of "red rooster" films indeed looms large. There is perhaps no better evidence of Pathé's threat than a letter from George Eastman, head of Eastman Kodak, which at the time supplied 90 percent of the negative film stock used throughout the world.[1] According to Eastman's figures, by the fall of 1907, the French company was selling on the American market between thirty and forty million feet of positive film stock per year, nearly twice as much as all the American companies combined.

FENCING IN THE ROOSTER

That the French company was seen as a potentially powerful competitor as early as 1904 is clear from the extant correspondence between Pathé and the Edison company. When Charles Pathé first wrote Edison, on 1 July 1904, of his intention

to open a sales office in New York and accused the American company of dupli-
cating its films for more than a year, Edison interpreted this move as a challenge—
as was evident in a 21 July letter to W. E. Gilmore from Frank Dyer, then head of
the company's legal department.[2] If Edison responded to Pathé, the letter no
longer survives, but the French company went ahead with its plans to have J. A.
Berst open the New York office in late August, which quickly proved profitable. In
an exchange of letters with Kleine Optical, one of its chief sales agents, on 24 August, Edison admitted that it now saw Pathé as its chief competitor, along with Biograph, on the American market.[3]

Three months later, Alexander Moore wrote to Edison's London representative, James White, arguing there was no point in buying Pathé films in England (for
shipment to the United States) now that the French company could supply its own
product quickly and efficiently.[4] As Pathé prospered, with the initial aid of Kleine
Optical, Edison included the French company within its string of patent suits,
which, although the specific one against Pathé never came to trial, clearly was intended to curtail the latter's expansion.[5] Pathé retaliated by marketing its films in
the United States several weeks prior to their release in Europe and by under-
selling Edison, charging twelve cents per foot for all of its subjects, a move that
effectively erased a distinction the American company had been trying to establish
between class A and class B films.[6] By the fall of 1906, Pathé's success was such
that, according to a letter from J. Hardin to Moore, Edison's representative in
Chicago, the French company (together with Vitagraph) was far outselling Edison
there and even offering a 30 percent discount to its largest buyers, which by then
would have included nearly all of the important film rental exchanges.[7]

As Pathé-Frères expanded worldwide through more than a dozen sales offices
between 1904 and 1906, Charles Pathé apprised his stockholders of plans to build
factories for printing positive film stock in those countries where the company was
selling the highest volume of film subjects.[8] Such factories would reduce the high
costs that the company already was paying for transportation and import duties,
especially in the United States. In the spring of 1907, Pathé was preparing to construct such a facility in Bound Brook, New Jersey, based not only on its expanding
business but also on its understanding that a March 1907 court decision partly up-
holding Edison's camera patent (against Biograph) did not apply to perforated
film.[9] Alarmed by the French company's move to embed itself more firmly in the
American market, Edison set up negotiations with Pathé in April through G.
Croydon-Marks, a London patents expert, threatening the company with litigation but also softening that threat with a "generous" proposition.[10] To counter the
Bound Brook factory plans, Edison made what at first seemed a lucrative proposal,
offering to print Pathé's positive film stock (from the shipped negative, already
edited) at its own facilities and to serve as the principal sales agent for its film subjects in the United States. Tempted by the offer, the French company responded
favorably, assuming that Edison would print the sum total of its weekly negative
output and that, in turn, it might gain exclusive rights to sell Edison films in Europe.

However, more than a month passed before the Edison company responded by refusing to accept Pathé's full list of weekly subjects and demanding the right to select which French films would be released on the American market.[11] After that,
the deal quickly collapsed, and Pathé accused Edison of costing it a good deal of
lost revenues.[12]

Edison's delaying tactic stalled the French company at a critical point in its expansion. Construction could not begin on the Bound Brook factory until early that
summer, and Charles Pathé himself hurried across the ocean to join Berst for the
factory's groundbreaking, as well as for Pathé Cinematograph's incorporation as
an American company.[13] Despite the company's record-setting business that fall,
the New York and Chicago offices remained uneasy because of the persistent
"unsettled conditions" created by the proliferating nickelodeons and rental exchanges.[14] The practice of duping prints continued to such an extent that Kalem's
Francis Marion, for instance, warned it could drive manufacturers like Pathé into
the rental business.[15] And Pathé's recent decision to stop selling films in France
and to establish its own rental system and exhibition circuit there raised fears that
it was about to initiate a similar move in the United States.[16] Another practice that
worried Berst, among others, was the unauthorized subrenting of films. Lewis
Swaab of Philadelphia condemned those who participated as "scavengers," citing
as examples several of his competitors "supplied with Pathé films." [17]

In order to curb these practices, Berst sent out new contracts to the exchanges
and exhibitors that fall, setting forth tighter restrictions on reselling, duping, and
"bicycling" prints (that is, illegally sharing them with other exhibitors), and encouraging customers to take all of the company's weekly releases en bloc rather
than select titles from among them.[18] As reported in the trade press, representatives of the leading rental exchanges convened in Pittsburgh in November and,
one month later, in Chicago to remedy these and other problems.[19] Their solution
was the United Film Service Protective Association (UFSPA), which promised to
combine all sectors of the industry into a single national "regulatory" organization, led by men such as Kleine, Aiken, Swanson, and J.B. Clark of Pittsburgh
Calcium Light and Film.

Behind the scenes, however, Edison was maneuvering to gain control of the
new association. Emboldened by a Chicago court decision, in October, which up-
held one of its patent suits against Selig, and by the evidence accumulating in its
case against Vitagraph—both of which strengthened its legal position—Edison
set out to negotiate a licensing agreement with the other manufacturers that would
allow them, for an annual fee, to exploit its patent.[20] Its purpose, besides the obvious one of self-interest, was to draw the industry's profits away from renters and
exhibitors and increasingly toward the manufacturers. Again, Edison set up negotiations with Pathé, assuming that once the world's leading film producer fell in
line, along with Vitagraph, the others would, too. Although its threat of litigation
still loomed large, Edison now focused on assuring the French company that its licensing agreement would disallow or discourage "foreign imports" other than

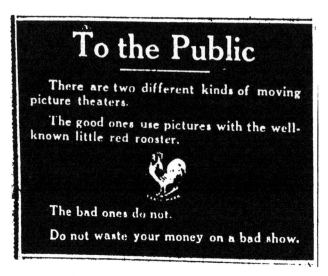

Figure 31. Pathé ad, *Chicago Tribune* (5 April 1908), 3.2.

those from Pathé itself. It was this assurance, Berst later testified, that persuaded Pathé to accept Edison's plan, as well as its insistence on paying only half the fee percentage the other manufacturers did.[21] The Association of Edison Licensees (AEL) then began securing contracts with members of the UFSPA, transforming it into the Film Service Association (FSA) and, in the process, excluding from its ranks George Kleine, the man who had brokered the original organization and the only other major dealer in "foreign imports."[22] Because it "shut out the importation of foreign stuff . . . not suitable or good enough for the American market,"[23] the AEL-FSA combine seemed to secure Pathé's position not only as the largest film supplier for that market but also as the only significant foreign producer (Méliès no longer counted), a position that supported the French company's own strategies of dominance within Europe, especially in its rivalry with the Italian company Cinès.[24] Moreover, the Edison agreement permitted Pathé to begin manufacturing its camera and projector, as well as printing positive film stock at the Bound Brook facility when it finally opened in late 1907—and began processing its order of fifty million feet of Eastman Kodak negative.[25]

However, not long after Biograph, together with Kleine, in February 1908,[26] set up its own rival licensing group to serve the foreign companies and importers excluded from AEL-FSA, Pathé began to sense that its operations were being blocked, its red rooster films fenced in. First of all, Biograph promised to offer "a regular weekly supply of from twelve to twenty reels of splendid new subjects" and soon had commitments from a sufficient number of rental exchanges and exhibitors' associations, especially in Chicago, to sustain what was being dubbed the

"Independent Movement."[27] That Chicago was the base for these Independents may explain why, in April, Pathé took the unusual step of placing an ad in the *Sunday Chicago Tribune,* claiming that only good theaters showed "pictures with the well-known little red rooster."[28] Then, not only did Biograph refer to AEL-FSA as the "Edison-Pathé combination," but Kleine, often evoked as the leader of the Independents, pointedly blamed Pathé more than Edison for its exclusionary strategies and for the ensuing "film war."[29] As if that were not enough, according to Georges Sadoul, with the revenue from the FSA contracts (which, at its peak, came from 150 rental exchanges, as well as the eight manufacturers), Edison's gross profits equaled and then exceeded those of Pathé for the first time in years.[30] Even as it continued to amass high revenues on the American market, the French company found itself being outflanked by rivals both within and without the AEL-FSA. Early in the summer of 1908, as a means of regaining some measure of control, Berst floated an idea that Pathé had used successfully before: if the AEL producers were to cut prices on their film subjects, the Independents would be unable to compete with them for long.[31] When that suggestion failed to win approval, the French company considered something more drastic. Now Charles Pathé himself came to the United States once again to explore the viability of establishing a circuit of film rental exchanges modeled on the system he had recently put in place in France, a system that, in its exploratory stages, may well have included Vitagraph and some of the Independents.[32]

That Pathé finally decided against making this move is revealing. The recession and monetary crisis threatening the United States economy at the time could have played a role in the decision, but the company's revenues, according to its own internal reports, seem not to have been much affected by that threat.[33] More to the point, Berst later admitted that Pathé found itself overextended in its investment and could not afford to set up the kind of rental exchange system that such a huge country as the United States would require.[34] Perhaps most crucially, the French company's internal records reveal that Pathé and his directors were all too aware that, despite the best efforts of Berst in New York and E. H. Montague in Chicago, "they continued to be considered . . . foreigners."[35] Pathé was no more able to exert a leadership role in the American cinema industry now than either it or the *Index* had been two years earlier at the start of the nickelodeon boom.[36] In late September 1908, the *Mirror* made a cryptic reference to one of the first signs of the French company's retreat. Whereas Vitagraph and Edison were increasing their outputs, respectively, to three and two reels per week, Pathé's "issue of new subjects" was being cut "to four reels per week as against the five reels" released previously that year.[37] As I have argued elsewhere, this would mark a profound shift in the French company's economic interests worldwide, leading it to rely less on the American market and redirect its investments back to Europe and the material base of the industry to which it had been committed from the very beginning.[38]

ROOSTERS AND LEMONS.

No. 25.   **April 20th, 1908.**

Figure 32. *Pathé-Frères Weekly Bulletin* (20 April 1908), cover.

To the extent that the AEL stimulated American film production (in part, inadvertently), it also fostered the wholesale adoption of trademarks, which previously had been unique to Pathé (and Méliès).[39] In October 1907, well before the AEL-FSA combine officially coalesced, Vitagraph already was including a trademark eagle V in its weekly trade press ads.[40] Early in 1908, as Biograph and Kleine still were negotiating their rival licensing group, Biograph adopted its own trademark, an encircled AB, which appeared in its trade press ads, on its posters, and on the title cards of its films.[41] Within two months, the Chicago firm of Essanay (another AEL member) began promoting its films through a script logo based on its owners' initials (somewhat like Gaumont's well-known "ELGE").[42] By the summer of 1908, Selig, too, had a new trademark, a Diamond S "brand," aptly chosen for its production of "Indian and Western subjects."[43] Instead of a distinct mark, Kalem (also an AEL member) designed a different cutout figure, in silhouette, for each of its films.[44] Finally, Edison would co-opt Méliès's earlier "authoring" strategy for industrial ends by "branding" the inventor's own signature on its film product. Trademarks not only allowed manufacturers to exert greater control over their supply of product to rental exchanges and exhibitors but also educated consumers in product differentiation. In other words, they helped audiences more quickly distinguish among the increasing number of American (as well as "foreign") film subjects.[45] The Selig or Essanay mark, for instance, assured a potential spectator that he or she would see a particular kind of film — a western or comedy, respectively.[46] By the fall of 1908, according to the *Mirror*, "the trademarks that now accompan[ied] all films" were a familiar sign of dependability and quality for almost any "confirmed visitor to moving picture theatres."[47]

Throughout the spring and summer of 1908, however, the rivalry between the two licensing groups led to more instability in the industry than either Edison or Biograph had imagined. The AEL-FSA set up a regularized schedule of weekly releases, writes Musser, in order to ensure "a steady, predictable flow of new subjects to the exchanges and then on to the exhibitors."[48] Yet soon there were complaints that the schedule was too inflexible and rental prices were too high, which increased the operating costs, especially for nickelodeon owners.[49] Then, in July, the AEL-FSA pegged its pricing system to a film's release date, making those shown on the very first day of their release, as Bowser writes, the only "truly 'fresh' and valuable" commodities.[50] Among the trade weeklies, only the *Index* strongly endorsed the AEL-FSA, earning it a reputation as a mouthpiece for "Edison and its allied interests."[51] The *Mirror* and *Show World* (and, to a lesser extent, the *Clipper* and *Billboard*) actively supported the Independents, while the *World* maintained a middle ground (accepting ads from both factions) and tried to mediate between the two in its editorials.[52] Finally, as Musser has documented, for the first time exhibitors were complaining, at least in New York, about a dearth of subjects.[53] By July, consequently, Edison was negotiating with Biograph and Kleine to merge the rival groups into a single patent association (and Pathé's absence from those discussions signaled its waning influence).[54] By September, the Motion Picture Patents Company (MPPC) was all but in place; still, Eastman and Pathé (after a brief flurry of publicity over its proposed rental exchange) delayed the MPPC's official institution until December.[55] That the MPPC provisions limited foreign imports even more than before surely addressed one of Pathé's demands, yet they also restricted each licensed producer to a maximum of four thousand feet (or four reels) of new positive film stock per week.[56] That restriction contractually bound the company to the concession previously made in September, and a weekly maximum of four thousand feet was considerably less than its full production capacity.

The power of the MPPC initially seemed impressive. It not only linked nearly all the major manufacturers but also licensed perhaps 80 percent of all rental exchanges in the country.[57] It also worked to develop affordable, regularized fire insurance for licensed exhibitors, and, for Pathé's benefit, pressured Congress (unsuccessfully) not to lower the tariff on imported positive film.[58] Yet the "Trust," as it was soon dubbed, excluded several important European manufacturers (Great Northern, most Italian firms) and, more important, a number of large rental exchanges (Chicago Film, Globe, Royal).[59] Moreover, its weekly licensing fee did not sit well with exhibitors, soon provoking the withdrawal of other rental exchanges, the most important being Swanson, Laemmle, and Fox (all former Pathé advocates).[60] Within weeks, a new group of Independents began to form around the International Projecting and Producing Company (IPPC), with its initial center of strength in the Midwest, especially Chicago, Saint Louis, and Cincinnati.[61] At first, the IPPC relied on releasing "unlicensed" foreign imports and recirculating older films, but the market demand was strong enough to encourage new manufacturers such as the New York Motion Picture Company (NYMPC), Centaur (later renamed Nestor), IMP (Laemmle's new company), Powers, and Thanhauser.[62] It also received support, sometimes much qualified, from the trade press: the *Mirror* noted Independent releases as early as February and began printing an "official" weekly listing in May; a month later, the *World* did likewise.[63] By summer's end, the new Independents were holding their own in competition with the MPPC, particularly as more American productions became available: the NYMPC's ads, for instance, listed twenty-five exchanges renting its weekly Bison films.[64] That fall, as the IPPC's influence waned, the various factions of the group gathered into a national alliance that, although itself unsuccessful, eventually would lead the following spring to a much more viable alternative to the MPPC: the Sales Company (organized by IMP and NYMPC).[65] For Pathé, this would present one more costly consequence of its decision, however grudgingly given, to align itself with the Trust.

In the struggle to ensure that "American interests" rather than "foreign interests" controlled the cinema market, the formation of the AEL-FSA and then the MPPC played a significant role by curbing Pathé's considerable, if far from invulnerable, economic power at a crucial stage in the new industry's development. And the emergence of a strong national Independent movement only added to the French company's dilemma. The initial steps had been taken toward the cinema's Americanization.

"OUTING" THE ROOSTER AS A "FOREIGN BODY"

This struggle for control was hardly confined to the economic arena, or even specifically to the production and distribution of films as fresh and valuable commodities. It also encompassed their venues of exhibition, and especially their reception and efforts to control or mediate that reception. And that involved an intense public debate over how best to regulate moving picture shows for "morally" beneficial ends, whether to repress or censor them through prohibitions of one kind or another or to ensure that they were "properly conducted" through a system of licenses and inspections and a voluntary adherence to standards of taste.[66] Evidence of this struggle is unmistakable in the trade press, national magazines, and daily papers. It is expressed perhaps most openly in a 1908 article in *World Today*, where Lucy France Pierce notes that competition between French and American manufacturers had become very keen, but then frames that competition in terms of taste and morality, marking the French with "bad taste" and immorality.[67]

This kind of moral discourse appears repeatedly throughout the previous year and is often invoked to describe Pathé films in circulation. Beginning in December 1907, for instance, the reviews in *Variety* are especially striking: *The Female Spy* was described as "chaotic" and "disagreeable"; *Avenged by the Sea* was so "gruesome and morbid" that it "should not be on the market"; *Christmas Eve Tragedy* was "as well conceived for children as an interior view of a slaughter house" and so reprehensible as to justify censorship.[68] Even if the trade weekly was rebuking Pathé for not advertising in its pages, the "horrified" language (not unlike that which greeted the published translations of Zola's novels) made these more than just bad reviews. Yet this attitude emerged even earlier, in the spring of 1907, in the correspondence reporting on Edison's refusal to negotiate further with the French company—a refusal couched self-servingly in terms of moral objections to Pathé's subjects.[69] When Charles Pathé visited the States, in May 1908, in order to assess the FSA's operations, he responded implicitly to such criticism by insisting (probably tongue in cheek) that, as a responsible businessman, he would personally select the films his company released in the American market.[70] All this controversy suggests that, in the United States, Pathé was situated near the center of a debate over early cinema's status as a modern form of mass culture and, more important, its ideological function as "a new social force" within an increasingly contested public sphere.[71]

The conflicted discourse about Pathé reveals how the company and its products served a double role in legitimating the cinema in the United States.[72] Initially, that role was to align certain perceived attributes of French culture with the American cinema. This can be seen in Pathé's own appeal, in its early ads, to the acknowledged high quality of French technology, demonstrated most clearly by the photography industry (where the Lumière name was held in high regard) or the new automobile industry and emblematized by such engineering marvels as the Eiffel Tower and the Gallery of Machines at the 1889 Paris Exposition.[73] Exhibitors, journalists, and others consistently celebrated the cinema by invoking the marvels of Pathé's "high quality"—from its unique stencil-color process to the "flickerless images" produced by its superbly crafted cameras, projectors, and perforating machines.[74] Pathé films also allowed many exhibitors to treat their programs like a new, but inexpensive, and continually renewed version of the European theatrical

No. 36   July 6th, 1908

Figure 33. *Pathé-Frères Weekly Bulletin* (6 July 1908), cover.

tour, a significant form of French cultural influence in this country in the late nine-teenth century.[75] And one of the more famous of those tours just happened to co-incide with Pathé's rise to dominance in the American market—the "Farewell America Tour" of Sarah Bernhardt, from 1905 to 1906.[76] Finally, Pathé films may well have benefited from the turn-of-the century American belief that France was "the center of civilized or 'enlightened' consumption." This meant "that the mag-ical link to everything Parisian was a near guarantee" of sales, Leach argues, es-pecially for department stores like Wanamaker's in Philadelphia, as in its mass market introduction of "Paris" fashion shows.[77] In other words, the nickelodeon showing Pathé films may have served as a social space analogous to such nearby

Figure 34. Lubin ad, *New York Clipper* (2 March 1907), 68.

stores, where the quality and taste associated with "Frenchness," initially, could be admired, consumed, and enjoyed.

Just as often, however, and more frequently after 1907, such appeals were replaced by another long-standing conception of French culture as risqué, deviant, and morally suspect—and allegedly different from American culture—especially in its display of sexual behavior, violence, and distasteful comic business.[78] Yet this change did not come until after a highly publicized attack on moving pictures that focused on an American film.[79] In April 1907, the *Chicago Tribune* printed a series of exposés on nickelodeons and arcades, calling special attention to where they were most concentrated—on Milwaukee Avenue, South Halsted, and lower State Street.[80] The films attacked were largely stories of crime and violence, among them Selig's *Bandit King* and Pathé's *From Jealousy to Madness*, which, much to the *Tribune*'s distress, was attracting "a large crowd at Friedman's nickel theater on Halsted."[81] Yet the one title singled out most often, and not only in Chicago, was Lubin's *Unwritten Law*, a reenactment of the lurid "Thaw-White Case," whose trial was front-page news across the country from January through April.[82] According to the *Clipper*, this film "created a sensation at the theatres and exhibition halls" for months after its release in March, and Lubin had trouble keeping up with the "continuing demand."[83] In Lowell, it "drew immense crowds" at the Rollaway Rink (and was held over for a second week), and in Atchison,

Kansas, it attracted as many people as *The Passion Play;* in cities like Houston, Worcester, and Chicago, showings occasionally were halted by the police; in others like New York, it provoked arrests.[84] One reason, the *Tribune* alleged, was that, when *The Unwritten Law* was shown at the "downtown 5 cent theatres" in Chicago (for a full week), the "[four o'clock] audiences were composed largely of schoolgirls" who, unlike "a good many grown women" who left shocked, "remained sometimes for two or three views of the pictures."[85] "This one film alone," the *World* concluded, "has been the cause of more adverse press criticism than all the films manufactured before, put together."[86]

The response to this public outcry was conflicted, contradictory, and, for Pathé, ultimately ironic. In New York, the "crisis" coincided with Police Commissioner Bingham's report, urging Mayor McClellan to follow the line of prohibition and cancel the licenses for most nickelodeons and arcades.[87] Exhibitors quickly banded together to form the Moving Picture Exhibitors Association (MPEA), signaling their acceptance of self-regulation, now that pictures were "a part of the home life of Greater New York," and protecting their interests.[88] In Chicago, after several investigations, moral reformers from the settlement movement and other civic groups confronted the "crisis" with a "counter-*attraction*" that put moving pictures "under proper supervision."[89] That summer, Jane Addams opened a theater for children at Hull House to compete with the surrounding shows on South Halsted (or the "slums of Chicago").[90] Those who spoke out in defense of moving pictures, however, always invoked Pathé films above all others as models of the "clean and wholesome" subjects best suited for their audiences.[91] In a letter blasting the *Tribune*'s charges, for instance, Kleine singled out the French company's newly released *Passion Play,* its fairy tale of *Cinderella,* "an industrial covering the manufacture of bottles" (*Bottle Industry*), and travelogues such as *Picturesque Canada* for being respectable, instructive, and popular "in churches as well as Five Cent Theatres."[92] Laemmle supplied Hull House with domestic scenes, moral dramas, fairy tales, and foreign scenes, but the films that got noticed in *Show World* were Pathé's *Cinderella, Aladdin,* and *Picturesque Java.*[93] In separate interviews, a Chicago Film Exchange spokesman lauded the "demand for fairy pictures such as *Cinderella* [and] *The Rajah's Casket,*" and a nickelodeon owner cited *The Passion Play* as one of his best draws ever.[94] As the previous chapter has shown, Pathé's *Passion Play* would go on to become the one film most Americans saw, and most frequently enjoyed, of all those (whether American or foreign) released over the course of the year.

Within months, however, the concern over crime and violence in films such as *The Unwritten Law* was shifting to French *grand guignol* melodramas.[95] During the nickelodeon boom, Pathé versions of such melodramas were not only accepted but quite popular.[96] This was clearly the case in Des Moines, where in March 1907 a dramatic critic cited the combination of "tense one-act drama . . . short character plays, vivid pathetic flashes from human life, a whirl of comedy . . .

which claims prominent attention on the French stage" (a reference to the Grand Guignol theater in Paris) as a model for the city's vaudeville programs.[97] One month later, when the Colonial Theatre opened there with an entire program of Pathé titles, *The Female Spy* played as a prominent feature.[98] Two weeks after that, the same film ran at the Nickeldom, whose programs the local paper was then praising for their well-chosen variety, with "scenes from foreign countries, unique adventures on land and water, and skillfully posed grotesque pictures."[99] By the summer, however, several rental exchange men interviewed in *Billboard* and *Show World* were claiming the demand for sensational melodramas was on the wane (at least in large cities); that is, they all joined the chorus now denigrating them.[100] In the trade press, it was the French tradition of *grand guignol* melodrama specifically that was decried as inappropriately sensational: witness *Variety*'s later review of *The Female Spy*, the censoring of Pathé's popular *Police Dogs* at a South Halsted show in Chicago, or Morris Fleckles's expression of distaste at the French sense of a moral lesson (which tended to offer negative examples or none at all).[101] That tradition now was sharply differentiated from an American tradition of "ethical melodrama" and its "bright, happy denouements,"[102] or what Leach, paraphrasing the department store magnate John Wanamaker, has described as the American "quest for pleasure, security, comfort, and material well-being."[103] Laemmle (Fleckles's boss) put it succinctly: "Let's cater more to the happy side of life. There's enough of the seamy side without exposing it to further view."[104]

This shift also was mapped onto Pathé's trademark use of color. In 1907, Pathé had revealed the details of its newly mechanized stencil-color process: as many as three positive prints were made from the film negative and then perforated in such a way as to produce three different stencils, each of which, when passed over rollers and brushes, in turn, applied a separate color to a fourth positive, resulting in a final three-color print.[105] At the same time, the company began pushing its "mono-tinting" process, which produced a similar effect, according to *Billboard*, "but cost much less" and would be equally "welcome wherever shown."[106] Pathé ads called this "special tinting," but the "twilight effect" described in *A Case of Arson*, released in August 1907, clearly marked this as a combination of toning and tinting: "The reflection of the mellow tint of the heavens in the greenish water is a pretty accomplishment."[107] For nearly a year, Pathé advertised these "special tint" films with the same regularity as its "colored" films. The two processes, however, were applied to different subjects. Stencil color was reserved for fairy tales like *Ali Baba* and *The Pearl Fisher*, trick films like *The Wonderful Mirrors*, or historical dramas like *The Vestal* and *Don Juan*.[108] Toning and tinting, by contrast, were used for *grand guignol* melodramas, whether set in the present, like *Christmas Eve Tragedy* or *Children's Reformatory*, or in the past, like *Blacksmith's Revenge* or *The Pirates*.[109] And it was these sensational films, no matter how striking their color effects, that were condemned so roundly in the trade press. As a consequence, Pathé was forced to reduce the number of *grand guignol* melodramas released on the American market; for the same reason, perhaps, it also dropped most references in its ads to toning and tacitly accepted the restriction of promoting only its trademark stencil color (and the genres to which it attached: scenics, historical dramas, religious films, and fairy tales), the one form of coloring that seemed to remain an asset.[110]

This illicit or "low-other" conception of French culture grew more and more persistent over the next year or so. And, despite the company's efforts, it seeped out across the spectrum of French films, encompassing much more than the sensational and the grotesque.[111] In *Harper's Weekly,* for example, Currie drew attention to the New York nickelodeon that advertised its program as "FRESH FROM PARIS, *Very Naughty.*"[112] In the *World,* Hans Leigh ("manager of a large theatrical circuit") inveighed against both old and new Pathé titles, from *The Hooligans of Paris* to *Christmas Eve Tragedy.*[113] The *World* also reported favorably on the Philadelphia ministers who loudly complained of Pathé's "bottle pictures": "That sort of thing may be all right on the other side of the pond, but it won't do over here."[114]

The refrain was the same for *The Clown's Daughter* and *The Acrobatic Maid:* the latter might "suit the Moulin-Rouge of Paris but is not a very proper film to show to an American audience."[115] *Military Prison* made a *World* reviewer wonder if it could ever pass muster with the "French Government."[116] Even W. Stephen Bush felt compelled to chide the French manufacturer for outdoing Lubin in terms of "wretched films" and to suggest eliminating such features in deference to "American taste."[117] In a similar yet even more xenophobic vein, *Variety* assumed any film that "could possibly cause offense" was French and repeatedly vilified Pathé's films well into 1909, as in the disgust it expressed at a Max Linder comedy, *The Servant's Good Joke,* which exploited the unexpected effects of a salad deliberately dressed with castor oil.[118] Ironically once again, the language of approbation which the AEL-FSA (including Pathé) had once invoked to exclude that "foreign stuff" from the American market shifted to target and tar the French company itself.[119]

This process accelerated in parallel with increasing pressures for a greater measure of control over this new arena of the "cheap" and the "low." After the Hull House experiment proved less than a resounding success in Chicago, the city passed an ordinance in late 1907 (apparently without even seeking the explicit support of moral reformers) "requiring a police permit for every film shown . . . and prohibiting the display of 'immoral or obscene' movies."[120] In New York, the MPEA exerted more and more influence, especially after Fox took over as its leader, gained court injunctions against attempts to deny permits to some halls (in tenement districts) and to close Sunday shows (which catered to working-class audiences), and forged links with the Tammany Hall political machine, as well as the People's Institute.[121] When, in a politically expedient move, Mayor McClellan halted all moving picture shows in late December 1908, the MPEA and the People's

Institute were ready to force his hand in the courts, with some short-term success.[122] The outcome of this famous confrontation was that one middle-class notion of regulation, which favored "rationalized discipline," triumphed over another, which insisted on prohibition.[123] And this victorious "uplift" position had the backing of an influential economist, Simon Patten, who saw the nickelodeon as a source of regeneration for the masses—"it appeals to the foundational qualities of men"—and who encouraged the construction of cinemas that would be as spacious and elegant as "legitimate" theaters and, therefore, more suitable for the "better classes."[124] As moving pictures increasingly became inscribed within the rhetoric of moral reform or uplift (with its imperialist notions of responsibility for "others less fortunate"), and the nickelodeon boom was described, by Hansen, as a "detour . . . through the lower regions of the entertainment market,"[125] Pathé found itself in danger of no longer being "useful" to those defending the cinema's legitimacy. Instead, for friend and foe alike in the trade press, its films too often were being circumscribed within public discourse as representative of what was "low" and "illegitimate" about the cinema.

As the demands for social control of the cinema converged with those of economic control, the need to deal with Pathé's illegitimacy took on ever greater urgency. This is perhaps no more evident than in the actions of the National Board of Censorship (which emerged out of a strategic move by the MPEA and the People's Institute, and quickly won the MPPC's approval), at least for the first year or so after its formation in March 1909.[126] According to documents housed at the Edison National Historical Site, throughout 1909 and 1910, Pathé films were either rejected or returned for alteration, proportionately, more frequently than were the films from American producers.[127] In May 1909, for instance, the board "condemned" two Pathé titles it had asked to be altered (*Le Parapluie d'Anatole* and *Le Boucher de Meudon*) but accepted Biograph's *Two Memories* after changes were made.[128] One month later, no less than six of thirteen Pathé titles were rejected outright or recommended for alteration.[129] As late as February 1910, the board found Alfred Machin's *Le Moulin maudit* so deeply offensive that, in order to eliminate its adultery, murder, and suicide, it suggested that Pathé simply lop off the second half of the film.[130] An October 1910 article in *World Today* unequivocally supports this pattern: "In the early days of the censors about one in every ten French pictures had to be condemned."[131] So does H. N. Marvin's testimony in the antitrust court case against the MPPC, in which he specifically refers to the great number of "indecent and obscene . . . pictures imported from foreign countries" as a principal reason for the board's formation.[132]

In effect, the early work of the National Board of Censorship neatly complemented that of the MPPC: the one curbed Pathé's economic power while the other curtailed what was perceived as its undesirable, immoral, "foreign" influence. "The day of the 'three murders and robbery per hundred feet' film seems to (Thank Heavens!) be passed," intoned the *World*, but the "good cheer" would prove premature.[133]

Figure 35. "The Current of the Drama," *Des Moines Tribune* (18 February 1909), 4.

DOCUMENT 5

"Music and Films," *Views and Films Index* (16 May 1908), 4

It may interest our readers to know that in one of the five-cent moving picture theatres in New York city a pianist is being employed who is a sure-
enough graduate from the Berlin Conservatory of Music, having studied

there and completed a course under the tutorship of Prof. Phillip Schar-
wenka.

The theatre is Harry Altman's house at 108th street and Madison avenue, and Arthur A. Barrow is the pianist. To begin with, be it known that
the adults in that section of the great city are people who, as a rule, have
enjoyed greater prosperity on the other side of the ocean, and being
mainly of that very appreciative class, namely, Russian, Roumanian, and
Hungarian Jews, it is no easy matter to win their appreciation for things
musical unless truly meritorious. When Mr. Altman opened this theatre he
decided that, while he would certainly welcome the children of the neighborhood, who are a necessary element for the success of every show of the
kind, he would cater somewhat to the adults of the neighborhood and
bring them there after their day's labors. But what especial treat, novelty or
invention could he offer? After conducting the place on the ordinary system for a few weeks an idea came to him—he would make a little greater
investment and procure good music. It was with this idea in mind that he
secured the services of Arthur A. Barrow, and the desired result came almost instantly.

The few adults who attended the performances soon became aware of
the fact that a hand with a brain behind it was manipulating the keyboard
of the piano, and the news spread quickly. To make matters brief, at the
present time there can be found nightly an audience of grown-ups who,
knowing good music when they hear it, smile indulgently to one another as
fantasies of Wagner, Rubinstein, Mendelssohn and Beethoven float from
beneath the player's hands, in company and proper mood with the story
and scene portrayed on the sheet.

"It has always been my idea," said Mr. Barrow, when seen by a FILMS
INDEX reporter, "that the pianists who at present furnish the accompaniment for the majority of the picture shows fail to use sufficient judgment in
their work. It seems to me as if the prevailing style of musical accompaniment to moving picture films is not the kind which might appeal to the
very best class of people. Of course it is very true that the main object for
which folks come to the shows is to see the pictures; but, to my way of
thinking, the next important factor to good films is good music. The public
is now thoroughly familiar with the nationality of action of the various
films. They know perfectly well that when the title of a subject bears the
trade mark of the rooster they are to witness a French film by Pathé. Taking as an example a comic film showing gendarmes, officers, firemen,
characteristic French citizens, women, children, etc., running through the
streets, where are seen typical French cafés, 'pâtisseries' and other estab-
lishments, over which hang signs in French, is it good judgment to play any
of our good old American coon rag-time? The scene portrayed necessarily

conveys to the audience a strong atmosphere of foreign life, and the strains of 'The Girl Who Threw Me Down,' 'Harrigan,' 'Popularity' or the like must certainly strike the audience as woefully out of place.

"But if, on the other hand, the pianist played for this scene a few bars of some classical, double-time, rippling, bubbling, trippling melody, doesn't it appear as if that would be more appropriate? Keeping on the subject of foreign scenes, would one of those pathetic scenes between a lover and his peasant girl sweetheart strike home very strongly to the tune of 'That's What the Rose Said to Me,' 'Love Me and the World Is Mine,' or 'Sweetheart Days'? You cannot make your audience imagine the French gallant or the demoiselle singing such a song; there is a feeling that if they heard it it would be Greek to them. On the other hand, doesn't it seem more appropriate that while the heartrending scene is taking place the soft tune of 'Hearts and Flowers' or the 'Melody in F' should be played in accompaniment? As a further instance, imagine the final scene of some foreign war drama (French, for instance); at the grand triumphant finish, when the French soldiers win whatever they have been fighting for or against, how dare any pianist ring out the strains of the 'Star Spangled Banner' or 'Hail, Columbia'? My choice for such a situation is 'Marseillaise,' now and always.

"The above are merely a few of the instances from a hundred which I can quote, but I use these as illustrations in my contentions that the knowledge of classical music makes a more sensible performance. There are selections in this class of music which will exactly fit situations purely by virtue of their melody for which no popular song ever written could be substituted. The better class of film lovers, I am glad to say, are quick to appreciate my style of accompaniment and it spurs one on to better effort."

Mr. Barrow's views on this subject are interesting, and if they could be presented to the general public it would prove to the advantage of the theatre owners. He doesn't deny that some popular songs often fit situations in the course of a film with a surprising degree of accuracy. But he contends that in such cases the value of the employment of such a song lies in its words; so that the spectator who doesn't happen to be familiar with the words of the song loses the entire effect; the virtue of classical music in this connection, on the other hand, lies purely in its melody—and only the deaf can lose such effect.

The operator of this house is D. J. Sheehan, of "Electroscope" fame. He is one of the oldest hands in the business, and what he doesn't know about the mechanism of any machine ever made anywhere is not worth record. He has been employed by Harry Altman since the first show given at this theatorium, and judging by the comment and frequent expressions of pleasure by the patrons the proprietor is justified when he says: "My two jewels—Barrow and Sheehan."

DOCUMENT 6

"Earmarks of Makers," *New York Dramatic Mirror* (14 November 1908), 10

The confirmed visitor to moving picture theatres learns in time to recognize almost at sight the product of different film manufacturers by certain peculiarities independent of the trademarks that now accompany all films. Some of these distinguishing characteristics are impossible to describe, being more in the nature of vague, general impressions than anything else; but there are other differences that are conspicuous and easily pointed out—infallible ear marks of the particular studios from which the pictures come. It may be the faces of the actors, the scene backgrounds, the style of the acting, the quality or peculiarities of the photography, or it may be the picture story itself and the manner in which it is constructed or handled that gives the information, but whatever it is, there is something about each manufacturer's films that distinguish them from the films of the others. It will be interesting to inquire into these differences of style and at the same time discuss the good and bad points of each maker.

First, let us classify the film product of the world as American and foreign. It is easy to recognize the imported dramatic or comedy pictures by a number of clear marks of difference. Most foreign pictures come from France and Italy, and if they are outdoor scenes we know them by the architecture of the buildings, by the costumes worn, or by the national characteristics of face and figure of the actors. We will also note that the French and Italian performers are more adept than any other nationality in talking with their hands, their shoulders, their bodies and their facial expressions. In this the French are rather better than the Italian, but both are better than the American, who in turn are so far ahead of the English as to be almost out of sight. Indeed, the English are easily the poorest pantomimists for moving pictures on the face of the globe. French and Italian pictures also rarely tell a long or complicated story. They are apt to consist of some simple episode or amusing situation worked out in the action with a nicety of detail that pictures from other countries seldom approach. Frequently, to American eyes, these episodes appear trivial and the comic situations silly and childish, but the excellence of the acting very often makes up for these objections. French comedy is superior to the Italian, but Italian makers exhibit generally a first-class ability to turn out pathetic or tragic pictures. Photographically foreign films rank high. They are clear and sharp in outline and one seldom sees in them the spots or imperfections noted so often in American pictures, due, it is said, to difference in atmospheric conditions between Europe and America. On this point the writer was informed by an official of the American Vitagraph Company that the atmosphere in America, being drier than in Europe, fine particles of dust settle on American films in the making, and appear as serious imperfections. However, this defect may be remedied in time, and in fact the French Pathe Company claims to have found the remedy and to be making practical use of it in its American studio, where films for the American trade are printed from negatives imported from its foreign studios. Before leaving the subject of foreign films it should be noted that colored, spectacular pictures, usually telling magic or fairy stories and sometimes religious allegories, are almost invariably French, coming either from the studios of Pathe Freres, Melies, or Gaumont. Suggestive or immoral pictures are no longer brought over from the other side — at least they are never shown in public, as the foreign makers long ago discovered that the American exhibitors would not accept them. Indeed, so careful have foreign producers become in this respect that they frequently go to the other extreme, and one rarely sees, even where stage dances are being represented, female performers displaying the lower limbs in tights above the knee.

While American dramatic or comedy pictures as a rule are not so good in pantomime as the French and Italian, they are very much superior in plot and in the literary merit of the stories they tell. Of course trash is too often produced on both sides of the ocean, but American trash generally has more novelty of idea than foreign trash. Some American manufacturers also will spend on elaborate scenic effects more money for a single picture than would ever be dreamed of in Europe for a dozen ordinary productions. In fact, nearly all American films are superior to the usual European output in this respect, and they appear to be improving constantly along this line, as they are in constructive and photographic qualities and in the acting ability displayed. However, in the last named particular the American still has much to learn from the foreigner. Take one instance to illustrate. When a foreign picture (not English) shows a farmer or peasant, the character appears to be real and genuine, not the work of an actor at all. Costume and action are faithful to the part represented. On this side, on the other hand, the actor, speaking generally, cannot conceal himself and his theatrical training. If he is a farmer he is too often a stage farmer, with the inevitable wisp of whiskers on the chin. Nevertheless, speaking still in a general way, American picture actors, as they become better trained in the art, are showing constant improvement all along the line, and American picture plot, construction and stage direction are growing better and better with each successive month and year. In the end THE MIRROR has no hesitation in predicting American films will lead the world in all essential qualities as they do now in the important particulars already referred to.

Let us now examine briefly some of the peculiarities, faults, and merits of individual manufacturers, advanced not in an over-critical sense, nor as an infallible verdict, but for what it is worth, as the conscientious opinion of a single writer.

Pathe Freres will be considered first because this firm is not only the largest producer of moving picture films in Europe but is the chief one of the world. What has already been said of French pictures as a class may be said in particular of this firm's output—only more so. Most Pathe actors have been long in the same employ and are readily recognized by the spectator. Like many dramatic stock players, they have become favorites with habitual patrons, and their appearance in a picture is usually hailed with delight. Pathe pictures are famous for their good photographic quality, superior pantomime, ingenious trick effects, beautiful colored results, and the clear, lucid manner of telling a picture story. The characters in a Pathe picture are usually of heroic size, more attention being paid to making the story plain to the spectator than to beauty of scenery, although outdoor scenes are often selected with a view to artistic prospect. One fault sometimes present is shallowness of plot and story, especially in comedy pictures. Another fault is the cheap and worn-out stock scenery often used for interiors. A few good scene painters might be profitably added to the Pathe employees.

Gaumont pictures are very similar to Pathe in general appearance, at first glance, but they do not display as much acting ability and they show careless haste in production, not often to be noted in the Pathe work.

Melies pictures usually run to the trick and spectacular style, with an occasional effort at comedy. Photographic quality of Melies films is invariably good, but the comedy has not often been of a character to find appreciation among American patrons of picture houses.

Urban-Eclipse films are manufactured in both England and France. Those done by English actors are awkward and bungling, but the travel pictures and views of events are usually well done.

The Radios, Italian films, are specially strong in photography and are usually darker in tone than is the product of houses named above. Pathetic dramatic subjects are frequently well done by this company, and travel views are of a high quality, but the comedy production is seldom of much account.

The Rossi films, another Italian product, are similar in character to Radios, but not so carefully prepared.

Lux French pictures resemble Gaumont in quality and character.

Great Northern films manufactured in Copenhagen are distinguished by clearness and perfection of photographic quality. The acting is not as spirited as the French, but it is invariably appropriate and conscientious. Scenery backgrounds are often specially beautiful.

Italian "Cines" productions are among the best of the Italian output. Photographic quality is always excellent and the subjects are usually well handled.

Eclair [*sic*] is a new French make of films, and from what has been seen of them on this side they give promise of gaining a very high reputation. They appear to resemble Pathe films in quality and general appearance.

American pictures are, of course, the best known on this side, next to the production of Pathe Freres, with which moving picture patrons the world over are familiar. American films which most nearly resemble Pathe in style of treatment are the pictures of the American Mutoscope and Biograph Company. These motion photographs are distinguished, like the Pathe, by their heroic size, enabling the actors to convey the ideas intended with the utmost clearness. Subjects produced by the Biograph Company are almost invariably of a superior character, whether melodramatic, tragic, or comic, and the acting and stage management are always able and skillful. Scenic backgrounds out of doors are usually well selected, but painted interiors are not marked by novelty or artistic excellence. On the contrary, they are usually rather meager. An excellent company of stock actors is employed and their faces are familiar favorites with moving picture patrons.

Edison pictures are noted for elaborate scenic productions and the artistic beauty of the scenes, whether natural or painted interiors, but these results are sometimes secured at the expense of clearness in telling a picture story. Important action taking place in artistic shadow or at a distance which permits of a beautiful and extended view may, and usually does, weaken the dramatic effect. This criticism is not always true of Edison pictures, as there are frequent occasions when art has been attained without loss of lucidity. Edison subjects are also nearly always of striking character, with novel effects.

The American Vitagraph Company produces a greater number of subjects than any other American firm, and while its comedy and dramatic work is not always distinguished by the most elaborate detail in scenic results, Vitagraph scenery is by no means inadequate. Indeed, in special cases the Vitagraph Company produces exceedingly expensive settings for important scenes, and it must be noted that an effort is always made to have scenery accurate and consistent. This is especially true of clever historical stories, for which this company is famous. Its comedy also is usually good and is marked by vivacity and frequently by rich humor. Vitagraph actors are a trained body of players, many of them favorites with spectators. The scenes are taken to a certain extent, like Biograph, at short range, although the figures are not so heroic in size. Occasionally weak and ineffective subjects are noted, but not often, considering the large output. We must not dismiss this company without mention of its occasional pictures of important events, which are always excellent and decidedly welcome.

The Kalem Company has not been in operation as long as the other New York producers, but it is showing marked improvement in its work. Obscurity in telling a story was formerly observed in the dramatic work of this company, but this tendency has lately been largely overcome. Like the other American producers, Kalem is clearly moved by constant endeavor to improve and elevate the character of its work, as witness the recent elaborate religious spectacles, Jerusalem in the Days of Christ and David and Goliath, mentioned favorably in a recent number of THE MIRROR.

The Selig Polyscope Company, of Chicago, is the one other American firm that rivals the Edison Company in large and striking scenic effects. Indeed, the Selig studio settings are on a larger scale, if anything, than the Edison, and it is the only company that has gone to the Rocky Mountains for the magnificent natural backgrounds to be found there better than anywhere else in the world. But all too frequently beauty of perspective has been accompanied by obscurity of dramatic action. The spectator remarks "How pretty! How realistic!" but he doesn't follow the story, and it is a question if more is not lost than gained by such a policy. It must be noted also that Selig picture stories are sometimes constructed without due regard to lucid narrative. However, the Selig Company is entitled to the highest praise for its ambitious and painstaking efforts in the direction of moving picture perfection.

The Essanay Film Manufacturing Company, of Chicago, has gained a wide popularity for clever comedy subjects, admirably acted and constructed. Recently this company has been producing a number of melodramatic stories with fair success, and it has just made a notable production of a high class drama with a star actor in the cast, but its comedy work will be best remembered by moving picture patrons, who will hope that the "comics" are not to be abandoned. Essanay pictures are always photographically good and clearly obvious to the spectators, although there are times when inconsistencies creep in.

The Lubin pictures, manufactured in Philadelphia, are among the earlier American productions, and consist of comedy, drama, and travel subjects. Of the three styles, the last named are the most meritorious, although not frequently enough produced. In comedy and drama there is much spirit displayed in the acting, but too often the stories are feeble or ragged and not handled with the best dramatic effect. The photography, however, is excellent.

ENTR'ACTE 4

"The Drummer and the Girl"

The Sound of Music in the Nickelodeon

Going to the movies in the fall of 1906 was different from what it would
be three years later, at least for most people. Among all the changes that
would occur during what Kleine privately called "the golden period of this
business,"[1] one of those least noted by cinema historians has to do with
sound.[2] Just as Pathé's dominance during these years presented a problem
for a truly American cinema, so too did sound—whether instrumental and
vocal music, the voices of lecturers and actors, or live sound effects and
noise, and whether that sound occurred separate from or in synchrony
with moving pictures. The industrial standardization of musical accompaniment began to develop rather late, Rick Altman writes, around
1909–1910; before then, sound in the nickelodeon was heterogeneous, irregular, or even nonexistent.[3] The trade press discourse generally supports
the dating of this change, but it also reveals that, prior to that date, sound
rather than silence (as Altman provocatively asserts) may have been more
prevalent; it not only took many forms but also served a variety of functions.[4] Broadly, however, in the fall of 1906, sound was closely tied to a particular site of exhibition and tended to interpolate the viewer as part of a
specific social *audience*. In other words, it played a significant role in the
communal moviegoing experience. Three years later, sound was becoming
less site-specific, more standardized; furthermore, as Altman argues, the
gradual move to continuous musical accompaniment began working in
parallel with other changes to transform the viewer into a *spectator,* caught
up in a specific film's narrativization of an individual character's desire.[5]
All this would have consequences for the reception of Pathé's films, especially in sharpening their sense of "foreignness."

Perhaps the first thing to point out about early nickelodeon programs is
that, from the very beginning, they almost always presented moving pictures *and* illustrated songs (a vocalist accompanied by a pianist and colored slides).[6] Although illustrated songs had existed as a regular vaudeville
act since the early 1890s,[7] their coupling with moving pictures may have
originated with Archie Shepard. Shepard first developed this format as a
touring exhibitor, Musser suggests, and continued the practice in the regular Sunday concerts he began to offer during the 1905–1906 theatrical
season, in parallel with the first nickelodeons.[8] The formula won immediate widespread acceptance, at least given the press reports on sites as
different as the Comique (Boston), the Nickel Family (Worcester), and the
Nickeldom (Des Moines), as well as the weekly listing of "latest song

Figure 36. "The Lost Child" song slide, 1896.

slides" in the *Index*, starting July 1906.[9] As a rule, moving pictures were the principal attraction on these programs, but it was not unusual for exhibitors to give more attention to illustrated songs, especially when the competition between nearby houses grew heated.[10] When the "nickel craze" hit Des Moines in the summer of 1907, for instance, the Radium distinguished itself by headlining its songs and special concerts: one week it even advertised its vocalists as former members of the local college quartet.[11] The alternating format of moving pictures and illustrated songs (rarely ever risqué) had a double effect, I would argue, in "localizing" the nickelodeon as a cheap amusement. It provided a venue of employment for talent, both well known and new, and it offered a unique mix of national mass-market culture (the widely circulating films, slides, and songs) and a local, more "popular" culture (the musicians, who often led sing-alongs with the audience).[12] In other words, illustrated songs may have helped to ensure that some nickelodeons at least did function as neighborhood family centers.

Figure 37. Radium Theater ad, *Des Moines Register and Leader* (29 May 1907), 6.

This was not the only kind of sound, however, that worked separately from, yet in conjunction with, moving pictures. Much more problematic were the ballyhoos (or graphophones) set up at nickelodeon entrances to attract passersby, aptly mechanical devices that combined the spieling functions of the circus parade and barker. These became an "obnoxious" problem in metropolitan areas like Philadelphia as early as the summer of 1906, when "property owners and influential shop keepers" (among them Wanamaker) objected to the dozen nickelodeons and "their noisy advertisements" stretching along Market Street.[13] A court injunction "prohibiting annoyances of this kind in the city of brotherly love" may have proved an example to other cities, as *Billboard* hoped, but the battle against ballyhoos flared up again one year later. This time the *World* followed "the situation in Philadelphia" closely, using the rhetoric of uplift to support the merchants of "the greatest retail street in the city" in their efforts to suppress "the nerve-wracking din and tawdry display" of the cheap showmen (backed by "realty brokers and speculators").[14] This time, too, there was a scapegoat in William Boogar, who cleverly hired an all-girl orchestra to play outside two of his three shows on Market.[15] Despite the testimony of the girls, whose repertoire included "between 150 and 200 pieces," none of which was played twice in one day, and who were never a "nuisance" (the trade weekly obviously was charmed), the court decided in favor of the merchants (and "responsible" showmen like Davis and even Lubin).[16] Thereafter, in Philadelphia and elsewhere, the sound of music (emanating from musicians or machines) largely retreated into the darkened halls of the nickelodeons.

Another, more recent debate has arisen over whether music actually accompanied the moving pictures. Altman contends that often it did not, at least in a systematic way, and that musical instruments often were used for "effects" or "props" (as well as "overtures" and "intermissions").[17] Early descriptions of nickelodeon programs and even Shepard's touring shows either bear him out or at least point up the heterogeneity of music's place and function on programs. In April 1905, for instance, when a Shepard company played Des Moines, the "mile of pictures" were shown with "every sound, vocal and mechanical, reproduced."[18] A year later, the first issue of the *Index* carried a report that contrasted a smoothly operating show (using a piano and drum) in the New York shopping district on lower Sixth Avenue with a poorly run, deceptive one in Harlem (with a gramophone outside playing monotonously).[19] In October 1906, the *Index* offered guidance not only for selecting and ordering the films on a program but also for making "music an important factor" in creating "realistic exhibitions": the film, in which a couple coming across a field stop and bow their heads, may have been a mystery in one theater, but it was perfectly understandable in another when accompanied by a tolling church bell.[20] By 1907, "most of the shows ha[d] musical accompaniments," according to Patterson; some already were using small orchestras.[21] When the Theatre Antique opened in Lowell, for instance, its orchestra and conductor (violinist Henry Pateneude) were cited as one reason for its quick success.[22] Another model "showhouse" was the Princess, in South Framingham, whose "three-piece orchestra afford[ed] music and effect."[23] Finally, individual performers were gaining some notoriety: one New York theater on the edge of Jewish East Harlem engaged a well-known pianist, Felix Simon, who was "delighting large audiences with his splendid straight and trick playing."[24]

During the spring and summer of 1908, further trade press reports confirmed the prevalence of music and took note of several new developments. A piano and drummer could be found in most moving picture shows, from the Chicago Orpheum or the New York Unique (*Variety* especially liked the drummer's "'effects' and 'props' for every picture") to the Idle Hour and the Lyric in Grand Rapids, Michigan (the latter employed "two sets of singers and musicians" because it was "pretty hard for a piano player to keep right on playing all afternoon and evening").[25] Small orchestras became the rule at new large cinemas like the Olympic in Lynn (five pieces) or Swanson's in Chicago (four pieces), but they always were linked to the moving pictures rather than to the illustrated songs or vaudeville acts.[26] Lecturers made a comeback, led by W. Stephen Bush, who gave "descriptive readings" of Pathé's *Passion Play*, Shakespeare adaptations, and other "classics" at theaters wishing to attract "the best class of people," all within "300 miles of Philadelphia."[27] Others had a more limited range of venues, like Herr Professor at Tompkins Square Vaudeville on New York's Lower East Side.[28] Some of the "better" theaters also tried out one of two "novelties" involving sound. The first involved enterprises seeking to commercialize the latest experiments in mechanical synchronization using phonograph disks.[29] The most publicized devices were the Cameraphone and the Chronophone, the latter of which Gaumont gradually built into a special attraction at People's Theatre and the Unique, in New York, before touring New England.[30] The second novelty was "talking pictures," which required a small troupe of actors to speak the characters' dialogue from behind the screen while a moving picture unreeled.[31] Two highly publicized companies for "talkies" were Actologue and Humanovo (the latter, one more Zukor investment that did not pan out well), but Harry Davis also had at least one company that toured the Midwest, playing for a month, for instance, at the Lyric in Des Moines.[32] Yet neither of these novelties succeeded in becoming standardized or widely distributed, largely because of added expenses and irregular synchronization.[33]

That year, the most detailed account of "music and films," however, came in an article devoted specifically to the subject in the *Index*.[34] It focused on Harry Altman's nickelodeon in Jewish Harlem and his "investment [in] good music" performed by a classically trained pianist, Arthur Barrow.[35] Barrow quickly learned that his audience knew "perfectly well" that "the trade mark of the rooster" meant a French film and that he had to choose his accompaniment accordingly. Although popular American tunes "often fit situations" in other films "with a surprising degree of accuracy," he said, they were "woefully out of place" here; instead, Barrow came up with variations on classical melodies to suggest "a strong atmosphere of foreign life," which offered added pleasure to "the better class of film lovers." At the same time, and in the same trade paper, Walter Eaton, the *New York Sun*'s drama critic, was describing Pathé's *Christmas Eve Tragedy* on a visit to the Fourteenth Street Bijou Dream.[36] Unlike *Variety*, Eaton found this *grand guignol* French film "a touching domestic tragedy" with an "irreproachable moral," but he also remarked on the ballad that followed, with the audience "invited to join in the chorus." This was a ballad "about a forsaken maiden 'in a village by the sea,'" and its conjunction with Pathé's film, along with Barrow's interview, raises an important question about how music before, during, and after a film could affect an audience's "reading." Although Eaton does not mention it (his focus is on the male characters), *Christmas Eve Tragedy* is unusual for the hint of interiority it gives the principal female character.[37] For some women spectators, at least, that ballad may have suggested a different sense of the film's "tragedy" from the one Eaton implied. These specific instances also reveal how sound could serve to sharpen and enforce the difference between American and "foreign" films, a difference that would work to the detriment of producers like Pathé in a period of "Americanization." And they suggest how Pathé's films could be associated with "high culture," which the company might exploit, but only to limited advantage.

During the months leading up to the fall of 1909, the trade press increasingly stressed how important instrumental music, and especially appropriate music, was to a good moving picture show.[38] Wurlitzer pipe organs began to turn up in ads and articles, and to appear in new theaters like the Alcazar in Atlanta.[39] The *World* especially began to take an interest in the "music question." Its "own critic" of New York houses frequently noted when music worked well as an attraction, praising the "good orchestra of ladies" at the Atlantic Palace on the Bowery, the "young lady who plays the piano" at Wonders Varieties near Union Square, as well as the pianist and drummer for their "excellent harmony" and "suitable symphonic accompaniment" at the Twenty-third Street Bijou Dream.[40] An editorial in the *World*, on 3 July 1909, singled out "the music that accompanies, illustrates, or . . . is supposed to harmonize with the pictures" as the only thing "lamentably deficient" about too many New York shows.[41] If engaging a small orchestra of strings was too costly, the trade paper recommended Keith houses as a model for how best to deploy the drum and piano. Writing as Lux Graphicus, Thomas Bedding positively gushed over "the drummer and the girl . . . , with the emphasis on The Girl," at the Fourteenth Street Bijou Dream.[42] "Never . . . have I heard, or seen, a girl enter so completely into the spirit of the pictures shown. . . . Every emotion, every sentiment, every movement, every mood illustrated on the screen, is duplicated by the tones of the piano. It is a perfect concordance of sound, movement and thought." It was that girl's performance, Bedding realized, that made "the pictures that *think*, here seem to me to *think* the most and the best." As he looked around at his "fellow visitors," all were absorbed in "the emotions portrayed by the performers," transfixed within an imaginary space of empathy induced and sustained by "The Girl" at the piano.[43]

Within months of its July editorial, the *World* took pride in noting, several manufacturers were offering advice to exhibitors in selecting the music most appropriate to accompany their films.[44] The first was Edison, which added a column called "Incidental Music" to its monthly *Kinetogram* bulletins. As reprinted in the *Index*, the first of these columns suggested "music cues" (an andante, an allegro, etc.) for each "scene" of such Edison films as *The Ordeal*.[45] Soon Vitagraph was announcing that it would be sending out specially composed scores for each of its "Films de Luxe": the music would be "written during rehearsals" and "played as the negative . . . is made, insuring absolute timing."[46] Significantly, Pathé did not join its fellow MPPC members in making available "music cues" or special scores for its films, even though the early Film d'Art productions it released were performed, at least in France, with scores written by well-known composers.[47] Given all the other innovations the French company exploited to remain competitive on the American market, it is worth pausing to ask why. The reason may lie in music's greater cultural specificity: what Pathé offered or might suggest as musical accompaniment for French audiences might not work for audiences in the United States (or even other countries). If many French films looked "strange" accompanied by American popular tunes, then with what music would they work effectively, how broad or limited was the range of that music, and how could Pathé keep that music from underscoring the foreignness of its films (except when that might work to their advantage)? Perhaps Berst and his associates realized that those best positioned to make such decisions were experienced musicians (such as Barrow) in the theaters, together with the trade press writers most committed to improving the quality of the moving picture show.[48]

For the *World*, the *Index*, and, to a lesser extent, the *Mirror* took their self-appointed task of "educating" exhibitors about music very seriously. Given their regular surveys of shows and audiences, they, too, could offer advice, even on specific film subjects. One of the earliest came in a report on the Senate, George Hines's model theater on Chicago's West Side, where Biograph's *Fool's Revenge* (loosely based on *Rigoletto*) "made a deep impression," accompanied by Schumann's "Träumerei" and Beethoven's "Moonlight Sonata."[49] In the *Mirror*, the manager of the St. Johns Nickel Theatre shared the choices his eight-piece orchestra made with several Pathé films: "the increasing feverishness of Suppé's 'Poet and Peasant Overture'" for the "weird *Bluebeard*," Faure's "The Crucifix" and Mendelssohn's "Priest's March" for *Joan of Arc*, and Tosti's "Goodbye" and Levbach's "Fifth Nocturne" to "enhanc[e] the dramatic situations" in *La Tosca*.[50] John Bradlet, the *World*'s representative in Chicago, contrasted the Orpheum and the Casino for how their music affected Biograph's *Cloister's Touch:* one increased its beauty, the other made it vulgar.[51] He also praised the Orpheum's handling of Pathé's *Violin Maker of Cremona:* whenever either Philippo or Sandro took up a violin on-screen, the orchestra stopped and the violinist played on alone, but more eloquently for Philippo so as to fit the film story's resolution.[52] Almost simultaneously, both the *World* and the *Index* gave free advertisements to perhaps the first book to collect "over 100 numbers of descriptive music . . . adapt[able] to any scene shown in the motion picture world," Gregg Frelinger's *Motion Picture Piano Music.*[53] By April 1910, in his weekly column for the *World*, S. L. Rothapfel (known later as "Roxy") was promoting Frelinger's book, encouraging musicians to use it as a guide for their own improvising, and reminding them, above all, that *"the picture comes first."*[54] According to *Nickelodeon*, it was soon being used in thousands of theaters in the United States and even Europe.[55]

Three points are worth reiterating. First of all, the *World*'s catchy phrase "the drummer and the girl" not only accurately references the musicians in many nickelodeons but also suggests that a good number of them, singers as well as pianists and other instrumentalists, initially at least, were young women. This is one more indication that, particularly in larger cities, early moving picture shows functioned for women as a "space apart and a space between," a new space of employment, socializing, or both.[56] Second, Pathé's reluctance to impose its own sense of what music should accompany its films further exposes the company's increasingly difficult or problematic position on the American market. Music culturally specific to the United States was blatantly out of sync with French subjects, but music "read" by Americans as culturally specific to France or even Europe could intensify the foreignness of the red rooster brand. This was an unenviable catch-22, and it was accentuated by the "American way of life" so often celebrated in the illustrated song slides. Finally, in conjunction with musicians and exhibitors, the trade press played a perhaps more significant role than did producers in standardizing or normalizing musical accompaniment and upgrading its quality.[57] But not in all theaters, as Mary Carbine has shown.[58] In Chicago's black theaters on the Stroll, what drew the "young people [who] thronged in large numbers" was not only the vaudeville acts and blues artists but also the musicians who "inappropriately" jazzed up the usual pictures.[59] By contrast, in Barberton, Ohio, at least one theater claimed that "all of its songs" were sung "in the Slavish language" of its many recent immigrants.[60] In the sense that the normalizing role of the trade press contributed to the transformation of most viewers into spectators, intellectually and emotionally engaging them now in the stories films told, it also coincided with another, perhaps even more important, of their functions, as polemicists for distinctive, exclusionary "American subjects."

CHAPTER FIVE

The Perils of Pathé
"Americanize or Be Foreignized," 1907–1910

For only five cents—kids, two for a nickel—the manager would let us stall all afternoon. So we would get comfortable, take off our slippers and nurse the babies for three, sometimes four films with illustrated songs in between. After we heard a song several times, with the pictures, and joined in the singing, most of us could understand what the song was about. That's how we learned to speak English. Ask anybody.

MRS. JOE FLEISHER, RECALLING HER EARLY MOVIEGOING ON THE LOWER EAST SIDE

What made Pathé's very presence, let alone its influence, especially undesirable at this historical moment, I would argue, was a conjunction of concerns about who went to the cinema, and about what and who were being constructed as "American." Of all those who constituted the nickelodeon's mass audience (and variations, of course, existed from one region or city to another), several groups especially attracted attention. One was the disproportionate number of recent immigrants from eastern and southern Europe, concentrated in urban centers throughout the Northeast and the upper Midwest. The "poorer sections of the cities where [these] innumerable foreigners congregate[d]," claimed George Walsh in 1908, were precisely where "the so-called 'nickelodeon' . . . held preeminent sway."[1] The other group was hardly mutually exclusive, consisting of women and children who, according to most accounts (however self-serving), made up the greater portion of nickelodeon audiences across the country. This was the case whether the two were taken together or separately, whether the women were single or married, working-class or middle-class, and whether the children were boys or girls. In Saint Louis in early 1909, for instance, some of the more conspicuous "regulars" were the "hundreds of young women employed downtown who [skip] their noonday luncheon . . . to visit the moving picture shows . . . and go back to the counter and the typewriter stomach hungry, but mentally fed."[2] Others, of course, saw this simply as impoverishment; and reformers such as Addams in Chicago and Davis in New York wrote and spoke tirelessly of their concern, especially for the "thousands of young people in every industrial city" for whom "going to the show" weekly or even daily had become habitual.[3]

Concern about the effect of "going to the show" on such groups of people was framed in terms of others: for instance, class mobility, a perceived "youth problem," and women's allegedly increasing independence, especially in public spaces, which Eleanor Gates summed up as that of "the girl who travels alone."[4] Yet each of these "problems" ultimately converged to feed a growing "crisis of anxiety" over the construction of an American identity. How would that identity be differentiated from others in an era of heightened nationalism? How would those without full citizenship—specifically immigrants, women, and children—best be trained to take up that identity and become "proper" social subjects within an American culture? Looking back at the crisis several years later, Maude McDougall offered this tongue-in-cheek summary: "From twenty to twenty-five per cent of the patrons of moving picture shows are children. And because the entertainment is inexpensive, and because it requires no translation, a very large percentage are immigrants. Immigrants and children! The entire raw material of future citizenship. No wonder the 'high-brows'—parents and teachers, legislators and entertainers—are concerned over the influence of these 'cheap' shows."[5] This anxiety was heightened, moreover, by the widespread popularity of all those undesirable "foreign" films. In the fall of 1908, the Grand Theater in Portland could still attract audiences with weekly bills that included "the latest French [Pathé] motion pictures."[6] And as late as June 1909, the British trade weekly *Bioscope* could file this report on moviegoing in the United States: "The quality of the Pathé picture is far and away ahead of that of its competition. . . . The public like Pathé pictures. . . . From this state of affairs there has arisen a condition of mind which one can only call Pathé-mentia."[7]

THE RHETORIC OF "NATIONAL MENACE"

Questions about these converging concerns became especially pertinent as the number of new immigrants rose from three hundred thousand in 1900 to a peak of nearly one million in 1907. Already in 1903, frankly racist editorials and political cartoons were representing this as an "alien invasion," a "national menace" threatening the very concept of a uniquely white American character.[8] The Italians and Jews, so "very different from the Irish and Germans who at former periods swelled our population," according to the Progressive weekly *The World's Work*, were "the least desirable part of the European population [and] add[ed] incalculable difficulties to our city life."[9] By the spring of 1906, a "New York morning paper" was reporting with alarm that fifty-two thousand immigrants had entered the city within a period of just four days.[10] These immigrants provoked an intense, often virulent debate over whether the so-called process of assimilation supposedly so crucial to Americanization was in jeopardy.[11] During the course of several months in 1906–1907, for instance, *Munsey's* ran Herbert Casson's thirteen-part series with the overall title "The Americans in America," celebrating "the leading races" that had contributed to the development of a "still unfinished" American character.[12] Six months later, in the *Century Illustrated*, Brander Matthews (a leading literary critic) insisted on the continuing success of this "melting pot" theory: "In some

Figure 38. Louis Dalrymple, "High Tide of Immigration—A National Menace," *Judge* (22 August 1903).

mysterious fashion we Americans have imposed our ideals on the Irish and on the Germans, as we are now imposing them on the Italians and on the Russian Jews." [13] Others were far less sanguine, and some even sounded like prophets of doom. After detailing the disproportionate strain the new foreigners were placing on the country's social institutions, the influential clergyman Josiah Strong demanded that "we Americanize the immigrants" or else "they will foreignize our cities, and in so doing foreignize our civilization." [14]

One of the more offensive strands of this debate intersected with the cinema in a very troubling way. In April 1907, *McClure's* published George Kibbe Turner's muckraking article on Chicago's "great immoralities," setting off a nationwide hysteria over an alleged "white slavery conspiracy." [15] Although Turner talked "cold business" about alcoholism, gambling, and especially political corruption, he saved some of his strongest attacks for prostitution, partly because it was obvious to him that "the chastity of woman is at the foundation of Anglo-Saxon society." [16] What Turner claimed to have found, in his investigations, was that "the largest regular business in furnishing women" was controlled by "Russian Jews." [17] And not only were they dominant in Chicago, they also had "a loosely organized association extending through the largest cities of the country." [18] Two years later, in another infamous article in *McClure's*, Turner focused exclusively on the "white slave trade" in New York. [19] Again, those controlling it supposedly were Jews, but now Turner traced its origins historically to eastern Europe, located its new center in the East Side ghetto, and introduced the French *maquereau* as an ear-lier, less successful rival to the Jew.[20] Dance halls were the "chief recruiting-grounds" for prostitutes, but Turner did not ignore moving pictures as a compet-ing entertainment.[21] His language had a disturbing parallel in trade press reports supporting McClellan's closing of New York nickelodeons. In *Moving Picture World,* those exhibitors accused of being greedy and disreputable, of giving the business a bad name, were "in almost every instance . . . foreigners who are not citizens."[22] The Protestant clergymen leading this campaign were more specific: the "princi-pal law-breakers" came from "the rapidly increasing Hebrew element."[23] Because many theaters were owned or managed by immigrant Jews, and their programs were full of French Pathé films, this concerted attempt to regulate or repress mov-ing picture shows has to be read, I think, within this wider discourse linking the "foreign" and the "criminal" or "diseased" as a serious threat, in Strong's words, to "our country."[24]

For writers of whatever persuasion, a vital component of the Americanization process for immigrants was education. "In urban centers such as New York City," write William Uricchio and Roberta Pearson, "the public schools constituted the first line of defense against the 'alien invasion,' charged with the responsibility for teaching immigrant children the language of their new country as well as its man-ners and morals."[25] Their point derives from a Carnegie Corporation study first published in 1920, which asserted: "If some degree of amalgamation has taken place in this country, if the kind of Americanism we now find may be likened to a stream with varying and unequal currents and not to a series of parallel water courses, then the school must be given credit for a considerable part in the achievement."[26] Yet "every conceivable mode of education," Michael Kammen argues, "was viewed as a potential contribution."[27] By 1908–1909, on the evi-dence of moral reformers from Jane Addams to John Collier and Michael Davis, all of them backed by Simon Patten's popular books, this concept of "education" included the cinema, especially the popular nickelodeons, which, according to the *New York Times,* now weekly attracted perhaps half the population of the United States.[28] As the previous chapters have shown, the trade press took up this notion, pointedly suggesting that if renters "listen[ed] a little more to country exhibitors and less to the Bowery" (another code word condensing Jew, French, and Italian into the "foreign," with links to the "criminal"), "they would soon find that the public does not call for highly sensational or silly films."[29] This idea would be sup-ported by the National Board of Censorship, through the principles guiding its at-tempt to mediate reception: that films offer appropriate rather than inappropriate models of behavior for immigrants and that women and children not be exposed to dubious, even deviant, values and attitudes. If "driving the French importer out of America" meant one thing to Turner, it meant something else for the uplift of the moving picture show.[30]

Underlying this thinking was a widespread assumption that the function of fiction within the new mass culture was to generate positive models of imitation for "building character." A good example was provided by the dime novels of Horatio Alger, which, Michael Denning argues, had their "largest readership between 1900 and 1915" (after the writer's death) and were soon transformed into an "archetypal narrative" of American capitalism in their "individualistic ethic of hard work and . . . self-improvement." [31] Yet even better examples were available in the mass magazines and Sunday newspaper supplements, where short stories enjoyed what even Brander Matthews admitted was "an immense vogue." [32] For the trade press, the "tons of good stories" resembled "playlets" (or scenarios), and the spectator was like a reader, except that "the moving picture narrates . . . in picture language instead of type." [33] In either case, what American readers wanted, according to F. Marion Crawford, a popular novelist of the time, was "to see before them characters whom they might really like to resemble, acting in scenes in which they themselves would like to take part." [34] In *Munsey's*, Hugo Münsterberg provided what seemed to be psychological "evidence" for this "theorizing": his experiments repeatedly showed that "the imitation of [a] suggestive sight suddenly brings to work [an individual's] stored-up powers." [35] In the same monthly, Casson asserted that Americans "demand[ed] that every story should have a happy ending"; and the *World* took up the cry with its promotion of "good cheer" films.[36] "We are all seeking happiness," *Nickelodeon* cheerfully concluded in a diatribe against tragedy, in the movies as in the mass magazines, "whether through money, or position, or imagination." [37] That fictional worlds consisted of fantasy trajectories for individuals to imitate in their own lives seemed as relevant for moviegoers as for readers of magazines, dime novels, and best-sellers.[38] It was better "brain food" than Post, Kellogg's, or Quaker Oats could offer in their cereal ads.[39]

RED-BLOODED REALISM VERSUS RED ROOSTER ARTIFICE

During these years, I would argue, Pathé's foreign subjects provided one of the principal "others" against which to construct an American difference. That difference began to surface in the trade press shortly after the essays in *Munsey's* and *Century Illustrated*, not only in *Variety* reviews but also in a host of trade press editorials and articles. From its initial issues in 1907, which coincided with the *Chicago Tribune*'s attacks, the *World* polemicized for "clean, wholesome" films, attributing its own moral reformist desire for them to "public opinion." [40] By the summer of 1908, that desire was so bound up with the debate over Americanization that James Law would turn it into a demand for "good, clean, wholesome, national, patriotic, educational films," which was hardly unrelated to his castigation of "the foremost French maker" for failing to conform to the standards of "American taste." [41] In *Show World*, Law even envisioned American companies soon "wrest[ing] the laurels from the foreigners, and . . . exporting the choicest films"; and the *Mirror* had a ready example in the "snap and go" of *Peck's Bad Boy*, a Kalem picture.[42] By the end of the year, the competition Pierce had observed between French and American manufacturers was turning, for the latter, into something like a national mission. Dyer promoted this mission, in *Show World* no less, insisting that "American manufacturers in particular [were] being extremely zealous" in their efforts "to eliminate any low class or vulgar subject."[43] At the same time, the *Mirror* was lauding "the great improvement in character and quality that has taken place in American film production."[44] By the following year, Carl Laemmle (now an important Independent figure) was putting the case bluntly as he moved into production: "I will make American subjects my specialty. . . . I want strong virile American subjects."[45]

This search for American subjects also became aligned with an aesthetic that the trade press increasingly marked off as different from Pathé's, in which color served as a lure, as a primary visual material of desire. The difference between the two is put succinctly, if bizarrely, by an article entitled "Films and Realism" in *Film Index* (October 1908).[46] Here, an unnamed writer conceptualized the initial decade of cinema history as an artistic development through three stages, with each one superseding the one before. First came the *actualité* of "Nature, pure and undefiled"; next came "Nature Humanized" in stories of realism or naturalism; and now comes what the writer calls "Romanticism." "Realism," interestingly, was associated not only with French writers like Balzac and Zola but also with the "murders, prodigies, and thrilling escapes" that Pathé's tinted-and-toned *grand guignol* melodramas had come to exemplify. "Romanticism," by contrast, offered stories in which "the camera . . . opens its imperturbable eye upon studio miracles, and . . . gives back symbolism more recondite than Ibsen . . . and a deus ex machina (photographica) which, as boldly as any Laura Jean Libbey, rearranges things that every dreamy little shop-girl would like to see."[47] Although this article never mentions color, and even appropriates the moralizing objectives of "ethical melodrama," it chiefly promotes an aesthetic of visual display, one that seems to project the future of cinema as an extension of the stencil-color films on which Pathé had built its reputation. Moreover, that future is envisioned in terms of "dream worlds" or "heavenly billboards" that particularly address women, and, more specifically, single, white-collar working women. In other words, this is a highly "feminized" cinema, seemingly well aware of its circulation as a "commercial enticement."

The "realist" aesthetic against which the *Index* imagined cinema's future, however, can be read as a displacement of the one actually coming into its own in the trade press. That aesthetic found an influential proponent, in the summer of 1908, in the review columns of *New York Dramatic Mirror*. The *Mirror*'s chief concern was to promote not visual display and certainly not color, but specifically American models for telling stories. These seem to have come chiefly from short stories, the market for which, by 1900, claimed Bliss Perry, was enormous, constant, and "perfectly adapted to our over-driven generation."[48] Handbooks now were available for beginning writers. One of the earliest came from Matthews, most of whose principles were then repeated by others—originality, unity, compression, brilliancy of style, action, form ("logical, adequate, harmonious"), and substance—

with this addition, "verisimilitude," including characters "drawn from life."[49] For examples, the *Mirror* reviewers could have looked to the "vivid and clear-cut prose" in *Munsey's* that Casson thought characterized American magazine fiction, or even to the "strong swift style" of the same magazine's ads that J. Angus Mac-Donald claimed were particularly effective for men.[50] They could have looked to the fiction cited by the *Nation:* "Our short stories move rapidly . . . every sentence must have 'go' in it, and stimulate the desire for the next sentence."[51] What went unsaid, however, was that most of these reviews were written by Frank Woods, who at the same time was selling scenarios to Biograph.[52] In short, a double sense of American self-interest guided this initial regulatory attempt to lay down a set of narrative principles for the American cinema.

Once upon a time, Pathé consistently had won accolades for its "lucid story telling."[53] Now, according to the *Mirror,* the company allegedly often "fail[ed] to tell a dramatic story so that the spectators [could] understand it."[54] Instead, it was American companies that were succeeding throughout the summer and fall of 1908. Edison's *Blue and the Gray,* for instance, was praised for its "consistent dramatic force, moving heart interest, and clearly told story."[55] Biograph's *Red-man and the Child* was rated "best film of the week" chiefly because "the story is original and consistent, and the scenes follow each other consecutively and naturally. Interest is aroused from the start, and is held with increasing power to the very end."[56] Other Biograph films such as *The Red Girl* and *The Call of the Wild* later served to point up "the particular elements that go to make up a successful moving picture story."[57] That meant "clever construction and acting of a well conceived and not too intricate plot," as in *The Guerrilla,* a thrilling war story that "was warmly applauded at the Unique" in New York.[58] In its summary of "the difference between foreign and American productions," the *Mirror* judged the latter "very much superior in plot" and again singled out Biograph for the "superior character" of its stories.[59] It was then, too, that the *World* joined the *Mirror*'s crusade, citing not only *The Guerrilla* and other Biograph films but also Selig's *One of the Bravest.*[60] The *World* also invoked the *Mirror*'s polemic in words that must have chilled Pathé: in surveying a large New England factory city that winter, it found even "foreigners" wanted "pictures with plenty of action" and "action so plain that it tells the story without the necessity of words" (now the prerogative of American films).[61] In contrast to the *Index,* the *Mirror* and now the *World* envisioned and promoted a cinema of "simple stor[ies], as all good stories should be,"[62] one that was decidedly—although this remained unstated—"masculine."[63]

These differences in aesthetics, in foreign and American subjects, in prescriptions for an American cinema: all can be seen as part of a larger change marking American culture at the turn of the century. Neil Harris offers one way of framing this change through what he has called the iconographic revolution, which, within a single generation, transformed the whole system of packaging visual information in the United States.[64] During the last decades of the nineteenth century, color chromos had circulated so widely that the United States sometimes was called the "chromo-civilization."[65] In the 1890s, chromolithography rapidly gave way to a new technology of halftone photoengraving, a process that allowed photographs to be reproduced on cheap paper (usually in black-and-white). Their use transformed newspaper and magazine journalism (a good example was *The World's Work*), where the photo now served to guarantee accuracy and authenticity.[66]

This change created new "categories of appropriateness," Harris writes, that gave certain kinds of visual reproduction more value than others.[67] It was bad enough that chromos sold in the millions, and ended up decorating the walls of many lower-class and even middle-class homes.[68] Often the quality of reproduction was unexceptional or far worse; as a consequence, the term "chromo" soon came to stand for all that could be labeled vulgar, debased, or simply old-fashioned in early mass culture.[69] These "categories of appropriateness" may well have functioned as significant criteria in the trade press efforts to limit or marginalize the reception of Pathé color films, particularly in contrast to the widespread effort, in 1908–1909, to valorize Charles Urban's Kinemacolor, based on G. Albert Smith's "scientific invention" of reproducing moving pictures in "natural color."[70]

Richard Slotkin offers an equally productive way of framing this change by making explicit the masculinism and racism of the discourse which argued that an "aesthetic of authenticity" must replace an "aesthetic of imitation" in American culture.[71] The latter assumed a fascination with replicas or reproductions of all kinds—from color chromos and stereographs for the home to a copy of the Republic statue (from the 1893 Chicago Exposition) installed in Siegel-Cooper's New York department store—and a faith in the power of machines to manufacture credible, inexpensive simulacra en masse.[72] This would remain the dominant aesthetic of the mass market, and it is not difficult to see Leach's "commercial aesthetic of color and light" as its logical extension. To counter what was seen as a cultural realm of "female" values and "female sensibilities," there developed what Slotkin has called a "*virilist* realism," which assumed a different kind of faith and fascination.[73] As early as 1895, the editor and publisher of *Munsey's*, for instance, was exhorting his writers to begin doing "men's work in fiction, as we are doing it in the industries of the world."[74] Similarly, in *The World's Work*, W. Churchill Williams, Frederick Emory, and others espoused a "red-blooded realism" that not only could inspire the "tough-minded" men (white, of course) now needed to "do the work" of an expanding American empire but also could teach immigrants and workers (both men and women) to accept their proper place within its hierarchical social order.[75] Here, writers like Owen Wister and Frank Norris were exemplary: they claimed to actively observe and reproduce the "real" in words, much in the manner of Alfred Stieglitz, whose exclusive medium was black-and-white photography.[76] Their subjects, along with those of Hamlin Garland, Frederic Remington, and others, were "new," inspired by "the drama of city streets, harbors, and quotidian scenes" or the "tremendous tales" of the frontier, where, Norris wrote, "there was action and fighting, and where men held each others' lives in the crook of a forefinger."[77] And they were addressed "intelligibly and simply," Norris insisted, to "the Plain People."[78] For moving pictures, such stories would soon become the quintessential American subject.

In other words, if one faction of the trade press discourse, represented by the *Index*, invoked a "feminized" aesthetic of imitation in order to imagine the cinema as a cultural space of consumption (in which color remained a privileged element of display), and perhaps something even approaching "high art," the other, represented by the *Mirror*, deployed a "masculinized" aesthetic of authenticity (in which color was unimportant) so as to envision the cinema as an arena of "realistic" storytelling, of "character-building," a new and influential form of "virile" American culture.[79] Could this be a crucial locus of the gender difference later marking so much of the theoretical work on cinema spectatorship, a difference mapped historically in terms of social activity (going to the movies) versus textual address and inscription (involving looking relations)?[80]

THE PATHÉ RESPONSE: DIFFERENTIATION AND ASSIMILATION

As the cries to restrict "foreigners" grew more frequent and more shrill, so, too, within the cinema market did they for restricting "foreign subjects," even those bearing the red rooster trademark. By the time the *Index* lent its support to this clamor, admitting that there was "a limit to the [number] of foreign subjects for which American audiences will stand" and that even some of Pathé's were "unsuited to American demands,"[81] it was clear that the French company would have to adjust its marketing strategies. By June 1908, Pathé had concluded that its rapid, perhaps overextended, growth was ending, at least in the United States, and that it had to ensure a stable basis of operations for steady profits (ever the bottom line). Briefly, that meant shifting film production financing onto affiliate companies, reorienting film distribution (to rely less on the American market), and investing more in the industry's material base—that is, apparatuses and film stock—and concentrating that investment in France.[82]

Apparently, Pathé never considered realigning its interests in the United States, even if it could have, with those of the Independents that emerged in opposition to the MPPC or helping them link up with any of the major exhibitors in New York or Chicago. Given its position of diminishing power within the context of open racism undergirding Americanization, it must have seemed hard enough coping with the "unsavoriness" of being "French"; taking on the slurs attached to other foreigners (especially Jewish immigrants) probably would have seemed unprofitable. At best, the French company maintained an ambivalent stance as that racism turned anti-Semitic in the trade press—perhaps best epitomized by all the cartoons

Figure 39. Laemmle ad, *Moving Picture World* (12 June 1909), 778.

equating the Independents and ghetto junkmen—and within the MPPC, where Smith and Blackton (of Vitagraph) and Kleine were especially hostile.[83] Instead, in order to remain competitive within the United States, Pathé sought to find positive, that is, acceptable, ways of further differentiating its commodities and addressing the normalizing demands of assimilation.

The first and perhaps most significant of Pathé's moves was to promote itself as the maker of "higher quality" films. In other words, it would reinvoke the high culture notion of Frenchness exploited earlier to legitimate the cinema. This strategy originated in France, in early 1908, with an investment in two new production companies, Film d'Art and SCAGL: in addition to financing the construction and equipment of their studios, Pathé contracted to edit, print, and distribute their films.[84] If Film d'Art initially drew on the talents of actors, directors, and playwrights associated with the prestigious Comédie-Française, SCAGL worked with authors of the Société des gens de lettres to produce adaptations of literary classics, as well as recent popular French plays and novels. Much like Vitagraph's "quality films," Pathé's *films d'art* had a double purpose: to "educate" the masses but also to attract and hold the "better classes."[85] On the one hand, such films

Figure 40. Ralph Ince, "Balked," *Film Index* (14 August 1909), 5.

could supply East Side Jewish "educational centers" like Tompkins Square Vaudeville, featured in *Theatre* (October 1908).[86] On the other, they could take advantage
of the emerging transformation in exhibition, as larger theaters (whether converted or newly constructed) began to compete successfully with nickelodeons
from New York and Chicago to Milwaukee and Des Moines.[87] Pathé's strategy,
moreover, was coupled with one of the company's more alluring "trademarks," its
automated stencil-color process, which allowed it to release at least one "beautifully tinted *film d'art*" each week.[88]

Throughout 1908, Pathé took great pains to publicize this move to quality films, not only in the *Index,* which promoted the French company's leadership, but also in major daily newspapers like the *New York Tribune.*[89] When the first Film d'Art productions previewed at the Salle Charras in Paris (late November 1908), the *Tribune* even treated them in the manner of a theatrical premiere.[90] That month, both the *Mirror* and the *World* praised the first SCAGL films, which were released in the United States as *films d'art.* *L'Arlésienne* (adapted from an Alphonse Daudet novella), for instance, set "a new standard of excellence" and served as "a moral object lesson for every American manufacturer."[91] For the *Mirror, Incriminating Evidence* was a "revelation" of cleverness as well as craft, for it starred the French pantomimist Séverin, who had been "one of the vaudeville sensations of the [past] year."[92] The term *film d'art* soon had such cachet that the *Mirror* bestowed it on exceptional films like *A Pair of White Gloves* not advertised as such — because "the story [was] so clever and subtle and the acting so finished and nearly perfect."[93] By May, the *Mirror* could claim that Pathé's *films d'art* had led the way in elevating the level of acting to "the same quality . . . that we see in Broadway theatres."[94] And the two weeklies were unanimous in their appraisal of *La Tosca:* one reported a spectator exclaiming, "What acting!"; the other sounded stunned, calling it simply "a polished work of art, almost flawless throughout."[95] All indications suggest that Pathé *films d'art* circulated extensively, from the Clement (a Keith theater) in Dover and the Princess in Lexington to the Family (formerly the Radiant) in Des Moines and the Savoy in Medford (Oregon).[96] And the success of certain titles supported *Bioscope*'s diagnosis of a persistent "Pathé-mentia": in June 1909, for instance, *La Tosca* did record business for three days at the Orpheum in Chicago.[97] The *Mirror,* seconded by the *Index,* would finally conclude: "In America, in particular, the finished work of the Pathé films d'art, both in a photographic and a dramatic sense, have spurred producers to greater efforts . . . and remarkable improvements."[98]

Still, despite this deliberate attempt to counter the mounting charges of illegitimacy, Pathé had to face continuing complaints, only now they were directed at French quality films as well. The famous *Assassination of the Duke of Guise* became an important test case. Initial reaction to the film was decidedly cool. In February, the *World*'s "Own Critic" saw it during his survey of "Fox's handsome and commodious Orpheum Theatre" in Harlem and noticed that the audience sat through what he thought was "the pièce de résistance" of the program in "respectful silence."[99] His explanation for such a cold reception, repeated the following week, was simply that "the Duke of Guise [was] unknown to the great bulk of the audience who gather in an American theater."[100] The *Mirror* had to agree, but it cited other, even more familiar, grounds: although *The Duke of Guise* had to be considered "one of the few masterpieces of motion picture production," its "gruesome" subject was difficult to ignore.[101] In the face of what seems to have been a lack of popular approval, the trade press set about "rehabilitating" the film. Introducing his new column on filmmaking in the *World,* Bedding singled out

Figure 41. Pathé ad, *Moving Picture World* (1 May 1909), 570.

The Duke of Guise as a model of the very latest "moving picture technique," especially in staging and photography.[102] A week later, he was citing the same film as a model of exceptional acting.[103] For the *Mirror*, which seconded Bedding's praise of the film's actors, *The Duke of Guise*'s alleged status as art also offered an added incentive to reverse "the increasing tendency of moving picture houses to change bills every day."[104] The Family Theater, in Des Moines, even drew on this defense in a planted news story, describing it as "a marvelously interesting film . . . one of the finest . . . ever brought" to the city.[105] A year after the film's initial release, however, *Nickelodeon* was mocking these efforts in a fictional interview that had a theater manager facetiously calling *The Duke of Guise* one of his "best coin collectors" ever.[106]

Others of Pathé's *film d'art* suffered even worse criticism. In November 1908, at the same time *L'Arlésienne* was receiving such high praise, *Variety* was describing *Mary Stuart* (drawn from the Victor Hugo novel), then playing at the Manhattan in New York, as incomprehensible to anyone unfamiliar with the story.[107] In fact, the reviewer was so vehement about such "floppers," with their "intended-to-be-gruesome finales" (in which Mary Stuart lost her head),[108] that he lambasted the "whole crowd" at Pathé for having the "dope" habit. The *World* was terribly conflicted about this film: one reviewer thought it "one of the finest productions of the season"; a week later, Bush found "only one good scene . . . the first; the rest are perfectly absurd."[109] In January, *Variety* cited another *film d'art* "starring the well-known Belgian actor Henry Krauss" as an example of the "blood-curdler," perhaps suitable for the Cirque d'Hiver in Paris but hardly for the "family ciné-hall" in New York.[110] In February, even the *Mirror* took Pathé to task for *The Scar:* its reviewer was "unable to understand readily scarcely any of the story."[111] Several months later, the *World*'s reviewers often were sounding much like *Variety*'s. Yes, *Cartouche* and *Père Milon* may be admirably staged and acted (and beautifully colored), but one's subject was unpleasant, and the other, unsuitable for American audiences.[112] Likewise, "the lesson taught" in *The Grandfather* was "insufficient to warrant so much death and gloom."[113] Later that year in the *Mirror*, Woods used two more Pathé films to serve as explicit warnings. On the one hand, *The Tower of Nesle* was too hurried and hard to follow: it tried to condense far too much of Dumas's novel into a single reel.[114] On the other, *The Wild Ass's Skin* (drawn from a Balzac story) showed all too clearly the point at which "high brow" films could become "too elevated for popular understanding."[115] Even in the eyes of a supposedly nonpartisan trade press, as well as some of the new theaters attracting the "better classes," the cultural capital of France seemed to have such diminishing exchange value that it hardly warranted export.[116]

This was not the case with another form of cultural capital the French company had long exploited: that of nonfiction. By the end of 1908, many nickelodeon programs included at least one nonfiction subject, whether a travelogue offering a quick "cheap tour" of the world or an "industrial" presenting the details of a new assembly line or a preindustrial labor process.[117] Both the *World* and the *Mirror* en-couraged their production, partly because they came "too rare[ly] from American makers."[118] As a global producer, Pathé supplied the majority of such films, and it seems to have realized, by 1909, that the educational value of nonfiction could help the company remain competitive on the American market.[119] One sign of nonfiction's legitimacy was an experiment at Keith's New York theaters (where Pathé subjects often were featured) in January 1909: for one week, the programs consisted of "only scenic, industrial, and educational pictures."[120] If unsuccessful, the experiment still underscored the cultural capital of nonfiction, and, when the reception of its *films d'art* proved mixed, Pathé seized on promoting its weekly nonfiction, which the trade press consistently praised.[121] The *World,* for instance, commended *Wood Floating in Morvan* ("nicely toned and tinted") and noted that au-diences "followed it very attentively."[122] Sanctimoniously, *Variety* argued that with more films like *Manufacturing Bamboo Hats,* "the moving picture business would benefit not alone in attendance but in its general standing with the public at large."[123] The *Mirror* found *Across the Island of Ceylon* "one of the few scenic pictures . . . to call forth applause from spectators."[124] But there was a hitch, especially as American firms entered the market in earnest: in comparison to Selig's *Shooting an Oil Well* or Essanay's *Sensational Logging,* the subjects Pathé was asked to supply were clearly foreign, and usually "primitive" or "exotic."[125] This strategy, then, was effective only to the extent that Pathé remained an important supplier of nonfiction, contributing a good number of titles to Kleine's influential catalog of educational films in early 1910.[126] Yet the genre, if it can be called one, would never be more than secondary to the American cinema industry.[127]

The severity and persistence of the criticism directed against its fiction films prompted Pathé to make even further adjustments, some related to the company's overall economic restructuring. In May 1909, for instance, Berst floated an idea that probably seemed little more than a bluff: Pathé was thinking of expanding its Bound Brook factory to produce negative film stock.[128] Although this did not hap-pen, the French company that year did lose its big contract with Eastman (for op-posing a European cartel that the American company aimed to control) and laid plans for manufacturing its own film negative, first in England and then in France.[129] Pathé also moved to market its apparatuses more widely, drawing on the still-unscathed reputation of French technology. In Europe, Pathé projectors and cameras had become standard; now, through the MPPC agreements, the com-pany made a concerted effort to duplicate that status in North America. This effort initially focused on an ad campaign for a new version of its projector, the "Professional."[130] Between May 1909 and May 1910, abetted by promotional arti-cles in the trade press, the Professional was being installed in venues from the best New York theaters to small nickelodeons throughout the country (from New Hampshire to San Francisco), and even on board U.S. Navy ships.[131] In short, it quickly rivaled Power's Cameragraph, which had long claimed to be "the only ma-chine for a first-class house."[132] Within another year or so, the Pathé Professional

Figure 42. Pathé ad, *New York Dramatic Mirror* (10 July 1909), 17.

camera also would become standard in American studios, not only for its mechanical simplicity and expert workmanship but also for its relatively low cost.[133]
If the American trade press looked unfavorably on French culture on the screen,
it readily accepted French technology "behind the scenes."

Other adjustments were geared even more specifically to the American market.
In April 1909, in order to accommodate exhibitor anxiety over its quality films, for
instance, Pathé cut the extra charge for stencil-colored prints by 50 percent.[134] Six
months later, now that Sunday shows seemed secure, it became the only company

Figure 43. Pathé ad, *Film Index* (4 December 1909), 11.

using Sundays as "a special release" day for *films d'art* such as *Rigoletto* or *La Grande Bretèche* (based on a Balzac short story).[135] Drawing on a format developed earlier for the popular *Passion Play*, it also sent these out with deluxe explanatory booklets, suggesting that "exhibitors use [them] to circularize the so-called better class in their towns."[136] The company also turned to less-French-specific subjects such as *Sister Angelica*, *The Prodigal Son*, and *The Legend of Orpheus*, all of which won praise for their acting, staging, and color effects.[137] In fact, *Variety* suggested,

Figure 44. Pathé ad, *Chicago Tribune* (6 February 1910), 2.6.

rather disingenuously, that if Pathé continued "to turn out subjects like this it [would] regain the old position of pre-eminence in the trade."[138] The company also experimented with marketing its version of *Drink*, the English stage adaptation of Zola's *L'Assommoir*, by releasing its two reels both at once rather than over consecutive weeks.[139] And the *Index* cited the poster for *Drink* as a model of design, with the Chicago Orpheum serving as an example for its display.[140] Shortly after the New Year, Pathé launched a national advertising campaign in several Sunday newspapers (Chicago, Cleveland, Detroit, Baltimore), reminding viewers of the "quality" the "Rooster brand" had long guaranteed.[141] This was a bold claim that Pathé had the same status as American companies like Kellogg's,

Coca-Cola, or Mennan's that distributed products nationally, but the campaign also had an immediate benefit for its new stencil-color *films d'art*, from familiar classics like *Carmen* and *Cleopatra* to specialized features like *Ouchard the Merchant* (from "an old Russian Folk Song").[142] Finally, the company was not above exploiting the Chicago Orpheum for testimonials like this: "Whenever we fail to show Pathé Pictures in our house our patrons are dissatisfied and they don't hesitate to tell us so."[143]

Yet all of Pathé's marketing moves, however innovative and even beneficial some were to the industry as a whole, however crucial some were to maintaining a standard of quality, would prove insufficient. *Variety* refused to stop vilifying French subjects, and *Show World* joined in the smear campaign.[144] Pathé was losing ground, *Variety* claimed, on the American market and elsewhere (specifically Australia), simply because its comic films were "ridiculous in the extreme" and its "more pretentious efforts . . . too heavy."[145] An "unpleasant" subject like *The Repentant Beggar* bore "all the marks of French drama": misery, want, threat of death by suicide.[146] The "ghastly tale" of *Ouchard* (one of the company's few subjects that may have addressed Jewish immigrants directly) made fools of the Board of Censors (it was approving "mudpies for commerce"); as for Pathé, it was "cordially invited to keep [its] bestialities at home."[147] Yet the *World*, which at least rebuked this xenophobic hysteria, along with the *Mirror*,[148] also could not refrain from printing a long, detailed letter from a viewer in Washington, who singled out an old Pathé film, *Scenes from Convict Life* (1906), as "not at all the kind of proper thing to present in a 'family' theater."[149] While the trade weekly may have argued, in its defense, that this letter justified the need, once again, for getting rid of old, worn-out films, it made no effort at all to correct the letter writer's mistaken assumption that *Scenes from Convict Life* was a new film. It was simply "common knowledge" that Pathé subjects often were inappropriate for the "happy, beautiful, virile age" in which (some) Americans supposedly imagined they were living.[150]

Most troubling for the French company, however, were the joint efforts of the *World* and the *Mirror* to promote "American subjects" over all others. That promotion now extended beyond a polemic for "clear, well-told stories." Throughout 1908, the two trade weeklies had praised the verisimilar acting style of Pathé's French films compared with the histrionic style of the Americans.[151] To Rollin Summers, for instance, "the French seemed natural adepts at pantomime"—able to express "shades of emotion" with "an arch of the eyebrows, a shrug of the shoulders, a gesture of the hands"—unlike Americans, who often seemed "lifeless and mechanical" or indulged in "orgies of gesticulation."[152] Woods repeated this praise of Pathé and, in a tongue-in-cheek guide for actors, linked it to the principle of making moving pictures "appear like events in real life."[153] Biograph "most nearly resemble[d] Pathé in style," Woods claimed, and within six months, despite the strong presence of the French *films d'art*, the American company's films had displaced Pathé's as exemplars of verisimilar acting. In January, according to the *World*, *The Maniac Cook* was remarkable in that "much attention [was] paid to the acting." [154] In March, the *Mirror* was more specific: the "clear facial expressions as well as the natural but intensely suggestive gestures" of the actors made *A Fool's Revenge* "the equal . . . of any of the Pathé 'film d'art.'" [155] A month later, while the *World* praised the superb acting in *Lady Helen's Escape*, the *Mirror* lauded *The Medicine Bottle*, whose story was "brought about so naturally and acted with such artistic restraint." [156] By May, with Biograph his primary reference point, Woods was condensing all this into an aesthetic of "intelligence and genuine realism" in acting, in order to complement the "photographic representation of genuine houses, streets, and outdoor localities." [157] Story, actor, and scene were being fused into an aesthetic privileging "authenticity" in representing not just life but *American* life.

These signs that Biograph was beginning to match and pass the French company coincided precisely with *Bioscope*'s remarks on the epidemic of "Pathé-mentia." They were evident not only in the films, at least as the two trade papers read them, but also in audience responses everywhere. In March, a "well known" theater figure in New York was stunned by the "dramatic construction and acting" in a Biograph film, comparing it to what he would expect in "any of the great Broadway theaters." [158] In June, on Fourteenth Street, *The Lonely Villa* provoked an audience to rise as one at the close and a woman to exclaim, "Thank God, they are saved!" [159] Just weeks later, when *The Way of Man* appeared (probably at the same theater), a man was overheard saying, "Now we shall see something good," and added, "Why, you can see them thinking." [160] This phrase, which Bedding later repeated, would also serve Woods to credit Pathé (now that it had lost its competitive edge) with earlier innovating the technique of placing the camera close to characters. [161] As in New York, so, too, it went in the Midwest, where Carl Anderson, a dedicated moviegoer in Spencer, Indiana, wrote that the company's stories had such finish, roundness, and completeness that a theater manager had "only to advertise a Biograph subject to fill his house." [162] In a weak defense of the Pathé *film d'art*, recognized worldwide for its unusually "well told story," *Nickelodeon* had to admit that "American picture manufacturers . . . have a little the best of it" because Americans preferred a "powerful plot," even if poorly written and acted, to "an artistically prepared story with a feeble plot." [163] Here, Biograph pictures had the extra advantage, wrote Woods (in a bit of self-flattery), of having powerful plots as well as superb writing and subtle acting that never went "over the heads of the public," making them "pioneers in the direction of higher work in America." [164] In short, throughout the country, the stories that now made "a lasting impression" (Woods's essential criterion) were American, even in "poetic" films such as *Pippa Passes*, which was specially featured one week at the Scenic Theater in Sioux City and, long after its initial release, according to an amazed *New York Times* reporter, still could draw tears in an Adirondack village. [165]

THE LAST STRAW

Through the 1909–1910 season, the *Mirror* and the *World* carried on a debate over what should be distinctive about "American subjects." The *Mirror* might not accept the *World*'s argument that "Indian and Western" films were the foundation of an "American school of motion picture drama" (the subject of the next chapter), but it could agree that American films should tell "simple life stories . . . represented by clean, good looking actors."[166] And that was perfectly in sync with the "Anglo-Saxon models" of youth now inhabiting the mass magazine ads (and clothing store windows), the "smoother, cleaner, more activist and athletic" figures, as T. J. Jackson Lears describes them, promoting everything from Mennen's toilet powder or Gillette safety razors to Arrow shirt collars, and who had "the country's future . . . written in [their] faces."[167] For Pathé, the increasing popularity of American films, so loudly ballyhooed in the trade press,[168] meant that its profits would continue to shrink if it kept supplying only "high art" or "exotic" subjects; it, too, would have to bow to the demands of assimilation.

Earlier, the French company had begun producing nonfiction films having a more direct appeal: examples would be *The Reception of the American Fleet in Australia*, which the Manhattan Theatre used to draw an audience from the Brooklyn Navy Yard, or *Wilbur Wright's Aeroplane*, which the *World* repeatedly recommended to exhibitors.[169] Pathé also added more "Indian and Western" subjects to its releases, something it had dabbled in with some success from *Indians and Cowboys* (1904) to *The Hostage* (1908).[170] The *World*'s harsh editorial criticism of *A Western Hero* (July 1909), which a good number of exhibitors had complained violated the basic rules of "realism," may have pushed Pathé to the brink of capitulation.[171] If not, six months later, the *World* would deliver the coup de grâce, contrasting the "American subject" with "the inadmissible subject," which was explicitly French.[172] The one remaining viable option (and perhaps it was lucky to have that) was to establish its own facilities in the United States for making "proper" American subjects, with "clean, good looking" American actors. The decision took some time, for the strategy first had to undergo extensive testing with Pathé affiliates in Russia, Italy, and Spain.[173] By the spring of 1910, Berst finally announced that Pathé was going ahead with plans to produce and market "American" films.[174] Although a studio for that purpose was not completed in Jersey City until the fall, the company already was shooting films on location, and it released its first title on 16 May 1910: appropriately a western, *The Girl from Arizona*.[175]

By 1909–1910, moving pictures were so deeply implicated in the discourses of nationalism and cultural or, more precisely, "racial" supremacy in the United States that Pathé had no choice but to meet what Berst called "the national tastes of America."[176] Much like the new Independent producer, Thanhouser, it would follow the dictate "The American People Prefer American Pictures."[177] In

Figure 45. Thanhouser ad, *Moving Picture World* (23 April 1910), 629.

conjunction with this new strategy of making American films, "with American actors and scenarios," the company also radically cut back its releases of French and
other foreign films to no more than three thousand feet or three reels per week.[178]
Thereafter, only half of its weekly releases in the United States would come from
France (and that would be a "choice selection"); the other half would demonstrate
its adherence to assimilation, its compliance with the demands of Americanization. No longer, it was hoped, would Pathé be tarred as a threat, as part of a "national menace." An ironic mark of this capitulation had been signaled earlier by

Woods in the *Mirror:* the "accepted term" for the moving picture machine no longer was *biograph* or *vitagraph* (now successful brand names) but *kinematograph* or *cinematograph,* a "ripped-off" trophy of assimilation that would later undergo even further shearing, to *cinema.*[179]

DOCUMENT 7

Thomas Bedding, "The Modern Way in Moving Picture Making," *Moving Picture World* (13 March 1909), 294

[The author of this important series of articles, which will form a complete hand-book to the most modern methods of producing moving pictures, is an accepted authority on the subject. He was for several years Editor of the "British Journal of Photography," in London; is well versed in all branches of the theory and practice of photography and production of "silent plays." These articles will be continued from week to week, and will be completed in about eighteen chapters.]

Introductory

If I were asked to give the reader my idea of what would be a good example of moving picture technique to take as a guide in the preparation of these films, I would select a recently published picture by Pathé, entitled "The Assassination of the Duke of Guise." It would be well if the student of these lines would see this picture for himself, because, then, he would more readily appreciate the piece of constructive criticism which I am about to pass on it.

In the first place, let us examine the picture in both its principal aspects, 1, as a piece of stage craft; 2, as a photograph. As a piece of stage craft it is comparable to the finest productions of Sir Henry Irving, who was, without doubt, the best stage producer of modern times. The scenes of the "Assassination" show accuracy of costume, accessories, archaeological and other details; the grouping, and what we commonly call the *mise-en-scene* are perfect; the acting such as only long and careful rehearsing under a master mind can produce. From this point of view, and I speak from experience of the Paris, London, and New York stages, I have no hesitation in pronouncing the film in question as an ideal piece of stage craft in the way of silent drama. It is an example to be studied, and studied again, until this lesson has been got thoroughly to heart. That the first essential for success in moving picture making is to have a suitable subject, well rehearsed.

Now, for the second aspect of this remarkable film. It was well, fully, evenly and naturally illuminated and exposed. There was nothing theatrical or stagey about the scenes; there were no obtrusively high lights or very dark shadows. The whole effect, as I have said, was natural, giving one the impression that the scenes shown actually took place in the beautiful rooms of a French court. Evidently Pathés are past masters in the art of illuminating their subjects. The exposure was accurate—accurate and full, which is a very great point in this kind of work. The negative was properly developed, for it had no defective marks on it to transmit to the positive, which was a richly toned piece of work. By "toned," I don't mean color-toned, I mean that the image of the positive was developed so as to give a pleasing variation of the silver pigment of the film; in other words the positive was of a rich warmish hue, in contradistinction to the soot and white-wash effects that are so common in moving pictures.

Such a picture as this is not made by accident. It was rehearsed by a world renowned French dramatist who is versed in the archaeological and historic lore of the period of French history at which the Assassination of the Duke of Guise took place. Then as regards the photographic end of the work, it has long since passed into proverb that Pathés are at the head of the world's producers of moving pictures. The reason for this is plain. They have studied the business scientifically; they go about it scientifically, that is to say, they apply the best available knowledge to the making of the picture in each of its departments. The result is success each time in point of technique.

Even better in some respects than the subject referred to is the dramatic rendering of "The Return of Ulysses," another film d'art which is about to be issued by this same house and which may again be referred to in illustrating the motif of these articles.

DOCUMENT 8

Lux Graphicus [Thomas Bedding], "On the Screen,"
Moving Picture World (25 December 1909), 918–919

. . . Everybody knows what a Pathe picture is in public. It is a marvel of steadiness, good photography and good acting. But to enjoy a Pathe picture at its very best, one must have the opportunity or privilege of examining a prominent release in Pathe's own little theater [on Twenty-fourth Street, New York]. Here you may sit at your ease in a quiet, spacious, tastefully appointed room and study Pathe drama almost by yourself, and realize beforehand something of the enormously pleasurable effect which those pictures are about to create on the great outside public.

. . . This appealed to me very convincingly the other day when, having seen a recent release the success of which depends very largely upon the well-timed dramatic action of the piece, Mr. Franconi, the courteous operator remarked, "I hope all the operators who handle this film will time it properly." He, himself, had properly timed it. The result was that not a single part of the dramatic action was misrepresented in the way of speed and so one got an impression that the movements on the screen were perfectly natural and synchronized with the emotions of the characters photographed. This is half the battle in properly representing a moving picture to an audience.

There is another and most important respect in which the Pathe theater commends itself favorably to me. It is this: That here one is able to judge of the color in the Pathe colored pictures at sufficient leisure to enable one to appreciate the beautiful effects which the Pathe people get on their positives. As I remarked on this page a few weeks ago, "Color is in the air just now." Everybody in the moving picture field is talking about it, discussing it, praising it, criticising it, wanting it; the phrase "natural colors" is passing finally into the vocabulary of the writer on this subject; into the minds of manufacturers; into the minds of the public. So that some general interest attaches to the Pathe colored films.

There is no question that the Pathe colored films, however they may be produced, are very beautiful things, are very satisfactory things, and are assuredly very artistic things. Many a time have I sat and appreciated them in the Pathe theater. They seem to me, as a mere member of the great moving picture public who pays five or ten cents several times a week, to have a most esthetically pleasing effect on the mind, as pleasing as a richly colored stage scene produced by a Belasco or a Mansfield. They are always in good taste, you never see any crudities or violences of color. It would appear that the tints, however they may be applied to the positive, are chosen with knowledge and discretion. And the result, as I have said, is this, that on the minds of the public a Pathe colored picture has a very satisfying effect. It may not be either "nature" or "science." But let us call it "art," and if we accept it as such, then it must be considered very good art indeed.

The Pathe colored pictures have won enormous popularity in this last year. They are certainly very cleverly done and they win the commendation of those who are authorities on the subject of the mechanical application of pigments to printing surfaces. Under this head comes of course color printing, moving picture positive making and the like. So that they are entitled to the respectful consideration of those technically interested. It must always be understood that the world's masterpieces in color from the Greek and Roman painters down to the present have been produced by hand or very largely so, and consequently we have every justification for placing the Pathe film in the category of the artistic production. At a time like the present, when so much general discussion is being devoted to the color of moving pictures, I thought it only right and just that special mention should be given to the peculiar form of coloring adopted by Pathe.

ENTR'ACTE 5

From "Delivering the Goods" to Adoring "Gods and Goddesses"

This final interlude serves as a kind of theme and variation, drawing together several earlier motifs and mixing them with others, as yet un-
sounded. Its general subject is less what the trade press called "the thea-
tricalization of the moving picture . . . at all ends of the game" than the
"magnitude of the business," as a *Munsey's* writer put it, especially with reference to exhibition or the experience of going to the movies.[1] According
to one of many estimates in circulation at the time, moving pictures were
"being witnessed in 8,000 theatres in the United States alone, to an average
possibly of 8,000,000 daily attendance."[2] In short, they were "delivering the
goods," and then some. Rather than rehearse much of the research already
done so well on this historical moment, I want to put in play a series of
"minor" notes and ideas (some only recently recovered) in order to under-
score what arguably has to be considered a break point in the emergence of
an American cinema. For if the period of 1909–1910 consolidated crucial
changes from the previous years—in industrial organization, in modes of
narration, representation, and address, in social and cultural function—it
also introduced others no less significant, especially in the context of Pathé's
diminishing presence and power on the American market.

Moving pictures may have been delivering the goods, but so was the
trade press.[3] The weeklies supporting the industry, wholly or in part, covered a spectrum of special interests. *Film Index* (now edited by James Hoff)
functioned as the official organ of the MPPC; *Show World, Moving Picture
News, Variety,* and *Billboard* all acted (but rarely in concert) as partisans of
the new Independents.[4] Although both initially supported the MPPC, the
World and the *Mirror* again sought out a middle ground, supposedly to treat
each faction with "impartiality" but also to resecure their own positions,
whichever won out.[5] To their extensive capsule reviews of new film releases, both soon added weekly columns that revealed different editorial
policies. At the *World,* Chalmers and Bedding introduced several series ob-
serving and evaluating theaters, audiences, and films in greater New York,
giving advice to projectionists and offering a "text book" on "picture making."[6] At the *Mirror,* "The Spectator" (Woods) spelled out an aesthetic of
narrative construction and spectator engagement, based on public screenings in the city, which, along with the paper's trenchant reviews, aimed to
"elevate the quality and character of moving picture subjects."[7] All this
confirmed New York as the industry's center, but the *World* did print a new
column by Bradlet on Chicago exhibitors after James McQuade, at the
Index, began writing a "Chicago Letter" on industry matters.[8] Given their

"nonpartisan" status, the *Mirror*'s and *World*'s joint polemic on American subjects assumes even greater significance, for it tended to pull the opposing industry factions toward one side of an axis dividing the American from the foreign. This circumscribed the discursive space within which favorable representations of Pathé could circulate even further, even in *Nickelodeon*. Despite the good notices this deluxe monthly sometimes gave Pathé, it was hardly averse to accepting ads from the new Independents or writing promotional pieces about them.[9]

The trade press undoubtedly did important educational and regulatory work, yet perhaps the most telling sign of the cinema's "coming of age" was the widespread acceptance of moving pictures in the general press. Attacks may not have ceased: *Collier's* (October 1908), the *American Review of Reviews* (December 1908), *Ladies' Home Journal* (July 1909), and several "Social Evil" tracts all repeated long-familiar charges.[10] But many more articles were enthusiastic or at least treated the movies seriously. The *Mirror* and the *World* both drew attention to this change in February and again that summer.[11] Several books now defended moving pictures as a "social force"; several national magazines—*Survey, Munsey's,* the *American,* and the *Independent*—carried long, constructive pieces championing the latest trends in production and exhibition.[12] That year, big-city dailies like the *New York Times,* the *Philadelphia Post,* and even the *Chicago Tribune* began allotting weekly space to moving pictures, especially in Sunday editions: in the *Tribune,* for instance, a Chicago University professor now "boosted" moving pictures as "the highest type of entertainment in the history of the world."[13] At the *New York Morning Telegraph,* George Terwilliger (who had worked with Woods at the *Mirror*) began to review films regularly, as "Gordon Trent."[14] By the spring of 1910, when another round of "social evil" attacks erupted, the *Mirror* could enlist big-city papers like the *Cleveland Plain Dealer* in defending "an institution against which so little can be said and in behalf of which so much praise should be given."[15] Yet economics as much as aesthetic and/or moral concerns prompted this change; only recently had theater managers in the largest cities been convinced of the advantage of advertising in a major daily, if only on Sundays.[16] This loosely coordinated defense of moving pictures also coincided with Pathé's national advertising campaign (which must have had an added ameliorating effect), and, throughout, the general press, well into 1910, the French company's *films d'art* and stencil-color process remained a familiar touchstone, invoking for readers the best in filmmaking.[17]

For the *World,* exhibitors were "the backbone of the business," and it is worth pausing to explore how their sites and practices were changing.[18] Not unexpectedly, the construction of large theaters continued—from Newark, Philadelphia, and Baltimore to Rochester, Detroit, and Milwaukee—as did the conversion of legitimate theaters—in New York, all those around Columbus Circle switched to moving pictures.[19] Major chains of cinemas were developing, from Loew's (which, with the Shuberts' backing, was reaching out from New York to New England and even Chicago) or the Stanley Corporation in Philadelphia (run by Mastbaum and Isman, who bought out Lubin) to Swanson in Chicago, the Skouras brothers in Saint Louis, or the Saxe brothers in Milwaukee (who had a small theater on Times Square in New York).[20] The programs of many larger theaters also were called "combination shows" because their reels of film were interspersed with vaudeville acts rather than illustrated songs. The extent of this phenomenon, sometimes called "small-time vaudeville," and what social groups were its chief patrons, is still open to debate.[21] Most research on this question has focused on New York, where many of the theaters visited by *Mirror* and *World* reviewers presented combination shows.[22] Outside New York, in 1909–1910, the evidence is conflicting: the largest theaters in Des Moines—the Lyric, Unique, Star, and Family—all programmed vaudeville and moving pictures; the Scenic and Bullock's Temple of Amusement (Providence), Keith's Bijou (Woonsocket), the Hippodrome (Lexington), and the Garrick (Ottumwa) also were successful with combination shows.[23] Yet the Bijou and Nickel in Providence presented only moving pictures and songs; the Olympic, Scenic, and Majestic in Sioux City did likewise; the theaters in Milwaukee avoided "cheap vaudeville" (or so it was said) "at any price"; and small-town exhibitors, Bradlet warned, often simply were not able to afford vaudeville.[24] On the whole, however, the trade press criticized the combination show and, as partisans of the new business, promoted what the *Index* called "the 'straight' picture show" in "purely picture houses," which, the *Mirror* claimed, now supposedly attracted "a higher quality of patronage."[25]

The range of moving picture shows, as Eileen Bowser usefully reminds us, remained quite extensive, with small and medium-sized houses perhaps still drawing the larger portion of moviegoers.[26] In spite of their commitment to "progress," the trade press recognized many different kinds of popular theaters. During the winter of 1908–1909, *Variety* included such typical "store shows" as People's Vaudeville (125th and Lennox) and 32 Park Row among its selective description of New York theaters.[27] The *World*'s "Own Critic" soon followed with a more extensive survey, from the Fourteenth Street Bijou Dream, the Unique, and Fox's Orpheum in Harlem to "The Ideas," the Scenic Theater, Wonders Varieties, an unidentified Park Row theater, and the Nicoland and Jacobs' in the Bronx.[28] A year later, a *New York Sun* reporter enjoyed working his way through the theaters, from Broadway above Fourteenth Street down into the Lower East Side.[29] Both *Variety* and the *World* repeated this kind of surveying in the Chicago area.[30] Overall, these forays bestowed praise and criticism equably, on the largest and smallest theaters, on the elegant as well as the plainly furnished. Of special interest to the trade press was the number of theaters contracted with rental exchanges dealing in Independent films compared with the "licensed" exchanges.[31] By fall 1909, the Independents were challenging the MPPC for dominance not only in the Chicago area (where they had twice the number of exchanges) but also in cities such as Cincinnati, Saint Louis, and Detroit.[32] Within a few more months, they also had the majority of theaters in Indianapolis and Baltimore.[33] Revealing here was Woods's admission, in June 1909, that the *Mirror* did not review Independent films for the simple reason that they were "exhibited in very few New York houses."[34] Although Laemmle sought to remedy this situation, beginning in September, by "furnishing first run service to the Fair" on Fourteenth Street, it did expose how narrow the *Mirror*'s initial public base for reviewing was compared with the *World*'s.[35]

Yet the progress continually ballyhooed by the trade press did not extend to everyone in that vast public of moviegoers, at least in the same way. In New York and other states, new ordinances were enacted to prohibit children from attending the shows except when accompanied by a parent or guardian.[36] Although there is some question about how strongly these were enforced, the *Mirror* would turn this stricter regulation of the young into a positive sign that moving pictures were not just for kids; they were "witnessed mostly by grown-up people."[37] The press also put the spotlight on several women who owned and/or managed shows: the most prominent was Mrs. Clement, who had run the Boston Bijou Dream since July 1909; another was young Leona Bryse at the Cub Theatre on South Halsted (Chicago).[38] Yet the shift to larger, more commercialized theaters like the Bijou Dream also curtailed a crucial function of nickelodeons for working women, as a site of socializing and employment. On his visit to Milwaukee, for instance, Bradlet complained of the women ushers in many theaters: "the tall handsome doorman," he thought, was the "sort of moral guardian" now needed to make a house "safe in every respect."[39] A different kind of concern erupted over the threatened "mixture of races" at the moving picture show. In the summer of 1909, the *Index* voiced the outrage whites expressed on Long Island and in Philadelphia when "coloreds" attended supposedly "white" theaters. The *Mirror* and *Variety* took another tack, promoting the opening of segregated theaters from San Antonio, Vicksburg, and Columbia (Missouri), to Springfield (Massachusetts).[40] In other words, the trade press readily accepted the Jim Crow laws restricting blacks as the norm, and, in the case of San Antonio, extended that as well to "Mexicans."[41] Whether, and in what ways, any of these segregated theaters may have served as alternative "spaces apart," resistant to the dominant white commercial culture, as Mary Carbine demonstrates that black theaters did in Chicago, remains to be discovered.[42]

Perhaps the most important development came in what might be called the audience's "taste for pictures." Early in 1909, the trade press still tended to consider audiences according to what theaters they frequented and where. In New York, for instance, the *World* made some stereotypical distinctions linking location to "class": Keith's Fifth Avenue theater (which still headlined vaudeville) had "an aristocratic clientele"; the Harlem Orpheum had "the bourgeoisie"; near Union Square, the Unique attracted "a mixture of all classes" (many probably shoppers); while the Dewey drew workers from the Lower East Side.[43] In Newark, theater owners told both the *World* and the *Index* that the "taste for pictures" differed "according to the neighborhood": the city's large Italian population, they thought, liked subjects "with plenty of action" (carefully qualified with "but not necessarily thrilling"), and especially "Wild West pictures."[44] Later that year, given the increasing standardization and differentiation of film manufacturers, the *World* suggested that people now sought out one or more familiar trademarks, and the kind of subjects associated with each.[45] If the Pathé rooster once had been synonymous with moviegoing in general, now there were "Biograph audiences, Pathé audiences, Selig audiences, Lubin, Vitagraph, and Kalem audiences." As the *Mirror* made clear, this may have been the case in New York, at least within limits, due to a standardized screening schedule at the Keith theaters: each day's "licensed" film releases played first at the Union Square and then circulated among the others.[46] The "regular" who preferred a specific brand of "licensed" film knew exactly when and where to expect new releases to appear. Whether anything like this standardized scheduling, which facilitated up-to-date reviewing for the *Mirror* and the *World,* was characteristic of other cities, however, remains to be determined, as does the question of exactly when the Independents were able to take advantage of something similar.

Throughout 1909, another "guarantee of satisfaction" was emerging. The first sign of this was "the pretty girl" the *World*'s "Own Critic" fell in love with one Sunday afternoon, in April, viewing *The Voice of the Violin.*[47] "Whenever there is a Biograph picture to be shown wherein this charming girl figures," he confessed, "I am there with my money to gaze upon her in silent, if unrequited, admiration." Within weeks, she was "the now famous Biograph girl," the subject of recurring praise.[48] By the following fall, the *World* was claiming that "the average citizen" in Chicago, no matter how much "he just raves" about this or that brand, "first and last . . . loves that Biograph girl."[49] As Richard deCordova points out, beginning in early 1909, several manufacturers already were exploiting the well-known names of theater actors to promote their "quality" films.[50] Pathé did this systematically with the French casts of its *films d'art* (some of whom, like Séverin, had toured the United States). In May, Vitagraph tried this once with Elita

Proctor Otis in *Oliver Twist;* that summer and fall, Edison followed Pathé's lead by releasing the cast lists for several films and by hiring Pilar-Morin, a female French pantomimist who recently had performed in American vaudeville.[51] All these efforts, however, sought to elevate moving pictures by investing them with the cultural capital of the legitimate theater (where the stars also tended to be women).[52] But the phenomenon of the Biograph Girl was different. Here was an unknown actress whom audiences had singled out and even forced the trade press to name; initially, in a sense, she was their creation.[53] Moreover, what made her attractive was not so much her acting ability, or how well her acting suited the story—which the *Mirror* so valued—but her *personality*. By early 1910, the *World* was speaking of a moviegoing public that had "its favorite actors and actresses" and of how this interest "in the personalities of the chief performers" could determine "the success of a particular film."[54]

The actor's "filmed body . . . as a site of textual productivity," deCordova deftly argues, changed "the status of film as a commodity" and introduced, for most manufacturers at least, an unusually "viable means of product differentiation" and of sustaining interest across a series of films.[55] It was Laemmle, an Independent, who first tried to exploit this growing public fascination for personalities, but not according to legend, as both deCordova and Gunning have shown.[56] In December 1909, one of his ads revealed, simply by reproducing a photo of her face, that the Biograph Girl was now "an IMP!"[57] Three months later, he was staging the infamous fake story of her death and bestowing on her a name, Miss Lawrence, in what the *World* admitted was adroit advertising.[58] Yet several MPPC manufacturers also engaged in promoting their leading actors. In January 1910, in a move given much more space in the press, Kalem released a large poster of its stock company for theater managers to use as a lobby display.[59] In April, Vitagraph not only put out its own poster for display but also launched a promotion for its "Vitagraph Girl," Florence Turner.[60] She already was so well known that the company could commission a popular song for her: when it was sung at the screening that opened the publicity campaign, in Saratoga Park, Brooklyn, "the applause was deafening."[61] Within a month, Kalem was mounting a similar campaign for Gene Gauntier, its longtime "Kalem Girl" (and chief scenario writer).[62] "The interest the public ha[d] taken in the personality of many of the picture players," wrote a stunned *World* columnist, was simply "astonishing."[63] And a Vitagraph publicist tossed out a label that would soon be permanently affixed to these new icons of worship: "moving picture Gods and Goddesses."[64]

The consequences of this emerging "movie star" system were enormous and multiple, but let me single out two in particular. The initial language in the *World* describing the Biograph Girl, along with the fact that

Figure 46. "The Vitagraph Girl" song sheet cover (April 1910).

most of these early stars were women,[65] points again to an anxiety over spectatorship in early cinema. The voycurism of the distinctly male gaze assumed in this review discourse looks a lot like a corollary to the "virile," "realistic" aesthetic of storytelling discussed earlier. In short, that discourse can be read as yet another attempt to regulate and even transform the cinema as a "feminized" space of consumption, where young women were often the principal spectators, the subjects of its looking relations. A further instance of this would be the assurance offered by "Our Man" in the *World* that there were as many young men as young women who "crav[ed] an autograph photo."[66] Despite these efforts to manage the boundaries of desire elicited by screen images and photos, for men as well as women,[67] however, manufacturers and the trade press alike quickly seized on their potential exchange value. The parallels between the shop window, theater lobby, and screen were so strong that both recognized that women viewers could be molded into desiring consumers in a double sense, not only to return again and again to adore their favorites but also to imitate them, especially in defining themselves through changes in fashion.[68] By the summer of 1910, the *World* was making this link between "dress and the picture" explicit,[69] revealing an attraction every bit as powerful as the *Mirror*'s clear, well-told stories and the growing insistence on American subjects. This contradictory discourse would continue in the earliest "fan" magazines, as Kathryn Fuller has shown, especially in their oscillation between acknowledging and regendering their audience of predominantly female readers/viewers/consumers.[70]

Movie stars and their fans, of course, presented another insurmountable problem for Pathé. In late 1908, the *Mirror* found that not only Biograph and Vitagraph actors but Pathé actors, too, were among the "favorites . . . habitual patrons . . . hailed with delight" whenever they appeared.[71] The new "gods and goddesses," however, now had to be as American as the stories in which they appeared and as "clean, good-looking," and youthful as the "Anglo-Saxon" models in mass magazine ads. The reputable French stage actors the company chose to publicize by name in its *films d'art* paled by comparison to all these American "girls": even the attempt to trade on the "exotic" Italian actress Victoria Lepanto as a "picture personality" fell flat.[72] Max Linder was another matter. There is some evidence that he was one of the "readily recognized" favorites alluded to by the *Mirror*, but Pathé was unable to exploit his star potential as fully as it did in Europe.[73] However marvelous his comic craft, after all, Linder had performed, and continued to perform, in films too often judged in "bad taste."[74] For Pathé, the phenomenon of the American movie star raised yet another barrier, further marginalizing French films and excluding them from the world's most lucrative market.

CHAPTER SIX

"Our Country"/Whose Country?
The Americanization Project of Early
Westerns, 1907–1910

*There are only certain pictures I like at the nickelodeons, such as those of cowboys, Indians, sol-
diers, wars; histories of men like George Washington, Lincoln, Grant and many more brave vet-
erans. Love stories I never do like because I hear so much about them.*

W. HORSTMEYER, SAN FRANCISCO *SUNDAY CALL,* "JUNIOR SECTION" (15 MAY 1910)

Do you like to go to the nickelodeon? Most every boy and girl likes to go, and so do I.
*I like to see historical pictures, like the battle of Bunker Hill or the battles of Lexington and
Concord. I would like to see Washington crossing the Delaware, too. The adventures of Daniel
Boone or Marcus Whitman I would like to see very much.*

VERNA NAUERT, AGE 13 YEARS, SAN FRANCISCO *SUNDAY CALL,* "JUNIOR SECTION" (15 MAY 1910)

In June 1908, the *New York Dramatic Mirror* had this to say about Pathé's *Justice of a
Redskin,* together with Gaumont's *Red Man's Revenge:*

> As both of these films are identical in story and almost identical in treatment . . . they
> will be treated together. Evidently one is borrowed from the other, but which film
> maker is guilty of the piracy it is impossible for THE MIRROR to determine, al-
> though it may be pertinent to state that the Gaumont film was advertised in America
> first.[1]

One week later, the *Mirror* returned to this "alleged pirating":

> THE MIRROR is now informed, however, that a similar film was produced nearly
> two years ago by the American Vitagraph company of New York under the title,
> "The Indian's Revenge," so that if Pathé pirated from Gaumont, Gaumont had pre-
> viously pirated from the Vitagraph.[2]

Manufacturers, of course, had been selling duped, pirated, and/or remade film titles on the American market for years, and the practice had not ended with the
FSA's formation six months earlier. So why would the *Mirror* make such a big deal
over this one instance of piracy? The question may seem trivial, but the *Mirror*
claimed to be printing not simply "press notices or advertisements" but "reviews
of films"—that is, "unprejudiced criticisms of the pictures and the story they tell."
At least two things are significant about this allegedly "unprejudiced criticism" of

"identical" films. First of all, the *Mirror* was marking the boundary not between "licensed" and "unlicensed" manufacturers, as one might expect, but between American and foreign (unmistakably French) film product—a boundary the trade weekly would draw even more sharply the following November.[3] Second, that boundary was being drawn according to which titles were more "original" or "authentic" among the "Western pictures" for which, *Moving Picture World* proclaimed, "everybody [was] clamoring" by the winter of 1908–1909.[4]

The *Mirror*'s review of these two French films points to a question that was beginning to preoccupy the trade press: What was distinctive, and of special value, about American films compared with foreign films? The question, of course, arose out of a specific historical conjuncture of conditions, which the previous chapters have described and analyzed in some detail. One, for instance, was the mass audience of moviegoers (many of them women and children) attracted to the nickelodeons and new larger theaters, where "foreign film product" (largely French Pathé titles) too often dominated the programs. Another was all the immigrants entering the United States, whose numbers and origins—allegedly "the least desirable part of Europe"[5]—threatened to jeopardize (for some) the concept of a uniquely "American character" or national identity. These conditions fostered various practices of excluding "foreign film product" on the American market, whether institutional (through the FSA, MPPC, and National Board of Censorship) or discursive (through the trade press and national magazines), but simultaneously they provoked efforts to create, promote, and exploit a distinctively American film product. Here, I would argue, the production and circulation of westerns played such a crucial role that, by 1909, the genre would become what the *World* described as the quintessential "American subject."[6] In this concluding chapter, I want to sketch out several explanations for the early westerns' rise to popularity, drawing on descriptions and commentaries in the trade press, as well as viewings of the few extant film prints. More important, I want to suggest how early westerns acted as a counter to "Pathé-mentia," functioning within a rejuvenated discourse of Americanization, an overtly racist discourse that sought to privilege the "Anglo-Saxon" (and the masculine) as dominant in any conception of American national identity.

"NATURAL WEALTH" IN STORY AND SPECTACLE

Early westerns played a significant role in securing the transition from a *cinema of attractions* to a cinema dominated by fiction films. They offered, I would argue, an exemplary model of negotiation between what Gunning has called "the desire to tell a story" and "the desire to display," between narrative engagement and spectacle attraction.[7] That is, westerns told a certain kind of story within the context of displaying particular, picturesque American landscapes. As the 1991 Smithsonian exhibition "The West as America" made clear, those landscapes had coalesced into an iconographic tradition already quite widespread in American popular culture by the turn of the last century.[8] Several generations of painters and photographers had produced a palimpsest of images in which the Great Plains from Texas to the Dakotas and Montana, the mountain ranges of Colorado and California, and the desert regions of the Southwest had turned, in Alan Trachtenberg's apt phrase, into a myth of "unimaginable natural wealth."[9] These images were broadly disseminated throughout the East and Midwest in magic lantern slide lectures, stereographs, and chromolithographs. Such works as Albert Bierstadt's *Sunset: California Scenery,* Fanny Palmer's *Rocky Mountains—Emigrants Crossing the Plains* or *Across the Continent,* and Andrew Putnam Hill's *George Hoag's Record Wheat Harvest,* for instance, all circulated as inexpensive chromo reproductions, for decorating the walls of urban lower- and middle-class homes.[10] Most of this iconography, Martha Sandweiss reminds us, served the interests of railroad and mining companies, land speculators, and local business enterprises—see, for instance, the chromo *California Powder Works*—as a way to attract immigrant settlers (and cheap labor) to the western states.[11] But it also served the interests of another kind of exploitation and consumption, that of tourism: by means of the railroads, William Cullen Bryant wrote, "we now have easy access to scenery of a most remarkable character . . . [to] Nature in her grandest forms."[12]

The Selig company of Chicago, as Robert Anderson has pointed out, was probably the first to systematically exploit the attraction of these landscapes and their "natural wealth."[13] This was becoming evident as early as 1906, specifically for the subjects used in Hale's Tours, the simulated railcar ride that enjoyed a brief season or two of popularity in summer amusement parks (and even in some cities).[14] Pathé initially supplied many of the scenic views for the "Tours of the World" programs, while American companies supplied those for "domestic" tours.[15] Yet Selig, as Raymond Fielding has shown, was the only one to issue a catalog supplement (in August 1906), listing twenty-five films specifically targeted for Hale's Tours.[16] And most of these offered tours through western locations like the Black Hills, the Royal Gorge, Utah, the Coeur d'Alene Mountains, or the Columbia River.[17] Selig's western manager and cameraman, H. H. Buckwalter, also was one of the first to recognize how moving pictures could serve as "promotional come-ons" for tourism in a state like Colorado: his "panorama of the Cripple Creek Short Line," he estimated, was shown to over fifty thousand people in Chicago's State Street theaters and to another twenty-five thousand in White City amusement park.[18] As the company shifted its marketing from Hale's Tours to the more popular nickelodeons, in early 1907, it continued to offer scenics like *A Trip through Yellowstone Park,*[19] but now it began to draw on its experience in location shooting for story films like *The Girl from Montana* and to take renewed interest in sensational melodramas set in the West like *The Bandit King.*[20]

Selig may not have had a monopoly on such films, but it did have an advantage. In advertising *Western Justice,* in June 1907, the company crowed that Edison, Vitagraph, and Kalem could never match the "magnificent scenic effects" of the film's western mountains and plains because they were confined to "some backyard in the East."[21] By early 1908, Selig could be even more explicit. The story of *The Squawman's Daughter*, for instance, "was re-enacted on the same ground" where it was said to have occurred, in a prairie landscape "that reache[d] as far as the eye [could] see."[22] That summer, outside Denver, the company used local cowboys to shoot several films that would "boost the State and create . . . [a] desire to visit the places where the pictures were made."[23] In its reviews of Selig films, the *Mirror* took up the spirit of these claims. Due to the "magnificently picturesque mountain[s]" in *An Indian's Gratitude*, the *Mirror* wrote, "no film, foreign or American, that has been produced in a long time can approach [it] in scenic splendor."[24] The spectacle attraction produced by such location shooting is still visible in a surviving print of *The Cattle Rustlers*, which includes an *actualité* sequence of rounding up and branding cattle in a mountain valley, repeated scenes of the rustlers' camp beside a swiftly flowing stream, and a climactic shoot-out at a log cabin, isolated on a treeless hilltop and backed by high, distant mountains.[25] Both the *Mirror* and the *World* took special note of the unusual popularity of Selig films in New York City the following winter and spring: *On the Warpath* (probably inspired by a well-known 1872 chromo), and *The Bad Lands*, for instance, were loudly applauded at the Manhattan and Union Square theaters.[26] And in Chicago, as *Show World* suggested, the "authenticity" of the Selig westerns functioned much the same as the railroad-sponsored travelogues boosting the southwestern states as a prime site for new settlements.[27]

In their display of distinctive American landscapes, then, some early westerns appropriated the iconographic tradition of the chromo and the travelogue, offering short, inexpensive tours of the Far West, especially appealing to urban audiences in the East and Midwest. Others, however, offered concise narrative formulas for standardizing the production of one-reel fiction films. That the long dime novel tradition of Wild West stories seems not to have been an explicit source for these is revealing.[28] In 1907, one scenario writer did make the link: his task was "much the same as that of the usual story writer," he told the *World*, "except that, like the dime novelist, he must have something happening every minute."[29] Yet a direct link went undeveloped, as Biograph's parody, *Terrible Ted*, attests.[30] The likely explanation was the public outcry that spring and summer in cities like Chicago over sensational films such as *The Bandit King* (with its bold robberies and climactic gun battle). In the new public space of mass consumption, of which the cinema was now a part, "working-class" dime novels were presumed "deplorable" or "odious."[31] Manufacturers may well have wanted to avoid any risk of offending their new allies, the Progressive reformers, with subjects that seemed "tainted." Still, by the spring of 1908, as the *World* editorialized, "an active demand . . . on the part of exhibitors" was beginning to reestablish that link to the dime novel tradition—in Selig's *Squawman's Daughter;* Essanay's "thriller from beginning to end," *The James Boys in Missouri* (the Chicago company also used "western" locations); and Edison's *Cowboy and the Schoolmarm*, whose horseback ride "crowded houses at Keith's" applauded for being "as good as a circus."[32]

THE

Moving Picture World

The Official Organ of the Moving Picture Exhibitors' Association.

The only Independent Weekly Journal published in the interests of Manufacturers and Operators of Animated Photographs and Cinematograph Projection, Illustrated Songs, Lantern Lectures and Lantern Slide Makers

PUBLISHED BY

THE WORLD PHOTOGRAPHIC PUBLISHING COMPANY, 361 BROADWAY, NEW YORK

Vol. 1., No. 17. June 29, 1907 Price, 10 Cents

Figure 47. Selig ad, *Moving Picture World* (29 June 1907), cover.

Yet this was the moment when Woods began to proselytize, in the *Mirror*, for "clear, well-told" stories to match the "vivid and clear-cut prose" so characteristic of middle-class mass magazines from *Munsey's* to *Saturday Evening Post*.

Certain western subjects did offer examples of strong plotting for Woods, but now it was Biograph and Vitagraph titles (made in the East) that took center stage.[33] As cited in the previous chapter, in August, Biograph's *Redman and the Child* rated "best film of the week" (and was "held over two days by special request" at the Manhattan): "The story is original and consistent, . . . scenes follow each other consecutively and naturally. Interest is aroused from the start, and is held with increasing power to the very end."[34] Months later, the *Index* and the *Mirror* noted that the film was still popular enough to be held over as far away as Natchez and San Antonio.[35] That fall, other Biograph films, such as *The Red Girl* and *The Call of the Wild* (also already cited), allowed Woods to single out "the particular elements that go to make up a successful moving picture story."[36] Coincident with the MPPC's formation, the *World* joined in the *Mirror*'s polemic to laud Selig films such as *A Montana Schoolmarm* and *In Old Arizona*.[37] Now Woods, too, cast his net wider, praising other "brands" as well: Selig's *On the Warpath* had a plot that was easy to follow and ended in a "big logical climax," while Essanay's *Road Agents* told a "straight story" uncomplicated by side issues or "maudlin sentiment."[38] As a type of recurring story, particularly in the films of Selig, Biograph, and Essanay, the western was coming to exemplify, for both the *Mirror* and the *World*, the kind of "simple story" that "all good film stories should be."[39] That Pathé films, including certain of the company's *films d'art*, continued to be cited as models of clear, coherent storytelling, comprehensible to any kind of audience, suggests just how significant these early westerns were as a "repeatable" American subject distinctively different from the "foreign film product."[40]

As the genre grew ever more popular during 1909,[41] however, an important difference began to emerge between one "school" of films that valued action above all else and another "school" that valued acting and logical plotting. In October, the *World* marked this as a difference not only between Selig and Biograph but also between one class of fiction aimed at the "masses" and another aimed at a "discriminating" audience.[42] In other words, the *World* argued, different "brands" attracted different class-based audiences. The school of action westerns had an "immense popularity with the people," but Selig was not its undisputed leader. As early as May, for instance, the *World* described *Why the Mail Was Late*, a "Western melodrama from Lubin," as having "all the snap and go for which these pictures have become known."[43] Once used to distinguish American from foreign films, the slang phrase now marked the westerns most filled with thrilling action, those involved in a rejuvenation of the dime novel tradition. It was precisely this kind of western that the new Independents, NYMPC (Bison), Centaur, and World Films, exploited in order to secure a niche on the American market.[44] In September, the *World* wrote that Bison's *Paymaster* had "all the dash and go of the usual melodrama and [held] the attention of the audience from the opening

Figure 48. Essanay ad, *Film Index* (18 December 1909), 901.

until the close."[45] In November, it headlined Essanay's new production unit, led by G.M. Anderson, that specialized in westerns "in which the wild and woolly plays the leading part."[46] By year's end, Bison's *Ranchman's Wife* could be compared to Selig's "wild and woolly" *On the Border* for thrills and applause.[47] Now, too, Bison films like *Romany Bob's Revenge* and *Government Relations* could be described, without a trace of a snicker, as "dime novel subjects."[48] The resurgent dime novel western was thriving in this "school of action," neatly epitomized in Essanay's *Heart of a Cowboy*, which beat, wrote the *World*, with "much of the true Western snap and go."[49]

One thing remained constant, however, as this new product differentiation cut across "licensed" and "unlicensed" manufacturers: the "foreignization" of Pathé. In May 1909, the *World* noted how audiences at a Keith Bijou Dream much preferred the "threadbare story" of Essanay's *The Indian Trailer* to the "more finished" *film d'art* of Pathé's *Père Milon*.[50] In a July editorial, it even reprinted a letter from an exhibitor excoriating the company for factual errors in *A Western Hero*, as if it were an act of piracy for Pathé to even try mining the genre. "The denizens of the far West are . . . jealous of their customs and characteristics," warned the *World*, "and telling a picture story at long range is treading on dangerous ground."[51] No matter how "beautifully colored" or "romantic and artistic" its scenes, the *Mirror* chimed in, they were not authentic—"they were not American."[52] That Pathé released *A Western Hero* in stencil color reveals its "foreignness" in another way.

Here, the trade press was unanimous: stencil color was perfectly appropriate for certain *films d'art* and "exotic" scenics, but not for American subjects, especially westerns.[53] For the latter, the realist aesthetic promoted by the *Mirror* and the *World* dictated a concern for the "orthochromatic," the accuracy of tonal values in "the black and white picture," which by 1909–1910, so went the claim, the public preferred, from whatever school it came.[54] The *World* singled out Biograph in particular as a model for other manufacturers to imitate, for its films' "fine, rich deposit in the shadows and clear, delicate lights."[55] The chiaroscuro of black and white could be enhanced by tinting and/or toning effects, but, as Woods argued, those had to serve the purpose of "approximating reality and at the same time making the story clear."[56] If *color* were to be invoked in the American cinema, it would be yoked to an aesthetic of "impressive realism" (to cite a Biograph ad), one imbued with a distinctive, historically specific American ideology.[57]

THE WESTERN AS WHITE SUPREMACIST ENTERTAINMENT

Whatever the distinction between "schools," the formulaic stories these westerns told closely adhered to the prevailing discourse of Americanization. The history of that discourse, and its construction of national identity, has been charted by Trachtenberg and others through a variety of written texts and visual images in the late nineteenth century.[58] Josiah Strong's widely reprinted tract, *Our Country: Its Possible Future and Its Present Crisis* (1885), for instance, made "race" its foundational concept: "The world [is entering] upon a new stage of its history—the final competition of races, for which the Anglo-Saxon is being schooled. . . . [T]he mighty centrifugal tendency, inherent in this stock, and strengthened in the United States, will assert itself."[59] So did John Fiske's infamous "Manifest Destiny" (1885), which envisioned a time in which "every land on the earth's surface . . . shall become English in its language, in its political habits and traditions, and to a predominant extent in the blood of its people."[60] The same goes for Theodore Roosevelt's popular *Winning of the West* (1889), which celebrated the appearance of the "American" (that new breed of Anglo-Saxon) as a culminating moment in "race-history."[61] This was nothing less than "ancestor worship" with a double function, argues Kammen: that is, "to enhance the prestige of the living more than to honor the dead" and "to marginalize or exclude the country's less 'desirable' inhabitants."[62]

This racist conception of an "American character" coincided with, and was partly determined by, "native-born" white middle-class fears of all the "undesirable" immigrants from eastern and southern Europe, who were settling in already densely populated cities like New York, Philadelphia, and Chicago.[63] Yet, in a tradition that went back at least to Thomas Jefferson, it was projected most forcefully upon the mythic (and now closed) frontier of "the West."[64] In that process of projection, perhaps best articulated by Frederick Jackson Turner (in his 1893 Chicago Exposition lecture), the West served to produce and entitle specifically "masculine" traits in this new breed of the "Anglo-Saxon."[65] Or, as Roosevelt put it in

Figure 49. Frederic Remington, "The Last Cavalier," in Owen Wister, "The Evolution of the Cow-Puncher," *Harper's* (September 1895), 605.

"The Strenuous Life" (1897), the frontier became an imaginary space for testing and renewing the "virility" of the race and its "fighting spirit."[66] Whereas the civilizing figure of a white woman once had represented "American Progress" in popular chromos, according to Ronald Takaki, now western heroes like General George Custer and even Buffalo Bill Cody were coming to personify "the masculine advance guard of civilization."[67] In 1896, for instance, Anheuser-Busch began packing chromos of Cassily Adams's *Custer's Last Fight* in its shipments of Budweiser beer, and the huge painting ended up on the walls of many local saloons.[68] In short, as Robert Rydell argues, the discourse of Americanization defused and deflected all kinds of perceived threats (chief among them class conflict) by asserting white male supremacy as the core of a new national identity.[69]

For early westerns, the parameters of this discourse are starkly exposed in Owen Wister's 1895 essay "The Evolution of the Cow-Puncher."[70] Only the "Anglo-Saxon" (male) supposedly had "the spirit of adventure, courage, and self-sufficiency" needed for survival "in the clean cattle country" of the American West. Unlike those *others*, those "hordes of encroaching alien vermin that [were turning] our cities to Babels and our citizenship to a hybrid farce," wrote Wister, the cowpuncher was a "direct lineal offspring" of Camelot: "In personal daring and in skill as to the horse, the knight and the cowboy are nothing but the same Saxon of different environments." The "inveterate enemies" of the cowboy, however, were the Mexican and the Indian, who had to be vanquished in order for

Wister to imagine a "clean cattle country." Acknowledging and even admiring "the Saxon contempt for the foreigner," Wister praised the cowboy for supplanting the Mexican, "this small, deceitful alien," and simply erased the Indian as one "whose hand was against all races but his own immediate tribe." This openly racist, covertly masculinized discourse framed Wister's own best-seller *The Virginian* (1902), but was widespread at the time.[71] It fueled what Slotkin has called the "*virilist* realism" or "red-blooded fiction" of two of Wister's friends, Frank Norris and Frederic Remington.[72] Norris said he drew inspiration from the "tremendous tales" of the frontier, where "there was action and fighting, and . . . men held each others' lives in the crook of a forefinger"; Remington was ready to blur any and all distinctions between fiction and life: "I've got some Winchesters and when the massacring begins, I can get my share of 'em ['the rubbish of the Earth'] and what's more, I will."[73] However toned down, "declawed," this discourse penetrated nearly every level of mass-market writing, from the short stories in *Saturday Evening Post* to the "moralistic adventure stories about clean-cut boys" in Frank Tousey's *Wild West Weekly* or Smith & Street's *Rough Rider Weekly*.[74]

Western films made up a small but increasingly influential component of what Rydell calls this "universe of white supremacist entertainments."[75] In June 1907, for instance, the ads for an early Kalem title, *The Pony Express*, heralded the express rider as one of the great figures in the history of the West, "harassed on every side by Indians and Highwaymen," but in this particular story waylaid by "Mexican vaqueros" or "Greasers."[76] The next year, similar stories cropped up in films from most "licensed" manufacturers. In Edison's *Pioneers Crossing the Plains in '49,* Indians massacre a wagon train of settlers and carry off "the [white] heroine," who then has to be rescued.[77] In Kalem's *The Renegade,* a falsely accused soldier restores his honor by freeing a little white girl from hostile Indians.[78] In Lubin's *The White Chief,* an "American" saves an "Indian girl" from an abusive Mexican and ends up being named chief of her tribe.[79] In Selig's *Cowboy's Baby,* the white child of the title survives a wagon train attack by Sioux Indians, is adopted by the cowboy hero, Joe Dayton, and then (to top things off) has to be rescued from the clutches of a wealthy Mexican, who wants revenge on Dayton and his new wife (whom he had once wooed).[80] In the already cited *Cattle Rustlers* (according to the story summary printed in the *Index*), the leader of the outlaws is a half-breed named Cherokee, their camp cook is a Mexican, and the log cabin site of the climactic shootout is home to Cherokee's "Indian sweetheart, Wahnita."[81] By the end of the year, the *World* was prompted to write, "theater managers [were] clamoring after" these kinds of "Wild West subjects."[82]

An important variant on Wister's "knight errant" appeared in early 1909, the horse soldier of the U.S. cavalry, a figure cloaked much more overtly in the mantle of national identity. Selig films developed the figure extensively, beginning with *In Old Arizona,* "a story of the plains, true to life," where soldiers come to the aid of white settlers against a jealous Mexican who has induced a band of Indians to attack them.[83] In *On the Warpath*, hostile Indians alone are the foe; in *Boots and*

Saddles, they take in a soldier dishonorably discharged for gambling and make a "good lieutenant" prisoner, only to suffer defeat at the hands of the latter's army troop.[84] These cavalry films culminated in Selig's *On the Little Big Horn,* which made Custer's martial masculine heroics unabashedly emblematic of "the advance guard of [American] civilization."[85] Other films deployed the soldier hero against more contemporary threats, whose locus shifted, as in the popular historical romance, to encompass and justify an expanding overseas empire.[86] In *Fighting Bob,* Selig sketched a naval lieutenant's chivalric rescue of a "native beauty" somewhere on the coast of Latin America.[87] In *A Soldier of the U.S. Army,* Kalem told a heroic story of a boy's "passage to manhood" in the Philippines and paired that with *The Japanese Invasion,* a xenophobic fantasy in which American military forces defend the West Coast against a deceptive enemy.[88] On the tenth anniversary of that "Splendid Little War" in Cuba, Selig perpetuated the myth of the Rough Riders in *Up San Juan Hill,* narrating not only "the famous feat of Lieutenant Bowen who carried the message to Garcia" at the war's outbreak but also the alleged charge up the hill against Valdez (which the *Mirror* discredited, along with Roosevelt's presence) and the rescue of Bowen's "sweetheart" from a treacherous act of vengeance.[89] In *Under the Stars and Stripes,* Selig returned to Cuba with a similar story full of "galvanic action," which made the *World,* in a patriotic outburst, "appreciate the influence which carries a man forward into battle, into what he may believe is almost certain death."[90]

Throughout 1909, however, the "purer" strain of Wister's formulaic offspring was far more prevalent. Mexicans continued to act as villains, as in Essanay's *Road Agents* or Lubin's *Mexican Bill.*[91] Indians went on harassing white settlers, as in Vitagraph's *Children of the Plains,* which complicated a massacre and rescue by separating two sisters, who recognize one another years later only by their matching lockets.[92] Even the Bison films that assured "unlicensed" exhibitors of one western (and probably more) per week often worked within this racist conception of "American character" as well. In late October, Bison exploited the tradition of chivalric romance in *Iona, the White Squaw,* in which a white girl raised by Indians becomes the object of a search and reward, is retrieved by a cowboy, and is "safely secured among her [white] friends."[93] Singled out as a top film by the *World* two weeks later, *Mexican's Crime* had "all the dash and go of the usual Western drama [with] cowboys, Mexicans [as the bad guys], careening horses [and] gun play."[94] In all these films, the *World* glibly noted, violence and "lively gun play" neither was "out of place" nor "create[d] unfavorable impressions."[95] What made it "seem proper and right"? These were American, not foreign (and especially not French), brands, and their action was determined by American assumptions about race.[96] One *World* reviewer even bolstered this attitude with claims of authenticity: in Selig's *Indian Wife's Devotion,* he found the representation of a "despicable . . . half-breed" fit perfectly with his personal experience of "many such cowardly characters."[97] Although the *Mirror* was less caught up in such posturing—a review of Lubin's *Bride Won by Bribery* wryly noted that Mexicans "exist in

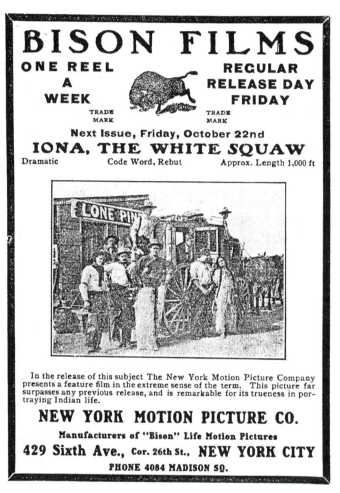

Figure 50. Bison ad, *Moving Picture World* (23 October 1909), 591.

this class of films solely to make trouble"—its reasons remained aesthetic and elitist.[98]

When, in late 1909, the *World* proposed "Wild West subjects" as "the foundation of American moving picture drama," it promoted them as an offshoot of the country's "national literature."[99] However ambivalent even the *World* may have been about many films' resemblance to dime novels, it recognized their educational (that is, ideological) potential: the westerns of thrilling action aimed at the masses were unusually popular with the young, especially boys.[100] Here, Michael Kimmel provides an important historical context: the new masculinity touted by

Figure 51. Home Merchandise ad for the Ikonograph projector,
People's Popular Weekly (February 1909), 17.

Roosevelt, Norris, Wister, and others arose, in part, to challenge a perceived threat
of "cultural feminization," through "the predominance of women in the lives of
young boys," within the social institutions of family, school, and religion.[101]
Among the new public spaces of mass consumption, nickelodeons (with their con-
gregations of women and children) exacerbated that sense of threat. Westerns

may well have offered boys—that is, "white boys," whether middle- or working-class, including some immigrants—a counter to this "feminization," something like a genre of their own to go along with the separate spheres of play, toys, and clothing that were becoming part of their training for manhood.[102] Westerns also had the advantage of being "distinctly American in characterization, scenery, and surroundings," and of having, in the *World*'s revealing phrase, "themes 'racy of the soil.'"[103] Their nostalgic backward glance served as a form of national memory, securing, in the midst of rapid social change, a fixed, exclusionary sense of identity—however false—for the "young and vigorous group of men of intellect, will and ceaseless activity" whose testing ground was the American city.[104] In short, westerns perfectly embodied the "good, clean, wholesome, national, patriotic, educational films" that the *World* insisted American manufacturers should be offering the American public to compete with, subjugate, and assimilate anything that was "alien."[105]

THE NOT SO "VANISHING INDIAN"

Not all westerns, however, were inscribed so unproblematically within the discourse of Americanization, and it is these others that demand to be considered more fully, and in some detail. As certain titles like *The Redman and the Child* or *The Red Girl* already should suggest, the previous pages deliberately have been constructed according to the principles of exclusion and co-optation defining the United States as "our country." For, in the trade press, the term designating such films was not "westerns" but "Indian and Western subjects," a point the *World* made clear in its polemic for American subjects and "an American school of moving picture drama." Half of the so-called westerns produced between 1907 and 1910, in fact, were actually Indian stories or had an Indian (or Mexican) as a central character or even the hero.[106] Nearly every manufacturer became involved in their production at some point, but there were differences. Edison and Essanay were least committed to Indian subjects; Selig and Vitagraph released a number of titles at crucial moments; Biograph, Kalem, and NYMPC more or less specialized in them.[107] Once again, the boundary between competing MPPC and Independent factions seemed less important than one distinguishing an American "school" of acting and logical plotting from an American "school" of action. In conjunction with that, there were significant differences in what kinds of stories the films told and for what audiences.

Early Indian subjects tended to follow one of two narrative trajectories. Beginning with Kalem's *Red Man's Way*, whose "Indian rites" were to be accompanied by specific "incidental music,"[108] a few worked out melodramatic stories of good versus bad characters (both usually played by white actors) within an Indian community. The attraction here, as in the same company's *Red Cloud*, according to the *Mirror*, was "the careful research" and "attention to detail" that went into depicting

"Indian pastimes and costumes."[109] In other words, these were promoted as "realistic" spectacles, meant to educate as well as entertain, much like the ethnographic displays or *tableaux vivants* mounted in museums and world's fairs. But *Red Cloud* did something especially devious: it transposed the name of the famous Oglala Sioux leader to an Indian addicted to gambling who, after being rejected by a chief's daughter, murders him and is hunted down and killed by another Indian who loves her and replaces her father as chief. Biograph's *Mended Lute,* whose "familiar love story" of generational conflict is resolved when an Indian brave "exhibits [unusual] fortitude" under tribal torture, extended this ethnographic impulse by using a Winnebago Indian, James Young Deer, to play its Sioux hero.[110] This film blended "poetry and romance," wrote the *World,* to display the unfamiliar in Sioux life for the contemplation of "discriminating" spectators.[111] When NYMPC began producing Indian subjects in 1909, with Young Deer and his wife, Red Wing, an integral part of its new California production unit, such contemplative spectacle (but not the attention to detail) began to dissipate, at least within this kind of story.[112] Instead, Bison films like *The Love of a Savage, A Redman's Devotion, Young Deer's Bravery,* and *Young Deer's Gratitude* all exhibited the "dime novel action and heroics" for which the company was now so noted.[113]

Most Indian subjects, however, told stories of Indian characters defined in relation to whites, with the hero or heroine demonstrating a sense of honor, justice, or self-sacrifice equal to or even surpassing that of his or her American "masters." A good example is Selig's 1908 film *An Indian's Gratitude:* because a young white woman has taught the lead character "that it is wrong to kill," he tracks a "white bully" who has insulted her and injured her lover, and then keeps a white vigilante mob from hanging the villain.[114] Something similar happens in Biograph's *Call of the Wild:* an Indian football hero (much like Jim Thorpe) and cavalry soldier is rejected by a "well-born white girl" and "abandons the ways of civilization"; kidnapping her in anger, he then "abandon[s] his revenge when she appeals to his higher nature."[115] Biograph's *Redman and the Child* offers a gendered variation on this: an Indian brave takes revenge on two outlaws who, in stealing a cache of gold, have killed a young white boy's grandfather and kidnapped the boy himself (whom the brave has befriended).[116] The same company's *Red Girl,* by contrast, has the title's heroine help capture, but not kill, a Mexican woman and a half-breed who have robbed white miners of their gold.[117] At least one film, however, Vitagraph's *An Indian's Honor,* defines its heroism as distinctive.[118] An Indian falsely condemned to death for murder has a friend take his place as a prisoner (until the day of execution) while he visits his home one last time, but he is robbed en route by friends of the gambler he killed in self-defense. In order to honor his vow to return, he travels fifty miles on foot, reaching the hangman's tree just in time, and falls dead from exhaustion. Here, the "noble savage" reemerges to die and be transformed into the enduring sign of a "natural" sense of morality that could even serve as a model for white American civilization.

Figure 52. Biograph ad, *New York Dramatic Mirror* (31 October 1908), 8.

Throughout 1909, all but a few films tracing the relations between Indians (or Mexicans) and whites defined their heroes in terms of a "natural" or learned goodness. Those that did not, from Kalem's *Trail of the White Man* to an early IMP effort, *Destiny,* usually drew harsh words from the trade press for "sensationalism," whether for a gruesome revenge exacted outside "the law" or for an overall sense of "death and depression and gloom."[119] When revenge killing was acceptable, as in Biograph's *Indian Runner's Romance,* it was because the story was historical (justifying a Sioux brave's vengeance on a cowboy who has kidnapped his wife), because Young Deer and Red Wing played the Sioux characters, and because the film was American-made.[120] It certainly was not acceptable if French-made, as in Pathé's otherwise absorbing *Justice of a Redskin,* where an Indian not only kills a white man "before the dead body of the [white] girl he murdered" but also "hurls the body into a stream and watches it sink from view."[121] In most films, however, the Indians (both men and women) who rescued or saved white Americans did so out of a sense of "innate" goodness, as in Essanay's *Indian Trailer,* Bison's *Cowboy's Narrow Escape,* and Selig's *The Indian,* or out of indebtedness to benevolent whites, as in Edison's *A Child of the Forest,* Bison's *Dove*

Eye's Gratitude, and Vitagraph's *Red Wing's Gratitude.*[122] In a variant on this plot, Essanay's *A Mexican's Gratitude,* a Mexican recognizes a sheriff who once saved him from hanging and rescues the white lawman (and his fiancée) from a "treacherous rival," who happens to be his own Mexican employer.[123] Only rarely did relations between whites and Indians (or Mexicans) become permanent; as a rule, the races were kept separate. Interracial marriage was carefully avoided, usually through an Indian woman's tragic death, as in Selig's *Daughter of the Sioux;* when it did occur, as in Bison's *Red Girl's Romance* or Essanay's *The Cowboy and the Squaw,* the couple remained isolated, as proscribed by the white man's law and its "prohibition of miscegenation."[124]

THE FICTIONS OF SUBJECTION AND ASSIMILATION

That Indian subjects were unusually popular with a wide range of audiences during this period demands an explanation.[125] That demand is especially acute because such stories no longer appeared frequently in other media, from dime novels and story weeklies to middle-class magazines.[126] As early as 1904, *The Bookman* asserted that "the Indian as a factor had dropped out" of the dime novel "about twenty years before."[127] That was true as well of the story weeklies that by then had replaced the dime novel, especially for middle-class juvenile readers. In *Wild West Weekly,* for instance, after Young Wild West saves his "sweetheart" Arietta from Indian captivity, the stories celebrate his "manly virtues" in adventures (financed by his gold mine and other properties) that pit him and his friends against outlaws and eastern criminals more often than Indians.[128] In *Rough Rider Weekly,* Ted Strong and Stella, his "Queen of the Range," are involved even less often with Indians.[129] In other words, the principal, if not exclusive, venue for Indian subjects at this historical moment seems to have been moving pictures. In seeking to explain this phenomenon, one has to ask whether Indian subjects functioned differently than did the westerns young boys were said to so love. One also has to ask whether it mattered if an Indian brave or an Indian maiden was the central character, and if he or she were played by an Indian or a white in disguise. Here, Bison's chief filmmaker, Fred Balshofer, offers a point of entry by attributing some films' success to the spectacle of the nearly naked male body: "the ladies simply went gaga over" Charles Inslee in "his naked Indian hero roles."[130] However smugly put, Balshofer's remark deserves consideration, since women (whether single or married, working- or middle-class) frequented the shows in large numbers and efforts to regulate the behavior of bodies, both in the audience and on the screen, were still being contested.[131] Indeed, it suggests that the popularity of Indian subjects may have been the result of a historically specific alignment of the "subordinated," according to race, gender, and class.

First of all, Indian subjects have to be situated within the iconographic tradition of the West. By the turn of the century, the Indian who earlier had been represented

THE AUDIENCE AT A MOVING-PICTURE THEATER—THE GALLERY BREATHLESSLY WATCHING
THE SCENE THAT APPEARS ON THE OPPOSITE PAGE

Figure 53. "The audience at a moving-picture theater . . . ," in William A. Johnson, "The Moving-Picture Show," *Munsey's* (August 1909), 636–637.

as opposing white civilization (whether "nobly" or "savagely"), in chromos such as "American Progress," had been transformed into the "Vanishing American" or what might be called, after Renato Rosaldo, a figure of "imperialist nostalgia." [132] The "thanatological tenderness" of that figure was strikingly captured in James Earle Fraser's sculpture of a defeated brave on horseback, "End of the Trail." [133] But the "Vanishing American" also circulated in all kinds of commercial attractions prior to moving pictures, from Buffalo Bill's Wild West to the "exotic" villages so popular at world's fairs from Chicago (1893) and Omaha (1898) to Saint Louis (1904) or Portland (1905). There, as Brian Dippie puts it, "Americans were invited to look with tenderness on the few living remnants of their own beginnings . . . 'the Alpha of the alphabet of American history.'" [134] Yet, whatever the attraction, including moving pictures, the Indian was presented as visual spectacle, commodified for mass consumption, within a nationalistic ideology of "racial progress." Accordingly, a hierarchy of types, from the highest (or closest to the "Anglo-Saxon" American) to the lowest, framed the distribution of Indian (or Mexican) characters in these films, just as it did, for example, the peoples inhabiting the Philippine Reservation at the Saint Louis Exposition. [135] Put simply, the "good" film Indian (or Mexican) served as a model of assimilation or an "object lesson" (encouraged by the Dawes Severalty Act of 1887), especially when that figure abandoned his or her culture and gratefully adopted the values and behavior of

A TRAGEDY OF THE FRONTIER—A THRILLING WESTERN SCENE
WHICH MAY HAVE BEEN POSED IN NEW JERSEY
OR LONG ISLAND

Figure 53. (*continued*)

the more "advanced" white American culture, predicated on private property and a male-dominated nuclear family, with its protective, paternalistic attitude toward women and children.[136]

As a model of assimilation, then, the Indian's appeal exceeded that of an elegiac nostalgia. For, as Slotkin has argued, throughout the last two decades of the nineteenth century, Indians often were conceived as displaced figures of the "working class [or] alien mob" and its threat of "savage war."[137] After the 1886 Haymarket "riots" in Chicago, for instance, one New York newspaper called for ending further immigration on the grounds that "such foreign savages . . . [were] as much apart from the rest of the people of this country as the Apaches of the plains are."[138] Nearly twenty years later, David Perry (then president of the National Association of Manufacturers) made a similar claim that "organized labor

Figure 54. Wladyslaw T. Benda, "They were permitted to drink deep of oblivion of all the trouble in the world," in Mary Heaton Vorse, "Some Moving Picture Audiences," *Outlook* (24 June 1911), 444.

know[s] one law, and that is . . . the law of the savage." [139] As Alex Nemerov suggests, the equation of "savage tribes" and "urban mobs" also can be traced in the paintings of Remington, Charles Schreyvogel, and others. [140] The "good" film Indian, then, could have had a special appeal for the working-class immigrants who made up a significant mass of the moving picture audience in metropolitan centers from New York and Philadelphia to Chicago. Mary Heaton Vorse gives evidence of this, particularly for women, in her sharply etched account of an East Side nickelodeon: one young Jewish woman repeatedly murmured aloud, so "rapt and entranced" was she by an Indian film. [141] And surely such films would have appealed to Progressive reformers interested in the assimilation of those immigrants. [142] For, if the Indian (or Mexican), despite his or her alleged savagery or deceitful nature, could acquire, embody, and enact the values of an "American" (being a white actor in disguise, of course, helped immeasurably), so, too, could the newly arrived immigrants from eastern and southern Europe, who were even closer to the "Anglo-Saxon" ideal. The "good" Indian (or Mexican) may well have been a more potent mirror image of cultural transformation, subjection, and assimilation (and managed social struggle) than the "clean, good looking actor" who played the more conventional western hero.[143]

EPILOGUE I: "HAPPY TRAILS," BUT FOR WHOM?

Whatever stories they told and whatever their reception, "Indian and Western subjects" circulated more or less securely within the racist ideology of Americanization. Nowhere near as secure, however, was their circulation within the trade press discourse preoccupied with "masculinizing" the cinema market. Indeed, several discursive "bits and pieces" dealing with westerns suggest that this masculinizing project was far from hegemonic, and that the cinema, in 1910, was far from being a tightly regulated, homogeneous social space. One is Louis Reeves Harrison's lengthy review, in the *World*, of Biograph's prestigious adaptation of the Helen Hunt Jackson best-seller *Ramona*, in which Mary Pickford plays a young woman (half Scottish, half Indian, but not Mexican) who suffers indignities at the hands of her family and other whites, eventually losing both her own baby and her Indian husband.[144] The others are capsule reviews, also in the *World*, of what at first might seem an anomaly: numerous "school of action" westerns in which "cowboy girls" perform heroic feats in stories of their own.[145] In Essanay's *Western Maid*, for instance, bandits are pursued "by a posse headed by a dashing Western girl"; in the same company's *Western Chivalry*, a young woman proves to a bunch of cowboys that she has the "right stuff" by "mounting and riding the worst horse on the ranch."[146] In Bison's *Female Bandit*, one of the "frightfully immoral" women that so upset Harrison in these westerns, so different from *Ramona*, exonerates herself by "rescuing a child from a burning house."[147] Selig's *Cowboy Girls* probably upset him as well: there, "a party of athletic New England girls take possession of a Western ranch" (while the men are away), redecorate the place and change its name from L. Z. to Lizzie, and take in a drifting cowboy and dress him in women's clothes; in the end, he helps them capture a band of rustlers and wins one girl for a wife.[148]

This discourse (perhaps too) neatly points to contrasting yet imbricated trajectories of historical change. Harrison writes within a familiar racist, masculinist, even classist ideology, extending its prerogatives beyond the "red-blood fiction" of his predecessors.[149] For the "popular New York theatre" where he saw *Ramona* one spring afternoon was full of men, "most of them . . . business men," attracted by "the occasion . . . of a special release."[150] They were quiet and respectful, a very different "ideal audience" from the one Vorse observed on the Lower East Side (and which Harrison derided as "the scum of the community"). Yet what most appealed to these men, according to Harrison, transcended the story; it was partly the self-sacrificial character Pickford played ("the ideal creature of our heartaches and dreams"), but mostly Pickford herself as an "exuberant and interesting personality"—in other words, her "genial glow" and "thrilling magnetism" as a movie star—and perhaps as a white woman who could "pass" as an "exotic" other. Although *Ramona* initially might seem an obvious site of cultural feminization, its elegiac nostalgia was readily available for reframing, or "re-branding," within a masculinized discursive space (one my grandfather inhabited), as a supposedly pious, yet sexually charged, corollary to the patriotic jingoism of more conventional westerns.

The "bits and pieces" clustered around the second western brand point in a different direction. Westerns like these, especially *The Cowboy Girls*, with its comedy of cross-dressing that precipitates the closural heroics and marriage, strongly suggest that young girls, even middle-class white girls, could be attracted to the genre. This brand has to be read in the context of the middle-class readership for girls' series books then emerging as an "offshoot of the boys' adventure series," from *Frank Merriwell* to *Wild West Weekly*.[151] These books had telling titles, like *The Motor Girls, The Ranch Girls,* and *The Outdoor Girls*, with active heroines, many of them "bands of sisters," as in *The Cowboy Girls*.[152] One thing this phenomenon suggests is that "cowboy girl" westerns may have prepared a wide range of female spectators for serial queen melodramas like *The Perils of Pauline* that would soon become so popular.[153] But it also reminds us that the surveys of children's viewing behavior, which proliferated in this period and concluded that boys, not girls, were the target audience for westerns, may be more representative of reformers' efforts to regulate leisure activities and channel children's desires according to conventional gender roles.[154] For girls may have gone to the movies not only to enjoy the "cowboy girl" westerns that seemed to target them but also to seek pleasure in others, just as they read across the boundaries that publishers and libraries tried to institute between girls' and boys' fiction.[155] Finally, this suggests that the feminization of the "movie fan," another middle-class, white phenomenon, probably occurred even earlier than recent studies have argued, and perhaps most tellingly in relation to a supposedly "masculine" genre like the western and in the face of a "masculinizing" discourse like Harrison's.[156]

If early westerns often did embody the "good, clean, wholesome, national, patriotic, educational films" called for by the *World,* they also opened up anomalous social spaces where the regulations against certain kinds of border crossing (and cross identification) could be tactically, tactfully elided or eluded.

EPILOGUE II: "THE END OF THE TRAIL" FOR PATHÉ

By 1910, according to Robert Anderson, "one out of every five pictures produced by American companies . . . was a western" or an Indian and Western subject, serving as a significant marker of product differentiation for at least a half dozen of them.[157] That summer, along with its regular films, Selig released a special feature, *Ranch Life in the Great Southwest,* starring "such celebrities as Henry Grammar, Tom Mix, Pat Long, Johnny Mullins, and Chas. Fuqua."[158] Kalem's series of Indian films remained consistently popular: among them was

The Exiled Chief, which depicted "the sad fate of the Seminole Indians" in the tradition of the "Vanishing American."[159] And Essanay began to exploit Anderson's popularity with what would become a highly successful *Broncho Billy* series.[160] But the genre was especially crucial for the Independents, as a reliably appealing staple of the weekly releases from exchanges like the Sales Company or a newcomer, Paramount.[161] The continued profitability of Bison's Indian and Western subjects prompted others to join the stampede. By that summer, Nestor was producing a new western nearly every week; that fall, Champion and a revitalized Columbia (which briefly used the Miller Brothers 101 Ranch in Oklahoma) were making westerns in order to secure a hold in the industry.[162] The biggest surprise, however, came when three exchange men—Harry Aitken and John Freuler (from Milwaukee) and Sam Hutchinson (from Chicago)—formed the American Film Company, with its trademark Flying A: almost all of its personnel were snatched from Essanay (leaving only Anderson's western unit intact).[163] Much like Thanhouser earlier that year, American boldly proclaimed it was making "American Film for the American People."[164] And that meant westerns.

As quintessentially American subjects and influential models of exclusion and inclusion sharply defined according to race, Indian and Western subjects also staked out a territorial claim against "foreign" incursions—which returns me to my opening. Prior to 1910, the few westerns Pathé released were often criticized for inauthentic landscapes or savage tortures and other "cold-blooded act[s]" deemed far too gruesome for American tastes.[165] Not unexpectedly, that criticism did not cease when the company had Louis Gasnier set about producing films in New Jersey, beginning with *The Girl from Arizona.*[166] For one thing, the kinds of westerns Gasnier chose were supposed moneymakers, "full of snap and go" like *The Cowboy's Sweetheart and the Bandit,* and that made them, the *Mirror* sniffed, "only too clearly of dime-novel origin."[167] Even though Gasnier had the audacity to hire Young Deer and Red Wing away from NYMPC, the *Mirror* continued to chide the company for "that sort of film" in *White Fawn's Devotion;* only with *A Cheyenne Brave,* which pitted a "noble" Cheyenne couple against the "savage" Sioux, did it begin to relent.[168] By then, however, it was the *World*'s turn, despite generally supporting the company's strategy, to chastise Pathé for "too much bloodshed" in a "yellow back type of story," *The Gambler's End.*[169] Even as an American company, Pathé still could not escape accusations of "bad taste." For another thing, and on this the *Mirror* and the *World* agreed, however well staged and photographed and whatever their "thrilling interest," the Wild West scenes in Pathé films looked woefully out of place in "unmistakable New Jersey rocks and woods."[170] In late 1910, Gasnier successfully addressed this problem by sending Young Deer to Los Angeles, as head of a separate production unit, to establish a West Coast studio (near Selig's, in Edendale).[171] Sensing that its ideological mission was nearly complete, the *World* cheerfully wrote: "So here we have the gratifying spectacle of a house of French origin getting down to the common sense view of things . . . producing American subjects for American audiences."[172]

Pathé's problems, however, were far from resolved by this carefully calculated move. As a regular supplier of westerns, it was coming rather late to the genre; whereas once the French company had led the way in producing all kinds of films for the American market, now it was being forced to play catch-up. Besides, Pathé could supply only a fraction of the hundreds of westerns released in 1910 and 1911, and far fewer than Selig, Essanay, Kalem, NYMPC, and American. Moreover, the company focused on Indian subjects as much as, if not more than, cowboy pictures, perhaps because of Young Deer's experience, and it never would find an actor who could compete with Essanay's Broncho Billy Anderson or Selig's Tom Mix, nor a filmmaker who could measure up to Allan Dwan at American or Thomas Ince, who would join NYMPC after working for IMP. Then, too, as Bowser argues, the vogue for Indian films, unlike westerns, turned out to be short-lived; their popularity (as well as their usefulness) began to decline within a year or so.[173] Finally, Pathé made an unusual commitment to having "burly" Indians, rather than "clean, good looking [that is, white] actors," play its major Indian heroes, a casting practice that was evident as early as *Justice of a Redskin* and one that Young Deer continued in the Indian and Western subjects of 1910 and 1911.[174] However commendable, this practice could never fully embody the requisite magic—or racist sleight of hand—of American assimilation.[175]

DOCUMENT 9

"An American School of Moving Picture Drama,"
Moving Picture World (20 November 1909), 712

A friend who is largely interested in moving picture production draws our attention to a striking fact in connection with the attitude of moving picture audiences towards the photographs shown. It is this: That the most popular subjects with those audiences are those which deal with Indian or Wild West themes. He points out that the audiences are largely composed of young people and he has ascertained by inquiry at moving picture theaters that these young people show preference for the subjects named. Independently of this we perceive, in our own experience, that these subjects are popular and that such themes as "Hiawatha," Indian dramas and Wild West plays commend themselves to manufacturers, producers, and audiences alike.

In this respect, therefore, we seem to see evidence of the foundation of an American moving picture drama; something around which sentiment clings just as it does in other countries. Sentiment is always strong where national life and character or history form the themes of pictorial or literary treatment. Here the question arises: Is there a national literature upon which film producers can draw with certainty and success? You have, of course, these Indian and Wild West subjects, as to which, perhaps, except in rare cases, the fullest justice is not always shown. But even so, these pictures form but a very small proportion of the pictures produced by American film manufacturers who too frequently, in our opinion, go abroad for their themes. For example: Comparatively few pictures dealing with the Revolutionary War are shown. Then, again, it is probable that the Civil War era has by no means been exhausted. The earlier period referred to is rich in the makings of history, a fact of which the average producer, or maybe the average scenario writer, seems to be somewhat ignorant.

On this occasion we are more concerned with the more popular sources of American subjects than with history. How rarely do we see a high class American novel dramatized in moving picture form! We write under correction, but we are very doubtful if the beautiful books of Nathaniel Hawthorne, one of the most fascinating American writers who ever lived, have been turned to account in moving pictures. Mention of the Scarlet Letter; The Blithedale Romance; Transformation; Mosses from an Old Manse, and others, will suffice to convince an intelligent producer or writer that there is a great field open for moving picture plays in the Hawthorne pages. Mark Twain has done duty on the stage and he, we think, is the only important American writer who has.

Then you have Mayne Reid, Fenimore Cooper, Artemus Ward, Judge Habberton, Max Adeler, W. D. Howells, Henry James, James Russell Lowell, Henry W. Longfellow (who by the way wrote a great many things besides "Hiawatha"). These writers are classical, but there are a whole crowd of moderns such as Winston Churchill, Marion Crawford, Mrs. Margaret Deland and others to draw from. Many of these people would no doubt be willing to trade the copyrights of their books to moving picture publishers.

We are only touching the fringe of an important matter which has been brought to our mind in reading through the stories of the films that are sent out by the manufacturers week by week. These are not American enough to suit our ideas. We do not want to see all American themes illustrated on the moving picture stage. That would be absurd, while there are so many of the world's masterpieces waiting for representation. But we do put in a plea for the creation of an American moving picture drama and we point out that the material lies ready to hand for adaptation by scenario writers and producers.

Afterword
The Amnesia of Americanization

In July 1910, Pathé used its weekly "manufacturer's notes" in *Moving Picture World* to make a series of claims about its historical role in the American cinema's emergence:

> Pathe Freres are the firm that boomed the film business of this country, and deserve all the recognition of this fact that exchanges and exhibitors can give them. Pathe Freres were the first to place titles and sub-titles on their films; the first to make regular releases on regular release dates; the first to release a reel at a time; the first to introduce posters for films; the first to produce colored pictures; the first to give advance information to the exhibitor and issue a weekly bulletin; the first to get out a trade paper; and lastly and most important, the first to get in touch with the exhibitor and study his requirements.[1]

Although several of these claims might be challenged, Pathé's overall role in expanding, as well as significantly shaping, the business in the United States cannot be contested. What is of particular interest, however, is that the company felt compelled to assert this version of history and even to plead for the recognition it felt it deserved. This was a clear sign not only that Pathé's position on the American market had weakened considerably, despite its balanced release schedule of "American-made" and European film product (the latter carefully selected for American tastes), but also that American companies, abetted by the trade press, were writing their own, equally self-serving, version of that history.

Thomas Bedding provides an early instance of that process, in January 1910, during an interview with Carl Laemmle (one of several industry leaders, from the Trust as well as the Independents, who had recently visited Europe). Allegedly surprised by Laemmle's "international grasp of the commercial situation," Bedding depicted the IMP company as a model for the American industry in that it embodied two "fundamental conditions for success, namely, a perfected organization of loyal helpers and an efficient system of distribution."[2] Ignoring any claims Pathé might have made about such conditions, as well as any difficulties the Independents overall may have been experiencing, he, too, with Laemmle's help, now saw that the industry's mission was not only national but also imperial.[3]

> There is no doubt in my mind that the American idea of commercial expansion, with the breadth of outlook which it takes, is a factor in the world commerce to-day. So that, listening as I did to Mr. Laemmle's ideas, and the possibilities of the American film taking a position in the markets of the world, was something in the nature of an intellectual treat.[4]

Others may have envisioned the spread of American films abroad as early as 1907, and Vitagraph may have done something about that, with some success, through its printing factory in Paris. Now that Pathé, the world's largest film supplier, had been contained on the American market and forced to fashion its product within the limits set by assimilation, the American industry was coming to see that its newly achieved competitive edge might be extended globally. As American production capacity continued to grow throughout 1910 and into 1911, and the American market again reached a level of saturation, the industry increasingly looked to foreign markets for added profits.[5] In other words, now that the American cinema had a "truly" American identity, however marked by internal division, American companies were ready to challenge and replace Pathé in other countries as well.

The *New York Dramatic Mirror* provides another instance of reimagining the history of American cinema. In October 1910, it initiated a campaign to come up with a "motion picture merit list," in what was perhaps the first attempt to establish a film canon of "the best ones ever produced."[6] This campaign asked the *Mirror*'s readers each to send in a list of ten best films, all of which it then compiled in early February 1911 (coincidentally, just as my grandfather, at the age of sixteen, took his first job arranging department store windows).[7] The *Mirror*'s "final count" in this campaign yields several points of interest. Among the 148 film titles "which received 25 or more votes," all were "licensed" subjects and nearly all had been released within the previous year, which meant that, with a couple exceptions, this was a "merit list" of "licensed" films from 1910.[8] More important, only Biograph and Vitagraph had titles receiving 75 votes or more, and Biograph's *Wilful Peggy* (with Mary Pickford) and Vitagraph's *The Three of Them* and *Rose Leaves* (with Florence Turner) each accumulated at least 120. Not unexpectedly, this reflects the aesthetic position of the *Mirror*, which polemicized for "quality" films stressing acting and logical plotting; the one surprise may be that Biograph placed second to Vitagraph. Perhaps the most significant thing about this "merit list," however, is the relative absence of foreign films. The few foreign titles turn out to be French: three from Gaumont and only six from Pathé, its biggest vote-getter being *Cleopatra* (with 42 votes).[9] This represents an astonishing shift over the course of a year or two. If the *Mirror* or the *World* were to have compiled such a list in late 1908 or early 1909, the majority of the film titles undoubtedly would have been Pathé's. Now, in late 1910, Edison, Kalem, and Essanay all had more 1910 films on the *Mirror*'s "merit list" than did Pathé.[10] In the United States at least, the cinema had been redefined as a "purely" American phenomenon, through Pathé's repositioning as a "structuring absence" in our country's cultural memory.

Invoking Horatio Alger, Michael Denning has argued that the history of the dime novel underwent a remarkable rewriting around the turn of the century.[11] Symptomatic of this rewriting was a nostalgic article in the *Atlantic Monthly*, which addressed such questions as "what did the dime novel stand for . . . and what forces did it represent in the evolution of American society?"[12] The answer came in platitudes: "The aim of the original dime novel was to give, in cheap and wholesome form, a picture of American wild life. . . . In reading them the American boy's soul soared and sang." Erased in this rewriting, Denning says, was any sense that the usual dime novel reader was "a factory girl" or that the reading focused on "the other, the 'lower classes' and the 'foreigners.'"[13] Something analogous happened to the Pathé films that flooded the American market between 1904 and 1908, and to the role they played, however contradictory, at a crucial stage in the development of an American cinema. Here, the erasure of a "foreign element," and the audiences for whom it was an attraction, has been nearly as complete. Once a crucial player in the cinema's expansion and legitimation, the French company now found its moves repeatedly blocked or deflected, stigmatized or appropriated. Once king of the market, the Pathé red rooster had to be suited up (to invoke language quite familiar to my grandfather) so as to appease its new masters just to keep from being run out of town. In the United States, where the cinema's industrialization constituted one of the defining moments of modernity—one that transformed the alternative social space of the nickelodeon into the commercial public sphere of an increasingly homogeneous consumer culture—the Americanization process acted as a significant framing, even determining, discourse. And, in the context of the debate over that process, Pathé came to serve as a crucial marker of the margin, ensuring that the American cinema would be truly American.

APPENDIX

Listed here are the titles of Méliès and Pathé French films released in the United States (in alphabetical order), followed by their titles as released in France. Exceptions include those titles that are the same in English and French and those for which the French title remains uncertain.

GEORGES MÉLIÈS

Arabian Nights or *Le Palais des mille et une nuits,* 1905
Astronomer's Dream or *La Lune à un mètre,* 1898
Automobile Chase or *Le Raid Paris–Monte Carlo en deux heures,* 1905
The Black Imp
Bluebeard or *Barbe bleue,* 1901
Cinderella or *Cendrillon,* 1899
The Clockmaker's Dream or *Le Rêve de l'horloger,* 1904
The Coronation of King Edward VII or *Le Sacre d'Edouard VII,* 1902
The Crystal Cabinet
Damnation of Faust or *Damnation du Docteur Faust,* 1903
Fairyland or *Le Royaume des fées,* 1903
Faust and Marguerite or *Faust et Marguerite,* 1904
The Impossible Voyage or *Le Voyage à travers l'impossible,* 1904
Joan of Arc or *Jeanne d'Arc,* 1900
Little Red Riding Hood or *Le Petit Chaperon rouge,* 1901
Magical Eggs or *L'Oeuf du sorcier,* 1902
Martinique Disaster or *Éruption volcanique à la Martinique,* 1902
Robinson Crusoe, 1903
A Trip to the Moon or *Le Voyage à la lune,* 1902
Wonderful Suspension and Evolution or *Équilibre impossible,* 1902

PATHÉ-FRÈRES

The Acrobatic Maid or *La Bonne des acrobates*, 1908
Across the Island of Ceylon or *A travers l'île de Ceylan*, 1909
Aladdin and His Lamp or *Aladdin*, 1901
Aladdin's Lamp or *Aladdin ou la lampe merveilleuse*, 1906
Ali Baba or *Ali Baba et les quarante voleurs*, 1907
Ali Baba and the Forty Thieves or *Ali Baba et les quarante voleurs*, 1902
Annie's Love Story or *Roman d'amour*, 1904
L'Arlésienne, 1908
Assassination of the Duke of Guise or *L'Assassinat du Duc de Guise*, 1908
August the Monkey or *Le Singe August*, 1904
Avenged by the Sea or *La Revanche des flots*, 1907
The Bewitched Lover or *L'Amoureux ensorcelé*, 1905
Blacksmith's Revenge or *Vengeance du forgeron*, 1907
Bluebeard or *Barbe bleue*, 1907
Bottle Industry or *Industrie de la bouteille*, 1907
Le Boucher de Meudon, 1909
Butterfly's Metamorphosis or *Métamorphose du papillon*, 1904
Camille, 1909
The Carman's Danger or *L'Automobile emballée*, 1907
Carmen, 1909
Carnival at Nice or *Carnaval de Nice*, 1907
Cartouche or *Cartouche roi des voleurs*, 1909
A Case of Arson or *Les Voleurs incendiaires*, 1907
Charlotte Corday, 1909
The Charmer or *Le Charmeur*, 1907
Children's Reformatory or *Le Bagne de gosses*, 1907
Christian Martyrs or *Les Martyrs chrétiens*, 1905
Christmas Eve Tragedy or *Nuit de Noël*, 1908
Christopher Columbus or *Christophe Colomb*, 1904
Cinderella or *Cendrillon*, 1907
Cleopatra or *Cléopatre*, 1910
The Clown's Daughter or *La Fille du saltimbanque*, 1908
The Clown's Revenge or *La Revanche de Pierrot*, 1906
Coffee Culture or *Culture du café au Brésil*, 1908
Crime on the Railroad or *Un Attentat sur la voie ferrée*, 1907
A Cure for Timidity or *Timidité vaincue*, 1910
The Deserter or *Le Déserteur*, 1906
Detective's Tour of the World or *Tour du monde d'un policier*, 1906
Different Hairdresses or *Coiffes et coiffures*, 1905
Distress or *École du malheur*, 1907
Dog Smugglers or *Chiens contrebandiers*, 1906

Don Juan, 1908
Don Quixote or *Don Quichotte,* 1903
The Downward Path or *Mariage de raison,* 1899
A Drama in the Air or *Un Drame dans les airs,* 1904
Drink or *L'Assomoir,* 1909
Eccentric Waltz or *Valse excentrique,* 1903
Fairy of the Black Rocks or *La Fée des roches noires,* 1902
Fancy Garden Party or *Nuit de carnaval,* 1906
Fantastic Fishing or *Pêche miraculeuse,* 1902
The Female Spy or *L'Espionne,* 1906
Fireworks/ Fire Cascades or *Cascades de feu,* 1905
The Fortune Hunters or *La Fortune de l'oncle d'Amérique,* 1908
From Christiana to North Cape or *De Christiana au Cap Nord,* 1904
From Jealousy to Madness or *Jalousie et folie,* 1907
The Gambler's Crime or *La Vie d'un joueur,* 1903
Gaul's Hero or *Vercingétorix,* 1909
Geneviève Brabant, 1907
Gold Prospectors, 1909
La Grande Bretèche, 1909
The Grandfather, 1909
The Great Steeplechase, 1905
Harlequin's Story or *La Légende de Polichinelle,* 1907
Hello Grinder or *Ohé! Ohé! Rémouleur,* 1906
The Hen with the Golden Eggs or *La Poule aux oeufs d'or,* 1905
Her Dramatic Career, 1909
Holiday or *En Vacances,* 1906
The Hooligans of Paris or *Les Apaches de Paris,* 1905
Hop o' My Thumb or *Le Petit Poucet,* 1905
The Hostage or *L'Otage,* 1908
The Idler, 1908
The Incendiary or *L'Incendiaire,* 1905
Incriminating Evidence or *Un Tuteur criminel,* 1909
Indians and Cowboys or *Indiens et cowboys,* 1904
Ingenious Soubrette or *La Soubrette ingénieuse,* 1903
Joan of Arc or *Jeanne d'Arc,* 1909
Joseph and His Brethren or *Joseph vendu par ses frères,* 1909
Joseph Sold by His Brothers or *Joseph vendu par ses frères,* 1904
Justice of a Redskin or *La Justice du peau-rouge,* 1908
The Language of Flowers or *Le Langage des fleurs,* 1905
The Legend of Orpheus or *La Légende d'Orphée,* 1909
Life of Louis XIV or *Le Règne de Louis XIV,* 1904
The Life of a Miner/ French Coal Miners or *Au pays noir,* 1905
Life of Napoleon or *Épopée napoléonienne,* 1903

Light Housekeeping, 1907
The Little Cripple or *Le Petit Béquillard,* 1908
Magic Roses or *Les Roses magiques,* 1906
Manufacturing Bamboo Hats or *Fabrication de chapeaux de bambous aux îles de la Sonde,* 1909
The Marathon Race or *The Stadium: Course du marathon,* 1908
Marie Antoinette, 1904
Martinique Disaster or *Catastrophe de la Martinique,* 1902
Mary Stuart or *Marie Stuart,* 1908
Mephisto's Son or *Le Fils au diable à Paris,* 1906
Military Prison or *A Biribi, disciplinaires français,* 1907
The Mill or *Le Moulin maudit,* 1909
Modern Brigandage or *Brigandage moderne,* 1905
The Moon Lover or *Le Rêve à la lune,* 1905
A Narrow Escape, 1908
Nest Robbers or *Les Dénicheurs d'oiseaux,* 1904
Othello, 1909
Ouchard the Merchant or *Ouchard le marchand,* 1909
A Pair of White Gloves or *L'Homme aux gants blancs,* 1908
Le Parapluie d'Anatole, 1909
The Passion Play or *La Vie et la Passion de Jésus-Christ,* 1902–1903
The Passion Play / Life and Passion of Christ or *La Vie et la Passion de N. S. J. C.,* 1907
Pathé-Journal, 1908–
Pathé Weekly, 1911–
The Pearl Fisher or *Le Pêcheur des perles,* 1907
Père Milon, 1909
Picturesque Canada or *Canada pittoresque,* 1907
Picturesque Java or *Java pittoresque,* 1907
The Pirates or *Les Forbans,* 1907
Police Dogs / Dog Police or *Les Chiens de police,* 1907
The Policeman's Little Run or *La Course de sergents,* 1907
A Poor Man's Romance or *Le Roman d'un malheureux,* 1908
The Prince of Wales at Lanori, 1906
The Prodigal Son or *L'Enfant prodigue,* 1901
The Prodigal Son or *L'Enfant prodigue,* 1907
Puss-in-Boots or *Le Chat botté,* 1903
The Rajah's Casket or *L'Écrin du rajah,* 1906
The Reception of the American Fleet in Australia, 1908
The Repentant Beggar or *Conscience de miséreux,* 1909
The Resourceful Waiter or *Comment on met son couvert,* 1901
Rigoletto, 1909
The River Ozu, Japan or *Les Rapides de la rivière Ozu,* 1906
Romance of a Poor Girl or *Le Roman d'une jeune fille pauvre,* 1909
The Runaway Horse or *Le Cheval emballé,* 1908

Russian Anti-Semitic Atrocities or *Atrocités antisémites russes,* 1905
The Scar or *L'Empreinte,* 1908
Scenes at Creusot's Steel Foundry or *La Métallurgie au Creusot,* 1905
Scenes from Convict Life or *Au bagne,* 1905–1906
The Servant's Good Joke, 1909
The Shipowner's Daughter or *La Fille du batelier,* 1908
The Shrimper or *La Pêcheuse de crevettes,* 1907
Sister Angelica or *Soeur Angélique,* 1909
Sleeping Beauty or *La Belle au bois dormant,* 1902
Sleeping Beauty or *La Belle au bois dormant,* 1908
Sleeping Sickness, 1910
Spring Fairy or *La Fée printemps,* 1902
Stag Hunt in Java or *Chasse aux cerfs à Java,* 1910
The Story of a Crime or *L'Histoire d'un crime,* 1901
The Strike or *La Grève,* 1904
A Stunning Creation or *Créations renversantes,* 1905
Tit for Tat or *La Peine du talion,* 1906
La Tosca, 1909
The Tower of Nesle or *La Tour de Nesle,* 1909
Trip through Algiers or *Vues d'Algérie,* 1902
Trip through Europe or *Fêtes à Sienne (Italie),* 1902
A Trip to the Stars or *Voyage autour d'une étoile,* 1906
Il Trovatore or *Le Trouvère,* 1910
Two Great Griefs or *Deux grandes douleurs,* 1908
Two Sisters or *Les Deux Soeurs,* 1907
Two Young Tramps or *Les Petits Vagabonds,* 1905
The Vestal or *La Vestale,* 1908
Victims of the Storm or *Les Effets de l'orage,* 1906
The Violin Maker of Cremona or *Le Luthier de Cremona,* 1909
A Visit to Bombay or *Une Visite à Bombay,* 1909
Voice of Conscience or *La Voix de la conscience,* 1906
A Western Hero, 1909
Wilbur Wright's Aeroplane or *L'Aéroplane Wright,* 1908
The Wild Ass's Skin or *La Peau de chagrin,* 1909
William Tell or *Guillaume Tell,* 1903
Witches Cave, 1907
The Wonderful Album or *L'Album merveilleux,* 1905
The Wonderful Mirrors or *Les Glaces merveilleuses,* 1907
Wood Floating in Morvan or *Le Flottage du bois dans le Morvan,* 1908

NOTES

To conserve space, the following abbreviations appear throughout the notes.

TRADE PRESS: WEEKLIES AND MONTHLIES

Bill	*Billboard*
FI	*Film Index*, 1908–1911
MPW	*Moving Picture World*
Nick	*Nickelodeon*
NYC	*New York Clipper*
NYDM	*New York Dramatic Mirror*
SW	*Show World*
Var	*Variety*
VFI	*Views and Films Index*, 1906–1908

DAILY NEWSPAPERS

CRH	*Chicago Record-Herald*
CT	*Chicago Tribune*
DMRL	*Des Moines Register and Leader*
DMT	*Des Moines Tribune*
LAT	*Los Angeles Times*
NYT	*New York Times*
NYTr	*New York Tribune*
Ore	*Oregonian* (Portland)

SPECIAL COLLECTIONS

ENHS   Edison National Historical Site, West Orange, New Jersey

GK   George Kleine Collection, Manuscripts Division, Library of Congress, Washington, D.C.

KA   Keith-Albee Collection, Special Collections, University of Iowa Library, Iowa City, Iowa

PREFACE

1. Charles Musser, *The Emergence of Cinema to 1907,* vol 1. of *History of the American Cinema* (New York: Scribner's, 1991).

2. Homi Bhabha, "Introduction: Narrating the Nation," *Nation and Narration* (New York: Routledge, 1990), 4.

3. Eric Hobsbawm, *The Age of Empire, 1875–1914* (New York: Pantheon, 1987), 34–83. For a discussion of early French cinema within the context of these discourses of imperialism and nationalism, see Richard Abel, "Booming the Film Business: The Historical Specificity of Early French Cinema," *French Cultural Studies* 1 (1990)—reprinted in Abel, ed., *Silent Film* (New Brunswick, N.J.: Rutgers University Press, 1996), 109–124.

4. Hobsbawm, *The Age of Empire,* 142–164.

5. Bhabha, "Introduction," 1–2.

6. Richard Ohmann, *Selling Culture: Magazines, Markets, and Class at the Turn of the Century* (London: Verso, 1996), 59.

7. I first laid out the parameters of this argument in "The Perils of Pathé, or the Americanization of the American Cinema," in Leo Charney and Vanessa Schwartz, eds., *Cinema and the Invention of Modern Life* (Berkeley: University of California Press, 1995), 183–223.

8. The initial Pathé distribution agencies, other than those in the United States, included Moscow (February 1904), Brussels (October 1904), Berlin (March 1905), Vienna (July 1905), Saint Petersburg (December 1905), Amsterdam (January 1906), Barcelona (February 1906), Milan (May 1906), London (July 1906), and Odessa (July 1906). For further information on Pathé-Frères, especially in France, where its rapid growth into a relatively large corporation was quite unusual, see Richard Abel, "In the Belly of the Beast: The Early Years of Pathé-Frères," *Film History* 5.4 (December 1993), 363–385; and Abel, *The Ciné Goes to Town: French Cinema, 1896–1914* (Berkeley: University of California Press, 1994), 20–22, 29–35.

9. See, for instance, "Moving Pictures," *NYC* (27 April 1907), 276, and (8 June 1907), 443.

10. One of the first important essays to deal with immigrants and early cinema is Judith Mayne's "Immigrants and Spectators," *Wide Angle* 5.2 (1982), 32–41.

11. Miriam Hansen provides an astute, useful conceptualization of the public sphere, drawing on Oscar Negt and Alexander Kluge's critique of Jürgen Habermas, as well as an excellent summary of the controversy over the social composition of nickelodeon audiences, in *Babel & Babylon: Spectatorship in American Silent Cinema* (Cambridge, Mass.: Harvard University Press, 1991), 7–15, 61–68, 90–125. Roy Rosenzweig offers a model case study of how working-class audiences in Worcester, Massachusetts, constituted an "alternative"

public sphere, in *Eight Hours for What We Will: Workers and Leisure in an Industrial City, 1870–1920* (Cambridge: Cambridge University Press, 1983), 191–221.

12. For other, quite insightful, essays reconsidering early cinema in terms of "the experience of modernity," see Tom Gunning, "Heard over the Phone: *The Lonely Villa* and the de Lorde Tradition of the Terrors of Technology," *Screen* 32 (Summer 1991), 184–196; Gunning, "'Now You See It, Now You Don't': The Temporality of the Cinema of Attractions," *Velvet Light Trap* 32 (Fall 1993)—reprinted in Abel, *Silent Film*, 71–84; Gunning, "Tracing the Individual Body: Photography, Detectives, and Early Cinema," in Charney and Schwartz, *Cinema and the Invention of Modern Life*, 15–45; and Gunning, "The Whole Town's Gawking: Early Cinema and the Visual Experience of Modernity," *Yale Journal of Criticism* 7.2 (Fall 1994), 189–201.

13. The first researchers to draw attention to Pathé's importance as a "foreign" presence in the early American cinema industry were Robert Anderson, "The Role of the Western Film Genre in Industry Competition, 1907–1911," *Journal of the University Film Association* 31.2 (Spring 1979), 19–27; and Kristin Thompson, "Regaining the American Market, 1907–1913," in *Exporting Entertainment: America in the World Market, 1907–1934* (London: British Film Institute, 1985), 1–27.

14. Anyone interested in the business operations of the Pathé company in the United States has to contend with the apparent disappearance of its internal records; to date, very few records of the American company have turned up in the newly opened Pathé Television Archive on the outskirts of Paris. For concise economic histories of early American cinema, see Janet Staiger, "Combination and Litigation: Structures of US Film Distribution, 1891–1917," *Cinema Journal* 23.2 (Winter 1984), 41–72; Robert Anderson, "The Motion Picture Patents Company: A Reevaluation," in Tino Balio, ed., *The American Film Industry*, rev. ed. (Madison: University of Wisconsin Press, 1985), 133–152; and certain sections of Staiger, "The Hollywood Mode of Production to 1930," in David Bordwell, Janet Staiger, and Kristin Thompson, *The Classical Hollywood Cinema: Film Style and Mode of Production to 1960* (New York: Columbia University Press, 1985), 85–153.

15. Barbara Klinger, "Film History Terminable and Interminable: Recovering the Past in Reception Studies," *Screen* 38.2 (Summer 1997), 109. The historical and/or theoretical research on exhibition and reception in early American cinema is extensive, but let me cite at least Russell Merritt, "Nickelodeon Theaters, 1905–1914: Building an Audience for the Movies," in Tino Balio, ed., *The American Film Industry* (Madison: University of Wisconsin Press, 1976), 59–82; Robert Allen, "Motion Picture Exhibition in Manhattan, 1906–1912: Beyond the Nickelodeon," *Cinema Journal* 18.2 (Spring 1979), 2–15; Robert Allen and Douglas Gomery, *Film History: Theory and Practice* (New York: Knopf, 1985), 156–157, 170–172, 202–212; Kathy Peiss, *Cheap Amusements: Working Women and Leisure in Turn-of-the-Century New York* (Philadelphia: Temple University Press, 1986); Dan Streible, "The Literature of Film Exhibition: A Bibliography," *Velvet Light Trap* 25 (Spring 1990), 81–119; Robert Allen, "From Exhibition to Reception: Reflections on the Audience in Film History," *Screen* 31.4 (Winter 1990), 347–356; Hansen, *Babel & Babylon*, 1–125; Janet Staiger, *Interpreting Films: Studies in the Historical Reception of American Cinema* (Princeton, N.J.: Princeton University Press, 1992), 3–123; Judith Mayne, *Cinema and Spectatorship* (New York: Routledge, 1993), 62–70, 77–102; Janet Staiger, *Bad Women: Regulating Sexuality in Early American Cinema* (Minneapolis: University of Minnesota Press, 1995), 1–115; Ben Singer, "Manhattan Nickelodeons: New Data on Audiences and Exhibitors," *Cinema Journal* 34.3 (Spring 1995), 5–35; Gregory Waller, *Main*

Street Amusements: Movies and Commercial Entertainment in a Southern City, 1896–1930 (Washington, D.C.: Smithsonian Institution Press, 1995); and Kathryn Fuller, *At the Picture Show: Small Town Audiences and the Creation of Movie Fan Culture* (Washington, D.C.: Smithsonian Institution Press, 1996).

16. Rather than list and annotate the specific writers and texts from which I derive my own sense of such crucial terms as *class, race, gender, mass culture,* and *pleasure,* let me direct the reader to later chapters where those issues are taken up in more detail. I should cite at least one exchange among historians that I will take up at several points later: "Dialogue: Sumiko Higashi, Robert Allen, and Ben Singer on Class and Manhattan's Nickelodeons," *Cinema Journal* 35.3 (Spring 1996), 72–128.

17. For a similar focus on discursive construction that I have found quite helpful, see William Uricchio and Roberta Pearson, "Constructing the Audience: Competing Discourses of Morality and Rationalization during the Nickelodeon Period," *iris* 17 (Autumn 1994), 43–54. This essay is part of Uricchio and Pearson's *Nickel Madness: The Struggle over New York's Nickelodeons,* forthcoming from Smithsonian Institution Press.

18. The cities whose newspapers I have searched most thoroughly include Des Moines (Iowa), Portland (Oregon), Cedar Rapids (Iowa), Council Bluffs (Iowa), Ottumwa (Iowa), and Medford (Oregon). The population of Portland rose from around 90,000 (1900) to more than 200,000 (1910); that of Des Moines, from almost 60,000 (1900) to nearly 90,000 (1910); that of Cedar Rapids, from 26,000 (1900) to 33,000 (1910); that of Council Bluffs, from 26,000 (1900) to 29,000 (1910); that of Ottumwa, from 18,000 (1900) to 22,000 (1910); and that of Medford, from less than 2,000 (1900) to nearly 9,000 (1910). See *Thirteenth Census of the United States* (Washington, D.C.: Government Printing Office, 1913), 62–63, 68, 72. The Keith-Albee Collection is at the University of Iowa (Iowa City, Iowa); the George Kleine Collection, at the Library of Congress (Washington, D.C.); the Edison materials, at the Edison National Historical Site (West Orange, New Jersey).

19. This notion comes from an intriguing little book, Lawrence Weschler's *Mr. Wilson's Cabinet of Wonder* (New York: Pantheon, 1995).

20. That is not to say that my previous work eschewed the personal altogether. *French Cinema: The First Wave, 1915–1929* (Princeton, N.J.: Princeton University Press, 1984), for instance, grew out of and addressed a great sense of indebtedness to Marie Epstein, who, in the 1970s, granted me a privileged position to view archive prints at the Cinémathèque Française in Paris. *French Film Theory and Criticism, 1907–1939* (Princeton, N.J.: Princeton University Press, 1988) was conceived initially as a joint venture with Stuart Liebman and then written partly for him, to compensate for his involuntary withdrawal from the project. *The Ciné Goes to Town: French Cinema, 1896–1914* and *Silent Film* were composed with and for friends who share a "burning passion" for early cinema, especially those active in the international association Domitor.

21. For a succinct appraisal of L. Frank Baum, see William Leach, *Land of Desire: Merchants, Power, and the Rise of a New American Culture* (New York: Pantheon, 1993), 55–61.

22. That title was given to my grandfather in a newspaper article—"Window Experts Build Ever Changing Show," *Canton Repository* (22 October 1941), n.p. My mother also recalls that in the late 1920s, before the Depression forced her parents to make a summer cabin their permanent home, she and her siblings watched movies on a home projector.

23. See Robert Rydell, *All the World's a Fair: Visions of Empire at American International Expositions, 1876–1916* (Chicago: University of Chicago Press, 1984), 6.

CHAPTER 1. TRICK OR TREAT

1. Charles Musser, *The Emergence of Cinema to 1907*, vol. 1 of *History of the American Cinema* (New York: Scribner's, 1991), 297–336. Musser first presented the argument for this "period of crisis" in "Another Look at the 'Chaser Theory,'" *Studies in Visual Communication* 10.4 (Fall 1984), 24–44. The research Musser amassed for this argument generally supported the position of Lewis Jacobs, in *The Rise of the American Film: A Critical History* (New York: Harcourt, Brace, 1939), 3–21. An earlier commonplace was that "nothing important" happened during this period—see, for instance, "Kinematography in the United States," *MPW* (11 July 1914), 175.

2. Robert Allen, *Vaudeville and Film, 1895–1915: A Study of Media Interaction* (New York: Arno Press, 1980), 181. Allen first took issue with Musser's argument in "Looking at 'Another Look at the "Chaser Theory,"'" *Studies in Visual Communication* 10.4 (Fall 1984), 45–50.

3. Andrew Higson makes a forceful argument for this position in "The Concept of a National Cinema," *Screen* 30 (Autumn 1989), 36, 42–46, as does Allen himself in "From Exhibition to Reception," *Screen* 31 (Winter 1990), 347–356. One problem with Musser's initial research, which he himself recognized, is that it focused on just three cities, as well as on a narrow range of sources—see Musser, "Another Look at the 'Chaser Theory,'" 44 n 11.

4. See George Kleine, "Progress of Optical Projection in the Last Fifty Years," *FI* (28 May 1910), 11, 27. A similar article appeared under the same title in *SW* (27 June 1908), 14–15, 38. See, also, the original dictation—Box 26: Historical File: General, GK. Terry Ramsaye also briefly mentions a short period of "decline" after the Spanish-American War and also asserts that Méliès and his "magic came to the rescue"—see Ramsaye, *A Million and One Nights: A History of the Motion Picture* (New York: Simon and Schuster, 1926), 394–395.

5. "Tony Pastor's Theatre," *NYC* (13 January 1900), 960.

6. "Tony Pastor's Theatre," *NYC* (27 January 1900), 1006.

7. See, for instance, Allen, *Vaudeville and Film*, 142–143; and Musser, *The Emergence of Cinema*, 273–276.

8. Allen also makes this point, specifically in relation to Méliès films but for a slightly later date, in *Vaudeville and Film*, 152–156.

9. For a detailed analysis of the entertainment sites within which moving picture exhibition first developed, see Charlotte Herzog, "The Archaeology of Cinema Architecture: The Origins of the Movie Theater," *Quarterly Review of Film Studies* 9.1 (Winter 1984), 11–32. For regular exhibition in dime museums such as the Eden Musée or Huber's Museum (in New York) and Brandenburgh's Ninth and Arch Museum (in Philadelphia), see Andrea Stulman Dennett, *Weird and Wonderful: The Dime Museum in America* (New York: New York University Press, 1997), 117–123.

10. Neil Harris, *Humbug, The Art of P. T. Barnum* (Chicago: University of Chicago Press, 1973), cited in Tom Gunning, "Crazy Machines in the Garden of Forking Paths: Mischief Gags and the Origins of American Film Comedy," in Kristine Brunovska Karnick and Henry Jenkins, eds., *Classical Hollywood Comedy* (New York: Routledge, 1995), 88.

11. See the ads for these vaudeville houses in *New York Journal* (4 April 1897), 61.

12. See the ads for this "legitimate" theater in *Iowa State Register* (22 May 1897), 6, and (25 May 1897), 6.

13. Charles Musser and Carol Nelson, *High-Class Moving Pictures: Lyman H. Howe and the Forgotten Era of Traveling Exhibition, 1880–1920* (Princeton, N.J.: Princeton University Press, 1991), 47–68.

14. Ibid., 69–104.

15. See, for instance, the published schedule of the 1899 Midland Chautauqua, which included two evening performances by "Mr. D. W. Robertson of New York," using "Edison's great projectoscope"—see "Programme Is Complete," *Des Moines Leader* (7 May 1899), 17. Robertson was still operating several touring companies in the Midwest as late as 1906—see "The Projectoscope," *VFI* (23 June 1906), 5; and the Shubert Theater ad in *Des Moines Mail and Times* (27 October 1906), 7.

16. My principal sources for this paragraph are the vaudeville listings (by state and/or city) in *New York Clipper* and *Billboard,* but see also Musser and Nelson, *High-Class Moving Pictures,* 58, 94–95.

17. For helpful profiles of George Spoor, see "Kinodrome Making Is an Art," *SW* (10 August 1907), 14; and "The George K. Spoor Co.," *FI* (28 May 1910), 8.

18. Prominent among these were the houses managed by Michael Shea, in Buffalo and Toronto. For a brief biographical sketch of Shea, see Robert Grau, *The Business Man in the Amusement World* (New York: Broadway, 1910), 315–316.

19. See, for instance, the American Vitagraph ad in *NYC* (13 May 1899), 217. George Kleine later acknowledged W. T. Rock of Vitagraph as "one of the first to grasp the possibilities of the new form of entertainment," in a sentence contained in the original 1908 dictation (GK) but deleted from the printed articles in *Show World* and *Film Index.* For the earliest reference to Rock, in *New Orleans Picayune* (3 July 1896), see Sylvester Quinn Breard, "A History of the Motion Pictures in New Orleans, 1896–1908" (M.A. thesis, Louisiana State University, 1951), 6—reprinted on microfiche for *Historical Journal of Film, Radio, and Television* 15.4 (October 1995).

20. "Vaudeville," *Bill* (8 December 1900), 7.

21. Unless otherwise noted, the primary sources for this and the following subheaded chapter sections are the vaudeville listings (by state and/or city), as well as moving picture ads in *New York Clipper* and *Billboard.*

22. Ainslee's, "Vaudeville Acts," *Bill* (29 December 1900), 8. This figure may be low because *Billboard* probably relied, as it did later with nickelodeons, on vaudeville houses themselves to fill out forms for compiling its list.

23. See the ad for Keith's Theatre (Boston) in *The Club Woman,* 1.1 (October 1897), 31. This monthly journal, published in Boston, was the official organ of the General Federation of Women's Clubs, established in 1890.

24. Allen first challenged the pejorative concept of a "chaser period" prior to 1903 or 1905 in *Vaudeville and Film,* 161–180. His research traced the "chaser theory" as an uncontested "myth" in the early histories of Gilbert Seldes and others, then simply repeated by later historians—see, for instance, Seldes, *An Hour with the Movies and the Talkies* (Philadelphia: Lippincott, 1929). For a series of even earlier pejorative references to a "chaser period," see Musser, "Another Look at the 'Chaser Theory,'" 25–27. As both attest, Robert Grau restricted the pejorative use of the term to the period "between 1898 and 1900"—see Grau, "Fortunes in the Moving Picture Field," *Overland Monthly* (April 1911), 395; and Grau, *The Theatre of Science* (New York: Benjamin Blom, 1914), 12.

25. Although their research data and interpretive frameworks do differ, both Musser and Allen more or less agree on this more positive definition of the "chaser"—see Musser, "Another Look at the 'Chaser Theory,'" 24–44; and Allen, "Looking at 'Another Look at the "Chaser Theory,"'" 45–50. For an early attempt to clarify the positive role of

the "chaser," see "Theatres and the Pictures: An Attitude Explained," *VFI* (7 September 1907), 3.

26. Gunther Barth, *City People: The Rise of Modern City Culture in Nineteenth-Century America* (New York: Oxford University Press, 1980), 205–206. Barth relies partly on Brett Page, *Writing for Vaudeville* (Springfield, Mass., 1915).

27. I generally follow Stuart Blumin's analysis of the lower middle class of white-collar or clerical workers, whose expanding numbers gave them unusual significance as targeted consumers or would-be consumers and whose paradoxical social position made the boundaries between a working class and a new, increasingly influential middle class of "professionals" (Ohmann's PMC) unstable, fluctuating, even porous. See Blumin, *The Emergence of the Middle Class: Social Experience in the American City, 1760–1900* (Cambridge: Cambridge University Press, 1989); Richard Ohmann, *Selling Culture: Magazines, Markets, and Class at the Turn of the Century* (London: Verso, 1996), 118–174; and "Dialogue," *Cinema Journal* 35.3 (Spring 1996), 72–74, 93–94, 111–112, 124–126.

28. Allen, *Vaudeville and Film*, 203–205. Perhaps Allen could "find no reference to the use of motion pictures in cheap vaudeville before 1906" because his information came largely from *Variety* and *Moving Picture World* rather than *Billboard* and *New York Clipper.* Douglas Gomery also argues, wrongly, that vaudeville was an insignificant venue for showing films between 1900 and 1905—see Gomery, *Shared Pleasures: A History of Movie Presentation in the United States* (Madison: University of Wisconsin Press, 1992), 16.

29. One of the earliest references to the success of "ten-cent" or "family" vaudeville stresses its popularity in the Northwest—see "War on Cheap Theatres," *NYDM* (31 December 1904), 20.

30. "Massachusetts," *NYC* (12 October 1901), 714, and (26 October 1901), 755.

31. "Massachusetts," *NYC* (16 November 1901), 819. Both Lowell and Lynn were cited as cities where crime was declining because so many workers were female—see Mary Gay Humphreys, "The New York Working-Girl," *Scribner's* 20 (October 1896), 512. For good historical studies of Lowell and Lynn, see Thomas Dublin, *Transforming Women's Work: New England Lives in the Industrial Revolution* (Ithaca, N.Y.: Cornell University Press, 1994), 77–151.

32. There is some evidence that moving pictures were shown in Chutes Park and Sans Souci Park as early as 1901 and 1902—see "Chicago," *NYC* (28 September 1901), 666, and (21 June 1902), 373. Musser says the Chutes had a moving picture theater at this time—"Another Look at the 'Chaser Theory,'" 33. Arthur Hotaling was said to manage a summer theater for Lubin's moving pictures in Sans Souci Park—see Linda Woal, "When a Dime Could Buy a Dream: Siegmund Lubin and the Birth of Motion Picture Exhibition," *Film History* 6.2 (Summer 1994), 160. For a quick synopsis of the Coney Island parks, see John Kasson, *Amusing the Million: Coney Island at the Turn of the Century* (New York: Hill and Wang, 1978), 34.

33. See, for instance, the Ingersoll Park ads in the labor-supporting *Des Moines Daily News* during the summers of 1901 and 1902; and "Iowa," *NYC* (14 June 1902), 352.

34. "The Biograph Wins," *NYC* (22 March 1902), 70.

35. Kasson, *Amusing the Million*, 8. Another venue was "black top" tent shows, in which later exhibitors like Archie Shepard and William Swanson got their start—see "The Evolution of Exhibiting," *MPW* (15 July 1916), 367; and W. H. Swanson, "The Inception of the 'Black Top,'" *MPW* (15 July 1916), 368–369.

36. This was probably the same W.A. Reed who, four years earlier, operated Vitagraph's exhibition service at West End Park, in New Orleans—see Breard, "A History of the Motion Pictures in New Orleans," 53.

37. See the Hennegan ad on the back cover of *Bill* (14 June 1902).

38. For an excellent study of S.Z. Poli's policies and practices as an independent vaudeville manager, in an expanding circuit of theaters that numbered more than twenty by 1905, see Kathryn Oberdeck, "Contested Cultures of American Refinement: Theatrical Manager Sylvester Poli, His Audiences, and the Vaudeville Industry, 1890–1920," *Radical History Review* 66 (Fall 1996), 40–91. Although Oberdeck does not discuss the moving pictures on Poli's programs, her statistical research does show that, as a percentage of total acts, they doubled in number between the period of 1894–1899 and 1902–1907.

39. "Washington," *NYC* (21 June 1902), 374.

40. See, for instance, the Krug Park ad in *Council Bluffs Daily Nonpareil* (29 May 1903), 8; and "Waterloo" and "Park Notes," *Bill* (27 June 1903), 5, 9.

41. Tom Gunning, "The Cinema of Attraction: Early Film, Its Spectator and the Avant-Garde," *Wide Angle* 8.3/4 (1986), 63–70. Various writers, including Gunning himself (in essays cited earlier), have argued that the "cinema of attractions" cannot be taken as a homogeneous category for early cinema—see, for instance, Charles Musser, "Rethinking Early Cinema: Cinema of Attractions and Narrativity," *Yale Journal of Criticism* 7.2 (Fall 1994), 203–232; and Abel, *The Ciné Goes to Town*, 59–178.

42. A magazine like *Harper's* proclaimed its "elite" status, in an editorial (September 1902), by claiming that it alone excluded "the 'timely' from its pages" (things like "volcanoes and Edward VII")—quoted in Ohmann, *Selling Culture*, 234.

43. See, also, the Ingersoll Park ad in *Des Moines Daily News* (21 July 1902), 2.

44. Gunning gives a good deal of attention to early Edison and Biograph comedies in "Crazy Machines in the Garden of Forking Paths," 90–93.

45. Allen notes the significant increase in trick films (most of them by Méliès) between 1901 and 1903, in *Vaudeville and Film*, 151–157. Although he also stresses a parallel increase in comic films, the trade press gives far less attention to them.

46. See the *New Orleans Democrat* (4 July 1900), 3—cited in Breard, "A History of the Motion Pictures in New Orleans," 97. After Ramsaye, Jacobs was one of the first to argue for Méliès's importance, saying this specifically about *Cinderella*: "Vaudeville managers ran the movie again and again on their programs," and it "spurred American movie makers to improve their own product"—see Jacobs, *The Rise of the American Film*, 26.

47. See the *New Orleans Democrat* (9 June 1901), 7—cited in Breard, "A History of the Motion Pictures in New Orleans," 108.

48. George Mehl also recalled screening "French pictures in Shea's Yonge Street theater" in Toronto at this time—see "Toronto, Canada, Claims Birthplace of 'Little Mary,'" *MPW* (15 July 1916), 410.

49. See the Ingersoll Park ad in *Des Moines Daily News* (21 July 1902), 2.

50. See Kleine, "Progress of Optical Projection in the Last Fifty Years," 27. See, also, "Picture Stories," *VFI* (21 September 1907), 3. Audience interest in Méliès's *A Trip to the Moon* must also have been predicated on the phenomenal success of Frederic Thompson and Skip Dundy's concession "ride" of the same name, first at the 1901 Buffalo World's Fair and then at Steeplechase Park on Coney Island, in the summer of 1902—see David Nasaw, *Going Out: The Rise and Fall of Public Amusements* (New York: Basic Books, 1994), 83. Such "ritual

spectacles of disaster" were feature attractions at the summer amusement parks—see Kasson, *Amusing the Million*, 72–82.

51. Most of these travel views are listed in the Vitagraph ad in *NYC* (11 April 1904), 168; the titles cross-check closely with those of Pathé catalogs from the period.

52. See the *New Orleans Democrat* (18 December 1902), 7—cited in Breard, "A History of the Motion Pictures in New Orleans," 126. For further references to houses serviced by Spoor's kinodrome, see "Indianapolis," *NYC* (3 January 1903), 994; and "Cincinnati," *Bill* (10 January 1903), 5.

53. "New York City," *NYC* (11 April 1903), 168. Musser quotes from this and several other Keith managers' reports on *A Trip to the Moon*, in April and May, in "Rethinking Early Cinema," 208–209. J. Austin Fynes, the former manager of Keith's Union Square Theatre, may have been a crucial figure in realizing "the importance of moving pictures as a vital part of the programs in the vaudeville theatres"—see Grau, *The Theatre of Science*, 21.

54. See, for instance, "Amusements," *LAT* (18 January 1903), 1.1, and (28 February 1903), 1.

55. Edison and Lubin sold different versions of this film, but other *Passion Plays* by Pathé and Gaumont may have circulated as well. For an analysis of the Edison and Lubin versions, see Charles Musser, "Passions and the Passion Play: Theatre, Film and Religion in America, 1880–1900," *Film History* 5.4 (December 1993), 419–456.

56. See Janet Staiger, "Combination and Litigation: Structures of US Film Distribution, 1891–1917," *Cinema Journal* 23.2 (Winter 1984), 45–46.

57. When Hennegan & Co. began selling a "new line" of "moving picture paper," it singled out *Martinique Disaster* and *King Edward's Coronation* as prime subjects—see the Hennegan ad on the back cover of *Bill* (14 June 1902).

58. See also the Selig Polyscope Catalog, supplement 36 (1 July 1902).

59. See the Edison and Biograph ads in *NYC* (4 October 1902), 712; and the Lubin ad in *NYC* (8 November 1902), 832.

60. See, also, the Edison catalog no. 135 (September 1902), 128, which lists Pathé's *Story of a Crime*.

61. See the Edison ad in *NYC* (1 December 1900), 896. For a good sense of the Christmas season as an "American tradition" by 1900, see Penne L. Restad, *Christmas in America: A History* (New York: Oxford University Press, 1995), 104–105, 123–131.

62. See the Edison ad in *NYC* (23 November 1901), 856.

63. See the Edison ad in *NYC* (15 November 1902), 856.

64. "San Francisco, Cal., Dates Back to the Year 1894," *MPW* (15 July 1916), 400.

65. Musser, *The Emergence of Cinema*, 331.

66. Ibid., 135–145, 177, 179; and Douglas Gilbert, "The Foreign Invasion," in *American Vaudeville: Its Life and Times* (New York: Dover, 1963), 135–151. See, also, the ads for Proctor's and Koster & Bial's in *New York Journal* (1 April 1897), 7; (4 April 1897), 61; and (4 December 1898), 34.

67. See the Geo. Méliès ad in *NYC* (9 May 1903), 276; and the "Star" Films ad in *NYC* (6 June 1903), 368.

68. Musser first developed this point in print in "Before the Rapid Firing Kinetograph," *Edison Motion Pictures, 1890–1900: An Annotated Filmography* (Washington: Smithsonian Institution Press, 1997), 33–36.

69. Musser, *The Emergence of Cinema*, 81–89, 263–264.

70. Nasaw, *Going Out*, 132–134.

71. See, for instance, "Coney Needs Cleansing," *NYTr* (15 July 1901), 12; and "Indianapolis News," *VFI* (4 May 1907), 7. In Austin, Texas, several early projectionists recalled that most townspeople did not consider the arcades or parlors "respectable"—see Burnes St. Patrick Hollyman, "The First Picture Shows: Austin, Texas (1894–1913)," *Journal of the University Film Association* 29 (Summer 1977), 3.

72. John Collier, "Cheap Amusements," *Charities and Commons* (11 April 1908), 75.

73. Herbert Mills, "How to Get Started in the Arcade Business," *VFI* (27 July 1907), 3.

74. F. James Gibson is quoted in "Advertising for Women," *Club Woman*, 1.1 (October 1897), 4. Marketers successfully had transformed shopping into "a form of *leisure*" by the turn of the century—see Ohmann, *Selling Culture*, 80. For further information on this gendering of consumption, see Ohmann, *Selling Culture*, 76 and 112.

75. "The Matinee Girl," *Munsey's* (October 1897), 137. See, also, Mary Gay Humphreys, "Women Bachelors in New York," *Scribner's* 20 (November 1896), 635.

76. It is worth reiterating that moving pictures first found a "home" in "refined" vaudeville, which for years had been a venue of "middle-class" family entertainment, rather than burlesque, which tended to address a "lower-class male audience." See Kathy Peiss, *Cheap Amusements: Working Women and Leisure in Turn-of-the-Century New York* (Philadelphia: Temple University Press, 1986), 142–143; and Robert Allen, *Horrible Prettiness: Burlesque and American Culture* (Chapel Hill: University of North Carolina Press, 1991), 197. Focusing on S. Z. Poli's New Haven programs in the 1890s and then in the 1900s, Oberdeck offers a more complicated reading of how "refined" vaudeville appealed deftly to a range of social groups defined by class and race or ethnicity—Oberdeck, "Contested Cultures of American Refinement," 40–91.

77. See *Providence News* (11 November 1903)—Clipping Book, 1903–1904, KA.

78. See the *New Orleans Democrat* (12 July 1900), 3—cited in Breard, "A History of the Motion Pictures in New Orleans," 97.

79. See *Providence News* (6 November 1903)—Clipping Book, 1903–1904. See, also, the Manager's Reports, Keith's New Theatre, Philadelphia, 5 October 1903, 12 October 1903, and 19 October 1903—KA.

80. See *Providence Journal* (10 November 1903) and *Providence News* (11 November 1903)—Clipping Book, 1903–1904. Perhaps it was only coincidence, but Mary C. W. Foote set up the Fairyland Doll Company shortly after this to manufacture "Fairyland" rag dolls—see Miriam Formanek-Brunell, *Made to Play House: Dolls and the Commercialization of American Girlhood, 1830–1930* (New Haven, Conn.: Yale University Press, 1993), 81, 83. An ad for the "Fairyland" Doll can be found in *Ladies' Home Journal* (November 1907), 88.

ENTR'ACTE 1. MARKETING FILMS AS A PRODUCT CATEGORY

1. Copyright law was extended, by the 1903 Edison versus Lubin and 1905 Edison versus Biograph court cases, to include an entire film subject, but as a material entity and not as a performance; hence, American companies did not often rely on this protection to "authorize" their products. For further information on this litigation, see Jeanne Thomas Allen, "Copyright and Early Theater, Vaudeville, and Film Competition," in John Fell, ed., *Film before Griffith* (Berkeley: University of California Press, 1984), 176–187; David Levy, "Edison Sales Policy and the Continuous Action Film, 1904–1906," in Fell, *Film before Griffith*,

207–222; Janet Staiger, "Combination and Litigation: Structures of US Film Distribution, 1891–1917," *Cinema Journal* 23.2 (Winter 1984), 42–47; and André Gaudreault, "The Infringement of Copyright Laws and Its Effects (1900–1906)," in Thomas Elsaesser, ed., *Early Cinema: Space, Frame, Narrative* (London: British Film Institute, 1990), 114–122.

2. Susan Strasser, *Satisfaction Guaranteed: The Making of the American Mass Market* (New York: Pantheon, 1989), 34–35.

3. Crowell is quoted in Arthur Marquette, *Brands, Trademarks, and Good Will: The Story of Quaker Oats* (New York: McGraw-Hill, 1967), 67. Crowell's comment seems typical—see, for instance, the quotes from turn-of-the-century writers, advertisers, and marketing entrepreneurs in Richard Ohmann, *Selling Culture: Magazines, Markets, and Class at the Turn of the Century* (London: Verso, 1996), 109.

4. Both Staiger and Hansen recognize the convergence of early cinema and consumerism through advertising: see Janet Staiger, "Announcing Wares, Winning Patrons, Voicing Ideals: Thinking about the History and Theory of Film Advertising," *Cinema Journal* 29.3 (Spring 1990), 3–31; and Miriam Hansen, *Babel and Babylon: Spectatorship in American Silent Cinema* (Cambridge, Mass.: Harvard University Press, 1991), 85.

5. Ohmann refers to *J. Walter Thompson Advertising* (1896) in *Selling Culture,* 193; but see, also, Emily Fogg Mead, "The Place of Advertising in Modern Business," *Journal of Political Economy* 9 (March 1901), 234.

6. This quote comes from Daniel Pope, *The Making of Modern Advertising* (New York: Basic Books, 1973), 5.

7. *Trade-Marks, Trade-Names, Unfair Competition* (Washington, D.C.: Williams C. Linton, 1923), 2. I found this legal treatise in the George Kleine Collection.

8. For a thorough study of trademarks in early cinema, see Harold Brown, *Physical Characteristics of Early Films as Aids to Identification* (Brussels: International Federation of Film Archives, 1990). Both Staiger and Leslie Midkaff DeBauche also focus on trademarks as an early advertising strategy, but for a slightly later period—see Staiger, "The Hollywood Mode of Production to 1930," in David Bordwell, Janet Staiger, and Kristin Thompson, *The Classical Hollywood Cinema: Film Style and Mode of Production to 1960* (New York: Columbia University Press, 1985), 99–100; Staiger, "Announcing Wares," 4–7; and DeBauche, "Advertising and the Movies, 1908–1915," *Film Reader* 6 (1985), 121–122.

9. For evidence of this, see the ads from around 1900 in such mass magazines as *Ladies' Home Journal, McClure's, Munsey's,* and *Saturday Evening Post.*

10. The story of Edison's patent strategy, and its enormous consequences for early American cinema, is well known; perhaps the best recent source is Charles Musser, *Before the Nickelodeon: Edwin S. Porter and the Edison Manufacturing Company* (Berkeley: University of California Press, 1991).

11. Biograph also tended to manufacture such film subjects—see, for instance, *Rip Van Winkle* (1903), *Kit Carson* (1904), *The Widow and the Only Man* (1904), and *The Moonshiners* (1904). Charles Musser, *The Emergence of Cinema to 1907,* vol. 1 of *History of the American Cinema* (New York: Scribner's, 1991), 349, 351, 352, 380, 390, 465.

12. Musser, *Before the Nickelodeon,* 263–264.

13. See, for instance, the Edison ad in *NYC* (9 January 1904), 1113.

14. "Hypnotized by a Poster Man," *Bill* (1 June 1901), 2. The poster itself is reproduced in *Bill* (18 May 1901), 3.

15. See, for instance, the "Star" Films ad in *NYC* (6 June 1903), 368. See, also, his claim in the 1903 "Star" Films Catalog that Georges Méliès's films "ha[d] given new life to the

trade at a time when it was dying out"—quoted in Lewis Jacobs, *The Rise of the American Film: A Critical History* (New York: Harcourt, Brace, 1939), 30.

16. Méliès also used a strategy on which some American companies relied—that is, copyrighting individual film subjects and depositing a paper print copy at the Library of Congress—which proved no more effectual in stopping the practice of duping.

17. Paolo Cherchi Usai, "(Ein kleines) Heldenleben. Die Entdeckung der Filme von Georges Méliès," *KINtop* 2 (1993), 83–92.

18. Paolo Cherchi Usai reminds me that, from the very beginning, Gaumont also adopted a similar strategy with its trademark marguerite, but Gaumont's presence on the American market was minimal until 1907 or 1908.

19. The earliest that seems to have survived is "Very Important Notice," *The Pathé Cinematograph-Films Catalogue* (London, May 1903), 12.

20. An early Pathé title card, from *The Ingenious Soubrette* (1902), is reproduced in Suzanne Richard, "Pathé, marque de fabrique: vers une nouvelle méthode pour la datation des copies anciennes," *1895* 10 (1991), 22. As Richard shows, the Pathé trademark design changed slightly from year to year, which has proved very useful in dating archive prints.

21. I borrow some language here from *Trade-Marks, Trade-Names, Unfair Competition*, 3.

22. Pathé's representative in the United States, J. A. Berst, also is said to have inserted a red rooster trading card in every reel of film the company sold, adopting a strategy American manufacturers of other commodities had used for several decades—see Ohmann, *Selling Culture*, 199, 201.

23. The one American company that did develop a trademark was not a manufacturer but a sales agent, Kleine Optical, and its distinctive brand of a K superimposed over an O (encircled in a double ring) circulated primarily in trade press ads (addressing rental exchanges and exhibitors), beginning in the summer of 1904.

CHAPTER 2. "PATHÉ GOES TO TOWN"

1. Charles Musser, *Before the Nickelodeon: Edwin S. Porter and the Edison Manufacturing Company* (Berkeley: University of California Press, 1991), 284.

2. Robert Allen, *Vaudeville and Film, 1895–1915: A Study of Media Interaction* (New York: Arno Press, 1980), 203–205. From more recent research done by students at the University of North Carolina, Allen concludes that, at least in that southern state, "each city's permanent film exhibition . . . was preceded by at least five years of irregular exhibition"—see "Dialogue," *Cinema Journal* 35.3 (Spring 1996), 97. My own research suggests that, in many other states and cities, film exhibition was much more regular, especially in family vaudeville.

3. Here, I draw on a schematic set of categories (preconditions of emergence, conditions of emergence, textual construction) for outlining the historical development of a major discursive practice, which itself is drawn from Michel Foucault—Marie-Christine Leps, *Apprehending the Criminal: The Production of Deviance in Nineteenth-Century Discourse* (Durham, N.C.: Duke University Press, 1992), 9. In doing so, I seek to offer not only a more accurate description of events but, to address Allen's challenge to cinema historians, also an analysis of "explanatory adequacy"—see "Dialogue," 76–77.

4. These catalogs are collected in Charles Musser, *Thomas A. Edison Papers: A Guide to Motion Picture Catalogs by American Producers and Distributors, 1894–1908: A Microfilm Edition* (Frederick, Md.: University Publications of America, 1985).

5. These managers' reports can be found in the Keith-Albee Collection at the University of Iowa Library. See M. Alison Kibler, "The Keith/Albee Collection: The Vaudeville Industry, 1894–1935," *Books at Iowa* (April 1992), 7–23.

6. Charles Musser, *The Emergence of Cinema to 1907*, vol. 1 of *History of the American Cinema* (New York: Scribner's, 1991), 297–417. See, also, Allen, *Vaudeville and Film*, 218; Fred C. Aiken, "Ethics of Film Renting Worthy of Deep Study," *SW* (27 June 1908), 24.

7. When the Orpheum reopened in Los Angeles, in the fall of 1903, it featured *A Trip to the Moon* on its initial program—see "Amusements," *LAT* (7 September 1903), 1.

8. Musser, *The Emergence of Cinema*, 325. See, also, Martin Sopocy, "French and British Influences in Porter's *American Fireman*," *Film History* 1.2 (1987), 137–148. Similarly, Porter had studied Méliès's *Bluebeard* in order to make his own *Jack and the Beanstalk* for Edison.

9. "Denver," *Bill* (19 September 1903), 6, and (5 December 1903), 10.

10. *New York Clipper* listed new sites in New Bedford, Fall River, Lowell, Lynn, and Lawrence (all cities of around 100,000 people in Massachusetts); other sites from Cleveland to Saint Joseph, Lincoln, and Duluth; and still others in Los Angeles, San Francisco, Portland, Seattle, and Tacoma.

11. Shepard first made a success of the Sunday concert of moving pictures at the Grand Opera House in Lowell, Massachusetts, but soon he was booking tours from Connecticut to Maine. Shepard operated somewhat like Lyman Howe, but he renewed his films much more frequently, repeatedly visited the cities on his circuit, and offered illustrated songs between reels of film. See Robert Grau, *The Theatre of Science* (New York: Benjamin Blom, 1914), 32–33; and Charles Musser and Carol Nelson, *High-Class Moving Pictures: Lyman H. Howe and the Forgotten Era of Traveling Exhibition, 1880–1920* (Princeton, N.J.: Princeton University Press, 1991), 142–144.

12. At least four summer parks in the Boston area were showing films—see "Massachusetts," *NYC* (25 June 1904), 407. Another four sites were reported in Oakland—"California," *NYC* (30 July 1904), 527. In Duluth, moving pictures were reported to be "a big card" at the Bijou Theatre—"Minnesota," *NYC* (13 August 1904), 571.

13. Musser, *The Emergence of Cinema*, 367. See, also, "Notes from Miles Brothers," *Bill* (27 June 1908), 31; "Kinematography in the United States," *MPW* (11 July 1914), 175; and Lewis Jacobs, *The Rise of the American Film: A Critical History* (New York: Harcourt, Brace, 1939), 52–53.

14. See the first Eugene Cline ad in *NYC* (27 February 1904), 15; and the first Film Rental Bureau ad in *NYC* (7 May 1904), 263. Within months, the latter was emphasizing its "superior weekly service"—see the Film Rental Bureau ad in *NYC* (9 July 1904), 458.

15. See the George K. Spoor ad in *NYC* (26 March 1904), 116; the Kleine Optical ad in *NYC* (9 April 1904), 164; and the Great Western Vaudeville Circuit ad in *NYC* (18 June 1904), 386.

16. "Massachusetts," *NYC* (14 May 1904), 271; "New Jersey," *NYC* (14 May 1904), 269; and "New Jersey," *NYC* (21 May 1904), 306.

17. Unless otherwise cited, the primary sources for this and the following paragraphs are vaudeville listings (by state and/or city) in *New York Clipper* and *Billboard*. "Amusements," *LAT* (23 September 1903), 1. The Iroquois Theater fire closed all of the theaters and vaudeville houses in Chicago for several months during the early spring of 1904. Recently found among my own parents' collections was a "memorial edition" probably handed down from my grandfather: an incomplete copy of Marshall Everett, *The Great Chicago Theater Disaster* (Chicago: George Cline, 1904).

18. "Amusements," *LAT* (4 October 1903), 1, and (1 November 1903), 1.1. See, also, the Keith Programme for 9 November 1903—Providence Clipping Book 1903–1904, KA.

19. See the Lyric Theater ad in *Ore* (22 May 1904), 19. *Robinson Crusoe*, however, was advertised as an Edison moving picture.

20. See, for instance, the *Pawtucket Gazette* article on the Keith Theatre program (1 January 1904)—Clipping Book 1903–1904, KA. As Ben Brewster reminds me, *The Poachers* was the United States title of *Desperate Poaching Affray*, produced by Haggar & Sons but distributed outside South Wales by British Gaumont.

21. See the *Providence News* article on the Keith Theatre program (15 March 1904)—Clipping Book 1903–1904, KA; and "Chicago," *Bill* (2 April 1904), 4.

22. Edison first advertised the film in *NYC* (7 November 1903), 896.

23. See the Kleine Optical ad in *NYC* (26 December 1903), 1067; and the Edison ad in *NYC* (9 January 1904), 1113.

24. Musser, *The Emergence of Cinema*, 366. See, also, the *Providence News* article on the Keith Theatre program (6 February 1904)—Clipping Book 1903–1904, KA.

25. See the Kleine Optical ads in *NYC* (18 June 1904), 400, and (3 September 1904), 647; and the Kinetograph ad in *NYC* (20 August 1904), 584. Edison and Lubin claimed to offer "original" versions of the film in side-by-side ads in *NYC* (23 July 1904), 508. A synopsis of Lubin's "original" (actually a remake) was published in the *Philadelphia Inquirer* (26 June 1904)—reprinted in Stanley Kauffmann and Bruce Henstell, eds., *American Film Criticism: From the Beginnings to Citizen Kane* (New York: Liveright, 1972), 5.

26. For one of the earliest "histories," which credits Méliès and Edison with "stirring up" interest in story films, see "Picture Stories," *VFI* (21 September 1907), 3.

27. Pathé's *Aladdin and His Lamp* (a 230-meter film released in 1901) was shown along with *The Destruction of Mt. Pelée* (perhaps also Pathé's version) as part of Selig Polyscope's program at the Ingersoll Park theater the last week of July—see the Ingersoll Park ad in *Iowa State Register and Leader* (22 July 1902), 2.

28. See the Edison catalogs of September 1902 and May 1903; the Edison ad in *NYC* (1 November 1902), 808; and the Lubin ad in *NYC* (28 February 1903), 36.

29. See the American Vitagraph ad in *NYC* (21 March 1903), 108.

30. See the American Vitagraph Catalog (ca. fall 1903), 3–6. *Don Quixote* was first announced in a special Pathé-Frères supplement, London, August 1903.

31. See, for instance, the Edison ad for Urban Trading's *Daylight Burglary* in *NYC* (20 June 1903), 408; and the Biograph ads in *NYC* (10 October 1903), 796, (31 October 1903), 872, (21 November 1903), 944, (28 November 1903), 968, and (12 December 1903), 1016.

32. See the Edison ad in *NYC* (7 November 1903), 896. The film also appeared in Edison's January 1904 catalog, entitled *The Rise and Fall of Napoleon the Great*.

33. See the Edison ads in *NYC* (2 January 1904), 1077, and (16 January 1904), 1136.

34. Pathé-Frères first referred to its trademark red titles in its London catalog, May 1903. According to later catalogs that year, both *Don Quixote* and *Puss-in-Boots*, for instance, were available in hand-colored versions.

35. See the Harbach & Co. ad in *NYC* (16 April 1904), 188.

36. Unless otherwise cited, the primary sources for this paragraph are the 1903–1904 Keith Managers' Reports, KA.

37. Musser and Nelson, *High-Class Moving Pictures*, 134–142. For thorough studies of the American fascination with Napoleon at the turn of the century, see Theodore P. Greene,

America's Heroes: The Changing Models of Success in American Magazines (New York: Oxford University Press, 1970), 110–165; and William Uricchio and Roberta Pearson, *Reframing Culture: The Case of the Vitagraph Quality Films* (Princeton, N.J.: Princeton University Press, 1993), 111–159.

38. Musser and Nelson, *High-Class Moving Pictures*, 143. See, also, the *Providence Telegram* article on the Keith Theatre program (5 April 1904)—Clipping Book 1903–1904—KA. By the turn of the century, in one biography or work of fiction after another (in English and French), Marie Antoinette had become a "sentimental" heroine, a model of "sisterly" tenderness and bravery—see Terry Castle, "Marie Antoinette Obsession," *Representations* 38 (Spring 1992), 19–20.

39. See the Kleine Optical ad in *NYC* (6 August 1904), 546.

40. See the Pathé Cinematograph ads in *NYC* (27 August 1904), 613, and (3 September 1904), 644. The first of these was positioned opposite a Lubin ad; the second was positioned just below an Edison ad.

41. "What Does It Mean?" *MPW* (26 October 1907), 535.

42. See the Pathé Cinematograph ad in *NYC* (24 September 1904), 718.

43. Kleine Optical Company, "Copied Films," *Complete Illustrated Catalogue of Moving Picture Machines, Stereopticons, Slides, Views* (October 1904), 2–3. The catalog, *Edison Films to July 1, 1904* (ca. September 1904), gives its collection of duped Pathé films unusual prominence. *The Life of Napoleon*, for instance, was still playing at the Saint Charles Orpheum in New Orleans in the fall of 1904, according to the *New Orleans Picayune* (18 October 1904), 12—cited in Sylvester Quinn Breard, "A History of the Motion Pictures in New Orleans, 1896–1908" (M.A. thesis, Louisiana State University, 1951), 154.

44. As Musser argues, once Kleine Optical began purchasing Pathé "originals" in June 1904, the company refused to distribute Edison dupes of those films and turned increasingly to Pathé and Biograph product. In October, for instance, Kleine Optical purchased $2,903 and $3,196 of films and merchandise from Pathé and Biograph, respectively, and only $1,650 of material from Edison. See Musser, *Before the Nickelodeon*, 278–279, 482.

45. Kleine Optical Company, "About Moving Pictures," *Complete Illustrated Catalogue*, 30. The first reference to *Christopher Columbus* comes in an Edison ad in *NYC* (18 June 1904), 395. Kleine himself summarized this break, singling out "the beautiful photographic quality" of Pathé prints in contrast to that of Edison's dupes ("in most cases bad, in some instances vile"), in an 11 October 1904 letter to the company—see Box 18: Edison Manufacturing Company, GK.

46. George C. Pratt excerpts this section from Kleine Optical's catalog, but only to focus on the success of *Great Train Robbery*, and Pathé is not identified as the maker of *Christopher Columbus*—Pratt, ed., *Spellbound in Darkness: A History of the Silent Film* (Greenwich, Conn.: New York Graphic Society, 1973), 36–37. Kleine himself pointed out that Kleine Optical had ordered fifteen prints of *The Great Train Robbery* that summer, in an 18 August 1904 letter to W. E. Gilmore—see Box 18: Edison Manufacturing Company, GK.

47. Small traveling exhibitors such as Bert Cook and Fannie Harris also relied on Pathé's entrance into the American market for new supplies of moving pictures—see Kathryn Fuller, *At the Picture Show: Small Town Audiences and the Creation of Movie Fan Culture* (Washington, D.C.: Smithsonian Institution Press, 1996), 10–12. This upsurge in moving picture exhibition may also have been facilitated by the move to consolidate vaudeville houses into circuits—see, for instance, "Vaudeville," *Bill* (26 March 1904), 3; "Big Vaudeville

Combine," *Bill* (25 June 1904), 2; the Keith circuit ad in *NYC* (25 February 1905), 30; the Western Vaudeville Association ad in *NYC* (11 March 1905), 78; and the Affiliated Western Vaudeville ad in *NYC* (15 April 1905), 207.

48. Unless otherwise cited, the primary sources for this and the following paragraphs are vaudeville listings (by state and/or city) in *New York Clipper* and *Billboard*.

49. Vitagraph took over the Colonial Theatre in Lawrence, 24–26 October, and then the Bijou Theatre in Fall River, 27–29 October—"Massachusetts," *NYC* (29 October 1904), 831, and (5 November 1904), 855. In the spring of 1905, Shepard even had one company that reached Des Moines: on 6–7 April, his "High-Class Moving Pictures" (with *The Moonshiners* and *Kit Carson*) was featured at Foster's Opera House; on 9 April, another program (with *The Inauguration of President Roosevelt*) was presented at the Grand Opera House—see the Foster's and Grand ads in *DMRL* (2 April 1905), 3.2, and (9 April 1905), 3.2.

50. See, also, the Film Rental Bureau ad in *NYC* (20 August 1904), 600.

51. See the Pathé ad in *NYC* (25 January 1905), 1141; and the first Miles Brothers ad in *NYC* (25 February 1905), 19. Crescent was the label of Paley & Steiner, a short-lived production company established by William Paley, whose kalatechnoscope service was used in Proctor's vaudeville houses in New York and Newark. Selig Polyscope also tentatively began to shift into film production at this time. See Musser, *The Emergence of Cinema*, 398–405.

52. Eugene Cline also began targeting the vaudeville managers in summer amusement parks—see the Eugene Cline ad in *NYC* (25 March 1905), 126.

53. See, also, "The Theatres," *DMRL* (27 November 1904), 2.6.

54. See, also, the Bijou ad in *DMRL* (23 January 1905), 5.

55. See, also, the Bijou ad in *DMRL* (1 January 1905), 3.3. Méliès's film returned to play for one more week in August at Ingersoll Park in Des Moines. Between January and March, in Lowell, the Boston, Casto, and People's theaters all reported specific film titles on their programs, perhaps a sign of heavy competition.

56. See the Auditorium ads in *Cedar Rapids Daily Republican* (12 July 1904), 8, (2 October 1904), 10, (6 November 1904), 11, and (20 November 1904), 10. *The Great Train Robbery* was shown the week of 13 November, but it received less publicity than *A Trip to the Moon*, the week of 14 August. *Annie's Love Story* or *Roman d'amour* was said to have sold one thousand copies worldwide—see Georges Sadoul, *Histoire générale du cinéma, II: Les Pionniers du cinéma, 1897–1908* (Paris: Denoël, 1948), 312–313.

57. See the People's Theatre ads in *Cedar Rapids Daily Republican* (18 December 1904), 8, (8 January 1905), 8, and (15 January 1905), 6.

58. See the Lyric Theater ads in *Ore* (24 July 1904), 19, and (31 July 1904), 19. The only reference to *The Great Train Robbery* was during that same week of 31 July, when it played at the Star Theater.

59. See the Bijou Theater ads in *Ore* (20 December 1904), 14, and (26 December 1904), 8.

60. See the Grand Theater ads in *Ore* (25 December 1904), 19, and (15 January 1905), 19.

61. See the Grand Theater ad in *Ore* (1 January 1905), 19; and the Star Theater ads in *Ore* (5 March 1905), 19, and (18 June 1905), 29.

62. See, for instance, the Grand Theater ads in *Ore* (18 December 1904), 19, (22 January 1905), 19, (5 February 1905), 19, (26 February 1905), 19, (19 March 1905), 19, and (16 April 1905), 19.

63. The Grand used these latter phrases only twice in its ads in *Ore* (14 May 1905), 27, and (21 May 1905), 29. The only other moving picture "brand" mentioned was Lubin's *The Counterfeiters*, by the Star Theater, in its ad in *Ore* (14 May 1905), 27.

64. Unless otherwise cited, the primary sources for this paragraph are the 1904–1905 Keith Managers' Reports, KA.

65. The Grand Opera House in Pittsburgh (managed by Harry Davis) came under Keith's control in September 1904 and immediately began showing moving pictures.

66. Several Méliès trick films also came in for praise: *The Clockmaker's Dream, The Black Imp,* and *The Crystal Cabinet.*

67. Other Pathé comic subjects and trick films receiving good notices included *Fantastic Fishing, August the Monkey, Fireworks, The Bewitched Lover,* and *The Clown's Revenge.* The managers' reports from Cleveland are particularly interesting because not once does *New York Clipper* refer to films being shown there.

68. *The Incendiary* also received a very favorable notice in the Philadelphia manager's report, 15 May 1905—KA.

69. *The Strike* also received good notices in the Cleveland manager's report, 7 November 1904, and the New York manager's report, 21 November 1904—KA.

70. For the sake of comparison, see the "deep interest" accorded a film of President McKinley's cortege at Proctor's Fifty-eighth Street theater—"New York," *NYC* (5 October 1901), 686.

71. See the Edison Films Catalog Supplement no. 222 (September 1904), and the Eugene Cline & Co. ad in *Bill* (24 September 1904), 40.

72. See the Lubin ad in *NYC* (22 October 1904), 824.

73. See the Pathé ad in *Bill* (31 December 1904), 32.

74. See *Lubin's Films,* May 1905. Fred Balshofer says that when he first came to work for Lubin, in 1905, all he did was make "duplicates of pictures that had been produced in France, by the Méliès company and Pathé-Frères"—see Fred Balshofer and Arthur Miller, *One Reel a Week* (Berkeley: University of California Press, 1967), 5–6.

75. See the Pathé ads in *NYC* (13 May 1905), 316, and (20 May 1905), 336. This coincided with congressional legislation, in 1905, establishing "trademark registration as prima facie evidence of ownership," which Pathé apparently could not take advantage of until the American branch office's incorporation in 1907—see Susan Strasser, *Satisfaction Guaranteed: The Making of the American Mass Market* (New York: Pantheon, 1989), 45.

76. See, for instance, the Pathé ad in *NYC* (6 May 1905), 290; and the Chicago Film Exchange ad in *Bill* (1 July 1905), 47.

77. "Pat-Chats," *Bill* (15 July 1905), 3.

78. Musser, *The Emergence of Cinema,* 386–393, 458.

79. For further information on the production of Vitagraph, Crescent, and Selig during this period, see Musser, *The Emergence of Cinema,* 398–412. Selig reported a big increase in sales of its few film titles that spring and summer—see "Pat-Chats," *Bill* (24 June 1905), 3; and "Pat-Chats," *Bill* (15 July 1905), 3.

80. For further information on Pathé-Frères in France, see Richard Abel, *The Ciné Goes to Town: French Cinema, 1896–1914* (Berkeley: University of California Press, 1994), 20–22.

81. This figure comes from the Pathé ad in *Phono-Ciné-Gazette,* 13 (1 October 1905), 209.

82. The Nickelodeon was credited with opening in 1903, in the special exhibition issue of *Moving Picture World* (15 July 1916), 405. This is a good example of why *Moving Picture World* itself warned readers that, in many of the issue's stories, showmen probably were "shooting the bull."

83. For a good summary of the amusement parlor or penny arcade at the turn of the century, see David Nasaw, *Going Out: The Rise and Fall of Public Amusements* (New York: Basic

Books, 1994), 155–160. See, also, Grau, *The Theatre of Science*, 16–19. The trade press gener-ally paid little attention to this form of commercial entertainment; an exception that links "coin operated machines" with "the moving picture industry" is "Moving Pictures," *Bill* (13 October 1906), 21. *Views and Films Index,* by contrast, tended to keep the two venues sepa-rate: see, for instance, "In the Defense of Slot Machines," *VFI* (21 July 1906), 3; and "Edi-torial Comments," *VFI* (23 February 1907), 3. Rollin Lynde Hartt was among the first to in-sist that "the mutoscope evolved into the biograph, substituting the screen for the peephole"—see Hartt, *The People at Play* (Boston: Houghton Mifflin, 1909), 122.

    84. Nasaw, *Going Out,* 158.

    85. For information on other earlier storefront theaters, see Musser, *The Emergence of Cinema,* 299–303.

    86. A fur merchant from Chicago who had relocated to New York, Adolph Zukor, to-gether with Morris Kohn, invested in the arcade business after a friend, Max Goldstein, drew their attention to Mitchell Mark's successful arcade on 125th Street (which Mark had first developed at the 1901 Buffalo Exposition). Whether or not Zukor opened the Crystal Hall in 1904 or 1905, and whether or not it was successful, still remains uncertain. See Will Irwin, *The House That Shadows Built* (Garden City, N.Y.: Doubleday, Doran, 1928), 3–8, 90–97; Adolph Zukor, *The Public Is Never Wrong* (New York: Putnam's, 1953), 36–40; and Neal Gabler, *An Empire of Their Own: How the Jews Invented Hollywood* (New York: Doubleday, 1988), 17–18, 22.

    87. See "Cincinnati's Contribution to Ancient Picture History," *MPW* (15 July 1916), 390; Marcus Loew, "The Motion Picture and Vaudeville," in Joseph Kennedy, ed., *The Story of the Films* (Chicago: A. W. Shaw, 1927), 286–287; Bosley Crowther, *The Lion's Share* (New York: Garland, 1985), 23–27; and Gabler, *An Empire of Their Own,* 20–21.

    88. For information on Wilson's theater, at 205 San Jacinto, Houston, see "Texas," *NYC* (25 February 1905), 24, and (29 April 1905), 263. Montgomery's theater in Fort Worth is cited prominently in Grau, *The Theatre of Science,* 293.

    89. Musser, *The Emergence of Cinema,* 418–420. See, also, the profiles of Harry Davis in C. G. Bochert, "Live News Notes from Iron City," *SW* (31 August 1907), 11; "Surprising Growth of Motion View Industry," *SW* (23 November 1907), 19; and "The First Nick-elodeon in the States," *MPW* (30 November 1907), 629.

    90. "Philadelphia: Gossip of the Week," *Bill* (21 October 1905), 3; "Philadelphia Pencil-ings," *Bill* (18 November 1905), 6; "Pat-Chats: Adopting the Pittsburgh Idea," *Bill* (2 De-cember 1905), 3; and "Philadelphia," *Bill* (20 January 1906), 7. A later report suggested there were perhaps a dozen in Pittsburgh by January 1906—"To Our Readers," *VFI* (30 June 1906), 3. According to ads in the *Philadelphia Public Ledger,* Lubin was showing films regularly at his Auditorium theater by September 1902—see Linda Woal, "When a Dime Could Buy a Dream: Siegmund Lubin and the Birth of Motion Picture Exhibition," *Film History* 6.2 (Summer 1994), 161. See, also, Musser, *The Emergence of Cinema,* 421–422.

    91. See, for instance, "Chicago," *Bill* (28 October 1905), 12; K. S. Hover, "Police Super-vision in Chicago," *Nick* (January 1909), 11; "Chicago Reports Many Variations in Picture Shows," *MPW* (15 July 1916), 413–414; Crowther, *The Lion's Share,* 27; and Musser, *The Emer-gence of Cinema,* 423. By December, a sign company on State Street was offering "signs for picture parlors and arcades exclusively"—see the Homer Saunders ad in *Bill* (9 December 1905), 40. Several months later, 20th-Century Optiscope was pushing its rental service in as-sociation with the International Theatre—see "Chicago," *Bill* (3 February 1906), 12. Chicago may have been the first city to clearly differentiate, through the disproportionate

licensing fees it charged them, nickelodeons or moving picture shows from penny arcades—see "Amusements," *Revised Municipal Code* (Chicago, 1905), 30–33.

92. "J. Austin Fynes Enterprises," *NYC* (17 March 1906), 108; Robert Grau, "Fortunes in the Moving Picture Field," *Overland Monthly* (April 1911), 396; Grau, *The Theatre of Science*, 18–21; William Fox, "Reminiscences and Observations," in Kennedy, *The Story of the Films*, 309–310; Crowther, *The Lion's Share*, 26–27; and Gabler, *An Empire of Their Own*, 65–66.

93. "Cleveland, O., Boasts of Some 'Pioneer' Picture Men," *MPW* (15 July 1916), 393. A year later, Bullock's company was running twelve nickelodeons in Cleveland—"Trade Notes," *VFI* (10 November 1906), 6. See, also, "Moving Picture News from Everywhere," *VFI* (19 October 1907), 4. About the same time, L. E. Quinnet opened the first moving picture theater in Montreal—see "Canada," *Bill* (27 June 1908), 37. It was then, too, that ads for printing posters and handbills specifically for "moving picture shows" began to appear with more frequency—see, for instance, the ad for Donaldson Litho Company of Newport, Kentucky, in *Bill* (28 October 1905), 36.

94. See the Miles Brothers ads in *NYC* (27 May 1905), 368, and (15 July 1905), 540, and in *Bill* (5 August 1905), 48. Miles Brothers, for instance, had Paul Howse of White City testify in support of its service in *Bill* (9 August 1905), 48. Edward Wagenknecht remembers seeing his first moving pictures at "The Chutes," a small West Side amusement park, in 1905 or 1906—see Edward Wagenknecht, *The Movies in the Age of Innocence* (Norman: University of Oklahoma Press, 1962), 8. See, also, the ad for National Film Renting (formerly Spoor's Film Renting Bureau) in *Bill* (9 September 1905), 48. National Film Renting claimed to have testimonials from at least two hundred clients, one of which may have been Ingersoll Park in Des Moines—see "Music and Drama," *Des Moines Mail and Times* (19 May 1906), 6.

95. See the Kleine Optical ads in *NYC* (9 September 1905), 723, and *Bill* (16 September 1905), 13, and the National Film Renting ad in *Bill* (9 September 1905), 48. One sign that many of the vaudeville houses were catering to women and children, especially with their matinee programs, came as a result of a fire at the Grand Opera House in Pittsburgh, 2 June 1905: most of the audience for the four o'clock show were "ladies and children"—see "Editorial Notes" and "Pittsburgh Disaster," *Bill* (10 June 1905), 10, 11. See, also, "Chicago," *Bill* (2 April 1904), 4.

96. Musser, *The Emergence of Cinema*, 374.

97. See the Kleine Optical ad in *NYC* (30 September 1905), 824.

98. Kleine Optical purchased $2,350 of material from Pathé in June, $5,292 in July, $2,345 in August, and $3,635 in September; only once during those months did it purchase more from Biograph, $3,802 in September—see Musser, *Before the Nickelodeon*, 482. See, also, Kleine Optical's *Complete Illustrated Catalog* (November 1905), 272.

99. Kleine Optical first began to assert its leading position in an ad in *Bill* (28 January 1905), 40.

100. At least two Méliès titles also received notice, *Faust and Marguerite* at the Metropolitan in Duluth and *The Automobile Chase* at the Aerial Garden in New York—see "Minnesota," *NYC* (1 July 1905), 483, and "New York City," *NYC* (8 July 1905), 504. Unless otherwise cited, the primary sources for this paragraph are the 1905–1906 Keith Managers' Reports, KA.

101. See, also, the Ingersoll Park ad in *DMRL* (27 August 1905), 2.6. The film also played at the Bijou in Duluth the first week of July—"Minnesota," *NYC* (8 July 1905), 508.

102. See, also, "Massachusetts," *NYC* (16 September 1905), 751.

103. The film also played at the Globe Theatre in Saint Louis in early October—"Missouri," *NYC* (7 October 1905), 831.

104. See, for instance, the 9 October 1905 program at Keith's Theatre in Boston, which featured four Pathé films out of a total of five, or the 5 February 1906 program at Keith's Theatre in New York, which featured four Pathé films—*The Prince of Wales at Lanori, Victims of the Storm, The Deserter,* and *The Fancy Garden Party*—all of which then were shown two weeks later at Keith's in Philadelphia—KA.

105. "Massachusetts," *NYC* (10 February 1906), 1303, and (17 February 1906), 1331. The only titles the *NYC* repeatedly called attention to, perhaps in a move to stigmatize the cinema's appeal, were Lubin's and Houseman's competing films of the Britt-Nelson fight.

106. One of the earliest descriptions of nickelodeon programs appears in "Our Head Office Boy Wants to Be a Reporter," *VFI* (25 April 1906), 10–11.

107. *Billboard*'s "Moving Picture Shows" column first appeared in the 7 April 1906 issue; it was appearing almost weekly by May. See, also, "Fire at the Circle Theatre," *Bill* (10 February 1906), 14; "Theatre Burns," *Bill* (10 March 1906), 14; and "Moving Picture Shows," *Bill* (7 April 1906), 6.

108. See the Bijou ads in *DMRL* (10 December 1905), 2.2, and (31 December 1905), 3.11.

109. See the Grand ad in *Ore* (30 July 1905), 29.

110. See the Grand ads in *Ore* (2 July 1905), 29, and (23 July 1905), 29.

111. See the Grand and Star ads in *Ore* (6 August 1905), 29, (20 August 1905), 29, (17 September 1905), 29, (8 October 1905), 29, and (22 October 1905), 29.

112. See the Star ads in *Ore* (26 November 1905), 29, (17 December 1905), 29, and (7 January 1906), 29.

113. "Pat-Chats: The Film Industry," *Bill* (30 December 1905), 7.

114. The "Family Theatres" of the Consolidated Vaudeville Managers Association were all located in Illinois, Michigan, Indiana, Ohio, and Wisconsin—see the association's ad in *NYC* (25 November 1905), 1032. A second circuit, Inter-State Amusement, was located in Texas, Arkansas, and Louisiana—see its ad in *Bill* (19 August 1905), 32. A third circuit called the Unique covered Minnesota, Manitoba, Wisconsin, and Illinois—see "Pat-Chats," *Bill* (9 September 1905), 3.

115. "Nickel Vaudeville," *Var* (17 March 1906), 4. For the trade weekly's initial distinction between "high-class" and "family" vaudeville, see *Var* (30 December 1905), 6. That the "high-class" vaudeville circuits were in the process of establishing a giant combine that linked Keith's, Proctor's, Poli's, and the Western Orpheum theaters all together, with Keith as the central booking agent, may also have encouraged the development of both "family" vaudeville and moving picture theaters—see, for instance, "Keith and Proctor Unite," *NYDM* (19 May 1906), 18; "Poli Joins the Merger," *NYDM* (26 May 1906), 18; and "The Big Merger Completed," *NYDM* (23 June 1906), 16.

116. George Kleine identified April 1906 as an important date in the emerging industry: because of the nickelodeons, film subjects began to acquire a much shortened "shelf life"—George Kleine, "Optical Projection in the Past Half Century," *SW* (27 June 1908), 15.

117. "Fire at the Circle Theatre," *Bill* (10 February 1906), 14; and "News," *VFI* (30 June 1906), 6.

118. See, for instance, "J. Austin Fynes Enterprises," *NYC* (17 March 1906), 108; "Nickel Theatre Pays Well," *CT* (8 April 1906), 3; "A General Outlook: Moving Pictures in Manhattan," *VFI* (12 May 1906), 4; and "Carl Laemmle Made Start in Chicago Storefront," *MPW* (15 July 1916), 420. According to an unpublished document, what convinced

Laemmle to open his own nickelodeon was a visit to Hollenberg's Chicago Theatre—see Carl Laemmle, "This Business of Motion Pictures" (AFI Center for Advanced Film Studies, Los Angeles), quoted in Musser, *The Emergence of Cinema*, 422.

119. "Louiseville," *Bill* (7 April 1906), 12; "Miscellaneous," *Bill* (6 May 1906), 30; "Special Correspondence from Important Points" and "The Moving Picture Shows," *Bill* (12 May 1906), 8, 9, and 37; "Davis a Ten-Center," *Var* (31 May 1906), 13; and "Moving Picture Shows," *Bill* (29 December 1906), 41. According to *Billboard*, "theatorium" came from one of the earliest moving picture entrepreneurs in Pittsburgh, T. H. Harion. The difficulties historians have in establishing precisely when viable storefront moving picture theaters first opened in many cities is particularly evident in Robert Kirk Headley, *Exit: A History of Movies in Baltimore* (Baltimore: Robert Kirk Headley, 1974).

120. Musser, *The Emergence of Cinema*, 425–427. After expanding his Sunday concerts to a dozen vaudeville houses (from New York City to Washington, D.C., Asbury Park, New Jersey, and Fall River, Massachusetts), Shepard took over the Savoy Theatre in New Bedford, Massachusetts, in May 1906, and began presenting regular moving picture programs—"Massachusetts," *NYC* (2 June 1906), 410, and (9 June 1906), 433. Grau credits Shepard and Isman with being the chief architects of the nickelodeon boom, in *The Theatre of Science*, 16, 28–35, 300.

121. "To Our Readers," *VFI* (30 June 1906), 3; and "Atlantic City," *Bill* (21 July 1906), 7. At least four new rental exchanges, all based in Chicago, began advertising in *Billboard* from April through June 1906: the American Film Company, the Inter-Ocean Film Exchange, the United States Film Exchange, and the Temple Film Company.

122. See, for instance, such family vaudeville houses as the Empire (Los Angeles), the Dewey (Oakland), the Dreamland (Decatur), the Electric Theatre (Waterloo), and the Zoo (Toledo), as reported in *New York Clipper* and *Billboard* throughout 1905. By October 1905, Davis also was using "cinematograph" to designate his film programs at the Grand in Pittsburgh—see "Pennsylvania," *NYC* (28 October 1905), 921.

123. See, for instance, the Kleine Optical ad in *NYC* (30 September 1905), 824; and the Miles Brothers ad in *Bill* (4 November 1905), 38. There were more than two hundred Pathé titles listed in the Eugene Cline Catalog (Chicago, 1906), 19–20. Kleine Optical also singled out its Pathé films of "foreign" views for Hale Tours, which the company originally had serviced at Electric Park in Kansas City in 1905—see the Kleine Optical ad in *Bill* (17 March 1906), 47.

124. See, for instance, the Pathé ads in *NYC* (30 December 1905), 1156; and in *Bill* (6 January 1906), 34.

125. Kleine, "Optical Projection in the Past Half Century," *SW* (27 June 1908), 15.

126. Throughout February 1906, according to its ads in *Billboard*, Pathé released two subjects per week.

127. "The Pictures: From the Standpoint of One Who Shows Them," *VFI* (19 May 1906), 6. The Muellers reported two hundred moving picture machines then in operation at Coney Island, a figure that probably included those in penny arcades.

128. "Pat-Chats," *Bill* (1 July 1905), 3, and (15 July 1905), 3. Even Edison implicitly acknowledged the city's importance by listing its Chicago dealers first (they constituted fully one-third of the total) in an ad in *NYC* (9 December 1905), 1088.

129. See, for instance, the Pathé ads in *NYC* (30 September 1905), 828, (14 October 1905), 869, and (28 October 1905), 930.

130. "Moving Picture Makers Organize," *NYC* (23 December 1905), 1118.

131. See, for instance, the Pathé ads in *Phono-Ciné-Gazette* (1 October 1905), 209; and in *Bill* (10 March 1906), 40. Balshofer recalls that Pathé also was selling its cameras and tripods in the United States, and he certainly was using a "Pathé field camera" when he first began making films in October 1907—see Balshofer and Miller, *One Reel a Week*, 6, 11–12. The French company might have wanted to keep such sales quiet in order not to provoke Edison to focus on its camera's possible infringement on Edison patents. Biograph's successful defense against Edison's litigation in U.S. Circuit Court, Southern District of New York, was reported in "Moving Pictures in Court," *Bill* (7 April 1906), 10; and in "Decision regarding Moving Pictures," *NYC* (7 April 1906), 206.

132. "To Our Readers," *VFI* (9 June 1906), 3. See, also, the Pathé ad for "MOVING PICTURES. MACHINES. SUPPLIES. FILMS," in *VFI* (25 April 1906), 12.

133. See the Grand Theater ad in *Ore* (8 April 1906), 29.

134. "Editorial," *VFI* (28 July 1906), 3.

135. Throughout May and June, Pathé ads in *Views and Films Index* listed three to six new subjects per week. See, also, the Pathé ad in *VFI* (4 August 1906), 11. All this suggests that a relatively reliable distribution system was in place by 1906 and that exhibitors now had advance notice each week of what film titles would be available and when; by contrast, Janet Staiger dates this development as coming much later, in 1909—"Announcing Wares, Winning Patrons, Voicing Ideals: Thinking about the History and Theory of Film Advertising," *Cinema Journal* 29.3 (Spring 1990), 5–7.

136. "Moving Pictures," *Bill* (13 October 1906), 21. This figure is for initial orders delivered from Paris, not for additional orders that may have been requested later for the more popular titles. If certain Edison films seem to have sold even more prints (the 1906 *Train Wreckers*, for instance, sold 157), that is because its figures were cumulative, covering one or more years—see Musser, *Before the Nickelodeon*, 317.

137. Musser, *Before the Nickelodeon*, 328. See, also, "Theatres and the Pictures: An Attitude Explained," *VFI* (7 September 1907), 3.

138. For the best analysis of these concepts, although applied to a later period, see Janet Staiger, "Standardization and Differentiation: The Reinforcement and Dispersion of Hollywood's Practices," in David Bordwell, Janet Staiger, and Kristin Thompson, *The Classical Hollywood Cinema: Film Style and Mode of Production to 1960* (New York: Columbia University Press, 1985), 96–112. The quote comes from Bill Brown, who argues that, fifty years earlier, the Beadles achieved something similar with the dime novel western—see "Reading the West: Cultural and Historical Background," in Brown, ed., *Reading the West: An Anthology of Dime Westerns* (Boston: Bedford Books, 1997), 22.

139. See *The Americanization of Edward Bok: The Autobiography of a Dutch Boy Fifty Years After* (New York: Scribner's, 1921)—quoted in Richard Ohmann, *Selling Culture: Magazines, Markets, and Class at the Turn of the Century* (London: Verso, 1996), 229. The analogy that Ohmann draws between mass magazines and stores may be usefully extended to include nickelodeons—see Ohmann, *Selling Culture*, 223–225.

ENTR'ACTE 2. THE COLOR OF NITRATE

1. Until recently, film archives could not or chose not to reproduce color viewing copies of surviving positive or negative film prints. Color in early cinema was the subject of the

1995 Amsterdam Workshop, organized by the Nederlands Filmmuseum, as well as the 1995 Udine conference in Italy.

2. William Leach, *Land of Desire: Merchants, Power, and the Rise of a New American Culture* (New York: Pantheon, 1993), 9.

3. Villiers de l'Isle-Adam's "The Heavenly Billboard" is quoted in Rosalind Williams, *Dream Worlds: Mass Consumption in Late Nineteenth-Century France* (Berkeley: University of California Press, 1982), 85–86. This story was first published in *La Renaissance littéraire et artistique* (30 November 1873) and then republished in *Contes cruels* (1883).

4. Williams, *Dream Worlds*, 84. See, also Christoph Asendorf, *Batteries of Life: On the History of Things and Their Perception in Modernity*, trans. Don Reneau (Berkeley: University of California Press, 1993), 160–161.

5. See, for instance, Theodore Peterson, *Magazines in the Twentieth Century* (Urbana: University of Illinois Press, 1956), 5; Robert Jay, *The Trade Card in Nineteenth-Century America* (Columbia: University of Missouri Press, 1987), 99–100; Leach, *Land of Desire*, 44–45; and Ellen Gruber Garvey, *The Adman in the Parlor: Magazines and the Gendering of Consumer Culture, 1880s-1910s* (New York: Oxford University Press, 1996), 19–25.

6. Peter Marzio, *The Democratic Art: Pictures for a 19th-Century America* (Boston: Godine, 1979), xi.

7. Neil Harris, "Color and Media: Some Comparisons and Speculations," in *Cultural Excursions: Marketing Appetites and Cultural Tastes in Modern America* (Chicago: University of Chicago Press, 1990), 320.

8. Richard Ohmann, "What Capitalists Needed," in *Selling Culture: Magazines, Markets, and Class at the Turn of the Century* (London: Verso, 1996), 48–61. See, also, Michael Orvell, *The Real Thing: Imitation and Authenticity in American Culture, 1880–1940* (Chapel Hill: University of North Carolina Press, 1989), 42–44.

9. Emily Fogg Mead, "The Place of Advertising in Modern Business," *Fame* 10 (April 1901), 163, 166. See, also, Ohmann, "Moving the Goods," in *Selling Culture*, 62–80; and Susan Strasser, *Satisfaction Guaranteed: The Making of the American Mass Market* (New York: Pantheon, 1989), 19.

10. *Art Amateur* (December 1894)—quoted in Marzio, *The Democratic Art*, 194. See, also, Williams, *Dream Worlds*, 84.

11. Ohmann, "Advertising: New Practices, New Relations," in *Selling Culture*, 81–117; and Strasser, *Satisfaction Guaranteed*, 89–123. See, also, Frank Luther Mott, *A History of American Magazines, 1885–1905* (Cambridge: Harvard University Press, 1957), 20–34.

12. Leach, *Land of Desire*, 55–61. Soon after its first issue in 1899, L. Frank Baum's *Show Window* became an indispensable journal to the "window-trimmers" responsible for decorating such department stores.

13. Leach, *Land of Desire*, 47.

14. Elizabeth Wilson, *The Sphinx in the City: Urban Life, the Control of Disorder, and Women* (Berkeley: University of California Press, 1991), 8. Descriptions of nickelodeons as products of Aladdin and his "magic lamp" appear quite early—see, for instance, "Kinematography in the United States," *MPW* (11 July 1914), 175. The best studies of women as primary spectators/consumers of early cinema are Kathy Peiss, *Cheap Amusements: Working Women and Leisure in Turn-of-the-Century New York* (Philadelphia: Temple University Press, 1986), and Lauren Rabinowitz, *For the Love of Pleasure: Women, Movies, and Culture in Turn-of-the-Century Chicago* (New Brunswick: Rutgers University Press, 1998).

15. These representative figures are drawn from "Our Head Office Boy Wants to Be a Reporter," *VFI* (25 April 1906), 10–11; and "An Unexplored Field and Its Possibilities," *VFI* (6 October 1906), 3–4.

16. See the Edison ad in *NYC* (5 July 1902), 424. See also the reference to "colored films" in the Harbach & Co. ad in *NYC* (17 May 1902), 284.

17. See the Edison ad in *NYC* (16 August 1902), 552.

18. See the Selig ad in *NYC* (22 November 1902), 875.

19. See the Lubin ad in *NYC* (7 May 1904), 244.

20. Managers' Reports, Keith Theatres, Boston (25 January 1904) and Philadelphia (22 February 1904)—KA. See, also, the *Providence News* article (15 March 1904)—Providence Clipping Book, 1903–1904, KA.

21. Musser suggests that Lubin may have been experimenting with a toning process, but evidence is lacking to support that possibility—see Charles Musser, *The Emergence of Cinema to 1907*, vol. 1 of *History of the American Cinema* (New York: Scribner's, 1991), 398.

22. Simultaneous with the Méliès office opening, British Gaumont ran a rare ad promoting its "biotint films in natural colors" (the titles were travel views)—see the Gaumont ad in *NYC* (23 May 1903), 324.

23. See the "Star" Films ad in *Bill* (7 November 1903), 24.

24. "Clever Moving Pictures," *LAT* (11 October 1903), 6.2. See, also, "Amusements and Entertainments," *LAT* (4 October 1903), 1.1, and (31 October 1903), 1.

25. Managers' Reports, Keith Theatres, Philadelphia (5 October 1903) and (19 October 1903) and Providence (9 November 1903)—KA. See, also, the Keith Programme for 9 November 1903—Providence Clipping Book 1903–1904, KA.

26. Managers' Reports, Keith Theatres, Washington (26 October 1903), Boston (11 November 1903), and Cleveland (23 November 1903)—KA.

27. Charles Musser and Carol Nelson, *High-Class Moving Pictures: Lyman H. Howe and the Forgotten Era of Traveling Exhibition, 1880–1920* (Princeton, N.J.: Princeton University Press, 1991), 134–136.

28. Ibid., 136–142.

29. Ten years ago, the Cinémathèque Française restored its color positive print of *Don Quixote—Tirages et restaurations de la Cinémathèque Française, II* (Paris: La Cinémathèque Française, 1987), 47. See the Managers' Reports, Keith Theatres, Washington (7 December 1903), Boston (22 February 1904), and Philadelphia (7 March 1904)—KA. See, also, a *Providence Telegram* article on the Keith Theatre program (5 April 1904)—Providence Clipping Book, 1903–1904, KA. Musser and Nelson, *High-Class Moving Pictures*, 143.

30. See the Lubin ads in *NYC* (7 May 1904), 244; and *Bill* (28 May 1904), 32.

31. See the Kleine Optical ad in *NYC* (20 August 1904), 594; the Eugene Cline ad in *NYC* (20 August 1904), 592; and the Film Rental Bureau ad in *NYC* (20 August 1904), 600.

32. For a good description of the kinds of color lithography developed during the nineteenth century, see Marzio, *The Democratic Art*, 9.

33. See the *Pathé-Frères Catalogue* (Paris, August 1904), 8; J. Marette, "Les Procédés de Coloriage Mécanique des Films," *Bulletin de l'association française des ingénieurs et techniciens du cinéma* 7 (1950), 3; Suzanne Richard, "A Beginner's Guide to the Art of Georges Méliès," in Paolo Cherchi Usai, ed., *A Trip to the Movies: Georges Méliès, Filmmaker and Magician* (Pordenone: Edizioni Biblioteca dell'Immagine, 1991), 43; and "Le Coloris," in Jacques Kermabon, ed., *Pathé, premier empire du cinéma* (Paris: editions Centre Georges Pompidou, 1994), 20–21.

34. The first announcement of Pathé's tinted red-block titles, including the trademark "Coq," appeared in the *Pathé Cinematograph Catalogue* (London, May 1903), 12. One of the earliest extant prints having a red-block title is *Valse excentrique* or *Eccentric Waltz* (1903–1904), at the National Film/Television Archive, London.

35. See the Pathé Cinematograph ad in *NYC* (27 August 1904), 613; and Kleine Optical, *Complete Illustrated Catalogue of Moving Picture Machines, Stereopticons, Slides, Views* (October 1904). See, also, Charles Musser, *Before the Nickelodeon: Edwin S. Porter and the Edison Manufacturing Company* (Berkeley: University of California Press, 1991), 278–279, 482.

36. See the Pathé ad in *NYC* (21 January 1905), 1141.

37. An example of this would be the insistence that the last part of *Joseph Sold by His Brothers* was "hand colored, not tinted"—see the Pathé ad in *NYC* (17 September 1904), 696.

38. See the Pathé ads in *NYC* (10 September 1904), 664, (31 December 1904), 1072, and (28 January 1905), 1161.

39. Managers' Reports, Keith Theatre, Boston, 5 December 1904 and 16 January 1905—KA.

40. See "Kansas City," *Bill* (3 September 1904), 10; "Iowa," *NYC* (31 December 1904), 1053; and the People's Theatre ads in the *Cedar Rapids Daily Republican* (18 December 1904), 8—(8 January 1905), 8.

41. Managers' Reports, Keith Theatres, Boston (19 and 26 December 1904), Providence (2 January 1905), and Philadelphia (30 January and 6 February 1905)—KA. During the period from 1904 to 1906, Georges Méliès seems to have adopted a strategy of producing ever more costly long films, particularly for exhibition at the most respected music halls and café-concerts in Paris. More important, Méliès never industrialized his production and distribution practices as Pathé did. See Richard Abel, *The Ciné Goes to Town: French Cinema, 1896–1914* (Berkeley: University of California Press, 1994), 19, 157–160.

42. Managers' Reports, Keith Theatres, Boston (21 August 1905 and 18 September 1905) and Philadelphia (31 July 1905 and 23 October 1905)—KA.

43. See the Managers' Reports, Keith Theatres, New York (21 and 28 August 1905), Philadelphia (4 September 1905), Providence (18 September 1905), and Boston (2 October 1905)—KA. The magician in *Wonderful Album* does turn out, ironically, to be a charlatan—see André Gaudreault, ed., *Pathé 1900* (Sainte-Foy: Les Presses de l'Université Laval, 1994), 73–75.

44. See the Pathé ads in *Bill* (21 October 1905), 42; and *NYC* (20 January 1906), 1237, and (17 February 1906), 1347.

45. See the Pathé ads in *Bill* (27 January 1906), 35; and *NYC* (27 January 1906), 1248.

46. See the Pathé ads in *Bill* (9 December 1905), 34; and in *NYC* (9 December 1905), 1069.

47. Kleine Optical, *Complete Illustrated Catalog* (November 1905), 272.

48. Throughout May and June, Pathé ads in *Views and Films Index* listed three to six new subjects per week. Slightly later ads flaunted the company's production of 80,000 feet of positive film stock per day—see, for instance, the Pathé ad in *VFI* (4 August 1906), 11.

49. "Pathé-Frères: A Chat with Mr. J. A. Berst," *VFI* (19 May 1906), 8.

50. "Tinting," *VFI* (9 June 1906), 10. Almost six months later, Edison described *The Night before Christmas* as "beautifully mono-tinted"—see the Edison ad in *NYC* (24 November 1906), 1067.

51. See, for instance, the Swanson ad in *Bill* (15 December 1906), xv. Swanson cited the following testimony from several of his customers: in Duluth, "the hand-colored pictures [brought] applause after applause"; in Green Bay, the "many Hand-Colored Subjects"

helped increase receipts by "over fifty percent." See, also, Marette, "Les Procédés de Colo-riage Mécanique des Films," 3. Pathé's first stencil-color machine, developed by Florimond, received a patent on 22 October 1906.

52. See the Edison ad in *NYC* (1 April 1905), 168.

53. See the Vitagraph ad in *NYC* (7 October 1905), 852; the Edison ad in *Bill* (10 March 1906), 35; and the Edison ad in *NYC* (16 June 1906), 472. André Gaudreault has found a ref-erence to tinting and toning in a 1906 Edison catalog, but it is uncertain how many tinted and toned prints the company actually sold.

54. See, for instance, Joseph Medill Patterson, "The Nickelodeons: The Poor Man's El-ementary Course in Drama," *Saturday Evening Post* (23 November 1907), 10; George Ethel-bert Walsh, "Moving Picture Drama for the Multitude," *The Independent* 64 (6 February 1908), 309–310; and Rollin Lynde Hartt, *The People at Play* (Boston: Houghton Mifflin, 1909), 129. When, in 1907, the Academy of Music, in Baltimore, "promised color moving pictures daily" on its vaudeville programs, very likely it was referring to Pathé stencil-color films—see Robert Kirk Headley, *Exit: A History of Movies in Baltimore* (Baltimore: Robert Kirk Headley, 1974), 41.

55. Although European films (by Raleigh & Robert, Gaumont, Pathé, Great Northern) primarily were praised for their fine toning effects, so were those of Selig and Edison—see "Editorial," *MPW* (5 September 1908), 171. Gaumont, for instance, released *The Waters of Life* and its own *Passion Play* in stencil color—see the Kleine Optical ads in *NYC* (21 De-cember 1907), 1232, and (11 January 1908), 1304. Barry Salt also refers to a tinted print (blue for night and red for fire) of Vitagraph's *The Mill Girl* (1907) at the National Film/Television Archive—see Salt, *Film Style and Technology: History and Analysis* (London: Starword, 1983), 101. After May 1908, Pathé no longer called attention to toning in its *Views and Films Index* ads, perhaps suggesting that the process was now in widespread use. Yet when the *World* first discussed toning, it summarized an article from a German source, *Das Bild*—see "Blue and Green Toned Films," *MPW* (25 January 1908), 57.

56. Paolo Cherchi Usai, "The Color of Nitrate," *Image* 34.1–2 (Spring-Summer 1991)—reprinted in Richard Abel, ed., *Silent Film* (New Brunswick, N.J.: Rutgers University Press, 1996), 29 n 12. Recently, Musser suggested a very practical reason for the absence of color in early American films: most have survived either in nitrate negative or in paper prints de-posited at the Library of Congress.

CHAPTER 3. THE FRENCH ROOSTER RULES THE ROOST

1. "Editorial: What Does It Mean?" *MPW* (26 October 1907), 536.

2. Testimony of Frank Dyer, *USA vs. MPPC* (1914), 1573. Dyer had been Edison's general counsel from 1904 until 1908, when he took over as the company's vice president—see, for instance, "William E. Gilmour and Thomas A. Edison Part," *Var* (1 August 1908), 13; and Charles Musser, *Before the Nickelodeon: Edwin S. Porter and the Edison Manufacturing Company* (Berkeley: University of California Press, 1991), 416.

3. Dyer, *USA vs. MPPC,* 1504.

4. "Notes from Manufacturers: Pathé," *MPW* (16 July 1910), 165.

5. A good indication of the uneven competition between "high-class" vaudeville houses and nickelodeons is the following comment: Vitagraph's *100 to 1 Shot* "is a very good film,

but it is being used in the cheap theatres here, which detracts very much from its value." Manager's Report, Keith Theatre, Detroit, 3 September 1906—KA.

6. See, for instance, the reference to the record growth in the moving picture business during the nine months after August 1906, in "Spirit of the Times," *VFI* (3 August 1907), 3. The Nickelodion, in Portland, provides a good example of limited newspaper advertising: after a half dozen small ads in the *Daily Oregonian* at the time of its opening, in August 1906, it placed only three more ads during the next nine months.

7. See Walter K. Hill, "About Moving Pictures," *Bill* (9 June 1906), 27; and "Growth of the Film Business," *Bill* (15 September 1906), 16. The latter editorial was reprinted, and reconfirmed, in *Bill* (13 October 1906), 20.

8. Bob Watt, "Philadelphia," *Bill* (29 September 1906), 11; "An Unexploited Field and Its Possibilities," *VFI* (6 October 1906), 3–4; and "Trade Notes," *VFI* (10 November 1906), 6. Chicago theaters were first described as residential or neighborhood venues in "Editorial: Stability of Moving Pictures," *VFI* (26 September 1906), 3. Most of these cities (the exception: Cleveland was more important than Boston) also were the centers of serious dramatic production and criticism—see, for instance, "The Molders of Opinion," *NYDM* (15 December 1906), 15.

9. "Massachusetts," *NYC* (22 September 1906), 851; and Roy Rosenzweig, *Eight Hours for What We Will: Workers and Leisure in an Industrial City, 1870–1920* (Cambridge: Cambridge University Press, 1983), 192, 201. *New York Clipper* reported that the Nickel was owned by Nickel Amusement Company of New York, but Rosenzweig lists several local and regional theater entrepreneurs, among them the Gordon Brothers and P. F. Shea.

10. "Massachusetts," *NYC* (8 September 1906), 765, and (29 September 1906), 845. See, also, Russell Merritt, "Nickelodeon Theaters, 1905–1914: Building an Audience for the Movies," in Tino Balio, ed., *The American Film Industry* (Madison: University of Wisconsin Press, 1976), 68. Soon after, Zukor's combination vaudeville–moving picture house, the Comedy Theatre on Fourteenth Street in New York, was mentioned in "Trade Notes," *VFI* (6 October 1906), 8.

11. "Electric Theatres and Nickelodeons," *Bill* (15 December 1906), 32–33. Despite its limitations, this directory is valuable for its specific information: each listing includes the street address, manager's name, seating capacity, and daily number of shows. Those offering fifty or more shows per day included the Bijou Dream in Cleveland, Happyland and the Moving Picture Parlor in Baltimore, and the Edisonia in Birmingham. Musser is the only historian to make use of *Billboard*'s directory—see *The Emergence of Cinema to 1907*, vol. 1 of *History of the American Cinema* (New York: Scribner's, 1991), 428–429.

12. See, for instance, the success of the Majestic Theater in Brooklyn, cited in "Trade Notes," *MPW* (28 September 1907), 470.

13. "Trade Notes," *VFI* (1 December 1906), 6; "Colorado's Best Advertisement," *VFI* (26 January 1907), n.p.; and "Moving Picture Shows," *Bill* (16 March 1907), 32.

14. "Ahoy, 1908!" *VFI* (4 January 1908), 3.

15. "War on Nickel Theatres," *NYDM* (23 March 1907), 18; "Moving Pictures at Dallas," *MPW* (23 March 1907), 40; "Electric Theatre Men Form Organization," *MPW* (20 April 1907), 102; "Texas," *NYC* (20 April 1907), 250, and (1 June 1907), 415; "Trade Notes," *MPW* (8 June 1907), 214, and (22 June 1907), 248. Although the number of nickelodeons in Boston went unmentioned, the organization of moving picture operators there had sixty-three members—"Trade Notes," *VFI* (23 February 1907), 6.

16. See, for instance, the profile of Harry Davis in "Trade Notes," *VFI* (2 March 1907), 6; and "Trade Notes," *VFI* (23 March 1907), 6. One of those Bijou Dreams shared the honor of initiating the nickelodeon boom in Detroit with the Casino (owned by Arthur Caille), which eventually became part of Casino Amusement Enterprises—see "Detroit, Michigan, the Home of the Famous 'Duplex,'" *MPW* (15 July 1916), 397.

17. "Massachusetts," *NYC* (12 January 1907), 1231, and (16 March 1907), 104; "Trade Notes," *MPW* (13 April 1907), 88; and "Massachusetts," *NYC* (13 April 197), 217, and (20 April 1907), 245. Lynn's first nickelodeon, the Dreamland, also soon doubled its original space—see "Massachusetts," *NYC* (12 January 1907), 1231.

18. "The Nickelodeon," *MPW* (4 May 1907), 140.

19. "Trade Notes," *VFI* (19 January 1907), 5.

20. "The Moving Picture Outlook," *VFI* (9 February 1907), 4.

21. See George Kleine's 10 April 1907 letter to the *Chicago Tribune,* printed in *MPW* (20 April 1907), 102; "Regulation of the Cheap Theaters," *CRH* (2 May 1907), 8; "Social Workers to Censor Shows," *CT* (3 May 1907), 3; and Sherman C. Kingsley, "The Penny Arcade and the Cheap Theatre," *Charities and Commons* (8 June 1907), 295.

22. "Editorial," *VFI* (29 June 1907), 4.

23. For a good introduction to the American film rental exchanges of 1905–1907, see Musser, *The Emergence of Cinema,* 433–438.

24. See the Inter-Ocean Film Exchange ad in *Bill* (7 April 1906), 37; and the U.S. Film Exchange and Temple Film Company ads in *Bill* (23 June 1906), 39 and 44.

25. All of these new rental exchanges first began advertising in *Billboard,* between July and December 1906. By early 1907, Chicago exchanges may have "controlled as much as 80 percent of the rental business in the United States"—see Musser, *The Emergence of Cinema,* 434. And, in a 31 December 1906 letter to Kleine, Frank Marion claimed that "the exhibition business is at the present time, as you know, almost wholly in the hands of the rental bureaus"—Box 29: Kalem Folder, GK.

26. See the first Swanson ad in *Bill* (8 September 1906), 56; and the first Laemmle ad in *Bill* (6 October 1906), 22. See, also, "Film News: Swanson Extends Field of Operations," *Bill* (27 June 1908), 31. The language of Laemmle's ads also sometimes had a parallel in the "Trade Notes" section of *Views and Films Index.* Laemmle's ads were unique in their attempt to create "a *feeling* of personal communication," a "personal voice," something E. A. Calkins (who wrote one of the first handbooks on advertising) considered crucial for a company's success—quoted in Richard Ohmann, *Selling Culture: Magazines, Markets, and Class at the Turn of the Century* (London: Verso, 1996), 187.

27. "Trade Notes," *MPW* (27 July 1907), 327; "Moving Picture News from Everywhere," *VFI* (12 October 1907), 4; and "Moving Picture Notes," *Bill* (19 October 1907), 53. Greater New York Film Rental also advertised on the cover of *VFI,* 20 April 1907.

28. Pittsburgh Calcium Light and Film also advertised on the cover of *VFI,* beginning on 1 June 1907.

29. By the winter of 1906–1907, most of the new rental exchanges were advertising not only in *Billboard* but also in *Views and Films Index.* The Western Film Exchange was run by John Freuler (with Harry Aitken), who entered the business with one of Milwaukee's first nickelodeons, the Comique, and later became president of the Mutual Corporation—see Robert Grau, *The Theatre of Science* (New York: Benjamin Blom, 1914), 56; "Where John R. Freuler Got His Start in Pictures," *MPW* (15 July 1916), 378; and Terry Ramsaye, *A Million and One Nights: A History of the Motion Picture* (New York: Simon and Schuster, 1926), 452.

30. See, for instance, the Miles Brothers ad in *VFI* (20 April 1907), 10; and the Kleine Optical ad in *VFI* (18 May 1907), 11.

31. See, for instance, the Chicago Film Exchange ad in *VFI* (6 July 1907), 12. The Chicago Film Exchange also reported a 50 percent increase in its business during the month of November 1906—"Trade Notes," *VFI* (15 December 1906), 6.

32. George Kleine pinpointed this change in the "shelf life" of individual film titles as occurring in April 1906—see Kleine, "Optical Projection in the Past Half Century," *SW* (27 June 1908), 14.

33. "For the Nickelodeon," *MPW* (4 May 1907), 134. For the best source of information on American film producers during this period, see Musser, *The Emergence of Cinema*, 449–488.

34. See, for instance, the profile of Lubin in *Bill* (22 May 1909), 8.

35. See the listings in "Latest Films," *VFI*, beginning on 15 September 1906; "Moving Pictures," *Bill* (13 October 1906), 21; and the Pathé ad in *VFI* (27 October 1906), 11.

36. See the Pathé ad in *VFI* (20 April 1907), 2.

37. Susan Strasser, *Satisfaction Guaranteed: The Making of the American Mass Market* (New York: Pantheon, 1989), 57.

38. See the 11 April 1907 letter from Kleine to Marion—Box 29: Kalem Folder, GK.

39. See, for instance, the Managers' Reports, Keith Theatres, New York City (16 July 1906), Detroit (23 July 1906), Boston (13 August 1906), and Cleveland (27 August 1906)—KA. For a description and analysis of *Dog Smugglers*, see Richard Abel, *The Ciné Goes to Town: French Cinema, 1896–1914* (Berkeley: University of California Press, 1994), 132.

40. See the Managers' Reports, Keith Theatres, Philadelphia (10 September 1907), Boston (17 September 1907), New York (17 September 1907), Detroit (24 September 1907), Philadelphia (22 October 1906), Detroit (31 December 1906), New York (7 January 1907), and Philadelphia (25 February 1907)—KA. For a description and analysis of these story films, see Abel, *The Ciné Goes to Town*, 175–176.

41. See the Managers' Reports, Keith Theatres, Philadelphia (18 February 1908), Boston (1 April 1908), and Philadelphia (15 April 1908)—KA. The only film that received even better notices than Pathé's was Edison's *Teddy Bears*—see the Managers' Reports, Keith Theatres, Providence (25 February 1908), Boston (4 March 1908), and Philadelphia (18 March 1908)—KA.

42. By 1907, Georges Méliès was no more than a minor film supplier in the United States, and Gaumont and Urban-Eclipse had just begun to distribute films on a regular basis (the latter mostly *actualités*) through Kleine Optical.

43. The Theatre Comique was one of the few nickelodeons (or even vaudeville houses) to have its weekly film programs reported in the trade press. See the weeks of 13 October, 17 November, and 15 December through 9 February, in *New York Clipper*. One of the first Pathé titles shown at the Comique was *Dog Smugglers*, a big hit on the Keith circuit the previous summer.

44. In order to compete with the Nickeldom, the Empire one week added a special feature to its vaudeville program, the "New French Motion Picture, *A Trip to the Stars*," the "first presentation" of this Pathé film "in Des Moines"—see the Empire ad in *DMRL* (23 September 1906), 3.7.

45. See the Colonial Theatre ad in *DMRL* (30 April 1907), 5. The Colonial lasted longer than any of the other nickelodeons that were operating in Des Moines that year (it was still thriving in 1914); whenever its initial manager, C. L. Mott, put ads in the local newspapers

(which was very infrequently), his programs featured Pathé films. For a description and analysis of two of these films, see Abel, *The Ciné Goes to Town*, 148–149, 151–152.

46. "The Nickelodeon," *MPW* (4 May 1907), 140. In reporting on the earliest nickelodeons in Toronto, W. M. Gladish remarked that the shows "consisted of one and a half reels of film, generally of French origin"—see "Toronto, Canada, Claims Birthplace of 'Little Mary,'" *MPW* (15 July 1916), 411.

47. "Moving Pictures," *NYC* (27 April 1907), 276, and (8 June 1907), 443. In Kansas City, Forest Park included among its summer attractions "Pathé from Paris"—see "Missouri," *NYC* (11 May 1907), 333.

48. See the Pathé ads in *VFI* (1 June 1907), 2, and (13 July 1907), 2. See, also, the testimonial letter reprinted in the Pathé ad in *VFI* (3 August 1907), 9.

49. William Bullock, "How Moving Pictures Are Made and Shown," *MPW* (10 August 1907), 359–360.

50. See, for instance, the first Kalem ad in *VFI* (15 June 1907) and "Trade Notes," *VFI* (3 August 1907), 4. See, also, Musser, *The Emergence of Cinema*, 485–486.

51. See "Moving Picture Industry" and "Moving Picture Industry Great," *SW* (29 June 1907), 16 and 28–29. By contrast, Pittsburgh was reported to have fifty "nickel amusements"—see "Live News Notes from Iron City," *SW* (9 September 1907), 10–11.

52. See the Laemmle ad in *SW* (6 July 1907), 2.

53. Barton W. Currie, "The Nickel Madness," *Harper's Weekly* (24 August 1907), 1246—reprinted in Gerald Mast, ed., *The Movies in Our Midst: Documents in the Cultural History of Film in America* (Chicago: University of Chicago Press, 1982), 47.

54. All six venues could be found among the "Amusement Houses of the City," in the women's club weekly, *Des Moines Mail and Times* (23 August 1907), 7. The population of Des Moines at the time was close to eighty-five thousand—see *The Thirteenth Census of the United States* (Washington, D.C.: Government Printing Office, 1913), 63. Similar conditions existed, according to the *Index*, in cities from Rochester, New York, to Vincennes, Indiana. In the small Iowa town of Ottumwa, for instance, the Electric Theatre and the Nickelodeon opened within a week of one other—see the Electric Theatre and Nickelodeon ads in *Ottumwa Courier* (15 June 1907), 5, and (22 June 1907), 4. Contrast this with Winona, Minnesota, where a family vaudeville house failed in 1904, two nickelodeons failed in 1906 and 1907, and the first successful nickelodeon did not open until November 1907—see David Thomas, "From Page to Screen in Smalltown America: Early Motion Picture Exhibition in Winona, Minnesota," *Journal of the University Film Association* 33 (Summer 1981), 8–12.

55. "Success of Nickel Shows Explained by Aaron J. Jones," *SW* (31 August 1907), 6.

56. "Large Profits in Motion Views," *SW* (6 July 1907), 16.

57. "Film Makers Slow," *SW* (13 July 1907), 10.

58. Pathé's *Dog Police* was "said to excel their famous *Dog Smugglers*," which was a big hit the previous summer—"Moving Pictures," *NYC* (15 June 1907), 464. See the Radium Theater ad, *DMRL* (29 May 1907), 6; "Today's Amusements," *DMRL* (30 July 1907), 5; "Correspondents," *SW* (10 August 1907), 12ii; and the Dreamland ads in *DMRL*, 30 July 1907, 1 August 1907, 8 August 1907, and 15 August 1907. Both *Two Sisters* and *Pirates* exemplify the relatively sophisticated system of representation and narration that Pathé's filmmakers had developed by 1907. For a description and analysis of these films, see Abel, *The Ciné Goes to Town*, 154–155, 188–190. In his 11 April 1907 letter to Marion, Kleine noted that he had "been struck by the rapidity of action" in Pathé, Gaumont, and Urban-Eclipse films—Box 29: Kalem Folder, GK.

59. See the Lyric Theatre ad, *DMRL* (23 July 1907), 3.7. The Lyric, as well as the Radium and the Dreamland, were the only nickelodeons in the city to advertise to the "cultured" middle-class readers of the *Des Moines Mail and Times.*

60. See "This Week's Bills," *DMRL* (9 June 1907), 3.6. Likewise, in Ottumwa, Pathé films appeared on both theaters' bills more frequently than did all others. One program at the Electric Theatre, for instance, had *Creusot's Steel Foundry* and *Light Housekeeping,* along with a *Cubs–White Sox Baseball Game;* another had *The Charmer, Magic Roses,* and *Around the World*—see the Electric Theatre ads in *Ottumwa Courier* (1 August 1907), 4, and (5 August 1907), 5. The Nickelodeon had *Voyage to the Star* and *Witches Cave* on one program and held over *Sleeping Beauty* for another—see the Nickelodeon ads in *Ottumwa Courier* (23 July 1907), 8, (25 July 1907), 8, and (7 August 1907), 8.

61. Currie, "The Nickel Madness," 1247.

62. This print may have been a "pirated" dupe (Currie's description fits the Pathé film closely), because several months later the company called unusual attention to the "excellency" of its new film, *The Pirates*—see "Moving Picture News from Everywhere," *VFI* (23 November 1907), 6.

63. "Trade Notes," *VFI* (8 June 1907), 4; "Trade Notes," *MPW* (24 August 1907), 391; "Film Correspondence," *Bill* (27 June 1908), 11. The "Home of Pathé" was owned and operated by the Chicago Electrical Theater Company (Aaron Gollos).

64. At least two sources other than the trade press cited this period as one of "wonderfully rapid" growth—see Asa Steele, "The Moving-Picture Show," *World's Work* (February 1911), 14,020; and "The Moving Picture Theatre," *Architecture and Building* 43.8 (May 1911), 319.

65. "Spirit of the Times," *VFI* (3 August 1907), 3.

66. Joseph Medill Patterson, "The Nickelodeons, the Poor Man's Elementary Course in the Drama," *Saturday Evening Post* (23 November 1907), 10. This article also began with a production photo from Pathé's *Two Sisters,* the first of ten illustrations in all, none of which was reproduced in the edited article reprinted in Pratt's *Spellbound in Darkness.* Others came from three Vitagraph films, *The Mill Girl, The Wrong Flat,* and *The Easterner,* Lubin's *Meet Me at the Fountain,* and the *Sharkey-Jeffries Fight.*

67. "Trade Notes," *MPW* (26 October 1907), 538, and (14 December 1907), 664; "Cincinnati Amusements Booming," *SW* (21 December 1907), 14; "Trade Notes," *MPW* (21 December 1907), 685; "Trade Notes," *MPW* (1 February 1908), 75; "Moving Picture News from Everywhere," *VFI* (22 February 1908), 6; and "Lubin in Cincinnati," *NYC* (21 March 1908), 129.

68. See, for instance, Eugene H. Stout, "Little Rock," *SW* (14 September 1907), 11; "Trade Notes," *MPW* (30 November 1907), 629; "Keith's Pictures All One," *Var* (22 February 1908), 10; "Nickel Theater Circuit," *SW* (7 March 1908), 4; and Grau, *The Theatre of Science,* 294–296. Casino Amusement controlled nine houses in Michigan—Sydney Wire, "The Casino Amusement Co.," *Bill* (23 November 1907), 20. A "Trenton concern" was said to operate "28 small theaters [in] New Jersey and Eastern Pennsylvania"—"Trade Notes," *MPW* (5 October 1907), 487. The Warner brothers also took the first steps toward what would become a major circuit of theaters—see "Trade Notes," *MPW* (14 September 1907), 440.

69. "News of the Nickolets," *MPW* (5 October 1907), 485; and "Trade Notes," *MPW* (19 October 1907), 521. Two main railway terminals anchored this stretch of Market Street,

so the nickelodeons appealed to out-of-town or suburban shoppers on their way to and from Wanamaker's—see "Among the Exhibitors," *MPW* (13 March 1909), 297.

70. These figures are derived from ads in *Billboard, Views and Films Index, Moving Picture World,* and *Show World.*

71. These included the Cincinnati Film Exchange, the Toledo Film Exchange, the Ohio Film Exchange (Columbus), the Columbia Film Exchange (Cleveland), the Nolan Film Exchange (Cincinnati), the Economy Film Exchange (Cleveland), the Southern Film Exchange (Cincinnati), and the Canton Film Exchange.

72. Sydney Wire, "The Moving Picture World," *Bill* (11 January 1908), 16.

73. See the People's Film Exchange ad in *VFI* (14 December 1907), 11.

74. See, for instance, the Eugene Cline ad in *Bill* (14 December 1907), 47; the Laemmle ad in *SW* (14 December 1907), 10; the Kleine Optical ad in *SW* (21 December 1907), 10–11; and the Swanson ad in *SW* (8 February 1908), 7. The Chicago Film Exchange also made much of its new branch office in Omaha—see its ad in *VFI* (21 December 1907), 21.

75. See, for instance, the Pittsburgh Calcium Light and Film ad on the cover of *VFI* (5 October 1907) and the Kleine Optical ad in *DMRL* (20 October 1907), 3.7.

76. F. C. McCarahan, "Chicago's Great Film Industry," *Bill* (24 August 1907), 4–5, 39.

77. "Moving Picture Notes," *Bill* (19 October 1907), 53.

78. See, for instance, the Pathé ad in *Bill* (16 November 1907), 27.

79. See the full-page Pathé ad in *Bill* (7 December 1907), 104.

80. See the full-page Pathé ad on the inside cover of *VFI* (21 December 1907).

81. See "Moving Pictures," *SW* (26 October 1907), 12; and "Trade Notes," *MPW* (23 November 1907), 614. If Kleine Optical had exclusive contracts with Gaumont and Urban-Eclipse, then the other exchanges had to rely heavily on Pathé.

82. See the Pathé ad in *VFI* (21 December 1907), 2. This Birmingham rental exchange already had specialized in Pathé films throughout the fall—see, for instance, the Baily Film Service ad in *VFI* (21 September 1907), 10.

83. See the Imported Film & Supply Company ads in *VFI* (30 November 1907), 4; and *Bill* (14 December 1907), 47.

84. See Laemmle's "Show World Junior" ad in *SW* (4 January 1908), 13.

85. See the Lyric ad in *DMRL* (22 December 1907), 3.7. The Lyric also called *Bluebeard* "a fit companion piece to *Ali Baba* shown several weeks before" and which Pathé itself singled out for its "coloring" as a "model fairy film" (and remake of the 1901 version)—see "Moving Picture News from Everywhere," *VFI* (23 November 1907), 6. See, also, "Laughter at the Lyric," *DMRL* (8 October 1907), 5; and the Lyric ad in *DMRL* (20 October 1907), 3.7.

86. See "The Rapper," *VFI* (17 August 1907), 8. The film's American release was first announced in *VFI* (2 March 1907), 11. This was Pathé's third version of *The Life and Passion of Christ* or the *Passion Play;* the other two dated from 1900 and 1902–1903.

87. See "Trade Notes," *VFI* (17 August 1907), 4, and (5 October 1907), 4. The printer for these booklets and posters was Hennegan & Co.—see, for instance, its ad in *VFI* (5 October 1907), 9. Patterson also devoted several paragraphs to the film in "The Nickelodeons," 11, 38. This long predates a similar move by Edison in the fall of 1909—see Janet Staiger, "Announcing Wares, Winning Patrons, Voicing Ideals: Thinking about the History and Theory of Film Advertising," *Cinema Journal* 29.3 (Spring 1990), 7.

88. See the Lyric ad in *DMRL* (29 September 1907), 3.7.

89. See "Moving Picture News from Everywhere," *VFI* (7 December 1907), 6; and "Trade Notes," *MPW* (14 December 1907), 667.

90. See "Moving Picture News from Everywhere," *VFI* (9 November 1907), 6; and Wire, "The Casino Amusement Co.," 20.

91. See "Iowa," *NYC* (14 December 1907), 1196; "Trade Notes," *MPW* (28 December 1907), 703; and "Moving Picture News from Everywhere," *VFI* (29 February 1908), 7.

92. See the People's Film Exchange ad in *VFI* (8 February 1908), 5.

93. "Editorial Notes and Comments," *MPW* (25 April 1908), 366.

94. For the 26 January 1907 issue, *Views and Films Index* redesigned its cover to represent a legitimate theater with a well-dressed audience of adults, their attention focused on a huge screen filling the stage space, below which a small orchestra is performing. *Show World* also supported the idea of larger, "first-class" moving picture theaters and cited Lubin's lease of the Park Theater in Brooklyn, as well as two 1,000-seat houses in Montreal, as models— "Moving Picture Industry Shows Marked Improvement, Activity and Development," *SW* (19 October 1907), 22. Lubin quickly gave up his lease on the Park when he was not allowed to change its facade; it is not certain when the Park actually began showing moving pictures exclusively—see "Arthur Hotaling Recalls the 'Good Old Days,'" *MPW* (15 July 1916), 381.

95. The *Mirror* published a series of interviews with managers on the sudden "falling off in the patronage of popular price houses devoted to melodrama"—see "What Is the Cause?" *NYDM* (18 April 1908), 5; "An Absorbing Problem," *NYDM* (25 April 1908), 3; "The Melodrama Theatre," *NYDM* (2 May 1908), 6; "Good and Bad Melodrama," *NYDM* (9 May 1908), 2; "The Popular-Price Theatre," *NYDM* (16 May 1908), 8; and "The Melodrama Theatre," *NYDM* (6 June 1908), 3. Among several causes given, the growth of moving picture shows was most cited. See, also, "The Drama of the People," *Independent* 69 (29 September 1909), 713–715.

96. See "New York City," *NYC* (27 April 1907), 280; "Trade Notes," *VFI* (4 May 1907), 6, and (11 May 1907), 4.

97. Each week, the *New York Clipper* mentioned the "big crowds" Shepard's moving pictures were attracting at the Manhattan. See, also, "Trade Notes," *MPW* (11 January 1908), 26; and Louis V. De Foe, "Theater Sees a Real Danger in the Growth of the Picture Play," *New York World*—reprinted in *MPW* (4 April 1908), 289. The lease on the Manhattan had to be renewed monthly—see Robert Grau, "Fortunes in the Moving Picture Field," *Overland Monthly* (April 1911), 396.

98. See "Moving Picture News from Everywhere," *VFI* (9 November 1907), 6; "Surprising Growth of Motion View Industry," *SW* (23 November 1907), 19; and Charles Morris, "The Chicago Orpheum Theater," *Nick* (January 1909), 3–5. The Orpheum was open for only seven weeks as a vaudeville house before shifting to moving pictures, and it became so popular that crowds were still blocking the sidewalks four months later—"Moving Pictures," *NYC* (28 March 1908), 164.

99. "Trade Notes," *MPW* (14 December 1907), 367; "Trade Notes: Sunday in New York," *MPW* (21 December 1907), 683–684; "Trade Notes," *MPW* (4 January 1908), 8; J. Austin Fynes, "Motion Pictures," *VFI* (11 January 1908), 4; and "Moving Picture News and Reviews," *Var* (15 February 1908), 11. The transformation in New York also was aided by the legislation increasing the licensing fee for a moving picture show so it was equal to that of a legitimate theater—see John Collier, "Cheap Amusements," *Charities and Commons* (11 April 1908), 75–76.

100. "New Name for Twenty-third Street," *NYDM* (4 January 1908), 14; "[untitled article]," *MPW* (11 January 1908), 22; and "Moving Picture News and Reviews," *Var* (25 January 1908), 11.

101. "Trade Notes," *MPW* (11 January 1908), 26; "Manhattan a Money Maker," *Var* (22 February 1908), 10; "The Moving Picture Field," *NYDM* (6 June 1908), 6; and Grau, "Fortunes in the Moving Picture Field," 396.

102. "Pictures at Union Square," *NYDM* (22 February 1908), 13; "Trade Notes," *MPW* (22 February 1908), 137; "Moving Pictures," *NYC* (21 March 1908), 140; J. L. Hoff, "Things Theatrical in Empire City," *SW* (21 March 1908), 7; De Foe, "Theater Sees a Real Danger in the Growth of the Picture Play," 289; and "Another Bijou Dream," *NYDM* (25 April 1908), 17. A Nicholas Power Company representative also singled out Keith and Proctor as leading this transformation—see "The Moving Picture Field," *NYDM* (30 May 1908), 7.

103. J. H. Hoff, "Things Theatrical in Empire City," *SW* (11 April 1908), 17; "Moving Pictures," *NYC* (18 April 1908), 246; "Editorial Notes and Comments," *MPW* (25 April 1908), 366; "Moving Pictures," *NYC* (25 April 1908), 272; "Busiest Picture Block," *Var* (13 June 1908), 11; "Nickelodeon Notes," *VFI* (25 July 1908), 7; "Among the Shows," *MPW* (11 December 1909), 843; and Grau, "Fortunes in the Moving Picture Field," 396. The Royal had been a burlesque house until acquired and transformed by Loew.

104. "Hopkin's for Pictures," *Var* (22 February 1908), 11; "Pictorial Vaudeville at Nelson Theatre, Springfield," *NYC* (7 March 1908), 85; "Haymarket and Olympic for Moving Pictures," *SW* (14 March 1908), 8; "Moving Pictures," *NYC* (21 March 1908), 140; the photo and caption, *VFI* (9 May 1908), 6; and Lewis E. Palmer, "The World in Motion," *Survey* 22 (5 June 1909), 358.

105. See "Trade Notes," *MPW* (29 February 1908), 160; and "Moving Pictures," *NYC* (28 March 1908), 164.

106. See "William C. Swanson's New Theatre," *SW* (27 June 1908), 26c; and "Film News," *Bill* (27 June 1908), 31. Swanson had departments for theaters, tent shows, parks and street fairs, and equipment repairs.

107. "A Modern Moving Picture Theatre," *NYDM* (6 June 1908), 6. The Star Theatre was unusual in that its "projecting machine [was] operated by electric motor instead of by hand," which the *Mirror* warned might not be permitted by fire insurance underwriters in other cities.

108. As Eileen Bowser reminds us, the nickelodeon "limit of 299 seats" in New York City was due, not to "the regulation of the common show license," but to "the building codes and fire laws," a condition that probably pertained in many other urban areas— Bowser, *The Transformation of Cinema, 1907–1915*, vol. 2 of *History of the American Cinema* (New York: Scribner's, 1990), 7.

109. See, for instance, F. G. Aiken, "The Business of Exhibiting," *VFI* (27 June 1908), 7; Bob Watt, "The Film Industry in Philadelphia," *Bill* (27 June 1908), 13; and "Chicago's 'Big 8' Picture Theatres," *FI* (11 September 1909), 1.

110. The Princess was praised for using two Power projectors—see "A Glance through the Trade," *VFI* (29 December 1907), 4–5.

111. See "Editorial," *FI* (7 November 1908), 3. Moreover, there were theaters like the Lyric in East Saint Louis, which, after expanding to seat one thousand, still was "packed both afternoons and evenings"—see "Moving Picture Shows," *Bill* (29 August 1908), 9.

112. See "Popular Price Drama Waning," *NYDM* (28 November 1908), 8. Yet, as Singer comments, a good number of these converted theaters—for instance, the Dewey, Fourteenth

Street Theater, and Royal in New York—attracted not middle-class audiences but the same crowds as before, when they played cheap melodrama or burlesque—see "Dialogue," *Cinema Journal* 35.3 (1996), 126 n. 2.

113. See Herbert J. Stryckmans, "Moving Picture Is Enemy of the Saloon," *SW* (30 May 1908), 7; and Kathleen McCarthy, "Nickel Vice and Virtue: Movie Censorship in Chicago, 1907–1915," *Journal of Popular Film* 5 (1976), 39.

114. See, for instance, "Moving Picture News from Everywhere," *VFI* (29 February 1908), 7; "An Amazing Growth," *NYDM* (28 March 1908), 4; De Foe, "Theater Sees a Real Danger in the Growth of the Picture Play," 289; "Trade Notes," *MPW* (23 May 1908), 457; "The Film Industry in Philadelphia," *Bill* (27 June 1908), 13; and "Film Makers' Tricks," *VFI* (12 September 1908), 7. "Between 1907 and 1908 the number of licensed theaters jumped from 116 to 320"—see McCarthy, "Nickel Vice and Virtue," 39. William Uricchio and Roberta Pearson take a more pessimistic attitude than does Ben Singer on dealing with the discrepancies in reporting these figures, in "Dialogue: Manhattan's Nickelodeons," *Cinema Journal* 36.4 (Summer 1997), 98–100, 108–109.

115. "Toledo All Pictures," *Var* (23 May 1908), 12; and "Moving Picture Notes," *NYDM* (4 July 1908), 7.

116. Fynes, "Motion Pictures," 4. Collier, "Cheap Amusements," 74. This report also put the number of New York nickelodeons at over 600.

117. John M. Bradlet, "A Tour amongst Country Exhibitors," *MPW* (6 February 1909), 142. This does not necessarily support Allen's contention, partly based on the research done by Thomas, Waller, Fuller, and others, that small towns and not large metropolises should be considered more representative of nickelodeon exhibition practices—see "From Exhibition to Reception: Reflections on the Audience in Film History," *Screen* 31.4 (Winter 1990), 349–350; and "Dialogue," 96–98. The statistic for moving picture shows in all cities of more than fifty thousand or even one hundred thousand people would be much higher; moreover, those in larger towns and cities tended to give more performances and to larger numbers of people and, hence, received greater attention in the trade press as profitable enterprises. See, for instance, "Motion Picture Theatres," *Bill* (5 December 1908), 76–77, (12 December 1908), 41–43, (2 January 1909), 41–43, (9 January 1909), 42–43, and (16 January 1909), 41–43.

118. See the front cover of *VFI* (29 February 1908).

119. See the Globe Film Service ads beginning in *Bill* (11 January 1908), 16.

120. See the Laemmle Film Service ads in *SW* (15 February 1908), 15, and (22 February 1908), 17; and the Swanson ad in *SW* (7 March 1908), 13.

121. Testimony of William Fox, *USA v. MPPC* (1914), 676. See, also, the tribute to Fox in "William Fox," *VFI* (8 August 1908), 3.

122. These figures come from "Pathé in New Quarters," *Var* (1 February 1908), 11; "Film Production Increasing," *NYDM* (27 June 1908), 7; and "Kinematography in the United States," *MPW* (11 July 1914), 176.

123. See "New York City," *NYC* (15 February 1908), 1396; and "Correspondence," *VFI* (15 February 1908), 10.

124. The new Pathé ad first appeared in *SW* (18 April 1908), 9, and then in *MPW* (23 May 1908), 466.

125. J. L. Hoff, "Moving Picture Art Is Spreading Like Wildfire," *SW* (27 June 1908), 6. See, also, a *Philadelphia Public Ledger* article, reprinted as "In the Maker's Studio," *VFI* (6 June 1908), 4.

126. Edward Wagenknecht, *The Movies in the Age of Innocence* (Norman: University of Oklahoma Press, 1962), 10–14. Although the *Passion Play* ran for a week at the Family Electric, the Wagenknecht family only saw it later at the Bijou Dream downtown. Wagenknecht also recalls seeing films at Balaban's "little Kedzie" and at the Victoria, on Twenty-second Street, west of California Avenue.

127. See "Moving Picture News and Reviews," *Var* (1 March 1908), 12, (21 March 1908), 15, and (18 April 1908), 13; and "Film Reviews," *Var* (25 April 1908), 13.

128. Walter P. Eaton, "New Theatrical Problem: Age of Mechanical Amusement," *VFI* (9 May 1908), 5.

129. "Moving Pictures," *NYC* (11 April 1908), 218, and (18 April 1908), 246.

130. See the Managers' Reports, Keith Theatres, Philadelphia (10 February 1908), Providence (24 February 1908), Washington (23 March 1908), and Detroit (20 April 1908)—KA. That *The Runaway Horse* was popular in nickelodeons at least a week or so before it began playing on the Keith circuit is clear from a note on recent releases in *MPW* (15 February 1908), 112. It was still being cited two years later, in Allan Meade, "All in the Day's Work," *Nick* (15 February 1910), 94.

131. All but one of the half dozen nickelodeons (Globe, Majestic, Theatorium, Parisian, and Orpheum) in Galveston were showing one or two Pathé titles on their two-film programs—see "Doing Things in Galveston," *VFI* (11 January 1908), 7. In Des Moines, the Lyric used Pathé's name in advertising several specific film titles—*The Shrimper* (7 January), *Ship Owner's Daughter* (21 January), and *The Idler* (20 April). In Ottumwa, the Electric Theatre showed Pathé's *Harlequin's Story* in two parts—see the Electric Theatre ad in *Ottumwa Courier* (26 December 1907), 6. According to Waller's unpublished research, two of the four films advertised at the Blue Grass Theater in Lexington, from April through May 1908, were from Pathé.

132. Of those 515 film titles, 458 were from "licensed" manufacturers (grouped in the Film Service Association), with most of the remaining 57 titles coming from Biograph and "independent" distributors of foreign imports. Of those 458 "licensed" films, 14 came from Méliès, 26 from Selig, 32 from Kalem, 40 from Lubin, 42 from Essanay, 45 from Edison, 82 from Vitagraph, and 177 from Pathé. McCoy's survey is reprinted in Musser, *Before the Nickelodeon*, 417.

133. "'A Square Deal for All' Is Thomas Edison's Promise," *Var* (20 June 1908), 12. Much later, in a 2 March 1914 letter on the occasion of Berst's "retirement" from Pathé, George Kleine also would praise "the high efficiency with which [he] conducted their affairs"—see Box 4: J. A. Berst, GK.

134. There are indications that the *Passion Play* was still popular in 1910—see "The Pathé Passion Play Undimmed in Popularity," *MPW* (29 October 1910), 988.

135. "The Elevation of Vaudeville," *MPW* (18 May 1907), 164. See, also, Charles Ulrich, "Comment on People and Affairs," *SW* (25 April 1908), 16.

136. "In the spring of 1906, a man could have gone into the film business modestly, with a capital of $3,000, and grown and prospered. Several have done it. To-day, the best posted men in the film business say that it is not advisable to enter the business under $15,000 or $20,000, and then the man must have an intimate knowledge of the business or he will lose all, or have on his hands only second-hand stuff that is worth little." McCarahan, "Chicago's Great Film Industry," 4.

137. Robert A. Woods and Albert J. Kennedy, eds., *Young Working Girls: A Summary of Evidence from Two Thousand Social Workers* (Boston: Houghton Mifflin, 1913), 1–6.

138. Christoph Asendorf explores this concept of "empty time" (derived from Walter Benjamin) from a different perspective in *Batteries of Life: On the History of Things and Their Perception in Modernity,* trans. Don Reneau (Berkeley: University of California Press, 1993), 140–152.

139. Collier, "Cheap Amusements," 75. Collier's words provided the conclusion for "Moving Pictures Past and Present," *Bill* (27 June 1908), 5. See Patterson's earlier comment on moving pictures as part of a "democratic movement" in "The Nickelodeons," 11. See, also, Mary Kingsbury Simkhovitch, *The City Worker's World in America* (New York: Macmillan, 1917), 123.

140. See "Film Maker's Tricks," *VFI* (12 September 1908), 7.

141. Kathy Peiss, *Cheap Amusements: Working Women and Leisure in Turn-of-the-Century New York* (Philadelphia: Temple University Press, 1986), 5–6. See, also, for the United States, Miriam Hansen, *Babel and Babylon: Spectatorship in American Silent Cinema* (Cambridge, Mass.: Harvard University Press, 1991), and Ohmann, *Selling Culture;* for England, Judith R. Walkowitz, *City of Dreadful Delights: Narratives of Sexual Danger in Late-Victorian London* (Chicago: University of Chicago Press, 1992); and, for France, Rosalind Williams, *Dream Worlds: Mass Consumption in Late Nineteenth-Century France* (Berkeley: University of California Press, 1982) See, also, Émile Zola, *The Ladies' Paradise* (Berkeley: University of California Press, 1992), 205, 219.

142. Kingsley, "The Penny Arcade and the Cheap Theatre," 295.

143. This was certainly the case with mass magazines — see Ohmann, *Selling Culture,* 252.

144. "The Propriety of Some Film Subjects," *VFI* (11 May 1907), 3. A good example would be the Funnyland, in Lowell, which was described as "the mecca of women and children in the shopping district" — see "Massachusetts," *NYC* (8 December 1906), 1107.

145. See "Three Points of View," *MPW* (13 April 1907), 89; and "The Nickelodeon," *MPW* (4 May 1907), 140.

146. See "Nickel Theaters Crime Breeders," *CT* (13 April 1907), 3. See, also, the description of State Street theaters, which served as a refuge for children after school, in "Audiences Like Pictures," *SW* (13 July 1907), 10.

147. "Editorial," *VFI* (21 September 1907), 4. In Knoxville, the local evening newspaper, *The Sentinel,* showed moving pictures to its one hundred delivery boys (ages six to fifteen) in order to "fill them with enthusiasm for their work" — see "Trade Notes," *MPW* (14 December 1907), 665.

148. See, for instance, "A Tribute to Moving Picture Shows [Galveston]," *MPW* (28 March 1908), 265; Collier, "Cheap Amusements," 75; "Picture Shows Popular in the 'Hub' [Boston]," *MPW* (16 May 1908), 433; "The Nickelodeon as a Business Proposition [Grand Rapids]," *MPW* (25 July 1908), 61; and Elizabeth Beardsley Butler, *Women and the Trades: Pittsburgh, 1907–1908* (New York: Russell Sage, 1909), 333–334.

149. "Editorial," *MPW* (14 March 1908), 203.

150. "Picture Shows Championed," *MPW* (20 June 1908), 525.

151. See "The Vogue of the Motion Picture," in *MPW* (1 August 1908), 83–84.

152. Hansen, *Babel and Babylon,* 118. The concept of *heterotopia* comes from Michel Foucault — see Hansen, *Babel and Babylon,* 107. See, also, Judith Mayne, "Immigrants and Spectators," *Wide Angle* 5.2 (1982), 32–41; and Peiss, *Cheap Amusements,* 148–153.

153. Mary Carbine, "'The Finest outside the Loop': Motion Picture Exhibition in Chicago's Black Metropolis, 1905–1928," *camera obscura* 23 (May 1990) — reprinted in Richard Abel, ed., *Silent Film* (New Brunswick, N.J.: Rutgers University Press 1996),

234–262; and Gregory Waller, "Another Audience: Black Moviegoing, 1907–16," *Cinema Journal* 31.2 (Winter 1992), 3–25.

154. In Topeka, several blacks sued the Novelty Theatre for refusing them seats in the "white patrons" section, and the case was described as a "victory over negroes"—see "Negro Question Settled," *Bill* (18 November 1905), 2. In Atlantic City, steps were taken to exclude blacks after visitors complained about "negroes . . . infesting" the place—see "Atlantic City," *Bill* (21 July 1906), 7. The industry's racist notion that moving pictures did not appeal to blacks is stated explicitly in "Trade Notes," *MPW* (8 June 1907), 216.

155. The Pekin opened in 1905, on Twenty-seventh and South State Streets, and was owned and operated by Robert Motts—see Carbine, "'The Finest outside the Loop,'" 241, 260. The Frolic opened in 1907, on West Main Street, "respectably" located on the edge of the downtown commercial district—see Waller, "Another Audience," 6–11. Other early black-owned businesses included the Africo-American Amusement Company operated "by and for the negro race" in Newport News, Virginia, and a Franklin Street theater "for colored people exclusively" in Natchez, Mississippi—see "Trade Notes," *VFI* (23 June 1906), 8; and "Trade Notes," *MPW* (15 June 1907), 232.

156. The Electric Theatre several times featured a Professor Hawley, who led a "colored quartette," and at least once it sponsored a "watermelon eating contest between little colored boys"—see the Electric Theatre ads in *Ottumwa Courier* (25 July 1907), 8, (5 September 1907), 5, and (18 September 1907), 2.

157. See "Trade Notes," *VFI* (6 October 1906), 6.

158. See "Trade Notes," *MPW* (15 June 1907), 4; "Business in Massachusetts," *VFI* (22 June 1907), 3; the Radium ad in *DMRL* (29 May 1907), 3.7; and the Lyric ad in *DMRL* (23 July 1907), 3.7.

159. McCarahan, "Chicago's Great Film Industry," 4. Amusement parks like Riverside in Chicago, in 1907, also catered to women and children by offering free admission—see Lauren Rabinovitz, "Temptations of Pleasure: Nickelodeons, Amusement Parks, and the Sights of Female Sexuality," *camera obscura* 23 (1990), 77.

160. "Moving Picture Industry Is in Great Uplift Movement," *SW* (21 September 1907), 18. In a 1994 interview, Edwin Stevens suggests that, as a boy, he got his parents to attend the moving pictures in Minneapolis—see Gregg Bachman, "Still in the Dark—Silent Film Audiences," *Film History* 9.1 (1997), 30.

161. See Aiken, "The Business of Exhibiting," 6.

162. J. Hartnett, "Theater Managers, Wake Up!" *MPW* (20 June 1908), 525.

163. See, for instance, Rosenzweig, *Eight Hours for What We Will*, 35–64, 93–126; and Peiss, *Cheap Amusements*, 16–21.

164. See Rosenzweig, *Eight Hours for What We Will*, 4.

165. As one example of this discourse, see the muckraking essay by George Kibbe Turner, "The City of Chicago: A Study of the Great Immoralities," *McClure's* 28 (April 1907), 575–592.

166. See, for instance, Josiah Strong, *The Challenge of the City* (New York: Eaton and Mains, 1907), 116–118; Currie, "The Nickel Madness," 1247; Collier, "Cheap Amusements," 75; "Film Shows Win the Press," *VFI* (23 May 1908), 5; Stryckmans, "Moving Picture Is Enemy of the Saloon," 7; "Moving Pictures and the Temperance Movement," *MPW* (4 July 1908), 6–7; "Strong Word for Pictures," *Var* (28 August 1909), 12; "'Spectator's' Comments," *NYDM* (4 September 1909), 16; "Picture Shows and Saloons," *Nick* (September

1909), 72; and Simon Patten on the nickelodeon's replacement of the saloon, in *Product and Climax* (1909), cited by Lewis E. Palmer, "The World in Motion," *Survey* (5 June 1909), 357.

167. George Shippy is quoted in K.S. Hover, "Police Supervision in Chicago," *Nick* (January 1909), 11.

168. See, for instance, Hugo Münsterberg, "The Prevention of Crime," *McClure's* 30 (April 1908), 756.

169. This link is made succinctly in "The Motion Picture Shows [Augusta]," *MPW* (29 August 1908), 154.

170. W. Livingston Larned, "The Public and the Filmmaker," *VFI* (25 January 1908), 3. Larned may have been a pseudonym for a young man J. Austin Fynes described as a freelance writer "of 'scenarios' for play-pictures."

171. For a comprehensive analysis of the system of representation and narration developed in Pathé films between 1904 and 1907, see Abel, *The Ciné Goes to Town*, 102–178. Janet Staiger argues that narrative comprehensibility *"within the film"* developed for the benefit of "working class, immigrant, and rural audiences" in the United States, but she confines her focus to American films—see Janet Staiger, *Interpreting Films: Studies in the Historical Reception of American Cinema* (Princeton, N.J.: Princeton University Press, 1992), 102, 119. Long before Larned's article, the *Index* had argued that films had to be understandable to a wide range of audiences—see "Moving Pictures for Audiences, Not for Makers," *VFI* (1 September 1906), 10.

172. See Walter Laidlaw, *Federation* 2.1 (April 1902), 26, 32; and *The Thirteenth Census of the United States*, 62, 95.

173. Between 1891 and 1900, according to the United States census, 52.8 percent of the new immigrants came from eastern and southern Europe; between 1900 and 1909, the figure rose to 71.7 percent—Frank V. Thompson, *Schooling the Immigrant* (New York: Harper and Brothers, 1920), 29–30. That most of those from Russia, and probably from Poland and Austria-Hungary as well, were Jewish has been established by Erich Rosenthal, "The Equivalence of United States Census Data for Persons of Russian Stock or Descent with American Jews: An Evaluation," *Demography* 12 (May 1975), 275–290. For information on the Jewish Pale region, stretching from near the Baltic Sea to the Black Sea, see Moses Rischin, *The Promised City: New York's Jews, 1870–1914* (Cambridge, Mass.: Harvard University Press, 1962), 19–33. See, also, Simon Kuznets, "Immigration of Russian Jews to the United States: Background and Structure," *Perspectives in American History* 9 (1975), 35–124.

174. William Fox, "Reminiscences and Observations," in Joseph Kennedy, *The Story of the Films* (Chicago: A. W. Shaw, 1927), 302.

175. "An Unexplored Field and Its Possibilities," *VFI* (6 October 1906), 3–4. "Foreigners" reportedly flocked to the summer amusement parks in Chicago, in 1906—see "Chicago Park Season," *Bill* (22 September 1906), 8.

176. "Censors Inspect Nickel Theaters," *CT* (1 May 1907), 6; and "Cheap Shows Lure: Police Aim a Blow," *CRH* (1 May 1907), 1.

177. "Correspondence: Low Priced Theatres," *MPW* (1 June 1907), 202; Currie, "The Nickel Madness," 1246.

178. Patterson, "The Nickelodeons," 10, 11. See, also, Collier, "Cheap Amusements," 75. In a part of this article excised in Pratt's *Spellbound in Darkness*, Patterson also singles out stokers and sailors attending the cheaper nickelodeons—see, also, the reprinting of this article in *MPW* (11 January 1908), 23. This reference suggests a further line of inquiry into the

audiences that frequented nickelodeons, at least if the sailor did epitomize a bachelor subculture closely linked to gay culture in turn-of-the-century New York—see George Chauncey, *Gay New York: Gender, Urban Culture, and the Making of the Gay Male World, 1890–1940* (New York: Basic Books, 1994), 34–44, 78–79.

179. Frederic Haskin, "Nickelodeon History," *VFI* (1 February 1908), 5. See, also, George Ethelbert Walsh, "Moving Picture Drama for the Multitude," *Independent* 64 (6 February 1908), 306; and the *New York Press* reporter describing a Bowery audience, in 23 February 1908—quoted in William Uricchio and Roberta Pearson, *Reframing Culture: The Case of the Vitagraph Quality Films* (Princeton, N.J.: Princeton University Press, 1993), 28. In December, *Show World* even estimated that "the population of New York City [was] 75 per cent foreign extraction"—"Sunday Closing Reduces Pay," *SW* (28 December 1907), 3.

180. Mayne, "Immigrants and Spectators," 33.

181. See Ben Singer, "Manhattan Nickelodeons: New Data on Audiences and Exhibitors," *Cinema Journal* 34.3 (Spring 1995), 5–35. To be fair, Musser also points to the importance of immigrant audiences for early New York moving picture shows, in contrast to the earlier influential study on Manhattan nickelodeons by Allen—see Musser, *Before the Nickelodeon*, 327. Judith Thissen is conducting research, much of it in the Yiddish press, for a forthcoming dissertation (University of Utrecht) on New York City's Jewish population as an audience for moving pictures during the silent period. She analyzes specific instances of her research quite cogently in "Dialogue: Manhattan's Nickelodeons," 102–107.

182. Fifty to seventy percent of the population on the Lower East Side was foreign-born—Laidlaw, *Federation*, 16–17, 30. See, also, Edmund J. James et al., eds., *The Immigrant Jew in America* (New York: B. F. Buck, 1907), 42–49; and Jeffrey S. Gurock, *When Harlem Was Jewish, 1870–1930* (New York: Columbia University Press, 1979), 49–55.

183. See Uricchio and Pearson, *Reframing Culture,* 19. See, also, Edward Ewing Pratt, *Industrial Causes of Congestion of Population in New York City* (New York: Columbia University Press, 1911), 29–31. By 1910, Jews constituted a quarter of New York City's total population—see Rischin, *The Promised City,* 94.

184. To be precise, Singer establishes a correlation between the location of the nickelodeons and the areas highest in population density as well as working-class residents; he is less interested in any correlation between nickelodeons and specific areas of ethnic concentration.

185. See, for instance, "Editorial," *VFI* (21 March 1908), 6; and "Moving Pictures," *NYC* (13 June 1908), 448. See, also, the description of a Jewish moving picture show by Montrose J. Moses, "Where They Play Shakespeare for Five Cents," *Theatre* 8 (October 1908), 264–265. For a good sense of the importance of "theatre-going" in the Jewish ghetto, see James, *The Immigrant Jew in America*, 226; and Nina Warnke, "Immigrant Popular Culture as Contested Sphere: Yiddish Music Halls, the Yiddish Press, and the Process of Americanization," *Theatre Journal* 48 (1996), 321–335.

186. James, *The Immigrant Jew in America,* 56–60, 251–252. The "Chicago Ghetto" also overlapped with one of the furnished room districts, which "housed a population of predominantly white service and factory workers," most of them women—Joanne Meyerowitz, "Sexual Geography and Gender Economy: The Furnished Room Districts of Chicago, 1900–1930," in Barbara Melosh, ed., *Gender and American History since 1890* (New York: Routledge, 1993), 43–71.

187. For specific data on the foreign-born population of those cities, see Laidlaw, *Federation*, 26–27; and *The Thirteenth Census of the United States,* 95. In 1900, "30 per cent of the

population . . . were foreign-born [in] 38 cities of 25,000 inhabitants or more"—Strong, *The Challenge of the City*, 152. Moreover, "more than two-thirds" of immigrants to the United States between 1900 and 1910 could be "found in the states of New York, Pennsylvania, Illinois, Massachusetts, Ohio, New Jersey, Texas, Wisconsin, and Michigan"—Thompson, *Schooling the Immigrant*, 28.

188. Early advertising practices on Park Row and the Bowery are described in "Store Show Advertising," *VFI* (22 February 1908), 5. See, also, "How to Advertise Picture Shows," *VFI* (14 September 1907), 3; James K. Meade, "Advertising the Show," *Nick* (February 1909), 43; and Meade, "A Picture Theater Newspaper," *Nick* (July 1909), 7.

189. See "Hull House, Chicago," *MPW* (29 June 1907), 262.

190. "Moving Picture News from Everywhere," *VFI* (28 March 1908), 6; "Music and Films," *VFI* (16 May 1908), 4; and Gurock, *When Harlem Was Jewish*, 49–51.

191. See "Chicago Notes," *MPW* (9 July 1910), 92. The writer also mentions Gaumont's *The Story of Esther* as being "deeply appreciated by the Jewish people who patronize these shows."

192. Lubin's *Hebrew Fugitive* and Biograph's *Romance of a Jewess* are reviewed in "Reviews of New Films," *NYDM* (19 September 1908), 9, and (31 October 1908), 8. Another Lubin film, *The Yiddisher Boy*, has a ghetto kid turn into a prosperous merchant and reward a friend who had once rescued him from a beating—see "Reviews of Licensed Films," *NYDM* (1 May 1909), 42. For a good content analysis of such films, see Patricia Erens, *The Jew in American Cinema* (Bloomington: Indiana University Press, 1984), 29–63. As Erens's research suggests, "ghetto films" in particular did not become more numerous until 1910 and later, when they could serve a different purpose for mainstream middle-class audiences. From 1905 to 1907, Pathé did make a number of Russian subjects that could have resonated with Jewish audiences, from *Russian Anti-Semitic Atrocities* (1905) to *The Female Spy* (1906).

193. Pathé had branch offices in Moscow (February 1904), Berlin (March 1905), Vienna (July 1905), Saint Petersburg (December 1905), Milan (May 1906), Odessa (July 1906), Budapest (June 1907), and Warsaw (July 1907). But the company's films circulated even earlier than that in most areas: in Poland, for instance, Malgorzeta Hendrykowska has found many Pathé titles on surviving cinema programs during the period between 1904 and 1908—Hendrykowska, "Was the Cinema Fairground Entertainment? The Birth and Role of Popular Cinema in Polish Territories up to 1908," in Richard Dyer and Ginette Vincendeau, eds., *Popular European Cinema* (London: Routledge, 1992), 112–125. On a four-month trip to Europe, Laemmle found that "Pathé seems to be the household word wherever there are moving pictures to be seen"—"Back from Europe," *VFI* (26 October 1907), 3. Berst even claimed that, by 1908, Pathé controlled "three-quarters of the business in Europe"—"Pathé's Position," *VFI* (13 June 1908), 4.

194. The phonograph could play an even stronger role in reinforcing ethnic identity: among Chicago workers, "the victrola helped keep Polish or Italian culture alive by allowing people to play foreign-language records, often at ethnic gatherings." Lizabeth Cohen, "Encountering Mass Culture at the Grassroots: The Experience of Chicago Workers in the 1920s," *American Quarterly* 41.1 (March 1989)—quoted in Hansen, *Babel and Babylon*, 113. My aim here is to extend Hansen's insight about how the cinema may have functioned for immigrant culture, specifically for its "chameleonlike quality," its "threshold function, oscillating between the tradition of family-centered ethnic entertainment and the more anonymous, more modern forms of commercialized leisure"—see Hansen, *Babel and Babylon*, 101–105.

195. Hutchins Hapgood, *The Spirit of the Ghetto* (New York: Funk and Wagnalls, 1902), 26–28. Hapgood also offers a glimpse of Jewish audiences at the Yiddish theaters on the Bowery—see *The Spirit of the Ghetto,* 113–116. See, also, Irving Howe, "The Lower East Side: Symbol and Fact," in Allon Schoener, ed., *The Lower East Side: Portal to American Life (1870–1924)* (New York: Jewish Museum, 1967), 10–14.

196. Herbert N. Casson, "The Jew in America," *Munsey's* 34 (January 1906), 394. See, also, Edward A. Ross, "The East European Hebrews," *The Old World in the New: The Significance of Past and Present Immigration to the American People* (New York: Century, 1914), 164–167; and Warnke, "Immigrant Popular Culture as Contested Sphere," 330–335.

197. Andrew Heinze, *Adapting to Abundance: Jewish Immigrants, Mass Consumption, and the Search for an American Identity* (New York: Columbia University Press, 1990), 3–7. See, also, Rischin, *The Promised City,* 101–102; and Uricchio and Pearson, *Reframing Culture,* 37. Both organizations, along with lecturers in the New York City public schools, were using stereopticons and moving picture machines—see "Lectures with Pictures," *VFI* (15 September 1906), 3.

ENTR'ACTE 3. A TRADE PRESS FOR THE "WORLD'S GREATEST SHOW"

1. "To Our Readers," *VFI* (25 April 1906), 3.

2. *Billboard* began publication in 1893; *New York Clipper* first appeared in 1852.

3. George Kleine, "Optical Projection in the Past Half Century," *SW* (27 June 1908), 15.

4. "Manufacturers and Dealers in Moving Picture Machines and Films," *NYC* (24 February 1906), ix. This photo page also marginalizes Edison and Vitagraph and gives much more attention to Méliès, Lubin, Selig, Spoor, and Kleine.

5. See the editorial page of *VFI* (25 April 1906) and (25 August 1906). See, also, "Announcement," *VFI* (3 November 1906), 3; and "Editorial," *VFI* (17 November 1906), 3.

6. Some historians claim Pathé and Vitagraph jointly owned *Views and Films Index*—see Charles Musser, *The Emergence of Cinema to 1907,* vol. 1 of *History of the American Cinema* (New York: Scribner's, 1991), 424; and William Uricchio and Roberta Pearson, *Reframing Culture: The Case of the Vitagraph Quality Films* (Princeton, N.J.: Princeton University Press, 1993), 45. As yet, however, there is no clear documentation of that, other than Pathé's own assertion that it was "the first to get out a trade paper," in "Notes from the Manufacturers," *MPW* (17 July 1910), 165. The Pathé and Vitagraph ads were the only ones that ran a full page, and they alternated each week inside the front and back covers.

7. See "Make a Note of This," *VFI* (19 May 1906), 8; and "To Our Readers," *VFI* (26 May 1906), 3, and (2 June 1906), 3. An early description of nickelodeons in New York, for instance, mentions four films, three of them by Pathé—see "Our Head Office Boy Wants to Be a Reporter," *VFI* (25 April 1906), 10.

8. Frank S. Munsey, "Advertising in Some of Its Phases," *Munsey's* 20 (December 1898), 477. For good studies of this language, see Richard Ohmann, *Selling Culture: Magazines, Markets, and Class at the Turn of the Century* (London: Verso, 1996), 185–193; and Christopher Wilson, "The Rhetoric of Consumption: Mass-Market Magazines and the Demise of the Gentle Reader, 1880–1920," in Richard Wightman Fox and T.J. Jackson Lears, eds., *The Culture of Consumption: Critical Essays in American History, 1880–1980* (New York: Pantheon, 1983), 39–64.

9. The first issue, for instance, reproduced "'The Lady with the Fan' by Abel Faivre, perhaps the most famous recent French painting" and "American Beauty" by Hamilton King. It is suggestive that most of these reproductions, which disappeared after six weeks, represented a woman in a state of emotion, and that several of the French placed them in Breton landscapes. Distributing visual reproductions en masse was a familiar advertising strategy, of course, but it also may have had a corollary in the art exhibitions and lectures organized by social settlements like Hull House in Chicago—see Allen F. Davis, *Spearheads for Reform: The Social Settlements and the Progressive Movement, 1890–1914* (New York: Oxford University Press, 1967), 41–43.

10. See, for instance, "Editorial," *VFI* (18 August 1906), 3; "Problems of the Trade and Their Solution," *VFI* (25 August 1906), 3; and "The Plan to Organize the Protective Association," *VFI* (27 October 1906), 3–4.

11. "Publishers' Note," *MPW* (9 March 1907), 3. In one of the first surveys of the early trade press, Robert Grau ignores *Views and Films Index* almost completely and gives priority to *Moving Picture World;* he also dismisses Saunders and claims that J. P. Chalmers founded the trade weekly (yet Chalmers was listed as associate editor on the masthead)—see Grau, *The Theatre of Science* (New York: Benjamin Blom, 1914), 246–247. In a 27 December 1906 letter to Frank Marion, George Kleine complained, without giving reasons, that *Views and Films Index* had become "unspeakable as a trade sheet"—see Box 29: Kalem Folder, GK.

12. The initial subscription rate for *Views and Films Index* was $4.00 per year; for *Moving Picture World,* it was only $2.00. The advertising rate for the former was $84.00 for a whole page; for the latter, it was $50.00.

13. See "The Nickelodeon," *MPW* (4 May 1907), 140; Barton W. Currie, "The Nickel Madness," *Harper's Weekly* (24 August 1907); and Joseph Medill Patterson, "The Nickelodeons," *Saturday Evening Post* (23 November 1907). See, also, "Moving Picture Combine," *MPW* (8 June 1907), 223; "Association News," *MPW* (22 June 1907), 250; and "Association Notes," *MPW* (29 June 1907), 270.

14. See, for instance, "Public Opinion as a Moral Center," *MPW* (11 May 1907), 147.

15. "Trade Notes," *MPW* (23 March 1907), 42. See, also, the reprinting of an article from the *Michigan Tradesman,* as "Unadulterated Fakes," *MPW* (5 October 1907), 487–488.

16. See, for instance, "Moving Picture Business Enjoys a Frenzied Boom," *MPW* (14 September 1907), 438–440; and F. C. McCarahan, "Chicago's Great Film Industry," *Bill* (24 August 1907), 4.

17. The Harold Washington Public Library in Chicago is one of the very few libraries to hold copies of the first volume of *Show World,* unfortunately in a rapidly deteriorating condition.

18. See, for instance, "Moving Pictures Industry," *SW* (29 June 1907), 16; and McCarahan, "Chicago's Great Film Industry," 4–5, 39.

19. "Editorial: What Will Pathé Do?" *SW* (19 October 1907), 18.

20. Pathé also was deliberately omitted from the list of "New Film Subjects," *SW* (12 October 1907), 11.

21. The company advertised the weekly bulletin in *NYC* (9 November 1907), 1044, and in *VFI* (21 December 1907), 13. In France, Pathé had been issuing monthly bulletins since 1905; it also consolidated its available titles into an annual bulletin in early 1907. Copies of the first two years of the American *Pathé Weekly Bulletin* are extremely rare; I have seen only five, all but one in the possession of a private collector in Paris.

22. Pathé's strategy here suggests that it was becoming wary of the trade press as well as rental exchanges (over neither of which it could exercise control), a wariness that would prove warranted as marketing and advertising eventually coalesced in the distribution branch of the industry—see, for instance, Leslie Midkaff DeBauche, "Advertising and the Movies, 1908–1915," *Film Reader* 6 (1985), 115–124.

23. See, for instance, McCarahan, "Chicago's Great Film Industry," 4–5, 39; and "The Film Industry," *Bill* (7 December 1907), 30, 74.

24. One of the first moving pictures reviewed was Edison's *Life of a Cowboy*, in "New Acts of the Week," *Var* (19 January 1907), 9. The first "Moving Picture News and Reviews" appeared in *Var* (25 January 1908), 11. Interestingly, the first industry ads were placed by Chicago rental exchanges such as Eugene Cline, 20th-Century Optiscope, and George Spoor. As editor of *Variety*, Sime Silverman also wrote many of the film reviews—see Robert Grau, *The Businessman in the Amusement World* (New York: Broadway, 1910), 238.

25. "An Amazing Growth," *NYDM* (28 March 1908), 4; and "The Moving Picture Field," *NYDM* (30 May 1908), 7.

26. After a full year without a designated editor, *Views and Films Index* made Leon Rubenstein its editor with the 23 May 1908 issue. Ellis Cohen left the trade weekly the following fall—see "Retired from *Film Index*," *NYDM* (17 October 1908), 11.

27. As editor of *Moving Picture News*, Saunders contributed an article, "Motion Picture Art," in *Bill* (27 June 1908), 6–7, 10. See, also, "Independents Talk of Organizing," *NYDM* (1 August 1908), 7; and Grau, *The Theatre of Science*, 246.

28. Saunders and Chalmers were listed jointly as editors for the 25 April 1908 issue, but Chalmers was the sole editor by the 2 May 1908 issue.

29. The first issue with the new format appeared on 4 September 1908: *Film Index* ran sixteen pages and used three columns per page (but with the same small typeface).

30. See, for instance, W. Stephen Bush, "Lectures on Moving Pictures," *MPW* (22 August 1908), 136–137; W. Stephen Bush, "The Coming Ten and Twenty Cent Moving Picture Theater," *MPW* (29 August 1908), 152–153; James D. Law, "Better Scenarios Demanded," *MPW* (29 August 1908), 153–154; W. Stephen Bush, "The Film of the Future," *MPW* (5 September 1908), 172–173; and Rollin Summers, "The Moving Picture Drama and Acted Drama," *MPW* (19 September 1908), 211–213—the latter reprinted in Stanley Kauffmann and Bruce Henstell, eds., *American Film Criticism: From the Beginnings to Citizen Kane* (New York: Liveright, 1972), 9–13. Bush began advertising as a film lecturer, based in Philadelphia, in *MPW* (27 June 1908), 547. He especially was noted for his lectures accompanying Pathé's *Passion Play*—see "Notes," *Bill* (10 October 1908), 9. Law promoted himself as a "leading American writer" and "Motographic" advertiser (also from Philadelphia) in ads in *SW* (27 June 1908), 27, and in *MPW* (27 June 1908), 545. See, also, Richard L. Stromgren, "The Moving Picture World of W. Stephen Bush," *Film History* 2.1 (Winter 1988), 13–22. Both Law and Saunders later became involved in the Colonial Film Company, which would specialize in educational films—see Grau, *The Theatre of Science*, 71–73.

31. "Reviews of Late Films," *NYDM* (13 June 1908), 10.

32. See "Comments on Film Subjects," *MPW* (10 October 1908), 279, and (14 November 1908), 378.

33. The editors of *Nickelodeon* were Ed J. Mock and Paul H. Woodruff; almost nothing is yet known about the Electricity Magazine Corporation.

34. See "'The Nickelodeon' as a Text Book," *Nick* (February 1909), 34. Grau spoke very highly of the magazine and its influence, by 1913, in *The Theatre of Science*, 248–249.

35. See "The Nickelodeon," *Nick* (January 1909), 1.

36. The Nickeldom reopened as the Unique in August 1908—see the special ad in *DMRL* (4 August 1908), 8.

CHAPTER 4. RECLAIMING THE MARKET

1. George Eastman's letter is reprinted in Georges Sadoul, *Histoire générale du cinéma, 2: Les Pionniers du cinéma, 1897–1909* (Paris: Denoël, 1948), 465–466. Although undated, it refers to his recent negotiations with Edison and Pathé representatives in the summer of 1907; it also coincides with the Eastman letter (dated 29 October 1907), which Pathé publicized in its ad on the inside cover of *VFI* (21 December 1907). Sadoul's account of the Film Service Association and Motion Picture Patents Company's formation in that volume (pages 461–478) is still one of the best available.

2. See the 1 July letter to the "Edison Import House" from Charles Pathé, and the 21 July letter to W. E. Gilmore from Frank Dyer—1904 Motion Picture Folder, ENHS. If any correspondence survives in the Pathé Télévision Archive, it has yet to be discovered.

3. See the 24 August 1904 letters to Gilmore from George Kleine and to Kleine from Gilmore—1904 Motion Picture Folder, ENHS.

4. See the 21 November 1904 letter to James White from Alexander Moore—1904 Motion Picture Folder, ENHS.

5. Between November 1902 and March 1905, Edison brought nearly thirty patent suits against its competitors—1905 Motion Picture Folder, ENHS. Again, good studies of the patent wars can be found in Janet Staiger, "Combination and Litigation: Structures of US Film Distribution, 1891–1917," *Cinema Journal* 23.2 (Winter 1984), 45–47; and Tom Gunning, *D. W. Griffith and the Origins of American Narrative Film* (Urbana: University of Illinois Press, 1991), 60–65.

6. See the Edison ad in *NYC* (12 July 1902), 444, as well as the contrasting Edison and Pathé ads in *NYC* (5 August 1905), 612, and (30 September 1905), 800. See, also, William E. Swanson's testimony in *United States vs. MPPC* (1914), 322.

7. See the 16 October 1906 letter to Moore from James Hardin—1906 Motion Picture Folder, ENHS.

8. "Compagnie Générale de Phonographes, Cinématographes et Appareils de Précision," *Les Assemblées Générales* (25 June 1906), 656, 658—Carton 1, Pathé Télévision Archive, Saint-Ouen.

9. "Trade Notes," *VFI* (16 March 1907), 6. For a more detailed analysis of Edison's negotiations with Pathé, see Kristin Thompson, *Exporting Entertainment: America in the World's Film Market* (London: BFI, 1985), 4–10. See, also, Martin Sopocy, "The Edison-Biograph Patent Litigation of 1901–1907," *Film History* 3.1 (1989), 19–22.

10. See the 15 March 1907 letter to Gilmore from G. Croydon-Marks, the 10 April 1907 letter to Croydon-Marks from Gilmore, and the 13 April 1907 letter to Gilmore from Dyer—1907 Motion Picture Folder: Pathé, ENHS. In a 5 May 1907 letter to W. E. Gilmore, George Kleine reveals that this proposal may have been a misguided part of Edison's plan, already in process, to negotiate a licensing agreement with most of the other manufacturers—see Box 18: Edison Manufacturing Company, GK.

11. See the 21 May 1907 letter from Croydon-Marks to Pathé and the 28 May 1907 letters from Gilmore to William Pelzer and to Thomas Edison himself—1907 Motion Picture Folder: Pathé, ENHS.

12. See the translation of the 22 May letter from Pathé to Croydon-Marks—1907 Motion Picture Folder, ENHS.

13. "Trade Notes," *VFI* (8 June 1907), 4; "Trade Notes," *MPW* (22 June 1907), 249. The "incorporators" of the new company were William H. Corbin, Collins and Corbin, Ernest A. Ivatts, and Charles Pathé. By locating in New Jersey, Pathé was taking advantage of new laws that gave corporations unusual "privileges, mobility, and powers"—see Richard Ohmann, *Selling Culture: Magazines, Markets, and Class at the Turn of the Century* (London: Verso, 1996), 60.

14. Fred Aiken later said of the nickelodeon and rental exchange explosion, in that first year or so, "there was little time for ethics"—see Aiken, "Ethics of Film Renting Worthy of Deep Study," *SW* (27 June 1908), 24–25.

15. "'Duping' of Fine Film Pictures Condemned," *SW* (9 November 1907), 16. In 21 January 1907 and 2 February 1907 letters to Kleine, Marion had reported that both Lubin and Miles Brothers continued to do a lot of duping, especially of Pathé films—see Box 29: Kalem Folder, GK.

16. See, for instance, "What Will Pathé Do?" *SW* (19 October 1907), 18; and "Editorial: What Does It Mean?" *MPW* (26 October 1907), 535–536. See, also, Richard Abel, *The Ciné Goes to Town: French Cinema, 1896–1914* (Berkeley: University of California Press, 1994), 33–34.

17. "Various Opinions on Organization," *VFI* (23 November 1907), 3, 7.

18. See "A New Move: The Pathé Contract," *VFI* (26 October 1907), 3; and "Editorial: What Does It Mean?" *MPW* (26 October 1907), 535–536.

19. See "American Moving Picture Captains Meet in Pittsburgh," *SW* (23 November 1907), 21; Warren Patrick, "Chicago Welcomes Captains of Moving Picture Industry," *SW* (30 November 1907), 18; "The United Film Service Protective Association," *MPW* (30 November 1907), 627; "Film Men's Association Needed, Says Swanson," *SW* (7 December 1907), 14; "Moving Picture Men Organize," *SW* (21 December 1907), 88; "James B. Clark," *MPW* (21 December 1907), 681; "The U.F.S.P.A.," *MPW* (21 December 1907), 682; "United Film Service Protective Association Meets," *Bill* (21 December 1907), 20; "Endorses New Film Organization," *SW* (28 December 1907), 10; "Moving Picture Men at Banquet," *SW* (28 December 1907), 11, 13; and "Film Convention and Moving Picture News," *Bill* (28 December 1907), 9. Except for a special supplement (23 November 1907), the *Index* was unusually reticent about the convention, having only one story devoted to it—"United Film Service Protective Ass'n," *VFI* (21 December 1907), 4–5.

20. See Charles Musser, *Before the Nickelodeon: Edwin S. Porter and the Edison Manufacturing Company* (Berkeley: University of California Press, 1991), 375–379. For a slightly different version of this history, see Robert Anderson, "The Motion Picture Patents Company: A Reevaluation," in Tino Balio, ed., *The American Film Industry*, rev. ed. (Madison: University of Wisconsin Press, 1985), 133–138.

21. See the testimony of J. A. Berst, *USA vs. MPPC* (1914), 1768–1770. See, also, Musser, *Before the Nickelodeon*, 377.

22. The initial listing of the UFSPA included rental exchanges only—"The U.F.S.P.A.," *MPW* (21 December 1907), 682. By February, the FSA was contractually bound to the following licensed manufacturers: Edison, Essanay, Kalem, Lubin, Méliès, Pathé, Selig, and Vitagraph—"Statement by the Licensed Manufacturers," *VFI* (29 February

1908), 3–4. For the details of Kleine's ill-rewarded diplomacy in the UFSPA's formation, see Eileen Bowser, *The Transformation of Cinema,1907–1915*, vol. 2 of *History of American Cinema* (New York: Scribner's, 1990), 26–27.

23. "Interview with FSA Members and Others," *MPW* (28 March 1908), 260. Among those foreign companies excluded from the AEL-FSA contracts were Gaumont, Urban-Eclipse, Cinès, and Great Northern (Nordisk), all of which had begun to carve out a niche in the American market.

24. See, for instance, the 11 February 1908 letter from J. A. Berst to George Eastman—MPPC Box no. 5, ENHS. Pathé also was allowed to hold an "INVENTORY SALE" of its "large stock of Films on hand"—see the Pathé ad in *VFI* (25 January 1908), 2. Pathé did make this concession: it would no longer use its *Weekly Bulletin* to "give the exact day of the issue of new films"—see "Editorial," *VFI* (22 February 1908), 6.

25. "Trade Notes," *MPW* (25 January 1908), 60. See, also, Martin Norden, "The Pathé-Frères Company during the Trust Era," *Journal of the University Film Association* 33 (Summer 1981), 16–17. The Bound Brook factory was producing thirteen thousand meters of positive film stock per day by the summer of 1908, with expectations of twenty thousand meters by the end of the year—see the "Rapport du Conseil d'Administration," Assemblée Générale Ordinaire, Pathé-Frères (2 June 1908)—Carton 2, Pathé Télévision Archive.

26. The Biograph licensing group was announced in an ad in *MPW* (22 February 1908), 130; and then in similar ads in *SW* (29 February 1908), 28, and *NYC* (29 February 1908), 52. As Gunning argues, Biograph had both legal and economic bases for defying Edison—see Gunning, *D. W. Griffith*, 63–65. Kleine had to sell the Kalem stock he controlled in order to avoid any conflict of interest. In a 28 February 1908 letter to Marion and Long, he speaks of his paradoxical situation—Box 29: Kalem Folder, GK.

27. See "Moving Picture Men Indorse Independent Movement in Chicago," *SW* (14 March 1908), 8; and "Trade Directory," *MPW* (25 April 1908), 378. See, also, Musser, *Before the Nickelodeon*, 380.

28. See the Pathé ad in *CT* (5 April 1908), 3.2.

29. See, for instance, "The Position of the American Mutoscope and Biograph Company" and "The Combine Viewed by the Daily Press," *MPW* (15 February 1908), 112, 115; "Trade Notes: The Film War," *MPW* (29 February 1908), 160–161; "Moving Picture Men Indorse Independent Movement in Chicago," 8; and "The Film Service Situation," *MPW* (4 April 1908), 287. Kleine may have been most peeved at Pathé because of the extraordinary costs Kleine Optical had incurred purchasing imported films in 1907 (a half million dollars), nearly triple the costs of film purchases from the companies that became the Edison licensees—see the untitled memo on 1907 purchases, in Box 18: Edison Manufacturing Company, GK.

30. Sadoul, *Histoire générale du cinéma*, 2:467.

31. "Pathé's Position," *VFI* (13 June 1908), 4.

32. See "Rumors regarding Pathé-Frères," *NYDM* (12 September 1908), 9; "Pathé Will Not Invade Rental Field," *MPW* (12 September 1908), 192; "Pathé Frères Not to Rent," *VFI* (19 September 1908), 4; and Bowser, *The Transformation of Cinema*, 28–29.

33. "Rapport du Conseil d'Administration" (2 June 1908)—Carton 2, Pathé Télévision Archive.

34. See the testimony of J. A. Berst, *USA vs. MPPC* (1914), 1778. As Gunning reminds me, no other manufacturer had tried to establish a rental exchange, not even Vitagraph, which still maintained an exhibition service.

35. "Rapport du Conseil d'Administration" (2 June 1908)—Carton 2, Pathé Télévision Archive.

36. The *Index* often had encouraged the formation of some kind of protective association for the new industry, beginning in the late summer of 1906—see, for instance, "Editorial: Association for Protection Against Dishonest Customers in the Moving Picture Trade," *VFI* (18 August 1906), 3; "Problems of the Trade and Their Solution," *VFI* (25 August 1906), 3; and "The Plan to Organize the Protective Association," *VFI* (27 October 1906), 3–4.

37. "Increasing American Output," *NYDM* (26 September 1908), 9.

38. For further information on this overall shift in Pathé's economic interests, see Abel, "In the Belly of the Beast: The Early Years of Pathé-Frères," *Film History* 5.4 (December 1993), 372–376.

39. In 1906, Pathé also began introducing its trademark into the diegetic world of story films such as *Holiday* and *Detective's Tour of the World:* it materialized as a small emblem or plaque attached to the set decor in one or more shots—see, for instance, Suzanne Richard, "Pathé, marque de fabrique: vers une nouvelle méthode pour la datation des copies anciennes," *1895* 10 (1991), 13–27; and Paolo Cherchi Usai, *Burning Passions: An Introduction to the Study of Silent Cinema* (London: British Film Institute, 1994), 104–105. For a brief analysis of how American companies used trademarks on their sets after 1907, see Bowser, *The Transformation of Cinema,* 137–139.

40. The first Vitagraph ad with this trademark appeared in *VFI* (5 October 1907), 2. When it first began producing films, Vitagraph briefly used a more elaborate trademark eagle clutching an American flag and shield—see the Vitagraph ad in *NYC* (5 October 1905), 852.

41. Biograph's circle AB first appeared in *NYC* (4 January 1908), 1279, and then in *MPW* (1 February 1908), 70. Within a month, another Biograph licensee, Great Northern, began promoting its trademark, a polar bear straddling a globe—see its ad in *MPW* (14 March 1908), 202. Soon Gaumont was using its name (rather than ELGE) encircled by marguerite petals to promote its "independent films"—see its ad in *MPW* (23 May 1908), 463.

42. Essanay's S & A logo first appeared in *MPW* (4 April 1908), 297.

43. Selig's Diamond S first appeared in *VFI* (13 June 1908), 12.

44. Kalem finally settled on a silhouette sunburst surrounding its name for a trademark—see its ad in *NYDM* (12 December 1908), 6.

45. Kleine Optical first displayed all the trademarks of the "Celebrated European Factories" whose films it exported in an ad in *MPW* (15 August 1908), 132.

46. Ben Turpin performed in many of these early Essanay comedies—see his account of that work in "Life of a Moving Picture Comedian," *MPW* (3 April 1909), 405. Some of that account is reprinted in Bowser, *The Transformation of Cinema,* 179.

47. "Earmarks of Makers," *NYDM* (14 November 1908), 10. It was at this time also that *Moving Picture World* began listing the precise release dates of films from both licensing groups—see "Latest Films of All Makers," *MPW* (7 November 1908), 370.

48. Musser, *Before the Nickelodeon,* 378. The FSA release schedule was first announced in *VFI* (11 April 1908), 3. As the largest supplier, Pathé had the most release dates: every weekday except Tuesday and Sunday. Vitagraph and Lubin each had two: the one, Tuesday and Friday; the other, Monday and Thursday. Selig, Essanay, Kalem, Méliès, and even Edison all had just one.

49. See, for instance, "Release Dates," *VFI* (11 April 1908), 3; "Now Is the Time," *VFI* (30 May 1908), 3; and "Association Renters Discuss Schedule," *VFI* (6 June 1908), 4.

50. Musser, *Before the Nickelodeon,* 378; and Bowser, *The Transformation of Cinema,* 28.

51. See, for instance, the front covers of *VFI* (22 February 1908) and (25 April 1908); and "The Moving Picture Field," *NYDM* (30 May 1908), 7.

52. See, for instance, "Words from the Knocker and Howler," *MPW* (1 February 1908), 72; "The Film Service Association and Ourselves," *MPW* (22 February 1908), 131; "About Ourselves," *MPW* (21 March 1908), 227; and "Editorial: The Sub Renter," *MPW* (8 August 1908), 99–100. One week, for instance, its cover would have an Edison ad; the next, ads from the "Independent" Eagle Film Exchange and Williamson and Company, importers of Italian "Cinès" films.

53. See "Scarcity of Film Subjects," *MPW* (4 April 1908), 283; "Editorial," *MPW* (11 April 1908), 311; and Musser, *Before the Nickelodeon,* 380–381. That older films continued to circulate, especially in small towns, is evident in Ottumwa, at both the Nickelodeon and the Electric Theatre, from 1907 through 1908, and at the Crystal Theatre in late 1908 and early 1909—this information is gathered from ads in the *Ottumwa Courier.* Still, the trade press did acknowledge that the FSA was responsible for the rapid system of distribution and exhibition now in place—see "Editorial Notes and Comments," *MPW* (25 April 1908), 366.

54. See, for instance, "Contemplates Consolidation of Film Interests," *Bill* (26 September 1908), 8; and "Motion Picture World Staggered by Combine," *Bill* (3 October 1908), 17. It was Frank Dyer, for Edison, and Harry Marvin and Jeremiah J. Kennedy, for Biograph, who headed these negotiations. For further information on the MPPC's formation, see Thompson, *Exporting Entertainment,* 10–19; Anderson, "The Motion Picture Patents Company," 138–142; Gunning, *D. W. Griffith,* 143–144; Musser, *Before the Nickelodeon,* 433–438; and Bowser, *The Transformation of Cinema,* 27–33.

55. The MPPC was even incorporated that September in New Jersey—Musser, *Before the Nickelodeon,* 435–437. For further information on the delay caused by Eastman and Pathé, see Bowser, *The Transformation of Cinema,* 31. Another reason that Pathé briefly considered opening its own rental exchange was to amortize the unsold film prints that were accumulating because of the AEL-FSA regulations, but it was able to sell off many of those prints between September and December, when the MPPC officially superseded the FSA.

56. See, for instance, the testimony of H. N. Marvin and Frank Dyer, *USA vs. MPPC* (1914), 26 and 1519.

57. See, for instance, the Motion Picture Patents Company ad in *FI* (6 February 1909), 15. The *Index* could be critical of the MPPC, especially in its reluctance to counter the Independents—see "Editorial: Tactics," *FI* (27 February 1909), 3. For positive appraisals of the MPPC, see "The Situation Reviewed," *FI* (24 April 1909), 4; "The Main Question," *FI* (1 May 1909), 3; "The Real Problem to Be Solved," *FI* (22 May 1909), 3; and "The Motion Picture Patents Company and Its Work," *MPW* (17 July 1909), 81–84.

58. See, for instance, "Insurance for Picture Houses," *NYDM* (10 April 1909), 14; "Fire and Liability Insurance," *NYDM* (17 April 1909), 13; "Fire Insurance for Exhibitors," *MPW* (17 April 1909), 468; and "Insurance for Picture Theatres," *FI* (17 April 1909), 4. Pathé imported film negative (at a lower tariff rate) and made positive prints at its Bound Brook factory—see "Proposed Tariff Change Favors Firm of Pathe Bros," *Var* (7 August 1909), 13. For a fuller analysis of this, the Payne-Aldrich tariff, see Thompson, *Exporting Entertainment,* 20–22.

59. See, for instance, "The Independents," *NYDM* (2 January 1909), 8; and "112 Exchanges Licensed," *Var* (30 January 1909), 13.

60. See, for instance, "The Patents Co. and the Independents," *MPW* (13 February 1909), 168; "Observations by Our Man about Town," *MPW* (6 March 1909), 263; the Laemmle ad in *MPW* (17 April 1909), 480–481; "Laemmle Is Independent," *NYDM* (24 April 1909), 14; "The Passing of Laemmle," *FI* (1 May 1909), 5; and "W. H. Swanson and the Independent Service," *MPW* (1 May 1909), 552. The Independents tried to redefine the MPPC as the "Modern Pocket Picking Coterie"—see "Observations by Our Man about Town," *MPW* (6 March 1909), 263.

61. See, for instance, the Independent Film Protective Association ad in *MPW* (16 January 1909), 66–67; "Independents Move," *Var* (23 January 1909), 13; "The Film Situation," *NYDM* (23 January 1909), 7; "The Independent Film Service Association," *MPW* (23 January 1909), 88; "The Independent Movement," *Nick* (February 1909), 39–40; "The Independent Movement and Its Progress," *MPW* (6 February 1909), 137; "The Film Situation," *NYDM* (13 February 1909), 12; "Conflicting Statements in St. Louis," *Var* (13 February 1909), 12; and "Strength of the Two Film Factions," *NYDM* (1 May 1909), 39–40. See, also, the relatively low number of exchanges leasing licensed films in these cities during May 1909—Box 26: Historical File: General, GK. For a much more in-depth analysis of these new Independents and J. J. Murdock, a prominent vaudeville owner who initially directed the IPPC, see Thompson, *Exporting Entertainment,* 19–27; Martin Sopocy, "Showmen and Tycoons: Friends and Enemies of the International Projecting and Producing Company," *Film History* 5.1 (March 1993), 96–115; and Charlie Keil, "Advertising Independence: Industrial Performance and Advertising Strategies of the Independent Movement, 1909–10," *Film History* 5.4 (December 1993), 472–488.

62. See, for instance, the first New York Motion Picture Company ad in *MPW* (29 May 1909), 734; the Laemmle ad in *MPW* (5 June 1909), 740; and "Independent Films: Centaur Film Company," *MPW* (7 August 1909), 207. The New York Company was formed by Fred Balshofer in partnership with Adam Kessel and Charles Bauman, owners of the Empire Film Exchange—see Fred Balshofer and Arthur Miller, *One Reel a Week* (Berkeley: University of California Press, 1967), 22, 24–25. Centaur was established in Bayonne, New Jersey, by David Horsley, and was renamed Nestor in early 1910; Horsley would be the first Independent to set up a studio in Hollywood—see Balshofer and Miller, *One Reel a Week,* 21, 57, 111. Horsley had monikers for some of his colleagues among the Independents, like "Lucky" Laemmle, "Foxy" Powers, "Erratic" Swanson, and "Road-Roller" Bauman—see Robert Grau, *The Theatre of Science* (New York: Benjamin Blom, 1914), 39.

63. See the Great Northern ad in *NYDM* (20 February 1909), 17; "Film Import Company Statement" and "Great Northern Independent Releases," *NYDM* (27 February 1909), 13; "Sample Independent Films," *NYDM* (6 March 1909), 14; "Release Dates of Independent Film," *MPW* (13 March 1909), 309; "Independent Releases," *NYDM* (17 April 1909), 13; "Independent Film Releases," *NYDM* (22 May 1909), 17; and "Independent Films," *MPW* (31 July 1909), 175.

64. See the New York Motion Picture Company ad in *MPW* (19 June 1909), 840. See, also, "Reports from the Field," *NYDM* (21 August 1909), 16, 18. Swanson especially argued that the Independents could "not possibly survive on European-made goods"—see Watterson R. Rothacker, "Chicago Film Men Discuss Motion Picture Outlook," *Bill* (11 September 1909), 26.

65. See, for instance, "A New Independent Movement," *Nick* (September 1909), 76; W. R. Rothacker, "National Independent Moving Picture Alliance," *Bill* (18 September

1908), 13; "Independent Alliance," *NYDM* (25 September 1909), 18; and "National Independent Moving Picture Alliance," *MPW* (25 September 1909), 410–412. By the end of 1909, Independent exchanges were boasting about, but hardly fulfilling, a release schedule of eleven American reels and seventeen European reels each week — see the Film Import and Trading Company ad in *MPW* (20 November 1909), 724–725; and National Independent Moving Picture Alliance ads in *MPW* (27 November 1909), 779, and *Nick* (December 1909), 4. For an early appraisal of the Sales Company, see "The Sales Company," *MPW* (21 May 1910), 822–823. See, also, Thompson, *Exporting Entertainment*, 22–25; and Keil, "Advertising Independence," 476–477.

66. A concise statement of these positions, attributed to a clergyman, politician, and physician, can be found in "Three Points of View," *MPW* (13 April 1907), 89.

67. Lucy France Pierce, "The Nickelodeon," *World Today* (October 1908) — reprinted in Gerald Mast, *The Movies in Our Midst: Documents in the Cultural History of Film in America* (Chicago: University of Chicago Press, 1982), 56.

68. See "New Acts," *Var* (7 December 1907), 10; and "Moving Picture News and Reviews," *Var* (14 March 1908), 13, and (18 April 1908), 13. *The Female Spy* ended with a young Cossack woman being killed and then dragged by a horse; *A Christmas Eve Tragedy* climaxed with a Breton fisherman throwing his wife's lover, along with his horse and cart, over a cliff into the sea. This discourse of moral disapproval contrasted, of course, with the respect that Collier, adhering to a position of regulation through uplift, used to describe New York nickelodeon films, in April 1908 — John Collier, "Cheap Amusements," *Charities and Commons* (11 April 1908), 74.

69. See the 28 May 1907 letter from W. E. Gilmore to T. Edison — 1907 Motion Picture Folder, ENHS.

70. "Chas. Pathé Makes a Statement," *VFI* (16 May 1908), 4.

71. Contrast this with Robert Sklar's statement that Pathé's success in the American market had notably little effect — Sklar, *Movie-Made America: A Cultural History of American Movies* (New York: Random House, 1975), 29.

72. William Uricchio and Roberta Pearson examine a similar contradiction in the appeals made to Italian culture in American discourse on the early cinema — see Uricchio and Pearson, "Italian Spectacle and the U.S. Market," in Roland Cosandey and François Albera, eds., *Images across Borders, 1896–1918* (Lausanne: Editions Payot, 1995), 95–105.

73. Perhaps the earliest evidence of this appeal comes in the Pathé ad in *NYC* (28 October 1905), 930. Between 1903 and 1905, Lumière's technical advances frequently were highlighted in the prestigious American monthly *Photo-Era Magazine*. In 1903, France exported fifty-one million francs' worth of automobiles and parts; in 1906, 140 million — Eugen Weber, *France Fin-de-Siècle* (Cambridge, Mass.: Harvard University Press, 1986), 207. See, also, Roger Magraw, *France 1815–1914: The Bourgeois Century* (London: Fontana, 1983), 232–233; and Paul Greenhalgh, *Ephemeral Vistas: The Expositions Universelles, Great Exhibitions and World's Fairs, 1851–1939* (Manchester, England: Manchester University Press, 1988), 154–155.

74. See, for instance, "Trade Notes," *MPW* (11 May 1907), 152–153. In 1906, Pathé already claimed that its projector was "the leading machine in Europe and South America" — see the Pathé ad in *VFI* (30 June 1906), 11.

75. Sarah Bernhardt made one of the earliest and most influential of such tours in 1880, then returned for another in 1900; Gabrielle Réjane made her first in 1895 and then

a second in 1904—see, for instance, Hamilton Mason, *French Theatre in New York* (New York: AMS Press, 1940), 6, 28–29, 31.

76. See, for instance, Arthur Gold and Robert Fizdale, *The Divine Sarah: A Life of Sarah Bernhardt* (New York: Knopf, 1991), 294–298.

77. William Leach, *Land of Desire: Merchants, Power, and the Rise of a New American Culture* (New York: Pantheon, 1993), 99–102. A similar point is made by Kathy Peiss, in "Making Faces: The Cosmetics Industry and the Cultural Construction of Gender, 1890–1930," *Genders* 7 (Spring 1990), 157–158; and Matthew Schneirov, *The Dream of a New Social Order: Popular Magazines in America, 1893–1914* (New York: Columbia University Press, 1994), 186–187.

78. For a good historical analysis of the sharp difference between France and the United States (as well as Great Britain) on matters of censorship in the late nineteenth century, see Walter Kendrick, *The Secret Museum: Pornography in Modern Culture* (New York: Viking, 1987), 95–124.

79. These attacks on moving pictures had begun the year before, in Chicago, Philadelphia, Cleveland, and Kansas City—see "News," *VFI* (7 July 1906), 8; "Do Moving Pictures Breed Immorality? An Unfair Attack," *VFI* (22 September 1906), 3; "Art Squad," *VFI* (29 September 1906), 3; and "Editorial," *VFI* (17 November 1906), 3. In Chicago, in particular, the newspapers were afraid that young girls were viewing peephole films like *The Opium Den* and *The Hold Up*, a subject John Sloan represented, from the working girl's point of view, in his 1905 engraving "Fun, One Cent"—reproduced in Janet Staiger, *Bad Women: Regulating Sexuality in Early American Cinema* (Minneapolis: University of Minnesota Press, 1995), 9. In March 1907, city officials also looked into closing "some of the five hundred nickel theatres in Greater New York"—see "The Closing of Nickelodeons in New York City," *MPW* (16 March 1907), 20; and "War on Nickel Theatres," *NYDM* (23 March 1907), 18.

80. See "The Five Cent Theaters," *CT* (10 April 1907), 8; "Nickel Theaters Crime Breeders," *CT* (13 April 1907), 3; "Traces Crime to Nickel Theater," *CT* (14 April 1907), 3; "War Is Declared on 5 Cent Shows," *CT* (27 April 1907), 5; "Would Suppress Vicious Shows," *CT* (28 April 1907), 1.10. "Censors Inspect Nickel Theaters," *CT* (1 May 1907), 6; "Cheap Shows Lure; Police Aim a Blow," *CRH* (2 May 1907), 1; "Curb Cheap Theaters," *CRH* (2 May 1907), 5; and "Trade Notes," *MPW* (11 May 1907), 153. Some Chicago newspapers like the *Daily News* challenged the *Tribune*'s attack—see Lauren Rabinovitz, "Temptations of Pleasure: Nickelodeons, Amusement Parks, and the Sights of Female Sexuality," *camera obscura* 23 (1990), 73. These three areas correspond closely to three of four immigrant neighborhoods that J. A. Lindstrom examines in her dissertation, "Getting a Hold Deeper in the Life of the City: Chicago Nickelodeons, 1905–1913" (Northwestern University, 1998).

81. See "Film Shows Busy; Panic Stops One," *CT* (15 April 1907), 4; "Cheap Shows Lure," *CRH* (1 May 1907), 1.

82. The Thaw case chronology was summarized in "Jerome's Merciless Attack on 'Angel Child' Evelyn Thaw," *DMRL* (10 April 1907), 1.

83. See, for instance, the Lubin ad in *NYC* (2 March 1907), 68; and "Moving Pictures," *NYC* (30 March 1907), 166, and (27 April 1907), 276. *The Unwritten Law* used a very conventional *tableau* style of narration and representation, illustrating a series of intertitles with "single-shot scenes of the famous moments in the case"—see Staiger, *Bad Women*, 62.

84. See "Nickel Theaters Crime Breeders," *CT* (13 April 1907), 3; "Houston Authorities Object to Picture of Thaw-White Tragedy," *MPW* (20 April 1907), 102; "Massachusetts," *NYC* (4 May 1907), 304; "Trade Notes," *MPW* (11 May 1907), 153, and (13 July 1907), 295;

and Roy Rosenzweig, *Eight Hours for What We Will: Workers and Leisure in an Industrial City, 1870–1920* (Cambridge: Cambridge University Press, 1983), 205, 207.

85. "Nickel Theaters Crime Breeders," *CT* (13 April 1907), 3. The previous summer, "great hordes of women . . . fought for a glimpse" of a White-Thaw mutoscope subject shown in a Luna Park arcade—see "Trade Notes," *VFI* (28 July 1906), 6.

86. "Editorial," *MPW* (25 May 1907), 159. Responding to the disastrous 1908 Boyerstown fire (wrongly attributed to an exploding projector), *Show World* later suggested that most of these attacks on moving pictures came from large daily newspapers because exhibitors did not often advertise in the daily press—see "The Press vs. Moving Pictures," *SW* (8 February 1908), 11.

87. See, for instance, "May Close Small Theatres," *NYDM* (8 June 1907), 17; and "Trade Notes," *MPW* (14 May 1907), 137, (8 June 1907), 214, and (20 July 1907), 312.

88. The quote is from Nicola Seraphine, the MPEA's first president, in "Association Notes," *MPW* (29 June 1907), 270. A different counterattack strategy was to suggest that censorship be extended to the Sunday comics pages—see "Moving Pictures Are Not Alone," *MPW* (17 August 1907), 375. Efforts to close down Sunday shows continued into the fall and winter—see, for instance, "Trade Notes," *MPW* (19 October 1907), 521; "The Matter of Sunday Shows," *MPW* (26 October 1907), 539; "In Brooklyn," *VFI* (2 November 1907), 5; "Brooklyn, N.Y., Notes," *MPW* (23 November 1907), 613–614; "Sunday in New York," *MPW* (21 December 1907), 683–684; and "The Sunday Trouble," *MPW* (28 December 1907), 703–704. See, also, Daniel Czitrom, "The Politics of Performance: From Theater Licensing to Movie Censorship in Turn-of-the-Century New York," *American Quarterly* 44.4 (December 1992), 533; and Staiger, *Bad Women*, 94–95. This strategy of self-regulation is similar to that developed by advertising agencies ten years before, when, in order to become "professional," they disavowed any connection with "disreputable" patent medicines—see Ohmann, *Selling Culture*, 97, 99.

89. See, for instance, "Public Opinion as a Moral Center," *MPW* (11 May 1907), 147–148. The City Club was the first organization to investigate Chicago's arcades and nickelodeons, in 1906—see Kathleen McCarthy, "Nickel Vice and Virtue: Movie Censorship in Chicago, 1907–1915," *Journal of Popular Film* 5 (1976), 43. The concept of "counter*attractions*" may have been developed by Charles Sprague Smith in an essay on the "saloon problem," *Federation* (March 1903)—see William Urrichio and Roberta Pearson, *Reframing Culture: The Case of the Vitagraph Quality Films* (Princeton, N.J.: Princeton University Press, 1993), 35. It appears as a crucial concept in Michael Davis's *The Exploitation of Pleasure: A Study of Commercial Recreations in New York City* (New York: Russell Sage Foundation, 1911), 4–5.

90. See, for instance, "Editorial," *MPW* (1 June 1907), 198; "Trade Notes," *MPW* (29 June 1907), 262–263; Jane Addams, *Twenty Years at Hull House* (New York: Macmillan, 1910), 386; McCarthy, "Nickel Vice and Virtue," 43; and Staiger, *Bad Women*, 63.

91. "Editorial: Public Opinion as a Moral Center," *MPW* (11 May 1907), 147.

92. See George Kleine's 10 April letter to the *Chicago Tribune*, reprinted in both *VFI* (20 April 1907), 5; and *MPW* (20 April 1907), 101–102. Most of these titles are listed in "Latest Films," *VFI* (20 April 1907), 5.

93. See, for instance, "Motion Views Win Jane Addams," *SW* (6 July 1907), 3; and the Laemmle Film Service ad in *VFI* (10 August 1907), 10.

94. See "Social Workers to Censor Shows," *CT* (3 May 1907), 3; and a *Chicago Record-Herald* interview reprinted in "Trade Notes," *MPW* (11 May 1907), 152. See, also, Swanson's and Laemmle's testimony in the Pathé ads in *VFI* (1 June 1907), 2, and (13 July 1907), 2.

95. For a good introduction to French *grand guignol,* see Mel Gordon, *The Grand Guignol: Theatre of Fear and Terror* (New York: Amok Press, 1988). "Thaw Case" films continued to circulate well into 1908, however, partly in response to a second trial, which resulted in Thaw's acquittal on the grounds of insanity—see the reprinting of a paragraph from the *Fresno Republican* as "More Adverse Criticism," *MPW* (8 August 1908), 155; and Bowser, *The Transformation of Cinema,* 42.

96. During this period, Vitagraph also briefly stressed the "sensationalism" of its films, but not of the "cheap, trashy dime novel melodrama" kind: see its ad for *The Automobile Thieves* in *VFI* (10 November 1906), 11.

97. "Vaudeville's Higher Aim," *DMRL* (24 March 1907), 3.6. About the same time, in a rare appeal, the Nickelodion sought to attract audiences in Portland by promoting Pathé's *Crime on the Railroad* as "a sensational film"—see the Nickelodion ad in *Ore* (12 February 1907), 11.

98. See the Colonial Theatre ad in *DMRL* (30 April 1907), 5.

99. See the Nickeldom ad in *DMRL* (13 May 1907), 5; and "This Week's Bill," *DMRL* (26 May 1907), 3.6.

100. See F. C. McCarahan, "Chicago's Great Film Industry," *Bill* (24 August 1907), 4–5, 39; "Moving Picture Industry Is in Great Uplift Movement," *SW* (21 September 1907), 18; and Fred Aiken, "Moving Pictures a National Industry," *SW* (14 December 1907), 24.

101. See "Public Taste in Pictures as Viewed by M. E. Fleckles," *SW* (7 September 1907), 9; and "Trade Notes," *MPW* (19 October 1907), 524.

102. See, for instance, "The Melodrama," *NYDM* (1 June 1907), 14; and "Public Taste in Pictures as Viewed by M. E. Fleckles," 9. For a further analysis of differences in French and American tastes, particularly in terms of the French penchant for *grand guignol* melodrama versus the American preference for "bright, happy denouements," see Richard Abel, "A Crisis in Crossing Borders, or How to Account for French 'Bad Taste,'" in Cosandey and Albera, *Images across Borders,* 299–313.

103. John Wanamaker's advertising editorial, in *North American* (5 April 1906), as cited in Leach, *Land of Desire,* 3. Ohmann describes something very similar in magazine ads around the turn of the century—see Ohmann, *Selling Culture,* 202–209.

104. "Moving Picture Industry Great," *SW* (29 June 1907), 29. See, also, Thomas Edison and his signed statement about "films of good moral tone" on the cover of *MPW* (21 December 1907), 677. This attitude was perfectly in sync with the "cheerful world" of consumption represented in most magazine advertising at the time—see Ohmann, *Selling Culture,* 210.

105. "Film Coloring," *VFI* (5 October 1907), 3. This revelation was then taken up in Joseph Medill Patterson's "The Nickelodeons, the Poor Man's Elementary Course in the Drama," *Saturday Evening Post* (23 November 1907), 11. See, also, David S. Hulfish, "Colored Films of To-day," *Nick* (January 1909), 15. According to Hulfish, "three classes of colored picture films" were available in the United States at that time: tinted and/or chemically toned, hand-colored, and machine-colored. Machine-colored films were the only ones to "exhibit all the colors of nature," and Hulfish attributed them solely to Pathé.

106. "Moving Picture Notes," *Bill* (19 October 1907), 53.

107. "Trade Notes," *VFI* (24 August 1907), 4.

108. See the Pathé ads in *VFI* (23 November 1907), 2, (7 December 1907), 2, (28 December 1907), 2, (21 March 1908), 2, and (6 June 1908), 13. W. Stephen Bush praised *Don Juan* as one of several models to follow, in "The Film of the Future," *MPW* (5 September 1908),

173. Gunning informs me that the Cinémathèque française showed a stencil-color print of *Dog Smugglers,* a *grand guignol* chase film, during the prescreenings for the 1996 Domitor conference.

109. See the Pathé ads in *VFI* (31 August 1907), 11, (21 September 1907), 11, and (23 November 1907), 2; and "Latest Productions," *VFI* (18 April 1908), 7.

110. After May 1908, the Pathé ads in *Views and Films Index* rarely refer to toning, but they continue to mark those films that were colored, that is, stencil colored.

111. Bowser was one of the first to note this pattern of objection to Pathé films, in *The Transformation of Cinema,* 40–41. A bizarre instance of this, unrelated to the cinema, appears in "The Bingville Bugle," a back-page parody of rural folks, occasionally printed in the *Sioux City Tribune:* one of its logos was the image of a rooster almost identical to Pathé's— see, for instance, the *Sioux City Tribune* (27 February 1909), 12.

112. Barton W. Currie, "The Nickel Madness," *Harper's Weekly* (24 August 1907), 1247— reprinted in Gerald Mast, ed., *The Movies in Our Midst: Documents in the Cultural History of Film in America* (Chicago: University of Chicago Press, 1982), 47.

113. Hans Leigh, "A Coffin for the Theatorium," *MPW* (22 February 1908), 135; and Hans Leigh, "Exhibitors Are Not Satisfied with Their Bill of Fare," *MPW* (23 May 1908), 454–455.

114. "A Reporter Visits Philadelphia," *MPW* (4 April 1908), 293. This referred to the frequent appearance of wine bottles in Pathé films.

115. "Comments on Film Subjects," *MPW* (12 December 1908), 476. Two weeks later, however, another reviewer found *The Acrobatic Maid* "a knockabout comic" very successful with audiences—see "Comments on the Week's Films," *MPW* (26 December 1908), 526.

116. See "Comments on Film Subjects," *MPW* (16 January 1909), 69. *Two Great Griefs* came in for similar criticism on the same page.

117. W. Stephen Bush, "The Coming of the Ten and Twenty Cent Moving Picture Theater," *MPW* (29 August 1908), 153; and "The Film of the Future," *MPW* (26 September 1908), 235.

118. See "Variety's Own Picture Reviews," *Var* (2 October 1909), 13. See, also, "Moving Picture Reviews," *Var* (19 December 1908), 13; "A French Sample," *Var* (2 January 1909), 10; "Auditorium," *Var* (9 January 1909), 10; "32 Park Row," *Var* (23 January 1909), 13; and "Moving Picture Reviews," *Var* (27 March 1909), 13, and (10 April 1910), 13.

119. In 1907, George Kleine had defended French films (especially Pathé's) against press attacks on Chicago's nickelodeons; one year later, allied with Biograph against the FSA, he was maligning French films as "racy, risqué, and sensational"—"Interview with George Kleine," *NYDM* (27 June 1908), 7. In criticizing American films, the *World* also used this "tarring" language; see, for instance, Selig's *The Ranchman's Love,* whose objectionable story "savor[ed] of the flavor of the French productions"—"Comments on Film Subjects," *MPW* (17 October 1908), 298.

120. K. S. Hover, "Police Supervision in Chicago," *Nick* (January 1909), 11–12. Recently J. A. Lindstrom has found evidence that the city's moral reformers knew nothing about this ordinance until months after it had been passed—see Lindstrom, "Many Bad Conditions Improved or Eliminated: Reform-Movement Groups and Chicago Nickelodeons," paper presented at the Society for Cinema Studies Conference, Ottawa, 17 May 1997. As expected, Chicago film manufacturers found the ordinance impractical—see "Film Men Oppose New Ordinance," *SW* (28 December 1907), 3–4. The Juvenile Protective Association would go on to conduct several other investigations much more in line with arguments for

censorship and prohibition—see Louise de Koven Bowen, *Five and Ten Cent Theaters* (Chicago: Juvenile Protective Association, 1909, 1911). The Chicago ordinance may have become a model for other cities like Detroit and Cleveland—see "Trade Notes," *MPW* (21 September 1907), 454, and (14 December 1907), 665. Yet several cities, including New Orleans, Charleston, and Norfolk, passed ordinances even earlier—see "Moving Picture Regulations: Reports from Mayors of Cities," *Insurance Engineering* (1909), 309, 319. See, also, McCarthy, "Nickel Vice and Virtue," 45; Musser, *Before the Nickelodeon*, 432; and Daniel Czitrom, *Media and the American Mind* (Chapel Hill: University of North Carolina Press, 1982), 51–52.

121. See "Sunday Shows Are Legal," *NYDM* (11 July 1908), 7; "Fox Again to the Rescue," *Bill* (8 August 1908), 9; Czitrom, "The Politics of Performance," 534–535; and Staiger, *Bad Women*, 95–97. See, also, the playground commissioner in Newark, who defended the moving pictures against an editorial in the *Evening News*—reprinted in "The Influence of the Pictures," *MPW* (5 December 1908), 446. For further information on the People's Institute, along with the Educational Alliance and the Bureau of Lectures in New York, see Nancy Rosenbloom, "In Defense of the Moving Pictures: The People's Institute, The National Board of Censorship and the Problem of Leisure in Urban America," *American Studies* 33.2 (Fall 1992), 41–60; and Uricchio and Pearson, *Reframing Culture*, 34–38.

122. For good summaries of New York nickelodeon closings, see "Wholesale Revoking of Licenses," *NYDM* (2 January 1909), 8; and "The Mayor of New York Stops Motion Picture Shows," *Bill* (2 January 1909), 9. Most of the city's daily papers also criticized McClellan's action—see, for instance, "Victory in Supreme Court," *FI* (16 January 1909), 4–5. See, also, Gunning, *D. W. Griffith*, 151–155; William Uricchio and Roberta Pearson, "Constructing an Audience: Competing Discourses of Morality and Rationalization during the Nickelodeon Period," *iris* 17 (Autumn 1994), 45–46; and Staiger, *Bad Women*, 98–102. The Association of Neighborhood Workers, to which the People's Institute belonged, and the East Side Boy's Institute also worked to counter McClellan's action—see "Victory in Supreme Court," 5; and "Commendation of Moving Pictures," *NYC* (16 January 1909), 1208.

123. This confrontation brought the new industry in line with a hegemonic alliance of Progressive industrialists, knowledgeable regulators, and reform-minded journalists—see Uricchio and Pearson, "Constructing the Audience," 47–51; Staiger, *Bad Women*, 87, 91; and Ohmann, *Selling Culture*, 293–294. The lengthy, acrimonious debate also may have provided a further incentive for reconciling the rival manufacturing interests, leading to the MPPC—see Musser, *Before the Nickelodeon*, 432. For a good survey of that "rationalized discipline" across the country, see "Moving Picture Regulations," 298–321.

124. See, for instance, W. Stephen Bush, "Who Goes to the Moving Pictures," *MPW* (3 October 1908), 378; "Editorial," *VFI* (7 November 1908), 3; "The Real Problem to Be Solved," *VFI* (29 May 1909), 3; Lewis E. Palmer, "The World in Motion," *Survey* 22 (5 June 1909), 357; and F. H. Richardson, "What Is in the Future?" *MPW* (28 August 1909), 280. For an analysis of Simon Patten's influential books, *The New Basis of Civilization* (1907) and *Product and Climax* (1909), see Daniel Horowitz, *The Morality of Spending: Attitudes toward the Consumer Society in America, 1875–1940* (Baltimore, Md.: Johns Hopkins University Press, 1985), 31–37.

125. These ideas come from Miriam Hansen, *Babel and Babylon: Spectatorship in American Silent Cinema* (Cambridge, Mass.: Harvard University Press, 1991), 66, 69; but the outlines of this redefinition of the nickelodeon period already were in place in H. F. Hoffman, "What People Want: Some Observations," *MPW* (9 July 1910), 77.

126. For a sense of the moral reformers' own perspective on this move, see "Censorship for Moving Pictures," *Survey* 22 (3 April 1909), 8. A good history is provided in "National

Board of Censorship of Motion Pictures," *MPW* (16 October 1909), 524–525. For later studies, see Gunning, *D. W. Griffith*, 155–160; Bowser, *The Transformation of Cinema*, 48–49; Staiger, *Bad Women*, 103–107; and Nancy Rosenbloom, "Progressive Reform, Censorship, and the Motion Picture Industry, 1909–1917," in Ronald Edsforth and Larry Bennett, eds., *Popular Culture and Political Change in Modern America* (Buffalo: State University of New York Press, 1991), 41–59.

127. This is not to say that American films were not rejected or returned for alteration, but proportionally fewer of them were censored. Probably because of Griffith's later reputation, most historians have focused on Biograph films that were criticized by the board. It should also be noted that, in April 1909, Pathé persuaded the board to take the unusual step of visiting its New York offices to approve nearly 150 films at one time, in order to maintain its release schedule, but this changed shortly thereafter—see "Censors Visit Pathé," *FI* (17 April 1909), 10; "'Spectator's' Comments," *NYDM* (8 May 1909), 16; Palmer, "The World in Motion," 363; Gunning, *D. W. Griffith*, 156–157, 160–162; and Bowser, *The Transformation of Cinema*, 50.

128. See the 10 May 1909 letter from John Collier to Frank Dyer—Motion Picture Folder, Censorship File, ENHS. Gunning reprints most of this letter in *D. W. Griffith*, 159–160.

129. See the 18 June 1909 letter from Collier to Dyer—Motion Picture Folder, Censorship File, ENHS. The trade press, however, sometimes wondered if censorship was little more than a "joke"—see the review of Pathé's *The Romance of a Poor Girl*, in *Var* (23 October 1909), 13.

130. See the 1 February and 9 February 1910 letters from Collier to Dyer—Motion Picture: Censorship Folder no. 1, ENHS. Ironically, Collier had detected not "one immoral or indecent picture" in his investigation of New York nickelodeons two years before—Collier, "Cheap Amusements," 74.

131. Charles V. Trevis, "Censoring the Five-Cent Drama," *World Today* (October 1910)—reprinted in Mast, *The Movies in Our Midst*, 69. Michael Davis also praises the work of the board in substantially decreasing the number of "morally objectionable" films—see Davis, *The Exploitation of Pleasure*, 34.

132. Testimony of H. N. Marvin, *USA vs. MPPC* (1914), 1282. Marvin may be referring to Independent films, but, if so, his chronology is mistaken, for any "problem" with Independent imports came after the board was established. See, also, the 15 January 1910 letter from Charles Sprague Smith, the board's first director, to Frank Dyer, arguing that Pathé should not be allowed to advertise its films as approved by the board for fear that would "tend to discredit the censorship"—Moving Picture: Censorship File, ENHS.

133. See F. H. Richardson, "A Few Pertinent Comments" and "Good Cheer Wanted," *MPW* (20 February 1909), 196. See, also, "The Week's Films," *MPW* (23 January 1909), 95; and "Comments on Film Subjects," *MPW* (13 February 1909), 172.

ENTR'ACTE 4. "THE DRUMMER AND THE GIRL"

1. See the 13 August 1909 letter to Léon Gaumont from George Kleine—Box 24: Gaumont, GK.

2. There are exceptions: Harry Geduld, *The Birth of the Talkies: From Edison to Jolson* (Bloomington: Indiana University Press, 1975), 30–70; and Eileen Bowser, *The Transformation*

of Cinema, 1907–1915, vol 2. of *The History of American Cinema* (New York: Scribner's, 1990), 13, 15, and 18–20. During the course of this book's rewriting, two other important texts appeared: Rick Altman, "The Silence of the Silents," *Musical Quarterly* 80.4 (Winter 1996), 648–718; and Martin Marks, *Music and the Silent Film: Contexts and Case Studies, 1895–1924* (New York: Oxford University Press, 1997). The Fifth International Domitor conference, held in Washington, D.C., 1–5 June 1998 and devoted to sound and early cinema, occurred too late for its findings to be included here.

3. See Rick Altman, "Naissance de la réception classique: la campagne pour standardiser le son," *Cinémathèque* 6 (1995), 98–111. Marks basically agrees with this argument about standardization, which Altman develops much more thoroughly in "The Silence of the Silents."

4. Altman and Marks do provide some substantive evidence for silence as an accepted practice: among them, F. H. Richardson, "Plain Talks to Theatre Managers and Operators," *MPW* (30 October 1909), 599–600; and the survey of San Francisco theaters in "Public Recreation," *Transactions of the Commonwealth Club of California* 8.5 (June 1913), 261.

5. Altman, "Naissance de la réception classique," 105–106.

6. For a good introduction to song slides, see John Ripley, "Song Slides Helped to Unify US Communities—and Sell Sheet Music," *Films in Review* (March 1971), 147–152; and "Romance and Joy, Tears and Heartache, and All for a Nickel," *Smithsonian Magazine* 12.12 (March 1982), 77–83. From the summer of 1906 well into the summer of 1907, the *Index* listed the latest song slides and films, according to their makers, side by side on the same page—see, for instance *VFI* (12 January 1907), n.p. Ads in the *Index* indicate that Alfred Harstn, an early sales and rental agent in New York, was specializing in the song slide business by 1907. According to Ripley, the largest cache of surviving song slides came from the St. Louis Calcium Light Company, which began advertising in the *Index* in the spring of 1907. Several young women who posed for song slides—among them Norma Talmadge, Anita Stewart, Alice Joyce, and even Florence Turner—later became movie stars, the first two at Vitagraph—see, also, Anthony Slide, *Early American Cinema,* rev. ed. (Metuchen, N.J.: Scarecrow, 1994), 137–138.

7. For contemporaneous accounts of illustrated songs and some of the problems connected with song slides, see "The Tremendous Demand of Song Slides," *MPW* (28 September 1907), 467–468; and "Song Slide Department," *FI* (18 December 1909), 18. After a quick survey of exhibition in Germany and France, Max Lewis (Chicago Film Exchange) claimed that illustrated songs were unique to the United States—see "Talking Moving Pictures Latest European Invention," *SW* (7 September 1907), 9. Illustrated songs were one form of what was called "act music" in vaudeville, in contrast to "house music," which was used for overtures and intermissions.

8. Charles Musser and Carol Nelson, *High-Class Moving Pictures: Lyman H. Howe and the Forgotten Era of Traveling Exhibition, 1880–1920* (Princeton, N.J.: Princeton University Press, 1991), 143, 160. Howe, Hadley, and other touring exhibitors offered piano overtures between their reels of film. Sigmund Lubin was a producer of song slides before he began manufacturing moving pictures—see Ripley, "Song Slides," 148–149.

9. See "Summer Shows," *DMRL* (6 May 1906), 3.6; [untitled], *DMRL* (20 May 1906), 3.6; "New Song Slides," *VFI* (21 July 1906), 3, 8; and "Massachusetts," *NYC* (8 September 1906), 765, and (29 September 1906), 851.

10. Such competition is mentioned in "Coming to the Front," *VFI* (16 March 1907), 4.

11. See, for instance, the Radium ad in *DMRL* (16 June 1907), 4.9. The Radium and the Lyric (which offered vaudeville and illustrated songs) were the only nickelodeons to regularly advertise in *Des Moines Mail and Times,* a local weekly for "cultured" middle-class readers, especially those belonging to women's clubs. Des Moines was recognized as a "city where musical endeavor is at the topmost height"—see Robert Grau, *The Businessman in the Amusement World* (New York: Broadway, 1910), 326–327.

12. The Woman's Municipal League inquiry in New York found much evidence of this sing-along practice in 1908—see John Collier, "Cheap Amusements," *Charities and Commons* (11 April 1908), 75. See also "Punishing the Music Publishers," *MPW* (6 February 1909), 141. It may well be that in larger cities, especially New York, "music publishers paid for singers to appear in nickelodeons in order to promote their latest songs"—see Ripley, "Song Slides," 147, 150; Ripley, "Romance and Joy," 78; and Bowser, *The Transformation of Cinema,* 15. Abe Balaban started his career as a singer at "The Kedzie" on Chicago's West Side, in the spring of 1907; by January, 1908, he and his brother, Barney (and their parents), were owner-managers and on their way to building the biggest circuit of cinemas in the country by the 1920s—see Carrie Balaban, *Continuous Performance: The Story of A.J. Balaban* (New York: A.J. Balaban Foundation, 1964), 24, 26; and Douglas Gomery, *Shared Pleasures: A History of Movie Presentation in the United States* (Madison: University of Wisconsin Press, 1992), 41.

13. See "Graphophone Spieling Prohibited," *Bill* (28 July 1906), 16.

14. See "The Situation in Philadelphia," *MPW* (26 October 1907), 540. See, also, "Short Talk to Busy Men," *VFI* (19 October 1907), 4; and Will Heck, "Agitation about Moving Picture Shows," *Bill* (26 October 1907), 46.

15. See "The Situation in Philadelphia," *MPW* (2 November 1907), 559. Boogar used a ballyhoo outside his other show.

16. See "From Philadelphia," *MPW* (16 November 1907), 596; "Philadelphia Items," *MPW* (23 November 1907), 615–617; and "When 'Music' Is a Nuisance," *MPW* (28 December 1907), 702. See, also, "Moving Picture Legislation," *VFI* (2 November 1907), 3; and "War in Philadelphia," *Bill* (2 November 1907), 28.

17. Altman, "Naissance de la réception classique," 100; and Altman, "The Silence of the Silents," 672–688. On "sound effects," see also Geduld, *The Birth of the Talkies,* 31–34. Altman's research on the whole is exemplary. However, he does rely perhaps too heavily on, and reads too selectively in, retrospective texts such as *Moving Picture World*'s anniversary issue on exhibition (15 July 1916) and George Benyon's "The Evolution of Picture Music," *Musical Presentation of Motion Pictures* (New York: Schirmer, 1921), 3–14. Marks assesses Benyon's memory, more persuasively, as "remarkably fuzzy"—see Marks, *Music and the Silent Film,* 63. Altman also puts a little too much stock in other texts, such as a 1909 guide for theater managers, which targets small theaters and advises the use of electrical switches and machines, and fewer employees, all of which serve the principle of greater efficiency—see L. Gardette, "Conducting the Nickelodeon Program," *Nick* (March 1909), 79–80.

18. See the Foster's ad in *DMRL* (2 April 1905), 3.2. Drawing on a long tradition in magic lantern shows and the theater, Lyman Howe became "the pioneer in introducing sound effects in a motion picture exhibition"—see "About Sound Effects," *FI* (26 February 1910), 7. See, also, Musser and Nelson, *High-Class Moving Pictures,* 90–91; and Bowser, *The Transformation of Cinema,* 13, 15.

19. In the one nickelodeon, the piano and drum complemented Pathé's comic *Hello Grinder,* but only the piano probably accompanied the song "Where the Morning Glories

Twine around the Door"—see "Our Head Office Boy Wants to Be a Reporter," *VFI* (25 April 1906), 10. Six months later, another report in the *Index* recommended music and mechanical effects during the performance, but the reference could have been to the program as a whole rather than the film screening—see "An Unexploited Field and Its Possibilities," *VFI* (6 October 1906), 4.

20. See "The Demand for Realistic Exhibitions," *VFI* (13 October 1906), 3. The moment "realizes" the well-known painting *Angelus* by Jean-François Millet. Another example was a warning: an audience attracted by a prize fight film had to sit through all or part of Pathé's *Passion Play* and actually cheered and applauded the crucifixion. Pathé produced a good number of films that incorporated sound cues (often "bridging" shots) between 1906 and 1908—see Richard Abel, *The Ciné Goes to Town: French Cinema, 1896–1914* (Berkeley: University of California Press, 1994), 131, 135, 147, 185. See, also, the references to specific sound effects in "Trade Notes," *MPW* (13 July 1907), 297.

21. Joseph Medill Patterson, "The Nickelodeons, the Poor Man's Elementary Course in the Drama," *Saturday Evening Post* (23 November 1907), 10. A cryptic reference in *Billboard* to the Nickelodeon Theatre in Fall River, Massachusetts, suggests that orchestras at least played in some theaters as early as the summer of 1906—see "Moving Picture Shows," *Bill* (11 August 1906), 15. Altman cites 1907 as "the tentative beginnings of film accompaniment practice"—see Altman, "The Silence of the Silents," 677.

22. See "Massachusetts," *NYC* (27 April 1907), 271.

23. See "A Successful Little Showcase," *VFI* (28 December 1907), 4–5. Opened in June 1907, the Princess originally seated 240 but was so successful that the seating was expanded to 515. The Princess also was unusual in using two Power projectors.

24. See "Moving Pictures," *NYC* (21 March 1908), 141. The theater was located on Second Avenue near 106th Street.

25. See "Unique Theatre," *Var* (15 February 1908), 11; "The Nickelodeon as a Business Proposition," *MPW* (25 July 1908), 61; W. Stephen Bush, "Hints to Exhibitors," *MPW* (24 October 1908), 317; and "The Chicago Orpheum Theater," *Nick* (January 1909), 3–5. Sam Katz began his career as a pianist "in a small moving picture theatre" on Chicago's South Side; later he would become a partner in the Balaban & Katz cinema circuit—see "Appendix A: Samuel Katz," in Joseph Kennedy, *The Story of the Films* (Chicago: A. W. Shaw, 1927), 350–351; and Gomery, *Shared Pleasures*, 41.

26. See the photo and caption in *VFI* (9 May 1908), 6; and "William Swanson's New Theater," *SW* (27 June 1908), 26c.

27. Bush first advertised his lectures in *MPW* (27 June 1908), 547. He also offered a guide for the practice in "Lectures on Moving Pictures," *MPW* (22 August 1908), 136–137. Bush specialized in doing lectures for the *Passion Play*—see his ad in *NYDM* (26 December 1908), 9. See, also, Stromgren, "The Moving Picture World of W. Stephen Bush," 17.

28. Herr Professor, a Dr. Lamberger, was featured in "Where They Perform Shakespeare for Five Cents," *Theatre Magazine* 8 (October 1908), 264–265, xi–xii. See, also, "Editorial," *MPW* (26 September 1908), 231; "The Lectures," *MPW* (13 February 1909), 167; "On the Screen," *MPW* (10 July 1909), 47; and "Lecturing the Show," *Nick* (December 1909), 167–168.

29. Bowser, *The Transformation of Cinema*, 19.

30. See "Failures of Nickelodeons," *MPW* (13 June 1908), 507; "Cameraphone Development," *NYDM* (4 July 1908), 7; "The Gaumont 'Chronophone,'" *NYDM* (5 September 1908), 8; "Gaumont Talking Pictures," *NYDM* (31 October 1908), 8; "Cameraphone Experiments,"

MPW (23 January 1909), 90; and "Cameraphone's New Policy," *NYDM* (6 March 1909), 12. The Cameraphone and Chronophone already were operating in 1907—see "Trade Notes," *MPW* (10 August 1907), 358, and (14 September 1907), 440. For some sense of the difficulties with these systems, one written by Cameraphone's former manager, see Carl Herbert, "The Truth about Talking Pictures," *MPW* (20 March 1909), 327–329; and "The Singing and Talking Picture," *MPW* (7 May 1910), 727–728. See, also, Geduld, *The Birth of the Talkies*, 56–58, 63–65.

31. This, too, may have originated with Howe, who first began promoting "his use of actors behind the screen as 'Moving Pictures That Talk' in August 1907"—see Charles Musser, *The Emergence of Cinema to 1907*, vol. 1 of *History of the American Cinema* (New York: Scribner's, 1991), 439. See, also, Musser and Nelson, *High-Class Moving Pictures*, 184–189.

32. See the Humanovo ad on the front cover of *VFI* (30 May 1908); the Lyric ads in *DMRL* (21 June 1908), 3.7, and (26 July 1908), 3.7; "Twenty-Two Humanovo Companies," *NYDM* (18 July 1908), 7; the Humanovo ad in *NYDM* (14 November 1908), 11; and "The Actologue in Cleveland," *MPW* (5 December 1908), 450.

33. See, for instance, "Editorial," *MPW* (28 November 1908), 419; and "Difficulties of Talking Pictures," *NYDM* (26 December 1908), 8.

34. See "Music and Films," *VFI* (16 May 1908), 4.

35. Barrow, the trade paper was quick to point out, had graduated from the Berlin Conservatory of Music.

36. See Walter Eaton, "New Theatrical Problem: Age of Mechanical Amusement," *VFI* (9 May 1908), 5–6.

37. For a detailed description and analysis of *Christmas Eve Tragedy*, or *Nuit de Noël*, see Abel, *The Ciné Goes to Town*, 202–204.

38. In Saint Louis, when the musicians' union tried to organize the moving picture shows, it found more musicians employed there than in the other theaters—see "Musicians in Nickelodeons," *Nick* (February 1909), 48. There is some indication that, by the 1909–1910 season, illustrated songs no longer figured as a significant attraction. Woods especially criticized the quality of the songs and singers—see, for instance, "'Spectator's' Comments," *NYDM* (3 July 1909), 15; "'Spectator's' Comments," *NYDM* (1 January 1910), 16; and "'Spectator's' Comments," *NYDM* (5 February 1910), 16. See, also, "Music in Picture Theaters," *Nick* (July 1909), 4; and H. F. Hoffman, "The Singer and the Song," *MPW* (4 June 1910), 935. Yet, the week before Christmas in 1909, the theaters advertising in the *St. Louis Times* listed quite a number of singers and illustrated songs—see "Picture Theatre Advertising," *FI* (15 January 1910), 19.

39. See, for instance, "An Innovation in Philadelphia," *NYDM* (9 January 1909), 9; "Atlanta's Alcazar Opens," *FI* (8 May 1909), 3; the Wurlitzer ad in *Nick* (June 1909), [inside cover]; and "The Music Question," *MPW* (4 December 1909), 804. For a wealth of information on the pipe organs and electric pianos used in theaters, see Q. David Bowers, *Nickelodeon Theatres and Their Music* (Vestal, N.Y.: Vestal Press, 1986), 127–203. See, also, the Yerkes ad for "High Grade Sound Effects for Moving Pictures," in *MPW* (29 May 1909), 719.

40. See, for instance, "Weekly Visits to the Shows," *MPW* (27 February 1909), 235; and "Weekly Comments on the Shows," *MPW* (13 March 1909), 305, and (1 May 1909), 552. Kleine Optical's special road show of Gaumont's *L'Enfant prodigue* required a twelve-piece orchestra, at least according to the program booklet for Sioux City, Iowa, the week of 2 August 1909—see Box 26: Historical File: General, GK. See, also, Pilar Morin, "Silent Drama Music," *MPW* (30 April 1910), 676.

248 NOTES TO PAGES 115–117

41. See "The Musical End," *MPW* (3 July 1909), 7–8.

42. See "On the Screen," *MPW* (4 September 1909), 312.

43. As the next chapter suggests, the pictures Bedding is referring to here probably were Griffith's Biograph films.

44. See "Musical Accompaniments for Moving Pictures," *MPW* (23 October 1909), 559. Kalem apparently considered sending out music with its version of *The Merry Widow* (1908) but decided against doing so because publishing it could infringe on copyright and, besides, the music was well known — see the 2 February 1908 letter from Marion to Kleine, Box 29: Kalem Folder, GK.

45. See "Incidental Music," *FI* (18 September 1909), 13. See, also, Altman, "Naissance de la réception classique," 108; and Marks, *Music and the Silent Film,* 68.

46. See "Vitagraph's Incidental Music," *NYDM* (2 October 1909), 30.

47. *The Assassination of the Duke of Guise,* for instance, had a score composed by Camille Saint-Saëns; the score for *The Scar* was composed by its writer, Fernand le Borne. See, for instance, "'Film d'Art' Plays," *NYTr* (13 December 1908), 2. Neither film apparently was accompanied by those scores in the United States. For a detailed analysis of Saint-Saëns's score for the *Duke of Guise,* see Marks, *Music and the Silent Film,* 50–61.

48. Pathé did not prepare specially arranged music for a film released in the United States until *Il Trovatore,* which used a collage of Verdi music — see "Music and the Picture," *MPW* (31 December 1910), 1518–1519; and Marks, *Music and the Silent Film,* 71–73.

49. "Notes From Chicago," *MPW* (13 March 1909), 300.

50. See the letter from Walter Golding, reprinted as "Music and Pictures," in *NYDM* (16 October 1909), 18. Golding also cited the music for one film each by Edison, Lubin, and Vitagraph.

51. "Increase the Beauty of the Pictures," *MPW* (12 February 1910), 217.

52. See "Chicago Notes," *MPW* (5 February 1910), 171–172, (19 March 1910), 423, and (23 April 1910), 650. Bradlet even worked with William King, the Orpheum's orchestra director, to arrange a special score (using an organ, orchestra, and chorus) for Gaumont's *A Penitent of Florence*—see "Remarkable Demonstration of Moving Pictures," *MPW* (7 May 1910), 728–729; and "A Film That Stirs the Audience," *MPW* (7 May 1910), 743. See, also, the comments on the "special music and sound effects" for Biograph's *The Way of the World* at Keith's Twenty-third Street theater, in "The March of Progress," *MPW* (7 May 1910), 724.

53. See "Motion Picture Music," *MPW* (18 December 1909), 879; "Motion Picture Music," *FI* (1 January 1910), 22. See, also, "Moving Picture Music," *Nick* (1 January 1910), 23; and Gregg Frelinger's letter reprinted as "Music for Moving Picture Houses," *MPW* (26 February 1910), 303. The *World* called Frelinger, of Lafayette, Indiana, "one of the greatest descriptive pianists of the day."

54. See S. L. Rothapfel, "Music and Motion Pictures," *MPW* (17 April 1910), 593. The same issue included two other articles, "The Music and the Picture" and "Feature Films for Feature Music," 590–591. Rothapfel's first column was "Dignity of the Exhibitor's Profession," *MPW* (26 February 1910), 289. See, also, Andrew Heinze, *Adapting to Abundance: Jewish Immigrants, Mass Consumption, and the Search for an American Identity* (New York: Columbia University Press, 1990), 213–214. Not until October 1910 would *Film Index* initiate the first regular trade column devoted solely to music — see Clyde Martin, "Playing the Pictures," *FI* (22 October 1910), 13. A month later, *Moving Picture World* would introduce Clarence Sinn's column, "Music of the Pictures," *MPW* (26 November 1910), 1227. Altman credits

both of these with playing "a major role in the campaign to standardize sound after 1910"—see "The Silence of the Silents," 680–685, 705.

55. See "Motion Picture Piano Music," *Nick* (1 May 1910), 239.

56. See, for instance, a description of the girl pianists in Pittsburgh, in "Trade Notes," *MPW* (25 May 1907), 180. This also may well have been especially significant for Jewish immigrant women, given the unusual value that the piano had in the process of their assimilation, partly because of its association with American popular music—see Heinze, *Adapting to Abundance*, 133–144. In a 1994 interview, Ralph Cole recalls that "girls we knew started to play," for wages, at the local nickelodeon in Princeton, Minnesota—Gregg Bachman, "Still in the Dark—Silent Film Audiences," *Film History* 9.1 (1997), 38.

57. Altman aptly describes this as a shift from music that was punctual and intermittent to music that was continuous—see "The Silence of the Silents," 663, 677, 682, 684.

58. See especially the pages devoted to music and stage performance in Mary Carbine, "'The Finest outside the Loop': Motion Picture Exhibition in Chicago's Black Metropolis, 1905–1928," *camera obscura* 23 (May 1990)—reprinted in Richard Abel, ed., *Silent Film* (New Brunswick, N.J.: Rutgers University Press, 1996), 245–256.

59. The quote is from Sylvester Russell, "Musical and Dramatic," *Defender* (9 April 1910) and (5 August 1911)—reprinted in Carbine, "'The Finest outside the Loop,'" 241. Dave Peyton, an orchestra leader at one theater, later wrote a column for the *Defender* that assumed the normalizing position of the trade press and strongly criticized this "jazzing up" practice—see Carbine, "'The Finest outside the Loop,'" 250–255.

60. See "Trade Notes," *MPW* (20 July 1907), 312.

CHAPTER 5. THE PERILS OF PATHÉ

1. Walsh, "Moving Picture Drama for the Multitude," *Independent* 64 (6 February 1908), 306.

2. "St. Louis Business," *FI* (20 March 1909), 10.

3. Jane Addams, *The House of Dreams* (New York: Macmillan, 1909)—reprinted in Gerald Mast, ed., *The Movies in Our Midst: Documents in the Cultural History of Film in America* (Chicago: University of Chicago Press, 1982), 72; and Michael Davis, *The Exploitation of Pleasure: A Study of Commercial Recreations in New York City* (New York: Russell Sage Foundation, 1911), 29–30, 34–35. See, also, Louise de Koven Bowen, *Five and Ten Cent Theaters* (Chicago: Juvenile Protective Association, 1909 and 1911), 1.

4. See, especially, David Nasaw, *Schooled to Order: A Social History of Public Schooling in the United States* (New York: Oxford University Press, 1979), 87–104. Walter Kendrick has argued that the "Young Person"—that fictional subject in most need of careful censorship practices at the turn of the last century—was more often described as male in the United States (in contrast to Europe, especially France), but this was not so much the case in the discourse representing the threats of moving picture exhibition—see Walter Kendrick, *The Secret Museum: Pornography in Modern Culture* (New York: Viking, 1987), 88–94, 142.

See, for instance, Eleanor Gates's series of stories and articles, "The Girl Who Travels Alone," which concludes with "Making Her Way in the World," in *Cosmopolitan* 62 (November 1906), 2–13, (December 1906), 163–172, and (January 1907), 308–315; and Margaret Deland, "The Change in the Feminine Ideal," *Atlantic* 105 (March 1910), 289–302. For more recent studies, besides that of Peiss's *Cheap Amusements,* see Margaret Gibbons Wilson, *The American Woman in Transition: The Urban Influence, 1870–1920* (Westport, Conn.: Greenwood, 1979); Susan Porter Benson, *Counter Culture: Saleswomen, Managers, and Customers in American Department Stores, 1890–1940* (Urbana: University of Illinois Press, 1986); Joanne Meyerowitz, *Women Adrift: Independent Wage Earners in Chicago, 1880–1930* (Chicago: University of Chicago Press, 1988); and Elizabeth Wilson, *The Sphinx in the City: Urban Life, the Control of Disorder, and Women* (Berkeley: University of California Press, 1991). For other studies that focus on women and cinema at the turn of the century, see Elizabeth Ewan, "City Lights: Immigrant Women and the Rise of the Movies," *Signs* 5.3 (1980), 45–65; Judith Mayne, "Immigrants and Spectators," *Wide Angle* 5.2 (1982), 32–41; Miriam Hansen, *Babel and Babylon: Spectatorship in American Silent Cinema* (Cambridge, Mass.: Harvard University Press, 1991), 90–125; Lauren Rabinovitz, "Temptations of Pleasure: Nickelodeons, Amusement Parks, and the Sights of Female Sexuality," *camera obscura* 23 (1990), 71–88; and Janet Staiger, *Bad Women: Regulating Sexuality in Early American Cinema* (Minneapolis: University of Minnesota Press, 1995).

5. Maude McDougall, "The Mission of the Movies: The Theatre with an Audience of Five Million," *The Designer* (January 1913), 160—quoted in William Uricchio and Roberta Pearson, *Reframing Culture: The Case of the Vitagraph Quality Films* (Princeton, N.J.: Princeton University Press, 1993), 29. A similar point is made in William Inglis, "Morals and Moving Pictures," *Harper's Weekly* (30 July 1910), 13.

6. See, for instance, the Grand Theater ads in *Ore* (4 October 1908), 43, and (22 November 1908), 43.

7. T. B., "News from America," *Bioscope* (24 June 1909), 25.

8. See, for instance, Louis Dalrymple's cartoon "High Tide of Immigration—A National Menace," which was the centerfold in *Judge* 45 (22 August 1903)—reprinted in William Truettner, ed., *The West as America: Reinterpreting Images of the Frontier, 1820–1920* (Washington, D.C.: Smithsonian Institution Press, 1991), 305. Racist epithets had been common for years, of course: in 1890, an *American Tribune* article complained about all those "foreign born rotten banana sellers, thieving rag dealers, Italian organ grinders, Chinese washmen and Bohemian coal miners, whose aspirations would make a dog vomit"—quoted in Uricchio and Pearson, *Reframing Culture,* 18.

9. "The Burden of the New Immigration," *World's Work* 6.3 (July 1903), 3601–3602. See, also, "Immigration and the Purity of the American Race," *World's Work* 6.4 (August 1903), 3716; and F. W. Hewes, "Where Our Immigrants Settle," *World's Work* 6.6 (October 1903), 4021–4024. According to William Ripley's influential *The Races of Europe* (1899), there were "three European races" (Teutonic, Alpine, Mediterranean), distinct from the Slavs and Semites of Eastern Europe. In elevating the Anglo-Saxon, however, lower categories in the hierarchy tended to be conflated, as in this example from economist John Commons: "The peasants of Europe, especially of Southern and Eastern Europe, have been reduced to the qualities similar to those of an inferior race that favor despotism and oligarchy rather than democracy"—see Commons, *Races and Immigrants in America* (New York: Macmillan, 1907), 10–12.

10. Cited in Brander Matthews, "The American of the Future," *Century Illustrated* 74 (July 1907), 474. At the same time, in his travel book, *The American Scene* (1907), Henry James was describing Manhattan's Lower East Side as if it were a "very foreign" country.

11. Matthews, "The American of the Future," 477. Commons makes a telling distinction between *amalgamation* and *assimilation,* in *Races and Immigrants in America,* 17–21, 198–238.

See, also, Michael Kammen, "Millions of Newcomers Alien to Our Traditions," in *Mystic Chords of Memory: The Transformation of Tradition in American Culture* (New York: Knopf, 1991), 228–253. Alex Zwerdling offers a concise summary of this debate in "Anglo-Saxon Panic: The Turn-of-the-Century Response to 'Alien' Immigrants," *Ideas from the National Humanities Center* 1.2 (Winter 1993), 32–45.

12. See Herbert N. Casson, "The Americans in America," *Munsey's* 36 (January 1907), 436. The series began in January 1906 and proceeded in this order: "The Jew in America," "The Sons of Old Scotland," "The Germans in America," "The Irish in America," "The English in America," "The French in America," "The Canadians in America," "The Scandinavians in America," "The Welsh in America," "The Italians in America," "The Dutch in America," and "The Spanish in America." That the first was devoted to Jewish immigrants seems a calculated (if later, contradictory) attempt to counter a growing, widespread anti-Semitism.

13. Matthews, "The American of the Future," 476. Interestingly, Matthews also drew attention to the contribution (out of all proportion to their numbers) of early French Protestant immigrants to the American concept of citizenship; yet consistent with the racist exclusions of the period, he also deliberately ignored both African Americans and Asian Americans.

14. Josiah Strong, *The Challenge of the City* (New York: Eaton and Mains, 1907), 65–67, 153. See, also, Frances Kellor, "The Immigrant Woman," *Atlantic* 100 (September 1907), 401–407.

15. George Kibbe Turner, "The City of Chicago: A Study of the Great Immoralities," *McClure's* 28 (April 1907), 575–592. Shelley Stamp Lindsey links this "white slavery conspiracy" to a series of American films in "Wages and Sin: *Traffic in Souls* and the White Slavery Scare," *Persistence of Vision* 9 (1991), 90–102; and "Is Any Girl Safe? Female Spectators at the White Slavery Films," *Screen* 37.1 (Spring 1996), 1–15. See, also, Staiger, *Bad Women*, 44–52, 110–111, and 116–146.

16. Turner, "The City of Chicago," 582. Turner also is revealing in his belief that the "European peasant" and the "vicious negro" were the primary sources of "savage crime"—see ibid., 580.

17. Ibid., 581.

18. Ibid., 582.

19. George Kibbe Turner, "The Daughters of the Poor: A Plain Story of the Development of New York City as a Leading Center of the White Slave Trade of the World, under Tammany Hall," *McClure's* 34 (November 1909), 45–61. For an excellent history of Jewish involvement in prostitution in New York, which though considerable was nowhere near that claimed by Turner, see Edward Bristow, *Prostitution and Prejudice: The Jewish Fight against White Slavery, 1870–1939* (New York: Schocken, 1982), 146–180.

20. Turner, "The Daughters of the Poor," 46–47. Turner also draws a link between "the Apaches, the bands of city savages in Paris," and the "white slave traders" in New York—see ibid., 60.

21. Ibid., 55.

22. See "Comments on the Mayor's Action by an Exhibitor and a Renter," *MPW* (2 January 1909), 5. See, also, the police commissioner's inflammatory article on which some of this xenophobic language draws—Theodore Bingham, "Foreign Criminals in New York," *North American Review* 188 (September 1908), 383–394. In describing the exhibitors meeting to oppose McClellan, the *New York Tribune* also used this language—see Tom Gunning, *D. W.*

Griffith and the Origins of American Film (Urbana: University of Illinois Press, 1991), 153. See, also, "Vincent Pisarro, chief investigator of the Society for the Prevention of Cruelty to Children," quoted in Uricchio and Pearson, *Reframing Culture*, 30. A further link to "disease" and "contamination" can be seen in descriptions of "the nickel theatres where Yiddish, Greek, and Italian are spoken by the owners [and] the performers," on Chicago's West Side, as an "epidemic"—see "All Kinds in Chicago," *Var* (29 February 1909), 13.

23. See "Sunday Show Protest," *MPW* (30 January 1909), 116–117. The resolution passed by this group pressed Jewish businessmen to accept Sunday as the "Sabbath" on the grounds that this was the "moral duty" of all American citizens. In May, as New York theater licenses came up for annual approval, the *World* at least did challenge this argument—see "Observations by Our Man about Town," *MPW* (1 May 1909), 548–549.

24. That the majority of New York theaters had Jewish owners or managers has been confirmed recently by Ben Singer, at least during the period 1908–1910—see Singer, "Manhattan Nickelodeons: New Data on Audiences and Exhibitors," *Cinema Journal* 34.3 (Spring 1995), 26–27. Edison's *Cohen's Fire Sale* makes this link explicit in that the film's central comic character, a Jewish merchant, owns a "'French' millinery store"—see the Edison ad in *MPW* (27 July 1907), 325.

25. Uricchio and Pearson, *Reframing Culture*, 22.

26. Frank V. Thompson, *Schooling the Immigrant* (New York: Harper and Brothers, 1920), 15.

27. Kammen, *Mystic Chords of Memory*, 244. See, also, "Correspondence: Low Priced Theatres," *MPW* (1 June 1907), 202.

28. See "Nation-Wide Wave of Motion Pictures," *NYT* (3 January 1909), 5.10.

29. See John Bradlet, "A Tour amongst Country Exhibitors," *MPW* (6 February 1909), 143. This smearing of "the east side of New York and the slums of other big cities" would be picked up a year later in the *Council Bluffs Daily Nonpareil* and reprinted in "Important If True," *FI* (5 February 1910), 2. And it would be reiterated in "The East Side Standard," *MPW* (24 September 1910), 698.

30. See Turner, "The Daughters of the Poor," 58.

31. Michael Denning, *Mechanic Accents: Dime Novels and Working-Class Culture in America* (London: Verso, 1987), 172, 202–203.

32. Brander Matthews, "The Study of Fiction," in *The Historical Novel and Other Essays* (New York: Scribner's, 1901), 81. Matthews was taken as an authority on the short story at the turn of the century—see, for instance, Bliss Perry, "The Short Story," *A Study of Prose Fiction* (Boston: Houghton, Mifflin, 1902), 301–302. See, also, Kristin Thompson, "From Primitive to Classical," in David Bordwell, Janet Staiger, and Kristin Thompson, *The Classical Hollywood Cinema: Film Style and Mode of Production to 1960* (New York: Columbia University Press, 1985), 164. Frank Munsey, for one, was very explicit about the kinds of stories he published in his magazine, including "Storiettes," or "brisk tales of a thousand or two thousand words," for "readers who wanted to *consume* fiction in batches"—see Richard Ohmann, *Selling Culture: Magazines, Markets, and Class at the Turn of the Century* (London: Verso, 1996), 292.

33. See, for instance, Hans Leigh, "A Coffin for the Theatorium," *MPW* (22 February 1908), 135; and "The Demand for New Subjects," *NYDM* (19 December 1908), 7. That Brander Matthews served as an arbiter of taste, even for the trade press, is evident in "The Influence of the Pictures," *MPW* (5 December 1908), 446.

34. F. Marion Crawford, *The Novel: What Is It* (New York, 1893), 23—quoted in Tom Lutz, *American Nervousness, 1903* (Ithaca, N.Y.: Cornell University Press, 1991), 29. See, also,

Matthews, "The Study of Fiction," 82. David Thomas suggests that, in small towns like Winona, Minnesota, the middle-class family practice of oral readings of classic and popular novels also may have set a precedent for moving pictures (in terms of narrative interest and "moral values")—see David Thomas, "From Page to Screen in Smalltown America: Early Motion Picture Exhibition in Winona, Minnesota," *Journal of the University Film Association* 33 (Summer 1981), 5–7.

35. Hugo Münsterberg, "The Prevention of Crime," *Munsey's* 30 (April 1908), 753. See, also, the turn-of-the-century French sociologist Gabriel Tarde, whose influential theory of imitation included the notion that imitative behavior took place in a semiconscious state. Matthews was quite familiar with his work—see Matthews, "The Study of Fiction," 83. For an analysis of Tarde's social theories, see Susanna Barrows, *Distorting Mirrors: Visions of the Crowd in Late Nineteenth-Century France* (New Haven: Yale University Press, 1981), 137–161; and Rosalind Williams, *Dream Worlds: Mass Consumption in Late Nineteenth-Century France* (Berkeley: University of California Press, 1982), 342–384.

36. Casson, "The Americans in America," 434; and "Good Cheer Wanted," *MPW* (20 February 1909), 196.

37. "Tragedy," *Nick* (November 1909), 135. This reads very much like a 1909 *New York Evening Post* editorial describing the "happy world" of current newspaper and magazine advertising—quoted in Ohmann, *Selling Culture,* 210. See, also, the claim that the "stories of the films" printed weekly in the *World* were "fit for home reading, for both young and old of both sexes"—"The Stories of the Films," *MPW* (2 April 1910), 502.

38. For two excellent studies of the construction of an "American" subject in turn-of-the century magazines, advertisements, and best-sellers, see Amy Kaplan, "Romancing the Empire: The Embodiment of American Masculinity in the Popular Historical Novel of the 1890s," *American Literary History* 2 (Winter 1990), 659–690; and Richard Ohmann, "History and Literary History: The Case of Mass Culture," in James Naremore and Patrick Brantlinger, eds., *Modernity and Mass Culture* (Bloomington: Indiana University Press, 1991), 24–41. Ohmann's essay is revised and expanded in *Selling Culture,* 287–339.

39. See, for instance, the Quaker Oats ad on the back cover of *Saturday Evening Post* (29 September 1900). See, also, James Whorton, "Eating to Win: Popular Concepts of Diet, Strength and Energy in the Early Twentieth Century," in Kathryn Grover, ed., *Fitness in American Culture* (Amherst: University of Massachusetts Press, 1990), 105–111.

40. See, for instance, "Editorial: Public Opinion as a Moral Center," *MPW* (11 May 1907), 147–148; and a *Baltimore Sun* article reprinted as "Moving Picture Business Enjoys a Frenzied Boom," in *MPW* (14 September 1907), 439. See, also, the call for "good, clean subjects," in "Words from the Knocker and Howler," *MPW* (1 February 1908), 72; and Hans Leigh's admonition to American manufacturers, in "A Coffin for the Theatorium," *MPW* (22 February 1908), 135. Laemmle also did his bit by calling for "good, clean, wholesome, entertaining" films, in his own earlier challenge to the *Chicago Tribune*—see, for instance, the Laemmle Film Service ad in *Bill* (27 April 1907), 34.

41. James D. Law, "Better Scenarios Demanded," *MPW* (29 August 1908), 153–154. Vitagraph had advertised one of its first films, *The Green Goods Man,* as an "American Film for American Audiences," in *NYC* (6 January 1906), 1188. The first manufacturer to insist that all of its productions were "American Films" was O. T. Crawford—see the company's ad in *VFI* (23 November 1907), 12. Crawford soon abandoned production and concentrated on renting and exhibiting; his company did have one of the first American trademarks: an Indian in headdress, in profile. Lary May refers to another critic asking for "American subjects"

in June 1908, but he does not provide a specific citation for the reference—May, *Screening Out the Past: The Birth of Mass Culture and the Motion Picture Industry* (Chicago: University of Chicago Press, 1980), 64.

42. See "Reviews of Late Films," *NYDM* (6 June 1908), 6; and James D. Law, "Moving Picture Drama Becoming a Vital Force," *SW* (27 June 1908), 20. One year before, Robert Bachman had predicted that "the United States will supply the films of the world as it supplies wheat and cotton," in "The Popularity of Films Grows," *SW* (13 July 1907), 10.

43. Frank L. Dyer, "The Progress and Mission of Moving Pictures," *SW* (19 December 1908), 9.

44. "Reviews of New Films," *NYDM* (12 December 1908), 6. See, also, "Earmarks of Makers," *NYDM* (14 November 1908), 10—reprinted in Stanley Kauffmann and Bruce Henstell, eds., *American Film Criticism: From the Beginnings to Citizen Kane* (New York: Liveright, 1972), 13–18.

45. "Interview with Carl Laemmle," *MPW* (5 June 1909), 740.

46. "Films and Realism," *FI* (24 October 1908), 11.

47. Laura Jean Libbey was one of the most popular writers of working-girl fiction from the 1880s through the 1900s. She published stories in the *New York Ledger, Fireside Companion,* and *Family Story Paper,* and they were frequently reprinted in cheap libraries. That her stories were being taken up by middle-class women readers is clear from "The Novelette and the Superwoman," *Living Age* 42 (16 January 1909), 182–184. For analyses of Libbey's work, see Denning, *Mechanic Accents,* 188–200; and Jean Carwile Matsteller, "Romancing the Reader: From Laura Jean Libbey to Harlequin Romance and Beyond," in Larry Sullivan and Lydia Cushman Schurman, eds., *Pioneers, Passionate Ladies, and Private Eyes: Dime Novels, Series Books, and Paperbacks* (New York: Haworth Press, 1996), 263–284.

48. Perry, "The Short Story," 329–330. For a good introduction to short story production as an industry by 1900, see Fred Lewis Pattee, "The Journalization of the Short Story," in *The Development of the American Short Story* (New York: Harper and Brothers, 1923), 337–356.

49. Pattee, *The Development of the American Short Story,* 293–294, 364–366.

50. Casson, "The Americans in America," 435; and J. Angus MacDonald, *Successful Advertising: How to Accomplish It* (Philadelphia: Lincoln, 1906), 241.

51. This undated quote from *Nation* comes from Pattee, *The Development of the American Short Story,* 369.

52. See, for instance, Terry Ramsaye, *A Million and One Nights: A History of the Motion Picture* (New York: Simon and Schuster, 1926), 512–513; Robert Henderson, *D. W. Griffith: The Years at Biograph* (New York: Farrar, Straus and Giroux, 1970), 56; Myron Lounsbury, *The Origins of American Film Criticism, 1909–1939* (New York: Arno Press, 1973), 12–28; Bordwell, Staiger, and Thompson, *The Classical Hollywood Cinema,* 106–107; and Gunning, *D. W. Griffith,* 186 n. 66.

53. The *Mirror* sometimes still maintained Pathé as the standard against which to judge American manufacturers—see, for instance, "Earmarks of Makers," 10.

54. "Reviews of Late Films," *NYDM* (25 July 1908), 7.

55. "Reviews of Late Films," *NYDM* (20 June 1908), 6. Kalem's *Lady Audley's Secret* was faulted, by contrast, because "unless one has read the book and knows the plot he finds it difficult to understand what it is all about"—see "Reviews of Late Films," *NYDM* (4 July 1908), 7.

56. "Reviews of New Films," *NYDM* (8 August 1908), 7. See, also, "Moving Picture Reviews," *Var* (1 August 1908), 13.

57. "Reviews of New Films," *NYDM* (26 September 1908), 9, and (7 November 1908), 8. *The Call of the Wild* "was liberally applauded" at Keith's Fourteenth Street theater in New York.

58. "Reviews of New Films," *NYDM* (21 November 1908), 8.

59. "Earmarks of Makers," 10. See, also, the remarks on plotting in Biograph's *Where the Breakers Roar* and *Money Mad*, as well as Selig's *A Dual Life*—in "Reviews of New Films," *NYDM* (3 October 1908), 8, and (12 December 1908), 6.

60. See, for instance, "Comments on Film Subjects," *MPW* (24 October 1908), 318, (21 November 1908), 398, and (12 December 1908), 478.

61. See Burton Allbee, "What Does the Public Want?" *MPW* (12 December 1908), 472. See, also, the review of Kalem's *The Girl at the Mill* as "an eloquent picture without words"—"Comments on Film Subjects," *MPW* (23 January 1909), 93. For a similar response, see "Reviews of New Films," *NYDM* (30 January 1909), 16.

62. This phrase comes from a review of Biograph's *Heart of O'Yama*, which never once mentions its "beautifully tinted scenes"—see "Reviews of New Films," *NYDM* (26 September 1908), 9; and the Biograph ad in *NYDM* (19 September 1908), 9.

63. There is a concise instance of this in the *Mirror*'s review of Edison's *Where Is My Wandering Boy:* "the story, the first and most important consideration in every film"—see "Reviews of New Films," *NYDM* (23 January 1909), 7.

64. Neil Harris, *Cultural Excursions: Marketing Appetites and Cultural Tastes in Modern America* (Chicago: University of Chicago Press, 1990), 307–308.

65. Peter Marzio, *The Democratic Art: Pictures for a Nineteenth-Century America* (Boston: Godine, 1979), xi.

66. Harris, *Cultural Excursions*, 305–306, 340. See, also, Richard Slotkin, *Gunfighter Nation: The Myth of the Frontier in Twentieth-Century America* (New York: Atheneum, 1992), 158.

67. Harris, *Cultural Excursions*, 307.

68. Marzio, *The Democratic Art*, 116–128; and Harris, *Cultural Excursions*, 322.

69. Even in France, by the 1880s, *chromo* meant "vulgar"—see, for instance, Henri Beraldi, *Les Graveurs du XIXe Siècle* (Paris: Librairie L. Conquet, 1888), quoted in Marzio, *The Democratic Art*, 209. Robert Jay, however, suggests a very different reason that might have affected trade press attitudes toward Pathé color films: namely, the higher quality of German chromolithography, in "cigar bands, labels, post cards, and other color work" that also had flooded the United States at the turn of the century—see *The Trade Card in Nineteenth-Century America* (Columbia: University of Missouri Press, 1987), 102–103.

70. See, for instance, "Cinematography in Natural Colors," *MPW* (12 September 1908), 197; "Color Kinematography," *MPW* (14 November 1908), 375; and "Color Photography Realized," *FI* (30 January 1909), 11–12, (6 February 1909), 4, 11, and (13 February 1909), 5. Neither Urban nor Smith tried to market Kinemacolor in the United States until the following summer, and they did not succeed until December—see "Urban to Introduce Color Photography on This Side," *Var* (26 June 1909), 13; and "Kinemacolor: First American Exhibition of Moving Pictures in Natural Colors," *MPW* (18 December 1909), 873–874.

71. I take these terms from Michael Orvell, but I follow Richard Slotkin in insisting on the way gender and race governed how they functioned. See Michael Orvell, *The Real Thing: Imitation and Authenticity in American Culture, 1880–1940* (Chapel Hill: University of

North Carolina Press, 1989), xv–xvi; and Slotkin, *Gunfighter Nation*, 156–157. For further arguments about a masculine (Anglo-Saxon) "turn" in American mass culture generally at the turn of the last century, see John Higham, "The Reorientation of American Culture in the 1890s," in *Writing American History* (Bloomington: Indiana University Press, 1970), 73–102; Christopher Wilson, *The Labor of Words: Literary Professionalism in the Progressive Era* (Athens: University of Georgia Press, 1985); Christine Gledhill, "The Melodramatic Field: An Investigation," in Gledhill, ed., *Home Is Where the Heart Is* (London: British Film Institute, 1987), 34; Denning, *Mechanic Accents*, 204–206; Kaplan, "Romancing the Empire," 659–690; Ohmann, "History and Literary History," 24–41; and Jane Tompkins, *West of Everything: The Inner Life of Westerns* (New York: Oxford University Press, 1992).

72. Orvell, *The Real Thing*, 36–38, 41.

73. Slotkin, *Gunfighter Nation*, 156–157.

74. Frank S. Munsey, "Publisher's Desk: A Generation of Writers," *Munsey's* (July 1895), 438—cited in Ellen Gruber Garvey, *The Adman in the Parlor: Magazines and the Gendering of Consumer Culture, 1880s to 1910s* (New York: Oxford University Press, 1996), 181.

75. See, for instance, W. Churchill Williams, "Red Blood in Fiction," *World's Work* 6 (July 1903), 3694–3700. See, also, Slotkin, *Gunfighter Nation*, 156–160.

76. In the 1895 preface to *Red Men and White*, Wister "claimed realism and authenticity for his tales"—Christine Bold, *Selling the Wild West: Popular Western Fiction, 1860–1960* (Bloomington: Indiana University Press, 1987), 41. See, also, Orvell, *The Real Thing*, 101–104, 114–119, 198–211.

77. Frank Norris, "The Frontier Gone at Last," *World's Work* 3 (1902)—reprinted in Donald Pizer, ed., *The Literary Criticism of Frank Norris* (Austin: University of Texas Press, 1964), 111.

78. Frank Norris, "Salt and Sincerity," *Critic* (1902)—quoted in Pattee, *The Development of the American Short Story*, 338.

79. Michael Kimmel provides a related context within which this difference in aesthetics operated: the concept of *masculinity*, in opposition to *femininity*, was replacing that of *manhood*, in opposition to *childhood*, at the turn of the century, and the behavior and attitudes defining it "had to be constantly demonstrated." See Kimmel, *Manhood in America: A Cultural History* (New York: Free Press, 1996), 119–120.

80. Hansen broaches something close to this point in *Babel and Babylon*, 123. See, also, Rabinovitz, "Temptations of Pleasure," 72.

81. "American vs. Foreign Films," *FI* (10 April 1909), 7.

82. For further information on this change in Pathé's investment and marketing strategies, see Richard Abel, "In the Belly of the Beast: The Early Years of Pathé-Frères," *Film History* 5.4 (December 1993), 372–378.

83. See, for instance, Ralph Ince's "Balked," in *FI* (14 August 1909), 5; and the same cartoonist's "Phew!" in *FI* (21 August 1909), 5. Laemmle, by contrast, cleverly played on Mother Goose rhymes, folk songs, and even popular films—see, for instance, the Laemmle ads in *MPW* (22 May 1909), 656, (12 June 1909), 778, (19 June 1909), 818, and (7 August 1909), 207. Earlier, Lux Graphicus had praised "the cogently written advertisements of Carl Laemmle" in "On the Screen," *MPW* (13 February 1909), 167. Like Lubin, Laemmle also produced comedies that could appeal to Jewish audiences—see, for instance, the IMP ad for *Levitsky Sees the Parade* in *MPW* (20 November 1909), 708.

Kleine, for instance, insisted on pronouncing the final *e* in his name, so as not to be mistaken for a Jew—Anthony Slide, *Early American Cinema*, rev. ed. (Metuchen, N.J.: Scarecrow,

1994), 49. See, also, the 4 February 1908 letter to Marion, in which Kleine describes Max Lewis's Chicago Film Exchange (then a member of the FSA but later excluded from the MPPC) as following the "Hebraic rule of taking everything that is allowed and then some"—Box 29: Kalem Folder, GK. See, also, Hansen, *Babel and Babylon*, 70.

84. For further information on this strategy, see Richard Abel, *The Ciné Goes to Town: French Cinema, 1896–1914* (Berkeley: University of California Press, 1994), 39–41.

85. Vitagraph was the American company most involved in a similar strategy of producing "quality films" at this time—see Uricchio and Pearson, *Reframing Culture*, 55–194. Although it produced several films fitting this category during 1908, from *Francesca da Rimini* to *Julius Caesar*, it did not engage heavily in their promotion until *Napoleon*—see, for instance, the half-page Vitagraph ad in *NYDM* (3 April 1909), 14; *"Napoleon—The Man of Destiny,"* *MPW* (3 April 1909), 399; and "Vitagraph High-Art Production," *FI* (10 April 1909), 14. Other companies such as Edison, Lubin, and Biograph also took up this strategy, but slightly later and less directly.

86. Montrose Moses, "Where They Perform Shakespeare for Five Cents," *Theatre* 8 (October 1908), 264–265, xi–xii. Moses also publicized the soon-to-be-released Pathé *films d'art*. Condensed versions of this article circulated widely—see "Nickelodeon Theatergoing," *DMRL* (11 November 1908), 3.6. Moses was an influential drama critic who included a chapter entitled "The Kinescopic Theatre" (partly based on this article), in *The American Dramatist* (Boston: Little, Brown, 1911), 200–214.

87. For a list of New York vaudeville houses turned into moving picture theaters, see "The Moving Picture Field," *NYDM* (6 June 1908), 6. See, also, Robert Allen, "Motion Picture Exhibition in Manhattan, 1906–1912: Beyond the Nickelodeon," *Cinema Journal* 18.2 (Spring 1979), 170–174; Eileen Bowser, *The Transformation of Cinema, 1907–1915*, vol. 2 of *History of American Cinema* (New York: Scribner's, 1990), 121–129; and Douglas Gomery, *Shared Pleasures: A History of Movie Presentation in the United States* (Madison: University of Wisconsin Press, 1992), 29–37.

88. See David Hulfish, "Colored Films of Today," *Nick* (January 1909), 15; and Lewis E. Palmer, "The World in Motion," *Survey* 22 (5 June 1909), 356. The trade press also began to draw attention to the stencil-color process in Gaumont films—see, for instance, "Moving Picture Reviews," *Var* (8 May 1909), 13; and "Pictorial Effect in Moving Pictures," *MPW* (29 May 1909), 709.

89. A long article from the *New York Tribune*'s Paris correspondent was reprinted as "Pathé Backs 'Le Film d'Art,'" in *VFI* (30 May 1908), 4, and summarized in "A French Enterprise," *NYDM* (30 May 1908), 4. See, also, "Future Pathé Films," *VFI* (11 April 1908), 3; "Actor's Laurels," *FI* (24 October 1908), 4–5; and "Growing Importance of Moving Picture Shows," *Nick* (February 1909), 53–54. *Billboard* even devoted editorial space to the Paris premiere of *The Assassination of the Duke of Guise*—see "Drama on Canvas," *Bill* (2 January 1909), 12.

90. See "'Film d'Art' Plays," *NYTr* (13 December 1908), 4.2.

91. See "Stories of the Films," *MPW* (28 November 1908), 433; and "Reviews of New Films," *NYDM* (5 December 1908), 8.

92. See "High Art Film by Pathé," *NYDM* (6 February 1909), 18; and "Many Notable Films," *NYDM* (13 February 1909), 12. In cities from Des Moines, Iowa, to Medford, Oregon, nickelodeons used Séverin's name to promote this film—see the Family Theatre ad in the *Des Moines Capital* (8 February 1909), 9, and the Savoy Theater ad in the *Medford Daily Tribune* (1 April 1909), 3.

93. See "Reviews of New Films," *NYDM* (1 May 1909), 42.

94. See "'Spectator's' Comments," *NYDM* (22 May 1909), 17.

95. See "Notable Film of the Week," *MPW* (19 June 1909), 832; and "Reviews of New Films," *NYDM* (10 June 1909), 16—reprinted in Kauffmann and Henstell, *American Film Criticism*, 32–33.

96. See, for instance, the Princess ads in the *Lexington Leader* and *Lexington Herald* (1 December 1908); the Family Theatre ads in the *DMRL* (7 February 1909), 3.7, (14 March 1909), 3.7, and (22 March 1909), 5; the Star Theatre ad in *DMRL* (21 June 1909), 6; the Savoy Theater ads in the *Medford Daily Tribune* (6 March 1909), 3, (1 April 1909), 3, and (14 April 1909), 2; and "Moving Picture Notes," *NYDM* (27 March 1909), 15. The *Duke of Guise* also played at the Premier Scenic in Portsmouth, according to the *Mirror*, the same week it did in Dover.

97. See "A Boost for Pathé," *FI* (26 June 1909), 12. In Ottumwa, the new Majestic Theatre even promoted *The Grandfather* as "Pathé's Masterpiece"—see the Majestic Theatre ad in *Ottumwa Courier* (22 July 1909), 4.

98. See "First in Pantomime Art," *NYDM* (1 May 1909), 38; and "Looking Forward," *FI* (7 August 1909), 2. Gunning assesses the impact of Pathé's *films d'art*, especially on Biograph films, in *D. W. Griffith*, 172–174.

99. "Weekly Comments on the Shows," *MPW* (20 February 1909), 200.

100. "Comments on Film Subjects," *MPW* (27 February 1909), 236. See, also, "Correspondence," *MPW* (6 March 1909), 277. Had at least some audiences seen the film accompanied by Saint-Saëns's musical score, that reception may well have been very different.

101. "Reviews of New Films," *NYDM* (27 February 1909), 13.

102. Thomas Bedding, "The Modern Way in Moving Picture Making," *MPW* (13 March 1909), 294.

103. Thomas Bedding, "The Modern Way in Moving Picture Making," *MPW* (20 March 1909), 326.

104. See "Daily Changes of Films," *NYDM* (13 March 1909), 16.

105. See "Well Balanced Bill," *DMRL* (15 March 1909), 5.

106. See Allan Meade, "All in the Day's Work," *Nick* (15 February 1910), 94.

107. "Moving Picture Reviews," *Var* (28 November 1908), 10.

108. The ending of the initial scenario for this film, which was cut in the version released in the United States, had the executioner hold up Mary Stuart's severed head for spectators' approval—see the Pathé-Frères Scenario Collection, Département des Arts et Spectacles, Bibliothèque Nationale, Paris.

109. See "Comments on Film Subjects," *MPW* (28 November 1908), 422, and (5 December 1908), 448.

110. "A French Sample," *Var* (2 January 1909), 10. Another *Variety* review mocked *Gaul's Hero*—see "Moving Picture Reviews," *Var* (10 April 1909), 13.

111. See "Reviews of New Films," *NYDM* (6 February 1909), 16.

112. See "Comments on the Week's Films," *MPW* (5 June 1909), 753.

113. See "Comments on the Week's Films," *MPW* (3 July 1909), 12.

114. See "Reviews of Licensed Films," *NYDM* (2 October 1909), 32.

115. See "'Spectator's' Comments," *NYDM* (11 September 1909), 14—reprinted in Kauffmann and Henstell, *American Film Criticism*, 33–35. By then, too, Woods also was using Séverin as an example of "the old school," the very opposite of an acting style that was "natural" and "true to life"—see "'Spectator's' Comments," *NYDM* (20 November 1909), 15.

116. Throughout this period, from late 1908 to late 1909, much of the trade press wrote approvingly of Pathé's stencil-color fairy tales, and even some of its trick films, yet however successful these films may still have been with children and adults, they no longer were judged significant to the development of an American cinema.

117. See, for instance, "Merits of Canned Drama," *Bill* (19 December 1908), 12.

118. See, for instance, the review of Lubin's *Cotton Industry in the South,* in "Comments on Film Subjects," *MPW* (14 November 1908), 379; "Encourage Educational Pictures," *NYDM* (26 December 1908), 8; and the review of Kalem's *Sponge Fishers of Cuba,* in "Notes and Comments," *MPW* (9 January 1909), 33, and in "Reviews of New Films," *NYDM* (23 January 1909), 7. For a fine analysis of early travelogues, see Tom Gunning, "The Whole World within Reach: Travel Images without Borders," in Roland Cosandey and François Albera, eds., *Images across Borders, 1896–1918* (Lausanne: editions Payot, 1995), 21–36. See, also, Daan Hertogs and Nico de Klerk, eds., *Nonfiction from the Teens* (Amsterdam: Nederlands Filmmuseum, 1994).

119. In France, Pathé began to collect its nonfiction into a weekly newsreel, *Pathé-Journal,* in 1908. Gradually, the company introduced this newsreel, in different languages, throughout Europe by 1910.

120. See "Drawing the Line," *NYDM* (23 January 1909), 8.

121. This promotional tactic seems to have begun in earnest with the Pathé ad in *FI* (4 September 1909), 14. Throughout 1908 and early 1909, Pathé gave much more attention to its story films, and especially its dramas, at least in the ads in *Views and Films Index.* In 1909, the company also established an educational film division in Paris, where Dr. Jean Comandon was given laboratory space to do research on microscopic cinematography, research that was presented to the Académie des Sciences later that year—see Abel, "In the Belly of the Beast," 373.

122. See "Comments on the Week's Films," *MPW* (17 July 1909), 88.

123. See "Variety's Own Picture Reviews," *Var* (4 September 1909), 13.

124. See "Licensed Reviews," *NYDM* (13 November 1909), 15. In praising Pathé's stencil color, the *World* also cited the related industrial, *Culture of Tea*—see "Unfair Advertising," *MPW* (27 November 1909), 756.

125. See, for instance, "*Sensational Logging,*" *FI* (29 January 1910), 5; and "Comments on the Films," *MPW* (12 February 1910), 215. By contrast, at the same time, Pathé was being praised for *Stag Hunt in Java, A Visit to Bombay,* and *Coffee Culture.*

126. See, for instance, James McQuade, "Motion Picture Events in the Windy City," *FI* (15 January 1910), 1, 8; "The Motion Picture as Educator," *MPW* (29 January 1910), 119; "Educational Pictures," *FI* (5 February 1910), 3; McQuade, "Bad Outlook for Fight Pictures," *FI* (19 March 1910), 6; "The New Kleine Catalog," *FI* (16 April 1910), 6–7; and "On the Screen," *MPW* (9 April 1910), 550. Pathé also arranged a special screening of such films for the New York City Board of Education—see "Pathé Pointers," *FI* (5 March 1910), 3. When John Collier presented a series of films to the National Conference of Charities and Corrections that summer, the story films included Biograph's *Pippa Passes* and Vitagraph's *Napoleon* and *Washington;* the only notable Pathé film was an educational, *Sleeping Sickness,* which received less attention than Eclipse's *The Fly Pest*—see "Pictures at Civic Convention," *FI* (11 June 1910), 3.

127. Pathé eventually would introduce the first newsreel, *Pathé's Weekly,* on the American market in 1911—see the Pathé ad in *MPW* (29 July 1911), 179; and "*The Pathé Weekly,*" *MPW* (23 September 1911), 871.

128. See "Pathé Freres and the Motion Picture Patents Company," *MPW* (8 May 1909), 590.

129. For further information on this struggle between Pathé and Eastman, see Abel, "In the Belly of the Beast," 376; and Vincent Pinel, "Pathé contre Eastman," in *Le Cinéma français muet dans le monde, influences réciproques* (Perpignan: Institut Jean Vigo, 1988), 193–206. By 1912, Pathé was one of the three leading suppliers of film negative in Europe, and its production would be "the principal and most vital component" of the company's business for the next fifteen years.

130. See, for instance, the full-page Pathé ad and "New Pathé Machine," in *MPW* (3 April 1909), 390, 402. See, also, the Pathé ad on the back cover of *NYDM* (1 May 1909). In describing the Pathé Professional to correspondence school students, David Hulfish pointed out the advantage of its being constructed in Paris, but he also was careful not to seem to be "boosting the Pathé machine"—see Hulfish, *Cyclopedia of Motion-Picture Work*, vol. 1 (Chicago: American Technical Society, 1914 [1911]), 206–207.

131. See, for instance, "Pathé's New Projecting Machine," *MPW* (8 May 1909), 593; "French Machine Hits Iowa City," *FI* (5 June 1909), 4; "Pathé Professional Outfit," *NYDM* (31 July 1909), 15; L. F. Cook, "Of Interest to the Trade: Pathe Freres Moving Picture Machines," *Nick* (October 1909), 127–128; "Pleased with Pathé Machines," *NYDM* (30 October 1909), 17; "Quantitative Competition," *MPW* (5 February 1910), 158; "N.I.M.P.A. Meeting," *MPW* (12 February 1910), 214; "Pathé Pointers," *FI* (19 March 1910), 7; "Pathé Machines on U.S. Warships," *NYDM* (14 May 1910), 21; "The Pathé Professional," *MPW* (6 July 1910), 89; and the Pathé ad in *MPW* (16 July 1910), 171.

132. The first company to use the *Mirror* for advertising was Nicholas Power, for the Cameragraph—see *NYDM* (11 July 1908), 7.

133. See Kristin Thompson, "Initial Standardization of the Basic Technology," in Bordwell, Staiger, and Thompson, *The Classical Hollywood Cinema*, 266–267.

134. See "Pathé Film d'Art," *NYDM* (17 April 1909), 13. That month, the company also moved its southern sales office from Birmingham to New Orleans.

135. See "Film d'Art for Sunday Release," *NYDM* (30 October 1909), 16; L. F. Cook, "Pathé-Frères Sunday Releases," *Nick* (November 1909), 155; "Coming Headliners: *Rigoletto,*" *MPW* (6 November 1909), 645; and the Pathé ads in *MPW* (4 December 1909), 789, and (11 December 1909), 829.

136. See "Trade Notes," *VFI* (17 August 1907), 4; "Pathé Notes," *FI* (20 November 1909), 2; and the Pathé ad in *FI* (4 December 1909), 11. Kleine Optical also distributed a deluxe booklet for Gaumont's *L'Enfant prodigue,* which had a special showing at the New Auditorium in Sioux City, Iowa, the week of 2 August 1909—see Box 26: Historical File: General, GK. These booklets were different from the single-sheet "lectures" or "readers" that accompanied many films, whether French or American: examples range from Kalem's *The Padrone,* reprinted in *Bill* (22 August 1908), 9, to Pathé's *Charlotte Corday,* used by the Starland Theatre in Brandon, Manitoba, and reprinted in "Picture Theatre Advertising," *FI* (13 November 1909), 4.

137. See "Licensed Releases," *NYDM* (16 October 1909), 17; "Licensed Reviews," *NYDM* (13 November 1909), 16; "Comments on the Week's Films," *MPW* (20 November 1909), 721; and "Reviews of Licensed Films," *NYDM* (11 December 1909), 17. See, also, "Variety's Own Picture Reviews," *Var* (16 October 1909), 12, (13 November 1909), 12, and (4 December 1909), 12.

138. One *World* reviewer also cited Pathé's *Her Dramatic Career* as an object lesson in quality, far surpassing anything on one theater's program, yet wondered whether its "characteristically French . . . play of passion" would be popular with American audiences—see "Comments on the Week's Films," *MPW* (27 November 1909), 757. Bedding continued to hold Pathé up as a standard for film quality, at least for the Independents to match—see "On the Screen," *MPW* (2 October 1909), 448.

139. See, for instance, "A Great Pathé Film d'Art," *FI* (9 October 1909), 9; "Double Reel of Film d'Art," *NYDM* (16 October 1909), 19; the Pathé ad in *FI* (30 October 1909), 10; and "'Spectator's' Comments," *NYDM* (18 December 1909), 15. During this period, Vitagraph experimented with several multiple-reel subjects, which were released in consecutive weeks: *Napoleon* (two parts), *Washington* (two parts), *Les Miserables* (four parts), *The Life of Moses* (five parts). The *World* singled out *Drink*, along with Pathé's *Rigoletto* and *Prodigal Son*, as examples of the few subjects that justified a length of one thousand feet or more—see "A Note of Warning," *MPW* (27 November 1909), 751.

140. James McQuade, "Waking Up on Posters," *FI* (13 November 1909), 6. The *World* also took *Rigoletto*'s release as an occasion to praise Pathé's posters—see "The Poster End," *MPW* (27 November 1909), 752. For a good analysis of how manufacturers and exhibitors used posters differently, see Leslie Midkaff DeBauche, "Advertising and the Movies, 1908–1915," *Film Reader* 6 (1985), 117–121.

141. The first of these ads can be found in *CT* (6 February 1910), 2.6; or *CRH* (6 February 1910), 7.3. Succeeding ads promoted comedy, tragedy, travel pictures, educational pictures, juvenile pictures, and historical pictures. See, also, "Pathé Pointers," *FI* (26 March 1910), 6; and "Novel Advertising Campaign," *NYDM* (26 March 1910), 20.

142. See the Pathé ad in *MPW* (19 February 1910), 270; the Pathé ads in *NYDM* (5 February 1910), 17, (12 February 1910), 19, and (23 April 1910), 19; and "A Colored Film d'Art," *NYDM* (12 February 1910), 18. See, also, *Pathé Weekly Bulletin* 132 (9 May 1910), n.p.

143. See the Pathé ad in *FI* (6 November 1909), 11.

144. *Film Index* accused *Show World* of attacking Pathé in revenge for not agreeing to advertise in its pages—see "There's a Reason," *FI* (26 February 1910), 2; and "A Useless Expedient," *FI* (5 March 1910), 2.

145. See "Pathé Losing Ground," *Var* (19 February 1910), 14.

146. See "Variety's Own Picture Reviews," *Var* (22 January 1910), 14. See, also, "Variety's Own Picture Reviews," *Var* (4 December 1909), 13, (8 January 1910), 12, and (29 January 1910), 13.

147. See "Variety's Own Picture Reviews," *Var* (5 March 1910), 13.

148. See "Honi Soit Qui Mal Y Pense," *MPW* (5 March 1910), 328; and "'Spectator's' Comments," *NYDM* (23 April 1910), 17.

149. See "Some Film Manufacturers Slow to Rise to the Standard of Modern Exactitude," *MPW* (2 July 1910), 31–32.

150. The quote is from "Tragedy," *Nick* (November 1909), 135.

151. Although not her primary point, Roberta Pearson makes a good case for this in analyzing the shift from a histrionic to a verisimilar style of acting, as articulated in trade press discourse—see Pearson, *Eloquent Gestures: The Transformation of Performance Style in Griffith Biograph Films* (Berkeley: University of California Press, 1992), 120–139.

152. Rollin Summers, "The Moving Picture Drama and the Acted Drama," *MPW* (19 September 1908), 213—reprinted in Kauffmann and Henstell, *American Film Criticism,*

9–13. Summers also makes an interesting "technical point" in suggesting that shooting "at close range" for "moving pictures may present figures greater than life size without loss of illusion."

153. See "Earmarks of Makers" and "Rules for Moving Picture Actors," *NYDM* (14 November 1908), 10 and 11.

154. See "Comments on Film Subjects," *MPW* (9 January 1909), 37. See, also, Bedding's assertion that "better films than those of Kalem, Biograph, Selig, and others . . . are not produced anywhere," in "On the Screen," *MPW* (27 February 1909), 232.

155. "Reviews of New Films," *NYDM* (13 March 1909), 16. See, also, "Comments on Film Subjects," *MPW* (13 March 1909), 302. Similar language would mark a review of *His Duty,* in "Comments on the Week's Films," *MPW* (5 June 1909), 755.

156. "Notable Films of the Week," *MPW* (24 April 1909), 515; and "Reviews of New Films," *NYDM* (10 April 1909), 14.

157. "'Spectator's' Comments," *NYDM* (22 May 1909), 17. This was just weeks after the *Mirror* had lauded Pathé for leading the world in finished film production. See, also, "'Spectator's' Comments," *NYDM* (11 September 1909), 14.

158. See "Modern Art in Motion Pictures," *MPW* (27 March 1909), 363. This would have greatly pleased Griffith, Biograph's principal director, whose ambition it once was to succeed on the Broadway stage.

159. See "Comments on the Week's Films," *MPW* (19 June 1909), 834. This was the "famous Biograph picture" Bedding would recall in "The 'Dramatic Moment,'" *MPW* (12 March 1910), 372. The *Mirror,* by contrast, described *The Lonely Villa* as "badly constructed" and devoted a lot of space to detailing its serious flaws, yet concluded it would "no doubt prove more popular than it deserves"—see "Reviews of New Films," *NYDM* (19 June 1909), 16—reprinted in Kauffmann and Henstell, *American Film Criticism,* 31–32.

160. See "On the Screen," *MPW* (3 July 1909), 11.

161. See "'Spectator's' Comments," *NYDM* (21 August 1909), 22.

162. See "A Biograph Appreciation," *MPW* (31 July 1909), 165–166. Similarly, in Ottumwa, the Majestic Theatre now identified some film titles as Biograph's—see, for instance, the Majestic Theatre ad in *Ottumwa Courier* (16 August 1909), 4. In Boston as well, the Star Theatre manager claimed that, of the American manufacturers, only Biograph had "attained the Pathé standard"—see "Correspondence," *MPW* (29 May 1909), 716. Gunning uses Anderson's letter to support his argument that "moral discourse formed an essential element of [Griffith's] narrator system"—see *D. W. Griffith,* 161–162.

163. See "Films d'Art," *Nick* (August 1909), 37.

164. See "'Spectator's' Comments," *NYDM* (11 September 1909), 14. Thereafter, Woods consistently praised American acting as a "new pantomime" much superior to the "old pantomime" of Europe (including now the French)—see "'Spectator's' Comments," *NYDM* (13 November 1909), 15, (20 November 1909), 15, and (11 December 1909), 15.

165. See the Motion Picture Theaters ad in *Sioux City Tribune* (6 December 1909), 5; "Moving Pictures Sound Melodrama's Knell," *NYT* (20 March 1910), 7; and "'Spectator's' Comments," *NYDM* (9 April 1910), 17. The *New York Times* article is misdated as 10 October 1909 in Linda Arvidson, *When the Movies Were Young* (New York: Dover, 1969), 130–131.

166. See "An American School of Motion Picture Drama," *MPW* (20 November 1909), 712; W. C. S., "What Is an American Subject?" *MPW* (12 February 1910), 206—reprinted in Kauffmann and Henstell, *American Film Criticism,* 35–37.

167. For an incisive analysis of pertinent changes in advertising around the turn of the century, see T. J. Jackson Lears, "American Advertising and the Reconstruction of the Body, 1880–1930," in Grover, *Fitness in American Culture,* 47–66. See, for instance, the 1908 Mennen's ad reproduced in Lears, "American Advertising," 57; and the Arrow and King Gillette ads in *Saturday Evening Post* (10 April 1909), 34, and (18 June 1910), 41. One of the ironies of this change, especially for Pathé, was that the Gibson Girl, an early version of the "modern" female figure in advertising, once had as a model Evelyn Nesbitt, the woman of the scandalous love triangle that culminated in the Thaw-White case — see *Murder of the Century,* Arts & Entertainment Network (26 June 1996).

168. Hans Leigh put it bluntly: in the spring of 1908, he had wanted "a practically 'all European' service" for his theaters; in the fall of 1909, he wanted only "American makes"—see Leigh, "Acting and Action," *MPW* (2 October 1909), 443.

169. See "American Sailors Saw the Fleet Pictures," *NYDM* (21 November 1908), 8; "Notable Films of the Week," *MPW* (1 May 1909), 553; and "Notable Films of the Week," *MPW* (8 May 1909), 593. Another example would be *The Marathon Race,* run in London and won by an American—see the full-page Pathé ad in *Bill* (5 September 1908), n.p.

170. *Variety,* for instance, had singled out *The Hostage* as a "perfect example of Pathé craft and popularity"—"Moving Picture News and Reviews," *Var* (25 January 1908), 11.

171. See "The Producer's Art," *MPW* (31 July 1909), 151. This was exactly opposite the criticism six months earlier of Pathé's *Fortune Hunters,* a "French picture" that was "too American"—see "Comments on Film Subjects," *MPW* (7 November 1908), 358

172. See "What Is an American Subject?" and "The Inadmissible Subject," *MPW* (22 January 1910), 82 and 83.

173. See Abel, "In the Belly of the Beast," 373. For further information on Pathé's strategy in Russia, see Richard Abel, "Pathé's Stake in Early Russian Cinema," *Griffithiana,* 38/39 (October 1990), 242–247.

174. See, for instance, "American Studio for Pathé?" *NYDM* (4 December 1909), 18; "Pathé American Studio Announced by Mr. Berst," *FI* (9 April 1910), 1, 3; "New Pathé Studio," *NYDM* (9 April 1910), 21; "Pathé Progress," *MPW* (9 April 1910), 557; and "What Pathé Is Doing," *Nick* (15 April 1910), 216. The company also closed its New Orleans sales office at this time—see James McQuade, "Chicago Letter," *FI* (7 May 1910), 4.

175. See "Pathé's American Film," *FI* (14 May 1910), 5; and the *Pathé Weekly Bulletin,* 133 (16 May 1910), n.p. For information on the studio, see "New Pathé Studio," *FI* (6 August 1910), 3; and "Berst Returns," *FI* (8 October 1910), 2.

176. "Pathé American Studio Announced by Mr. Berst," 3.

177. See the first Thanhouser ad in *MPW* (23 April 1910), 629.

178. See "Pathé Film Selection," *NYDM* (23 April 1910), 20; and "Notes from the Manufacturers: Pathé," *MPW* (16 July 1910), 165.

179. See "'Spectator's' Comments," *NYDM* (3 July 1909), 15.

ENTR'ACTE 5. FROM "DELIVERING THE GOODS"

1. See "The Poster End," *MPW* (27 November 1909), 752; and William Allen Johnson, "The Moving-Picture Show, The New Form of Drama for the Million," *Munsey's* 41 (August 1909), 633.

2. "'Spectator's' Comments," *NYDM* (19 March 1910), 16.

3. The phrase comes in an early "'Spectator's' Comments," *NYDM* (26 June 1909), 11. Although unreliable before 1909 or so, Grau does offer a good survey of the trade press after that date, in *The Theatre of Science* (New York: Benjamin Blom, 1914), 246–257.

4. One of Woods's first columns situates the *Mirror* in relation to four of these other weeklies (ignoring *Variety* and *Billboard*), with the clear sense that the *World* would be its principal rival—see "'Spectator's' Comments," *NYDM* (15 May 1909), 15. Hoff became editor of *Film Index* in early April 1909, and most of its pages were filled with the licensed manufacturers' descriptions of newly released films, and their ads. Interestingly, Hoff had been the New York representative for *Billboard* and then *Show World*—see "James Hoff Manager of 'Films Index,'" *NYDM* (3 April 1909), 13. J. T. Murdock, a vaudeville magnate whose early leadership of the "Independents" was compromised by debts, owned *Show World* throughout much of 1909; thereafter, it was bought out by a Denver circus entrepreneur—see "There's a Reason," *FI* (26 February 1910), 2. *Billboard* introduced a "Motion Picture News" page in June 1909 but continued to offer little more than story descriptions from the manufacturers. *Variety*, *Show World*, and *Billboard* also spoke, it should be remembered, from a point of view committed to entertainment other than moving pictures.

5. The *Mirror* was particularly insistent on staking out this middle ground—see, for instance, "'Spectator's' Comments," *NYDM* (23 October 1909), 16. One sign of the *World*'s initial uncertainty was that, well into March 1909, it was very critical of the Independents in its editorials and columns, yet readily accepted their advertisements.

6. All of these columns were initiated between January and April 1909; they included "Weekly Comments on the Shows by Our Own Critic," "On the Screen by Lux Graphicus [Bedding]," "Observations by Our Man about Town," F. H. Richardson's "Operator's Column," and Bedding's "The Modern Way in Moving Picture Making." Thomas Bedding assumed joint editorship of the *World* in January 1910. Louis Reeves Harrison began writing regularly for the *World*, with "The Play," *MPW* (30 April 1910), 676–677. Unlike the *Mirror*, whose weekly "Motion Picture Field" generally ran three to four pages, each issue of the *World* ran twenty-five to thirty pages, all of them devoted to the industry.

7. This quote comes from the first "'Spectator's' Comments" in *NYDM* (1 May 1909), 38. In line with the *Mirror*'s interest in the legitimate theater, Woods already was claiming motion pictures as "a new form of combined literature and art," one in which "the story is the thing." His insistence on viewing new films in public theaters came in "'Spectator's' Comments," *NYDM* (11 September 1909), 14.

8. James McQuade's "Chicago Letter" first appeared when *Film Index* underwent another design format change, for the 4 September 1909 issue. McQuade headed the weekly's Chicago office, and his "Letter" usually opened on the first page. *Film Index* underwent yet another design format change, in its 28 May 1910 issue, and expanded to thirty-two pages in length. Once John Bradlet became the "Western Representative" for the *Moving Picture World*, in February 1910, he contributed a weekly column, "Chicago Notes" (which had appeared irregularly and anonymously before).

9. See, for instance, "The Independent Movement," *Nick* (February 1909), 39–40; the Independent Film Services ad in *Nick* (March 1909), [inside front cover]; and the photo of J. J. Murdock on the front cover of *Nick* (May 1909). *The Nickelodeon* served as an uplift organ for the entire industry; because it targeted exhibitors who wanted to upgrade their shows, it may well have provoked *Moving Picture World* to give more attention to exhibition.

10. See, for instance, the Laemmle ad in *Bill* (17 October 1908), 47; "Laemmle Raps 'Colliers,'" *FI* (17 October 1908), 4; the Laemmle letter reprinted in *MPW* (7 November 1908), 357; "Theater Manager Replies to Moving Picture Critics," *MPW* (5 December 1908), 451; "Moving Pictures Ad Nauseum," *American Review of Reviews* 38 (December 1908), 744–745; and "'Spectator's' Comments," *NYDM* (17 July 1909), 15, and (4 September 1909), 16. See, also, Louise de Koven Bowen, *Five and Ten Cent Theaters* (Chicago: Juvenile Protection Association, 1909, 1911).

11. See "Moving Pictures Recognized," *NYDM* (20 February 1909), 17; "Editorial," *MPW* (20 February 1909), 193; "'Spectator's' Comments," *NYDM* (26 June 1909), 11; and "*Munsey's Magazine* and Moving Pictures," *MPW* (10 July 1909), 48. See, also, "*Success* and Moving Pictures," *MPW* (26 December 1908), 523; and "Moving Pictures in Current Literature," *Nick* (September 1909), 70–71.

12. The books included Simon Patten's *Product and Climax* and Rollin Lynde Hartt's *The People at Play*; Jane Addams's *Spirit of Youth* had not yet appeared in late June. Hartt's book was based on articles published previously in the *Atlantic Monthly*—see Paul Gorman, *Left Intellectuals and Popular Culture in Twentieth-Century America* (Chapel Hill: University of North Carolina Press, 1996), 17, 19. The magazine articles were Lewis E. Palmer, "The World in Motion," *Survey* 22 (5 June 1909), 355–365; Walter Eaton, "Canned Drama," *American Magazine* 68 (1909), 493–500; Johnson, "The Moving Picture Show, the New Form of Drama for the Million," 633–640; and "The Drama of the People," *Independent* 69 (29 September 1909), 713–715. See, also, "The Point of View," *Scribner's* 46 (July 1909), 121–122; and William Inglis, "Morals and Moving Pictures," *Harper's Weekly* (30 July 1910), 12–13. Most of these texts continued to extol Pathé films as the best available.

13. See, for instance, "The Nation-Wide Wave of Moving Pictures," *NYT* (2 January 1909), 10; and Professor Frederick Starr, "The World, before Our Eyes," *CT* (7 February 1909)—reprinted in *MPW* (20 February 1909), 194–195, and in Stanley Kauffmann and Bruce Henstell, eds., *American Film Criticism: From the Beginnings to Citizen Kane* (New York: Liveright, 1972), 21–23. Starr's article was copyrighted by Selig, Kleine, and Spoor, all of whom also advertised that Sunday in the *Tribune*, suggesting it was planted or at least paid for—see "Editorial," *MPW* (20 February 1909), 193. The *Cleveland Leader* also "devote[d] a page regularly to motion pictures"—see Grau, *The Theatre of Science*, 235.

14. Grau, *The Theatre of Science*, 250. Terwilliger also wrote scenarios for Biograph and later joined Reliance as the company's scenario editor.

15. "'Spectator's' Comments," *NYDM* (26 March 1910), 16. See, also, "The Press and the Moving Pictures," *MPW* (31 December 1909), 952; "Moving Pictures Sound Melodrama's Knell," *NYT* (20 March 1910), 7; and "'Spectator's' Comments," *NYDM* (23 April 1910), 17.

16. Regular local advertising had long been a practice in smaller cities, of course, as evidenced by the Des Moines and Ottumwa theaters in 1907. Yet it may not have been done regularly in larger cities as late as the fall of 1909—see "Advertising the Show," *Nick* (February 1909), 43; "An Opportunity to Advertise," *FI* (11 September 1909), 2; and "The Modern Moving Picture Theatre: Advertising the Theatre," *MPW* (30 October 1909), 598–599. See, also, David Hulfish, *Cyclopedia of Motion-Picture Work*, vol. 2 (Chicago: American Technical Society, 1914 [1911]), 200. The *Index* first called attention to the need for newspaper advertising by reprinting an article from the *Philadelphia Dispatch*, as well as an amusements column from the Sunday *St. Louis Times*—see "Question of Advertising," *FI* (8

January 1910), 2, and (15 January 1910), 19. See, also, the full page of ads from the Sunday *St. Louis Republic* (6 February 1910), reprinted in *MPW* (26 February 1910), 295.

17. See, for instance, "The Moving Picture and the National Character," *American Review of Reviews* (September 1910), 315–320; and Asa Steele, "The Moving-Picture Show," *World's Work* (February 1911), 14018–14032.

18. "The Exhibitors' Golden Time," *MPW* (21 May 1910), 821. To be sure, this editorial criticized exhibitors for making more than their share of the business's profits, but it does reveal a greater interest in exhibition than expressed by the *Index*, which always favored the (licensed) manufacturers.

19. See "Weekly Comments on the Shows," *MPW* (12 June 1909), 794; "Among the Picture Theaters," *Nick* (January 1909), 28–29; "Big Detroit Theater," *Nick* (February 1909), 44; "New Lubin Theater," *Nick* (July 1909), 10; "New Theater Seats 1,300," *Nick* (July 1909), 30; Charles Morris, "The Milwaukee Princess Theater," *Nick* (1 February 1910), 61–62; "The March of Progress," *MPW* (7 May 1910), 723; and Robert Grau, *The Businessman in the Amusement World* (New York: Broadway, 1910), 117–118.

20. See, for instance, "Lubin Sells Philadelphia M. P. Houses," *Bill* (26 June 1909), 13; "The Isman-Lubin Concern Out for the Big-Small Time," *Var* (14 August 1909), 8; "Views of Independents" and "Picture Theatres Combine," *NYDM* (21 August 1909), 17 and 19; Morris, "The Milwaukee Princess Theater," 61–62; James McQuade, "Chicago Letter," *FI* (30 April 1910), 6; "Broadway Has Its Picture House," *MPW* (8 August 1910), 289; Douglas Gomery, *Shared Pleasures: A History of Movie Presentation in the United States* (Madison: University of Wisconsin Press, 1992), 36–40; and Eileen Bowser, *The Transformation of Cinema, 1907–1915*, vol. 2 of *History of American Cinema* (New York: Scribner's, 1990), 125–129.

21. Most recently this has involved Robert Allen and Ben Singer, in "Dialogue," *Cinema Journal* 35.3 (Spring 1996), 84–91, 113–122. Allen relies heavily on *Moving Picture World* and *Variety*, as well as the Loew's circuit, to support his argument that "combination shows" were a very important "marketing niche" that helped attract a middle-class audience; one architecture magazine, in May 1911, supports his contention that moving picture theaters had "developed into vaudeville houses"—see "The Moving Picture Theatre," *Architecture and Building* 43.8 (May 1911), 319. Singer is less convinced, drawing on a broad range of discourse, from the *World* to various reformist surveys, that complained about the level of vaudeville acts in the shows and their lack of appeal to the "better classes."

22. In January 1910, for instance, "the Dewey, Unique, Comedy, and Fourteenth Street Theatre gave liberal vaudeville bills while the Fair, Crystal, and until recently the Union Square have confined their programs to pictures and songs"—see "'Spectator's' Comments," *NYDM* (1 January 1910), 16. Grau also credits Fox with being "the pioneer" of the combination show, in *The Businessman in the Amusement World*, 131–132.

23. The information on Des Moines comes from ads in the *Des Moines Register and Leader*, 1909–1910; that for Lexington, Kentucky, comes from Gregory Waller, *Main Street Amusements: Movies and Commercial Entertainment in a Southern City, 1896–1930* (Washington, D.C.: Smithsonian Institution Press, 1995), 65–83; that for Ottumwa comes from the *Ottumwa Courier*, 1908–1909. The information on Providence comes from "From Larger Cities," *NYDM* (21 August 1909), 17. See, also, the Manager's Reports, Keith Bijou Theatre, Woonsocket, Rhode Island (10 May 1909–3 January 1910)—KA.

24. The information for Milwaukee—which mentions the Princess, but not the Saxe brothers' ownership—comes from "Among the Moving Picture Theatres," *MPW* (30 April 1910), 684. The Olympic, Scenic, and Majestic all advertised together—see, for instance,

the Motion Picture Theaters ad in *Sioux City Tribune* (22 November 1909), 12. See, also, John Bradlet, "A Tour amongst Country Exhibitors," *MPW* (6 February 1909), 142. Both Richardson and Bradlet complained that too many Chicago houses were "playing a mixed bill of pictures and vaudeville"—see "Vaudeville vs. Moving Pictures," *MPW* (16 October 1909), 525; and "Chicago Notes," *MPW* (5 February 1910), 171.

25. See "'Spectator's' Comments," *NYDM* (1 January 1910), 16; and "Straight Picture Shows," *FI* (18 June 1910), 2. See, also, Fred Marriott, "Some Impressions of the Moving Picture in St. Louis, Detroit, and Buffalo," *MPW* (2 October 1909), 446–447; "Vaudeville or Not?" *Nick* (November 1909), 134–135; "Cheap Vaudeville a Menace to the Exhibitor," *MPW* (8 January 1910), 8–9; "Vaudeville in Picture Theaters," *Nick* (15 February 1910), 86; H. I. Dillenback, "Looking into the Future," *Nick* (15 March 1910), 143–144; and the summary of an editorial from the *Christian Science Monitor,* in "Objectionable Vaudeville," *MPW* (19 March 1910), 415. As a writer for the *Index,* James McQuade recalls his own participation in this campaign against small-time vaudeville, in "Chicago Reports Many Variations in Picture Shows," *MPW* (15 July 1916), 414.

26. See Bowser, *The Transformation of Cinema,* 121–123. For a survey of the four kinds of theaters coexisting around 1910, see Hulfish, *Cyclopedia of Motion-Picture Work,* vol. 2, 176–192. For an incomplete, but still extensive, list of theaters, both licensed and unlicensed, see "Motion Picture Theaters," *Bill* (11 September 1909), 81–91. In a report on the Stair & Havlin circuit, formerly "the principal arbiters of melodrama," *Billboard* claimed that "the same class of people who had previously made melodrama so profitable" now followed moving pictures—see "Motion Picture Shows Replace Melodrama," *Bill* (30 October 1909), 5.

27. See "People's Vaudeville," *Var* (12 December 1908), 12; "Dewey Theatre," *Var* (19 December 1908), 13; "32 Park Row," *Var* (23 January 1909), 13; and "Manhattan," *Var* (13 February 1909), 13.

28. See the series of almost weekly "Comments on the Shows by Our Own Critic," in *Moving Picture World,* from 16 January through 19 June 1909.

29. This was reprinted as "Seeing the Pictures," in *FI* (25 December 1909), 3–4.

30. See, for instance, the South Side survey in "Late Chicago Theatres," *Var* (10 July 1909), 13; the survey of Madison Street in "Among the Chicago Shows," *MPW* (9 October 1909), 494; the survey of North Avenue in "Among the Chicago Theatres," *MPW* (23 October 1909), 575; and the survey of State Street in "Chicago Notes," *MPW* (5 February 1910), 171–172.

31. By August, the number of Independent Film Exchanges nearly equaled that of Licensed Exchanges; see "Directory of Film Exchanges," *MPW* (14 August 1909), 232.

32. See, for instance, the list of rental exchanges receiving licensed films in "Number of Reels of Film Leased during May 1909"—Box 26: Historical File: General, GK. Saint Louis was nearly as important as Chicago because it now had nearly two hundred theaters—see "From Larger Cities," *NYDM* (21 August 1909), 21. See, also, "A Week in Cincinnati, Ohio," *MPW* (13 November 1909), 682. Yet the *Mirror* insisted that licensed theaters remained dominant in cities from Kansas City and San Antonio to Fall River and Providence—see "From Larger Cities," *NYDM* (21 August 1909), 17; and "The Motion Picture Field," *NYDM* (2 October 1909), 30–31.

33. See "On the Road—Among the Exchanges and Exhibitors," *MPW* (22 January 1910), 88–89.

34. See "'Spectator's' Comments," *NYDM* (12 June 1909), 15.

35. See "Reviews of Independent Films," *NYDM* (25 September 1909), 17. Either Laemmle or United Film Renting extended service to the Fourteenth Street Theater in December—see "Independents Gain Opening," *NYDM* (18 December 1909), 17; and "Independent Films on Fourteenth Street," *MPW* (25 December 1909), 923.

36. See, for instance, John Collier, "Cheap Amusements," *Charities and Commons* (11 April 1908), 75–76; and "Observations by Our Man about Town," *MPW* (9 October 1909), 483–484. Other states considered such ordinances as well—see, for instance, "Prohibiting Child Attendance," *NYDM* (27 March 1909), 13; "Editorial," *MPW* (3 April 1909), 395; "Children Bill Defeated in New Jersey," *NYDM* (8 May 1909), 17; "Excluding the Youngsters," *Nick* (June 1909), 150; and "The Admission of Children to Moving Picture Shows," *MPW* (7 August 1909), 188. In arguments meant to counter such ordinances, the *World* and *Nickelodeon* heaped praise on theaters that appealed to children—see "Children and Moving Pictures," *MPW* (18 September 1909), 369; and "Admitting Children," *Nick* (November 1909), 135.

37. See "'Spectator's' Comments," *NYDM* (19 March 1910), 16. For a summary of these and other forms of regulation, see Boyd Fisher, "The Regulation of Motion Picture Theatres," *American City* 7.6 (December 1912), 520–522.

38. See, for instance, "Chicago's Woman Manager," *FI* (27 November 1909), 6; Palmer, "The World in Motion," 358; and "Mrs. Clement and Her Work," *MPW* (15 October 1910), 859–860. For others, see Bowser, *The Transformation of Cinema*, 47.

39. See "Among the Moving Picture Theatres," *MPW* (30 April 1910), 685.

40. See, for instance, "Picture Theatre for Negroes," *NYDM* (27 March 1909), 13; "Theatres for Negroes in Vicksburg," *NYDM* (15 May 1909), 15; "House for Colored People," *Var* (10 July 1909), 13; and "Licensed Predominate in San Antonio," *NYDM* (2 October 1909), 31. For others in Evansville, Louisville, Wilmington, and Cincinnati, mentioned in the *Indianapolis Freeman*, see Gregory Waller, "Another Audience: Black Moviegoing, 1907–16," *Cinema Journal* 31.2 (Winter 1992), 4. See, also, the *World*'s "technical solution" to the "problem" of keeping white and black patrons separate in Louisiana, while assuming that "we in North are not so keen on race prejudice"—"Drawing the Color Line," *MPW* (5 March 1910), 337.

41. The Hidalgo on the west side of San Antonio was "patronized almost exclusively by Mexicans"—see "Notes on the Far West," *FI* (18 June 1910), 12.

42. According to Carbine's research, Chicago's black theaters clearly served as alternative "spaces apart" by the middle or late 1910s and 1920s; before that, the evidence is less clear, as it is in Waller's research on Lexington's black theaters. See Mary Carbine, "'The Finest outside the Loop': Motion Picture Exhibition in Chicago's Black Metropolis, 1905–1928," in Richard Abel, ed., *Silent Film* (New Brunswick, N.J.: Rutgers University Press, 1996), 234–262; and Waller, "Another Audience," 3–25.

43. See "Weekly Visits to the Shows," *MPW* (27 February 1909), 235. See, also, the description of the Dewey as "a resort of the 'popular' family kind," in "Weekly Comments on the Shows," *MPW* (23 January 1909), 88. The Fourteenth Street Theater, formerly known as "the house of melodrama," drew an audience similar to the Dewey's—see "A Model Show," *MPW* (28 November 1908), 421. The *Index* made similar distinctions in a brief survey of Washington, D.C.—see "Picture Show Has Come to Stay," *FI* (14 August 1909), 4.

44. See "Motion Pictures in New Jersey," *MPW* (6 March 1909), 277; and "Good Report," *FI* (20 March 1909), 11.

45. See "The Variety of Moving Picture Audiences," *MPW* (25 September 1909), 406. In the spring of 1910, Woods was still tying popularity to trademarks and their "uniformity of excellence"—see "'Spectator's' Comments," *NYDM* (9 April 1910), 17.

46. See "'Spectator's' Comments," *NYDM* (6 November 1909), 13. Woods was appalled when the Keith theaters abandoned this practice in November, and it was not reinstated (and then with slight changes) until July 1910—see "The Keith & Proctor Release System," *MPW* (16 July 1910), 137. Although most licensed films still premiered at the Union Square, the number of reels released had grown so large that the Keith Theater on East 125th Street (in Harlem) became a secondary venue, but only for Lubin, Kalem, and Essanay.

47. See "Weekly Comments on the Shows," *MPW* (10 April 1909), 437. The "pretty girl" turned out to be Florence Lawrence, who was first singled out for her acting in *Song of the Shirt*—see "Reviews of New Films," *NYDM* (28 November 1908), 8. This review is reprinted in Kauffmann and Henstell, *American Film Criticism*, 19.

48. See, for instance, "Notable Films of the Week," *MPW* (24 April 1909), 515; "Notable Films of the Week," *MPW* (29 May 1909), 712; and "Comments on the Week's Films," *MPW* (3 July 1909), 12.

49. G. P. von Harleman, "Among the Chicago Shows," *MPW* (9 October 1909), 494. Von Harleman served as "western representative" to the *World* until February 1910, when Bradlet assumed that position. One reviewer also briefly compared "the very winsome girl" in Essanay's *The Two Brothers* with the Biograph girl—see "Comments on the Week's Films," *MPW* (9 October 1909), 489.

50. Richard deCordova, *Picture Personalities: The Emergence of the Star System in America* (Urbana: University of Illinois Press, 1990), 36–44. Janet Staiger examines this promotional strategy even earlier but focuses more on Edison in the fall of 1909, in "Selling Stars," *Velvet Light Trap* 20 (Summer 1983), 10–14.

51. Elita Proctor Otis was well known for playing the character of Nancy Sykes on stage—see the Vitagraph ad in *NYDM* (1 May 1909), 43. For similar reasons, Edison hired Miss Cecil Spooner to play a dual role in its adaptation of *The Prince and the Pauper*—see "Cecil Spooner on the Moving Picture Stage," *MPW* (28 August 1909), 277. Several of the new semiweekly Edison bulletins in August and September provided cast lists, and the one for *Ethel's Luncheon* was reprinted in "Stories of the Films," *MPW* (4 September 1909), 317. An article by Pilar-Morin published in an Edison bulletin was reprinted as "The Value of Silent Drama, or Pantomime in Acting," *MPW* (13 November 1909), 682. Essanay also tried to exploit this once, unsuccessfully, with Henry E. Dixey in *David Garrick*—see "Reviews of New Films," *NYDM* (14 November 1908), 10; and "Comments on Film Subjects," *MPW* (14 November 1908), 380.

52. Staiger looks at the development of a "star system" in legitimate theater for possible corollaries to that in moving pictures, in "Selling Stars," 11–12. In a parallel strategy, Edison hired well-known authors—Carolyn Wells, Edward Townsend, Richard Harding Davis, and Rex Beach—to write scenarios for the company—see, for instance, "On the Screen," *MPW* (11 September 1909), 342; "Comments on the Week's Films," *MPW* (18 September 1909), 377; "'Spectator's' Comments," *NYDM* (25 September 1909), 16; "Coming Edison Features," *NYDM* (11 December 1909), 15; and "Another Literary Work Filmed," *MPW* (8 January 1910), 9. At the same time, Vitagraph also hired Rev. Madison C. Peters "to write and produce . . . biblical subjects"—see "Vitagraph Advancement," *NYDM* (28 August 1909), 16. Most of the best early scenario writers, a good number of them women,

turned out to be lesser-known but "experienced writers of fiction for the magazines and newspapers"—see Grau, *The Theatre of Science*, 89–92.

53. For a more specific analysis of Florence Lawrence and her role as the first "film star," see Gunning, *D. W. Griffith and the Origins of American Narrative Film* (Urbana: University of Illinois Press, 1991), 218–220. As is well known, Biograph was the last company to reveal its principal actors' names. For an insightful analysis of why companies withheld the names of their actors for so long, see deCordova, *Picture Personalities*, 77–84. The main reason, deCordova suggests, may have been to exploit the value of secrecy as a way of stimulating the moviegoer's "desire for knowledge."

54. See "On the Screen," *MPW* (5 February 1910), 167; and "Giving Credit Where Credit Is Due," *MPW* (12 March 1910), 369. See, also, "Moving Picture Personalities," *Nick* (1 February 1910), 60.

55. See deCordova, *Picture Personalities*, 50, 84–89.

56. See ibid., 55–61; and Gunning, *D. W. Griffith*, 220–224.

57. See the IMP ad in *MPW* (18 December 1909), 866. That week, the *World* was alarmed that "our girl, our only girl, whom we have silently worshipped in effigy these many months," might no longer be with Biograph—see "Comments on the Films," *MPW* (18 December 1909), 881.

58. See the IMP ad in *MPW* (5 March 1910), 365; and "On the Screen," *MPW* (19 March 1910), 420. Photographs of "Miss Lawrence, the IMP Lady," circulated widely that spring, and the *World* spotted one in a Peoria newspaper ad—see "The Music and the Picture," *MPW* (17 April 1910), 590–591; and "Notes on the Trade," *MPW* (7 May 1910), 741.

59. See "Kalem Actors' Pictures for M. P. Theatre Lobbies," *FI* (15 January 1910), 1, 5; "Lobby Portraits," *NYDM* (15 January 1910), 13; and "Photographs of Moving Picture Actors," *MPW* (15 January 1910), 50. One year before, Kalem had released a photograph of its players, which appeared in "The Kalem Stock Company," *NYDM* (2 January 1909), 8.

60. See "Vitagraph Notes," *MPW* (2 April 1910), 515. See, also, "Vitagraph Notes," *MPW* (9 July 1910), 114; and "Picture Personalities: Miss Florence E. Turner, The Vitagraph Girl," *MPW* (23 July 1910), 187–188.

61. The cover for the sheet music was reproduced in "A Vitagraph Night for the Vitagraph Girl," *FI* (23 April 1910), 3. See, also, "The Vitagraph Girl," *NYDM* (23 April 1910), 20; "Vitagraph Girl Feted," *MPW* (23 April 1910), 644; "A Song Novelty for Licensed Exhibitors," *MPW* (28 October 1911), 300; and Anthony Slide, *The Big V: The Story of Vitagraph* (Metuchen, N.J.: Scarecrow, 1985), 38–39.

62. See "The Kalem Girl," *FI* (7 May 1910), 3. See, also, Anthony Slide, *Early American Cinema*, rev. ed. (Metuchen, N.J.: Scarecrow, 1994), 156.

63. See "Observations by Our Man about Town," *MPW* (21 May 1910), 825.

64. See "Picture Gods and Goddesses," *NYDM* (26 March 1910), 20; and "Moving Picture Gods and Goddesses," *FI* (26 March 1910), 10.

65. As early as July 1909, the *World* was quoting a newspaper to the effect that moving pictures were a boon to young actresses—see "Moving Pictures Help Women," *MPW* (10 July 1909), 54. Not all of these "stars" were women, of course; Vitagraph's Maurice Costello was one of several exceptions.

66. See "Observations by Our Man about Town," *MPW* (21 May 1910), 825.

67. Here again, the relationship between moving pictures and turn-of-the-century gay or, more precisely, lesbian subculture needs to be explored—see, for instance, the reference

to Jane Addams and the surveys cited in Peter Filene, *Him/Her/Self: Sex Roles in Modern America*, 2nd ed. (Baltimore, Md.: Johns Hopkins University Press, 1986), 48–49.

68. One of the earliest instances of this comes in conjunction with Bedding's reference to Florence Lawrence, in "On the Screen," *MPW* (19 March 1910), 420. See, also, "Play to the Ladies," *Nick* (February 1909), 33–34; and "The 'Show Window,'" *FI* (25 December 1909), 3.

69. See the editorial entitled "Dress and the Picture," *MPW* (9 July 1910), 73–74.

70. See Kathryn Fuller, *At the Picture Show: Small Town Audiences and the Creation of Movie Fan Culture* (Washington, D.C.: Smithsonian Institution Press, 1996), 133–149. *Motion Picture Story Magazine* was first announced, in December 1910, as a licensed monthly similar in format to "the *Century, Munsey's*, or any other popular magazine," which strongly indicated its appeal to middle-class males—see "Popular Magazine for Film Fans," *Nick* (15 December 1910), 339. For the first five years after its initial publication in February 1911, however, its "Answers to Inquiries" column revealed a fan readership that was at least 60 percent female.

71. "Earmarks of Makers," *NYDM* (14 November 1908), 10.

72. See "Picture Personalities: Victoria Lepanto," *MPW* (26 February 1910), 294. Lepanto appeared in *Camille* and also *Othello*, produced by Film d'Arte Italiana, a Pathé affiliate. This was the first of a series of columns that *Moving Picture World* used primarily to promote various men in various branches of the business.

73. In March 1910, Linder was promoted as "the famous comedian who for years has made such a hit all over America in the Red Rooster Films"—see "Pathé Pointers," *FI* (19 March 1910), 7; and L. F. Cook, "Of Interest to the Trade: Pathé Prospectives," *Nick* (15 March 1910), 161. The *Mirror* took up this promotion, along with a special photograph, in "The Popular Max Linder," *NYDM* (30 July 1910), 25, 26. See, also, the reference to Linder as "the popular Pathé comedian" in "Reviews of Licensed Films," *NYDM* (14 May 1910), 20. Since Linder had appeared in many Pathé films shown in the United States from 1906 on, this may well have some validity; it probably was not just an attempt to exploit the new fascination with personalities—see, for instance, the praise given to him, still unnamed, in "Comments on the Week's Films," *MPW* (9 October 1909), 489. For further information on Linder, crowned *le roi du cinématographe* in early 1910 (in France), and for analyses of his films, see Richard Abel, *The Ciné Goes to Town: French Cinema, 1896–1914* (Berkeley: University of California Press, 1994), 137, 140–141, 151, 217–219, 220–221, 226, 236–245.

74. See, for instance, the *Mirror*'s review of *A Cure for Timidity*, in which only "the inimitable acting of a Pathé comedian . . . could make this comic subject acceptable"—"Reviews of Licensed Films," *NYDM* (19 March 1910), 17.

CHAPTER 6. "OUR COUNTRY"/WHOSE COUNTRY?

1. "Reviews of Late Films," *NYDM* (13 June 1908), 10.

2. "Alleged Pirating of Films," *NYDM* (20 June 1908), 6.

3. "Earmarks of Makers," *NYDM* (14 November 1908), 10. However, the *Mirror* did pointedly praise a Great Northern western, *Texas Tex*, as "an American subject . . . although produced in Copenhagen"—see "Late Film Reviews," *NYDM* (1 August 1908), 7.

4. See, for instance, "Some Coming Headliners and a New Religious Subject," *MPW* (24 October 1908), 318; "Latest Films: Selig's *A Montana Schoolmarm*," *MPW* (19 December 1908), 512; John Bradlet, "A Tour amongst Country Exhibitors," *MPW* (13 February 1909), 169; and "Motion Pictures in New Jersey," *MPW* (6 March 1909), 277.

5. See "The Burden of the New Immigration," *World's Work* 6.3 (July 1903), 3603.

6. Robert Anderson first sketched out some of the lines of this argument in "The Role of the Western Film Genre in Industry Competition, 1907–1911," *Journal of the University Film Association* 31.2 (Spring 1979), 19–26. Here I disagree with Miriam Hansen, who writes, "Actually the 'Americanization' of the cinema seems to have been less a question of treating nationally specific themes (like Indian and Western films) than of developing a particular *type* of film"—see Hansen, *Babel and Babylon: Spectatorship in American Silent Cinema* (Cambridge, Mass.: Harvard University Press, 1991), 79. Bill Brown recently argued that, fifty years earlier, the House of Beadle promoted its dime novel westerns as "Purely American Novels" and as part of a "patriotic project"—see his "Reading the West: Cultural and Historical Background," in Brown, ed., *Reading the West: An Anthology of Dime Westerns* (Boston: Bedford Books, 1997), 21.

7. See, for instance, Tom Gunning, "'Now You See It, Now You Don't': The Temporality of the Cinema of Attractions," *Velvet Light Trap* 32 (Fall 1993)—reprinted in Richard Abel, ed., *Silent Film* (New Brunswick, N.J.: Rutgers University Press, 1996), 71–84.

8. The catalog edited by Truettner, *The West as America* (Washington, D.C.: Smithsonian, 1991), is an extraordinary source of images from that iconographic tradition, as well as an excellent compilation of essays rethinking that tradition.

9. Alan Trachtenberg, *The Incorporation of America: Culture and Society in the Gilded Age* (New York: Hill and Wang, 1982), 17–18.

10. See Truettner, *The West as America*, 123, 131, 231; and Peter Marzio, *The Democratic Art: Pictures for a Nineteenth-Century America* (Boston: Godine, 1979), 116–128, 312. See, also, Neil Harris, "Color and Media: Some Comparisons and Speculations," in *Cultural Excursions: Marketing Appetites and Cultural Tastes in Modern America* (Chicago: University of Chicago Press, 1990), 322.

11. Martha Sandweiss, "Views and Reviews: Western Art and Western History," in William Cronon, George Miles, and Jay Gitlin, eds., *Under an Open Sky: Rethinking America's Western Past* (New York: Norton, 1992), 193–194. See, also, Marzio, *The Democratic Art,* 339. There is some evidence that moving pictures exploiting this iconography were used on ships to induce Jewish immigrants "to go west . . . rather than settle in the congested cities of the east"—see "Moving Pictures to Get Immigrants West," *Nick* (May 1909), 130.

12. William Cullen Bryant, *Picturesque America* (1874)—quoted in Trachtenberg, *The Incorporation of America*, 18–19.

13. Anderson, "The Role of the Western Film Genre in Industry Competition," 22–24. See, also, the Selig ad in *NYC* (22 November 1902), 875.

14. Despite a few factual errors, the best study of this amusement ride remains Raymond Fielding, "Hale's Tours: Ultrarealism in the Pre-1910 Motion Picture," in John Fell, ed., *Film before Griffith* (Berkeley: University of California Press, 1984), 116–130. See, also, Charles Musser, *The Emergence of Cinema to 1907*, vol. 1 of *History of the American Cinema* (New York: Scribner's, 1991), 429–430; and Lauren Rabinovitz, "Temptations of Pleasure: Nickelodeons, Amusement Parks, and the Sights of Female Sexuality," *camera obscura* 23 (1990), 79–80.

15. Kleine Optical, which specialized in selling such films, made this distinction between "foreign" and "domestic" in its ad in *Bill* (17 March 1906), 47. See, also, the Kleine Optical ad in *NYC* (10 March 1906), 100; and the Edison ad in *NYC* (28 April 1906), 281. Hale's Tours may also have stimulated the production of an "omnibus" film like Pathé's

A Detective's Tour of the World, released in June 1906—see "Latest Films," *VFI* (16 June 1906), 4.

16. Fielding, "Hale's Tours," 126–127. See, also, "Latest Films," *VFI* (30 June 1906), 5.

17. Three of these films were still being offered in early 1907—see "Popular Films," *VFI* (12 January 1907), n.p.

18. See "Colorado's Best Advertisement," *VFI* (26 January 1907), n.p.

19. See the Selig ad in *NYC* (23 February 1907), 15. Edison released a film by the same title, "beautifully mono-tinted," one week earlier—see the Edison ad in *NYC* (16 February 1907), 1377.

20. See the Selig ad in *VFI* (16 March 1907), 10; and "New Films," *VFI* (20 April 1907), 6. Earlier Selig sensational melodramas included *Tracked by Bloodhounds or, A Lynching at Cripple Creek* (1904) and *The Hold-Up of the Leadville Stage* (1905)—see, for instance, the Selig ads in *NYC* (30 July 1904), 532, and (29 April 1905), 264.

21. See the Selig ads for *Western Justice* in *MPW* (22 June 1907), 251, and (29 June 1907), front cover; and "Comments on Film Subjects," *MPW* (7 March 1908), 195. Those competitors' films included Edison's *Life of a Cowboy* (1906) and *Daniel Boone* (1907), Vitagraph's *The Prospectors* (1906) and *The Indian's Revenge* (1906), and Kalem's *The Tenderfoot* (1907). The two Vitagraph films were the object of some scorn because they substituted Central Park and Brooklyn for the Wild West and a Coney Island beach for a Florida scene with "Seminoles"—see "Trade Notes," *MPW* (15 June 1907), 235.

22. "Comments on Film Subjects," *MPW* (7 March 1908), 195.

23. "Pictures of Real Western Life Coming," *MPW* (27 June 1908), 541. Although Buckwalter initially headed up Selig's western filmmaking unit in Colorado, G. M. Anderson wrote and directed the fiction films during the first half of 1907; after that, Francis Boggs was responsible for many of the Selig westerns.

24. "Reviews of Late Films," *NYDM* (18 July 1908), 7.

25. "This is an ambitious out-door production"—see "Reviews of New Films," *NYDM* (19 September 1908), 9. The 35mm print of *The Cattle Rustlers*, at the National Film/Television Archive, runs 862 feet.

26. "Reviews of New Films," *NYDM* (27 February 1909), 13. The 1872 chromo *On the Warpath* is reprinted in Marzio, *The Democratic Art*, 329.

27. "Motion Pictures to Boost Immigration," *SW* (19 December 1908), 22. See, also, "Immigration and the Purity of the American Race," *World's Work* 6.4 (August 1903), 3716.

28. Another possible source then in vogue also was rarely mentioned, western dramas on stage—see, for instance, "Blood and Thunder Plays Repudiated by the Public," *SW* (27 July 1907), 10; and James C. Dahlman, "The Cowboy in Drama," *SW* (21 December 1907), 24. From the evidence of theater ads in cities and towns from Des Moines and Ottumwa (Iowa) to Portland and Medford (Oregon), western dramas were popular at least through 1910. Dime novels and plays undoubtedly provided filmmakers with narrative and scenic elements on which to draw, as Bowser points out, but initially the connection seems to have been neither exploited nor made explicit in the trade press—see Eileen Bowser, *The Transformation of Cinema, 1907–1915*, vol. 2 of *History of American Cinema* (New York: Scribner's, 1990), 170–171.

29. See "Trade Notes," *MPW* (15 June 1907), 233–234.

30. Biograph itself described Ted as "a youthful victim of Dime Novelitis, emulating Roosevelt in the wild and woolly wilderness"—see the Biograph ad in *NYC* (5 October 1907), 892.

31. These terms come from George C. Jenks, "Dime Novel Makers," *Bookman* 20 (October 1904), 108.

32. See the Edison ad in *VFI* (11 April 1908), 15; "Our Visits," *MPW* (11 April 1908), 312; "The Manufacturer," *MPW* (18 April 1908), 339; and "Newspaper Comments on Film Subjects," *MPW* (2 May 1908), 415. This kind of "thrilling and sensational" film supposedly was a "strong attraction" in some western states, "the type of picture that takes so well" — see the Bijou Theater ad, for *A Western Romance*, in the *Medford Daily Tribune* (21 August 1908), 4.

33. See, for instance, the reviews of Vitagraph's *Twixt Love and Duty* and *An Indian's Honor*, in "Reviews of Late Films," *NYDM* (25 July 1908), 7, and (15 August 1908), 7.

34. "Reviews of New Films," *NYDM* (8 August 1908), 7. See, also, "Moving Picture Reviews," *Var* (1 August 1908), 13. Gunning cites this film as "show[ing] the first stirrings of the narrator system" that Griffith developed throughout 1908 and 1909 — see *D. W. Griffith and the Origins of American Narrative Film* (Urbana: University of Illinois, 1991), 69–74. At the same time, the *Mirror* pointedly criticized Biograph's *The Stage Rustlers* for "hold[ing] up an outlaw as a hero" — see "Reviews of Late Films," *NYDM* (18 July 1908), 7.

35. See "Around the Country," *VFI* (12 September 1908), 4; and "Moving Picture Notes," *NYDM* (7 November 1908), 8.

36. "Reviews of New Films," *NYDM* (26 September 1908), 9, and (7 November 1908), 8. See, also, the analysis of *Call of the Wild*'s concluding tableau, in Gunning, *D. W. Griffith*, 108–109.

37. "Comments on Film Subjects," *MPW* (26 December 1908), 525; and Bradlet, "A Tour amongst Country Exhibitors," *MPW* (13 February 1909), 169. *A Montana Schoolmarm* provoked considerable applause at New York's Columbia Theatre—see "Moving Picture Reviews," *Var* (6 February 1909), 13. The *Mirror* made a point of noting that *In Old Arizona* was filmed entirely in Selig's Chicago studio.

38. "Reviews of New Films," *NYDM* (23 January 1909), 7, (27 February 1909), 13, and (27 March 1909), 13. In Medford, Oregon, *On the Warpath* was promoted as "a thrilling Indian story of the plains, showing a rousing, realistic battle scene between Indians and settlers" — see the Savoy Theater ad in the *Medford Daily Tribune* (7 April 1909), 3.

39. Nanna Verhoeff makes a persuasive argument that the early western was less a genre than a set of texts united by a network of "family resemblances" — see her "Early Westerns: How to Trace a Family" (master's thesis, University of Utrecht, 1996).

40. See, for instance, Pathé's *L'Arlésienne*, which "sets a new standard of excellence" as "a model object lesson for every American manufacturer," and *Assassination of the Duke of Guise*—in "Reviews of New Films," *NYDM* (5 December 1908), 8; and Thomas Bedding, "The Modern Way in Moving Picture Making," *MPW* (13 March 1909), 294.

41. By the fall of 1909, the Scenic Theatre in Fall River was specializing in westerns, and Fred Aiken was told in Detroit that audiences wanted either comedies or westerns— see "All Good in Fall River," *NYDM* (2 October 1909), 31; and James McQuade, "Chicago Letter," *FI* (16 October 1909), 12.

42. See Hans Leigh, "Acting and Action," *MPW* (2 October 1909), 443. Frank Woods responded to Leigh by arguing that Biograph, at its best, really succeeded at acting and action equally well—see "'Spectator's' Comments," *NYDM* (2 October 1909), 32.

43. "Comments on Film Subjects," *MPW* (1 May 1909), 554. See, also, the review of Lubin's *The Falling Arrow*, in "Comments on Film Subjects," *MPW* (8 May 1909), 592; and that of Lubin's *A Nugget of Gold*, in "Comments on the Week's Films," *MPW* (24 July 1909), 125.

44. The first NYMPC film to get the *World*'s attention was *The Cowboy's Narrow Escape*—see "Comment's on the Week's Films," *MPW* (26 June 1909), 871. NYMPC was releasing one western per week by late summer. World Films sometimes did likewise—see its ad in *MPW* (19 June 1909), 848. Centaur westerns, *A Cowboy Escapade, The Cowboy's Sweetheart,* and *A Close Call,* appeared more irregularly—see the Centaur ad in *MPW* (29 August 1908), 158; "Independent Film Stories," *MPW* (24 April 1909), 532; and Centaur's full-page ad in *MPW* (2 October 1909), 468. The Powers Company also occasionally released a western—see, for instance, its ad for *A Red Man's Love,* in *MPW* (20 November 1909), 706.

45. See "Comments on the Week's Films," *MPW* (25 September 1909), 416. The *Mirror* was more critical of Bison westerns, finally granting some praise to *Iona, the White Squaw,* in "Reviews of New Films," *NYDM* (30 October 1909), 15.

46. See "Essanay Will Release Two Reels," *MPW* (6 November 1909), 638. That same week, the *Mirror* used much more circumspect language in its announcement, revealing a clear bias in favor of the other "school"—see "Essanay Two Reels," *NYDM* (6 November 1909), 16.

47. See "Comments on the Week's Films," *MPW* (20 November 1909), 722, and (4 December 1909), 799. One of Selig's more popular westerns, *The Cowboy Millionaire,* imports the "wild and woolly" directly into the city, where the "rough-house" action quickly loses its allure for the film's hero—see "Comments on the Week's Films," *MPW* (6 November 1909), 643. *The Cowboy Millionaire* survives in a 35mm print at the Nederlands Filmmuseum.

48. See "Comments on the Films," *MPW* (5 February 1910), 169, and (26 February 1910), 300. The company announced its own "phenomenal success," in "Bison Notes," *MPW* (12 March 1910), 387; this is supported by Fred Balshofer and Arthur Miller, *One Reel a Week* (Berkeley: University of California Press, 1967), 67.

49. See "Comments on the Films," *MPW* (8 January 1910), 17. The *World* had reprinted a *Denver Post* article on the film's production, which included a draft of the scenario, in "The Essanay Company Out West," *MPW* (4 December 1909), 801–802. For the *Mirror,* this Essanay film was "frankly a Western melodrama"; see "Reviews of Licensed Films," *NYDM* (1 January 1910), 17. See, also, its grudging praise of Essanay's *The Girl and the Fugitive,* in "Reviews of Licensed Films," *NYDM* (26 March 1910), 18. In its year-end wrap-up of the moving picture industry, *Film Index* praised Selig and Essanay for their "realistic Western subjects"—see "Reviewing the Year," *FI* (1 January 1910), 2.

50. See "*The Indian Trailer,*" *MPW* (22 May 1909), 672.

51. See "The Producer's Art," *MPW* (31 July 1909), 151. This editorial excoriation is significant because the *World* frequently criticized American westerns for inaccuracies, but never so harshly as in this case. From July through September, the *World* also published letters by someone calling himself Wild West who singled out eastern locations falsely representing western landscapes—see, for instance, Wild West, "Accuracy in Indian Subjects" and "Wild West in the East," *MPW* (10 July 1909), 48, 57.

52. See "Reviews of New Films," *NYDM* (10 July 1909), 15.

53. See not only the already cited reviews of Pathé scenics and *films d'art* in the *World,* the *Mirror,* and *Variety* but also "On the Screen," *MPW* (25 December 1909), 919. One boy, interviewed for the San Francisco *Sunday Call* (15 May 1910), singled out colored French films as the best scenics, and other children referred to specific Pathé titles—see "A Little Child Shall Lead Them," *MPW* (4 June 1910), 936.

54. See "Black and White Pictures. Do the Public Prefer Them?" *MPW* (19 February 1910), 245. See, also, "The Picture of the Future," *MPW* (17 December 1910), 1398–1399. By 1911, once the American cinema no longer was threatened by the "foreign," the *World* could return to the issue of color and praise "toned pictures"—see "Toning and Tinting as an Adjunct to the Picture," *MPW* (18 March 1911), 574.

55. Interestingly, the foreign manufacturer now cited as a model was Gaumont—see "Orthochromatic Moving Pictures," *MPW* (12 February 1910), 202; and "The Qualitative Picture: The Influence of the French School of Picture Making," *MPW* (25 June 1910), 1089–1090. This was another clear signal of Pathé's exclusion, for one year earlier the *World* had cited Pathé as a model for such pictorial qualities—see Bedding, "The Modern Way in Moving Picture Making," *MPW* (15 May 1909), 626–627.

56. See "'Spectator's' Comments," *NYDM* (13 November 1909), 15. See, also, the *World*'s review of *The Indian Runner's Romance,* in which "the reproduction of outdoor scenery is so good that it seems as though one were actually in the woods and fields"— "Comments on the Week's Films," *MPW* (4 September 1909), 315–316.

57. See the Biograph ad for *The Country Doctor* in *NYDM* (10 July 1909), 16.

58. See, for instance, Trachtenberg, *The Incorporation of America*, 11–37; and Alexander Saxton, *The Rise and Fall of the White Republic: Class Politics and Mass Culture in Nineteenth-Century America* (London: Verso, 1990), 321–347.

59. Josiah Strong, *Our Country: Its Possible Future and Its Present Crisis* (New York, 1885), 174–175. See, also, Trachtenberg, *The Incorporation of America*, 78–79, 102–104; and Saxton, *The Rise and Fall of the White Republic,* 343–344.

60. Fiske's "Manifest Destiny" was given as a lecture first in London, in 1880, and then some fifty times throughout England and the United States, until its publication in *Harper's Monthly* (March 1885), 578–590; and in John Fiske, *American Political Ideas Viewed from the Standpoint of Universal History* (Boston: Houghton Mifflin, 1885). This passage is quoted in Richard Drinnon, *Facing West: The Metaphysics of Indian-Hating and Empire-Building* (Minneapolis: University of Minnesota Press, 1980), 240.

61. See, especially, Richard Slotkin, *Gunfighter Nation: The Myth of the Frontier in Twentieth-Century America* (New York: Atheneum, 1992), 29–62. For the British version of this "Race Union," see William S. Stead, *The Americanization of the World, or the Trend of the Twentieth Century* (London: Review of Reviews, 1902; reprint, New York: Garland, 1972).

62. See Michael Kammen, *Mystic Chords of Memory: The Transformation of Tradition in American Culture* (New York: Knopf, 1991), 220, 222.

63. See, for instance, "The Burden of the New Immigration," *World's Work* 6.3 (July 1903), 3601, 3603.

64. See, for instance, Joyce Appleby, Lynn Hunt, and Margaret Jacob, *Telling the Truth about History* (New York: Norton, 1994), 108, 117.

65. See, for instance, Trachtenberg, *The Incorporation of America,* 13–17.

66. See, for instance, Slotkin, *Gunfighter Nation,* 51–52.

67. Ronald Takaki, *Iron Cages: Race and Culture in Nineteenth-Century America* (New York: Knopf, 1979), 171–173, 175–176. For a particularly good analysis of the figure of Custer in early films, see Roberta Pearson, "The Revenge of Rain-in-the-Face?, or Custers and Indians on the Silent Screen," in Daniel Bernardi, ed., *The Birth of Whiteness: Race and the Emergence of United States Cinema* (New Brunswick, N.J.: Rutgers University Press, 1996), 273–299. For an early analysis of Cody and Roosevelt as American heroes, see Dixon Wecter, *The Hero in America: A Chronicle of Hero-Worship* (New York: Scribner's, 1941), 341–391. For an

analysis of John Hay's *The Bread-Winners* (1883), which has a Custer-like hero, see Drinnon, *Facing West*, 261–266. Hay served as secretary of state during the "Splendid Little War," that is, the Spanish-American War.

68. See Kammen, *Mystic Chords of Memory*, 186. About the same time, *Harper's* worked up a publicity campaign to increase the popularity of Remington's western illustrations—see Kammen, *Mystic Chords of Memory*, 395–396.

69. Robert Rydell, *All the World's a Fair: Visions of Empire at American International Expositions, 1876–1916* (Chicago: University of Chicago Press, 1984), 2–8. See, also, Michael Denning, *Mechanic Accents: Dime Novels and Working-Class Culture in America* (London: Verso, 1987), 205–206.

70. Owen Wister, "The Evolution of the Cow-Puncher," *Harper's Monthly* 91 (September 1895), 602–617. This essay was accompanied by five Frederic Remington illustrations. Wister, Remington, and Roosevelt were easterners, friends who had "roughed it" in the western mountains or plains in order to "restore" their masculinity. Theirs was a story of "proven" regeneration sometimes told in films like Vitagraph's *The Easterner* (1907)—see "Film Review," *VFI* (17 August 1907), 6.

71. See, for instance, Saxton, *The Rise and Fall of the White Republic*, 341–342. Another example is Frederic Remington's short story "A Sergeant of the Orphan Troop," *Harper's Monthly* 95 (August 1897), 327–336.

72. See, for instance, W. Churchill Williams, "Red Blood in Fiction," *World's Work* 6.3 (July 1903), 3694–3700; and Slotkin, *Gunfighter Nation*, 156–157.

73. Frank Norris, "The Frontier Gone at Last," *World's Work* 3 (1902)—reprinted in Donald Pizer, ed., *The Literary Criticism of Frank Norris* (Austin: University of Texas Press, 1964), 111. Remington's words come from an 1893 letter to Wister, quoted in Saxton, *The Rise and Fall of the White Republic*, 344.

74. Examples of the former include Eleanor Gates's "A Round-Up in Central Park," *Saturday Evening Post* (6 August 1905), 2–4; and Wister's own story "Extra Dry," *Saturday Evening Post* (27 February 1909), 14–15, 39–40. On the adventure stories, see Christine Bold, *Selling the Wild West: Popular Western Fiction, 1860–1960* (Bloomington: Indiana University Press, 1987), 15–16. *Wild West Weekly* first appeared in 1902; *Rough Rider Weekly*, in 1904. Yet the discourse also could be "sent up" in films like Selig's *The Cowboy Millionaire* (1909): one of the hero's last acts is to turn his copy of Remington's "Cowboy on Horseback" to face the wall of his Chicago mansion.

75. Rydell, *All the World's a Fair*, 6. For an excellent analysis of Buffalo Bill's Wild West as a "white supremacist entertainment" operating in parallel with world's fairs, see Jonathan Martin, "'The Grandest and Most Cosmopolitan Object Teacher': Buffalo Bill's Wild West and the Politics of American Identity, 1883–1899," *Radical History Review* 66 (Fall 1996), 92–123. Another popular "white supremacist entertainment" that preceded both the world's fairs and the cinema was the touring Barnum & London Circus—see Bluford Adams, *E Pluribus Barnum: The Great Showman and the Making of American Popular Culture* (Minneapolis: University of Minnesota Press, 1997), 185–192.

76. See the Kalem ad in *MPW* (15 June 1907), 226. Peter Stanfield makes a good argument for analyzing the figure of Indian or Mexican villains in early westerns because they invariably "define the counterimage of the typically White hero." His own research focuses on surviving films from a slightly later period—see Stanfield, "The Western, 1909–1914: A Cast of Villains," *Film History* 1.2 (1987), 97–112.

77. See "Reviews of Late Films," *NYDM* (11 July 1908), 7.

78. See "Films of All Makers," *VFI* (25 July 1908), 11. A 35mm print of *The Renegade*, at the National Film/Television Archive, runs 778 feet.

79. See "Reviews of New Films," *NYDM* (8 August 1908), 7. See, also, Lubin's *Western Romance*, in "Reviews of Late Films," *NYDM* (18 July 1908), 7.

80. See "Latest Films of All Makers," *VFI* (8 August 1908), 11; and "Reviews of Late Films," *NYDM* (15 August 1908), 7.

81. "Latest Films of All Makers," *VFI* (12 September 1908), 11. There are no intertitles in the National Film/Television Archive print to identify the characters.

82. "Some Coming Headliners and a New Religious Subject," *MPW* (24 October 1908), 318.

83. See the Selig ad in *FI* (23 January 1909), 14; and "Reviews of New Films," *NYDM* (23 January 1909), 7.

84. See "Reviews of New Films," *NYDM* (27 February 1909), 13, and (27 March 1909), 13. *Boots and Saddles* was one of the few films the Family Theatre in Des Moines mentioned by name in 1909—see the Family Theatre ad in *DMRL* (28 March 1909), 3.3. See, also, Selig's *The Bad Lands*, in "Comments on Film Subjects," *MPW* (15 May 1909), 634. The *World* first noted the popularity of war films in its review of Selig's Civil War film *Brother against Brother*—see "Comments on Film Subjects," *MPW* (17 April 1909), 477.

85. See "Reviews of Licensed Films," *NYDM* (4 December 1909), 17. Selig took the unusual step of advertising this film in *NYDM* (13 November 1909), 16.

86. A good example would be Richard Harding Davis's best-seller, *Soldiers of Fortune* (1897). A later film celebrating this "soldier of fortune" figure is Kalem's *The Colonel's Escape* (1912). See Amy Kaplan's excellent analysis of the genre in "Romancing the Empire: The Embodiment of American Masculinity in the Popular Historical Novel of the 1890s," *American Literary History* 2 (Winter 1990), 659–690.

87. See "Reviews of New Films," *NYDM* (12 June 1909), 15. Another naval hero has to rescue an American girl in the Arabian desert in Selig's *Won in the Desert*—see "Reviews of New Films," *NYDM* (31 July 1909), 15.

88. See "Films of the Week," *FI* (3 July 1909), 7; "Reviews of New Films," *NYDM* (10 July 1909), 17; and "Comments on the Week's Films," *MPW* (17 July 1909), 89. In Vitagraph's *The Mexican's Revenge*, there is a melodramatic struggle between a U.S. naval officer, his Mexican lover, and jealous Mexicans, set in early southern California—see "Licensed Reviews," *NYDM* (30 October 1909), 14; and "Comments on the Week's Films," *MPW* (30 October 1909), 605.

89. See "Reviews of Licensed Films," *NYDM* (27 November 1909), 14. The 35mm print of this film at the National Film/Television Archive has German intertitles and runs 950 feet. *Up San Juan Hill* and *Custer's Last Stand* played at the Majestic and the Scenic, respectively, the same week in Sioux City—see the Motion Picture Theaters ad in *Sioux City Tribune* (13 December 1909), 12.

90. See "Comments on the Films," *MPW* (29 January 1910), 127. This kind of blatant jingoism was common even earlier in mass magazines like *McClure's* and *Munsey's*—see Richard Ohmann, *Selling Culture: Magazines, Markets, and Class at the Turn of the Century* (London: Verso, 1996), 277–278.

91. See "Films of the Week," *FI* (20 March 1909), 9.

92. See "Comments on Film Subjects," *MPW* (3 April 1909), 494.

93. See the reluctant praise of this film, whose title character is named after a Walter Scott heroine, in "Independent Reviews," *NYDM* (30 October 1909), 16.

94. See "Comments on the Week's Films," *MPW* (13 November 1909), 683. See, also, Bison's *The Message of the Arrow,* in "Comments on the Week's Films," *MPW* (18 December 1909), 882.

95. These specific phrases come from a review of Selig's *The Freebooters,* "which smacks very strongly of the Wild West," in "Comments on the Week's Films," *MPW* (25 September 1909), 415.

96. Even Pathé accepted "the duplicity and cunning of American aboriginals" in *A Western Hero,* and a *World* reviewer commented favorably on their depiction, well before exhibitors rebelled against the film's inaccuracies—see "Comments on the Week's Films," *MPW* (3 July 1909), 12.

97. See "Comments on the Week's Films," *MPW* (18 December 1909), 880.

98. See "Reviews of New Films," *NYDM* (5 June 1909), 15. See, also, its lukewarm review of Kalem's *The Indian Scout's Revenge,* which "satisf[ied] the demands of a certain class of renters and exhibitors who clamor for that sort of thing"—"Reviews of Licensed Films," *NYDM* (5 March 1910), 18.

99. "An American School of Moving Picture Drama," *MPW* (20 November 1909), 712.

100. One of the first indications of this comes in a rare ad for the Ikonograph projector, which was promoted as suitable for the home, as well as for halls, churches, and schoolrooms—see the Home Merchandise ad in *People's Popular Monthly* (February 1909), 17. The *World* began suggesting the popularity of westerns about the same time—see "Nemesis," *MPW* (27 March 1909), 366. See, also, the "boy expert" cited in Louis Reeves Harrison, "Stagecraft," *MPW* (14 May 1910), 774. The *World*'s ambivalence crops up in a review of Bison's *By His Own Hand*—see "Comments on the Films," *MPW* (12 February 1910), 217. It also can be seen in films like Vitagraph's comedy of a New York City newsboy, *Dime Novel Dan*—see "Comments on Film Subjects," *MPW* (22 May 1909), 676.

101. See Michael Kimmel, *Manhood in America: A Cultural History* (New York: Free Press, 1996), 121–122. A good example of this "threat" is Earl Barnes, "The Feminizing of Culture," *Atlantic* 109 (June 1912), 770–776. During the late nineteenth century, all kinds of middle-class fraternal organizations also developed as "masculinist alternatives" to these "female-controlled" spaces—see Kimmel, *Manhood in America,* 171–172. The attempt to "masculinize" moving pictures through "realist" narratives, and particularly westerns, could be seen, then, as part of a push to transform the "feminized" space of the nickelodeon into a juvenile or even adult complement to the fraternal organization.

102. See Kimmel, *Manhood in America,* 160–161. See, also, Mark Seltzer, *Bodies and Machines* (New York: Routledge, 1992); and Judy Wilkey, *Character Is Capital: Success Manuals and Manhood in Gilded Age America* (Chapel Hill: University of North Carolina Press, 1997).

103. "What Is an American Subject?" *MPW* (22 January 1910), 82.

104. See Frank W. Blackmar, "The Mastery of the Desert," *North American Review* 162 (May 1906)—quoted in Donald Worster, *Under Western Skies: Nature and History in the American West* (New York: Oxford University Press, 1992), 88. See, also, Albert Shaw, *The Outlook for the Average Man* (New York: Macmillan, 1907), 115. I borrow some language here from Kammen, *Mystic Chords of Memory,* 295. Ohmann presents a similar argument for western stories in mass magazines, in *Selling Culture,* 334.

105. Law, "Better Scenarios Demanded," *MPW* (29 August 1908), 153–154.

106. Eileen Bowser argues that "Indian films" constituted a separate genre from "Westerns" during these early years—see Bowser, *The Transformation of Cinema,* 173–177.

107. In November 1909, Kalem announced that it would be specializing in "juvenile subjects"—see, for instance, "Children's Pictures for Children's Theatre," *FI* (13 November 1909), 7. Three months later, the company took the advice of "Mr. Exchange Man" and shifted to specializing in "Indian pictures"—see, for instance, "Kalem Indian Series," *NYDM* (12 February 1910), 19; and "Programs for Children," *MPW* (19 February 1910), 246–247.

108. "Moving Picture High Art," *Bill* (19 October 1907), 20. See, also, the Kleine Optical ad in *MPW* (12 October 1907), 506. Kalem's ad stressed the film's authenticity and promoted it as "suitable for use at the most particular Chatauquan exhibition." A film entitled Pathé's *Indian Justice*, but whose story seems quite close to that of Kalem's *Red Man's Way*, can be found at the National Film/Television Archive; the 35mm print runs 474 feet.

109. See "Reviews of New Films," *NYDM* (2 January 1909), 8.

110. See "Comments on the Week's Films," *MPW* (14 August 1909), 226. Young Deer had performed with circuses like Barnum & Bailey and the 101 Ranch, worked briefly at Kalem (perhaps on *Red Cloud*), and then wrote, directed, and acted in Lubin westerns, including *The Fallen Arrow*—see "James Young Deer," *MPW* (6 May 1911), 999.

111. See, also, Gunning's analysis of compositional depth in the images of natural landscapes in *The Mended Lute*, in *D. W. Griffith*, 209–210.

112. Probably the first reference to Young Deer and Red Wing comes in the announcement for *Half Breed's Treachery*, in "Independent Films," *MPW* (21 August 1909), 267. See, also, the article reprinted from the *Los Angeles Examiner*, as "Los Angeles Home of Three Film Companies," in *MPW* (19 February 1910), 256; and "New York Motion Picture Company Notes," *MPW* (5 March 1910), 342. The company also was strong enough to attract Charles Inslee from Biograph to work in Bison films beginning in the summer of 1909. See Balshofer and Miller, *One Reel a Week*, 28–29, 33, 40, 41, 54, 55.

113. See "Comments on the Films," *MPW* (31 December 1909), 961, (22 January 1910), 92, and (26 February 1910), 300. The *Mirror* even found "a credible attempt to give us a poetic story" in *The Rose of the Ranch*—see "Reviews of Licensed Films," *NYDM* (19 March 1910), 18.

114. "Reviews of Late Films," *NYDM* (18 July 1908), 7. In *The Squawman's Daughter*, an Indian woman repays her "cowboy sweetheart," who has saved her from "a villainous desperado," by leading his friends on horseback to his rescue—see "Comments of the Week's Films," *MPW* (7 March 1908), 195.

115. "Reviews of New Films," *NYDM* (7 November 1908), 8. Biograph's *The Greaser's Gauntlet* (7 August 1908) provides a Mexican variation on this story in which a white woman first saves a Mexican and then, five years later, though a drunken participant in her kidnapping, he finally repays his debt.

116. "Reviews of New Films," *NYDM* (8 August 1908), 7.

117. "Reviews of New Films," *NYDM* (26 September 1908), 9. This film, along with *The Heart of O Yama*, appeared in the first Biograph ad in the *Mirror*—see *NYDM* (19 September 1908), 9. See, also, *The Girl and the Outlaw* (released just one week before *The Red Girl*), in which an "Indian maiden" dies helping rescue a young white woman from outlaws. The 16mm print of *The Girl and the Outlaw*, in the Library of Congress paper print collection, runs 315 feet.

118. See "Film Reviews," *VFI* (8 August 1908), 10; and "Reviews of Late Films," *NYDM* (15 August 1908), 7.

119. See, for instance, "Reviews of New Films," *NYDM* (9 January 1909), 9; and "Comments on the Week's Films," *MPW* (20 November 1909), 721. See, also, the review of Kalem's *Seminole's Revenge,* in "Reviews of New Films," *NYDM* (20 March 1909), 13.

120. See the Biograph ad in *NYDM* (28 August 1909), 16; "Reviews of New Films," *NYDM* (4 September 1909), 16; and "Comments on the Week's Films," *MPW* (4 September 1909), 315. See, also, the *World*'s criticism of Biograph's *Comata the Sioux,* which, in raising questions about historical accuracy, acknowledges with some reluctance that whites did force the Sioux to change their way of life and that perhaps that was worth representing in moving pictures—"Comments on the Week's Films," *MPW* (2 October 1909), 450.

121. See "Comments on Film Subjects," *MPW* (27 March 1909), 368; and "Reviews of Late Films," *NYDM* (13 June 1908), 10.

122. See "Comments on Film Subjects," *MPW* (29 May 1909), 714; "Comments on the Week's Films," *MPW* (26 June 1909), 871, and (4 September 1909), 313; "Reviews of New Films," *NYDM* (16 October 1909), 17–18, and (23 October 1909), 15; and "Comments on the Films," *MPW* (8 January 1910), 16. Young Deer and Red Wing also appeared in Vitagraph's *Red Wing's Gratitude*—see Bowser, *The Transformation of Cinema,* 173.

123. *A Mexican's Gratitude* was lauded for its "true atmosphere," as one of "Essanay's California series of sensational Western pictures"—"Reviews of New Films," *NYDM* (15 May 1909), 15. The 35mm print of *A Mexican's Gratitude,* at the National Film/Television Archive, runs 876 feet.

124. See "Comments on the Films," *MPW* (15 January 1910), 56, and (22 January 1910), 92; and "Reviews of Licensed Films," *NYDM* (5 March 1910), 16. Stanfield makes this argument forcefully in "The Western," 103–106.

125. A review of Lubin's *The White Chief,* for instance, begins with "Indian pictures are the fashion"—see "Reviews of New Films," *NYDM* (8 August 1908), 7.

126. In his analysis of western stories in turn-of-the-century mass magazines, Ohmann finds very few "Indian subjects"—see Ohmann, *Selling Culture,* 329–337.

127. Jenks, "Dime Novel Makers," 110.

128. See, for instance, Edmund Pearson, *Dime Novels* (Boston: Little, Brown, 1929), 218; and Bold, *Selling the West,* 15.

129. See, for instance, J. Edward Leithead and Edward T. Leblanc, *"Rough Rider Weekly* and the Ted Strong Saga," *Dime Novel Round-Up* 41.7 (July 1972), 1–27.

130. Balshofer and Miller, *One Reel a Week,* 40.

131. Balshofer's remark does not explain, of course, a spectator's interest (as later pages will explore) in *The Cowboy Girls* or even *The Female Bandit,* which he himself made for Bison.

132. See, for instance, Brian Dippie, *The Vanishing American: White Attitudes and U.S. Indian Policy* (Middletown, Conn.: Wesleyan University Press, 1982), 197–269; and Julie Schimmel, "Inventing 'the Indian,'" in Truettner, *The West as America,* 171–173. Rosaldo's concept is discussed in Ann Fabian, "History for the Masses: Commercializing the Western Past," in Cronon, Miles, and Gitlin, *Under an Open Sky,* 232–233.

133. The felicitous phrase "thanatological tenderness" comes from Ella Shohat and Robert Stam, *Unthinking Eurocentrism: Multiculturalism and the Media* (London: Routledge, 1994), 118. Fraser's "End of the Trail" was first modeled in 1894 and enlarged to monumental size for the 1915 Panama-Pacific Exposition in San Francisco—see Schimmel, "Inventing 'the Indian,'" 172–174, 353.

134. Dippie, *The Vanishing American*, 207. Dippie cites Mary Alice Harriman, "The Congress of American Aborigines at the Omaha Exposition," *Overland Monthly* 33 (June 1899), 508. See, also, Trachtenberg, *The Incorporation of America*, 35–36.

135. See, for instance, Rydell, *All the World's a Fair*, 167–178.

136. See, for instance, Trachtenberg, *The Incorporation of America*, 33–34. Stanfield mentions "assimilation by other means" than miscegenation for the Indian, but does not develop the point, in "The Western," 106.

137. Slotkin, *Gunfighter Nation*, 91–92.

138. This quote comes from the *State Sun*, as cited in Stanley Feldstein, ed., *The Poisoned Tongue: A Documentary History of American Racism and Prejudice* (New York: Morrow, 1972), 258.

139. David M. Perry, *Proceedings of the N.A.M.* (1903), quoted in Slotkin, *Gunfighter Nation*, 91.

140. Alex Nemerov, "Doing the 'Old America,'" in Truettner, *The West as America*, 297–303.

141. Although this essay probably was written in the spring of 1911, it is very suggestive of how immigrant spectators responded to "Indian and Western subjects." The audience of this nickelodeon on Houston Street was Jewish, "looking undersized according to the Anglo-Saxon standard." See Mary Heaton Vorse, "Some Picture Show Audiences," *Outlook* 98 (24 June 1911), 442–443, 445.

142. One of the *World*'s reviewers, commenting on Lubin's *Red Eagle's Love Affair*, however, suggests that, for many whites, there was a limit to this assimilation: "Whites can never be induced to accept [Indians] upon equal terms, no matter how well educated they are." See "Comments on the Films," *MPW* (2 July 1910), 24.

143. G. M. Anderson's Jewishness, which was not well known at the time (he had changed his name from Aaronson), offers an interesting corollary here for, as Broncho Billy, this "Yiddisher Cowboy" became, arguably, the first American film cowboy hero. Because Broncho Billy frequently was an outlaw who turned good, the figure offered a strikingly doubled model of assimilation. One of Bison's early releases had been a comic western, *Yiddisher Cowboy*—see the Bison ad in *MPW* (14 August 1909), 229.

144. Louis Reeves Harrison, "A Great Motion Picture and Its Lesson," *MPW* (4 June 1910), 933—reprinted in Stanley Kauffmann and Bruce Henstell, eds., *American Film Criticism: From the Beginnings to Citizen Kane* (New York: Liveright, 1972), 43–45. Chon Noriega has a fine analysis of Jackson's novel, Biograph's film, and Harrison's review in "Birth of the Southwest: Social Protest, Tourism, and D. W. Griffith's *Ramona*," in Bernardi, *The Birth of Whiteness*, 203–226. When Biograph relocated its production unit to California in early 1910, this elegiac nostalgia first reached a kind of culmination in *A Romance of the Western Hills*, where not only was Indian life allegedly depicted "as it exists today" but an "Indian maiden" (also played by Mary Pickford) and her lover served as forceful models of morality for a rich white family— see "Biograph Company Migrates to the Land of Sunshine and Flowers," *MPW* (29 January 1910), 120; "Los Angeles Home of Three Film Companies," 256; Balshofer and Miller, *One Reel a Week*, 55; and "Reviews of Licensed Films," *NYDM* (23 April 1910), 17.

145. These "cowboy girl" westerns have eluded historians partly because very few survive in film archives such as the Library of Congress (Washington) and the National Film/Television Archive (London); a good number of them only recently have been restored and made available at the Nederlands Filmmuseum (Amsterdam).

146. See "Comments on the Films," *MPW* (15 January 1910), 56, and (26 February 1910), 299.

147. See "Comments on the Films," *MPW* (19 February 1910), 258; and Louis Reeves Harrison, "Stagecraft," *MPW* (14 May 1910), 774.

148. See the Selig ad in *NYDM* (30 April 1910), 20; "Comments on the Films," *MPW* (14 May 1910), 785; and "Reviews of Licensed Films," *NYDM* (14 May 1910), 19.

149. For other reviews, see "Ramona in Picture Film," *NYDM* (14 May 1910), 21; "Realism in Moving Pictures," *MPW* (14 May 1910), 775; "Reviews of Licensed Films," *NYDM* (4 June 1910), 16; and "Comments on the Films," *MPW* (4 June 1910), 942. Gunning focuses on panoramic compositions in *Ramona*—see Gunning, *D. W. Griffith*, 270.

150. Some months later, there was an interesting pictorial contrast to this description in *World's Work:* one page had no less than six frame stills from *Ramona*, but the next had two photos of nickelodeon entrances that stressed how important women and children were as daytime audiences—see Asa Steele, "The Moving Picture Show," *World's Work* (February 1911), 14023–14024.

151. See Nancy Tillman Romalov, "Unearthing the Historical Reader, or, Reading Girls' Reading," in Larry Sullivan and Lydia Cushman Schurman, eds., *Pioneers, Passionate Ladies, and Private Eyes* (New York: Hawthorn Press, 1996), 87–101; and Sherrie Inness, "On the Road and in the Air: Gender and Technology in Girls' Automobile and Airplane Serials, 1909–1932," *Journal of Popular Culture* 30.2 (Fall 1996), 47–60.

152. *The Motor Girls* began publication in 1910; *The Ranch Girls,* in 1911; *The Outdoor Girls,* in 1913. They were preceded by series named after individual heroines, such as *The Bobbsey Twins* (1904) and *Dorothy Dale* (1908).

153. None of these early "cowboy girl" westerns seem to survive, but later ones do at the Nederlands Filmmuseum: for instance, Vitagraph's *A Girl of the West* (1912), *The Craven* (1912), and *How States Are Made* (1912); Essanay's *Broncho Billy's Escape* (1912); and Solax's *Two Little Rangers* (1913). See, also, Ben Singer, "Female Power in the Serial-Queen Melodrama: The Etiology of an Anomaly," *camera obscura* 22 (January 1990)—reprinted in Abel, *Silent Film,* 163–193. Interestingly, the first (and only mildly successful) of these serials, Edison's *What Happened to Mary?* (1912), was serialized in *Ladies' World,* a tabloid-size mail-order monthly that addressed "a poorer, more rural readership," in contrast to the more urban, middle-class readership of *Ladies' Home Journal*—see Gardner Wood, "Magazines and Motion Pictures" *MPW* (11 July 1914), 194. For an excellent analysis of these two monthlies, see Ellen Gruber Garvey, *The Adman in the Parlor: Magazines and the Gendering of Consumer Culture, 1880s to 1910s* (New York: Oxford University Press, 1996), 9, 137–147.

154. See, for instance, the highly selective quotes from student essays in the San Francisco *Sunday Call* (15 May 1910), reprinted in "A Little Child Shall Lead Them," *MPW* (4 June 1910), 936. The first "authoritative" survey of schoolchildren was done by the Child Welfare Committee of New York, in late 1910, and concluded that three-fourths of the boys liked "Cowboys and Indians" best—see "Pictures That Children Like," *FI* (21 January 1911), 3.

155. Romalov, "Unearthing the Historical Reader," 90–92.

156. See, for instance, Kathryn Fuller, *At the Picture Show: Small Town Audiences and the Creation of Movie Fan Culture* (Washington, D.C.: Smithsonian Institution Press, 1996), 115–168; and Gaylyn Studlar, "The Perils of Pleasure? Fan Magazine Discourse as Women's Commodified Culture in the 1920s," *Wide Angle* 13.1 (1991)—reprinted in Abel, *Silent Film,* 263–297.

157. Anderson, "The Role of the Western Film Genre in Industry Competition," 25 n. 65. See, also, Michael Davis, *The Exploitation of Pleasure: A Study of Commercial Recreations in New York City* (New York: Russell Sage Foundation, 1911), 29–30, 34–35.

158. See, for instance, the half-page ad in *FI* (25 June 1910), 7; James McQuade, "Famous Cowboys in Motion Pictures," *FI* (25 June 1910), 9–10; and the special poster for the film reprinted in *MPW* (2 July 1910), 23. Tom Mix, of course, would soon become a star for Selig. An incomplete 35mm print of *Ranch Life in the Great Southwest*, running 622 feet, survives at the National Film/Television Archive. As an instance of its importance, *Ranch Life in the Great Southwest* was featured by the Colonial Theatre in a special ad in *DMRL* (11 August 1910), 5.

159. See "Kalem Indian Stories Popular," *MPW* (25 June 1910), 1099; and "Reviews of Licensed Films," *NYDM* (18 June 1910), 19.

160. See the Essanay ad for *Broncho Billy's Redemption* in *FI* (30 July 1910), 20.

161. Paramount's first manager and general representative were, respectively, I. Bernstein (Union Film Exchange) and J. Levine (Imperial Film Exchange)—see "Notes of the Trade," *MPW* (7 May 1910), 741; and the Paramount ad in *MPW* (21 May 1910), 842.

162. See, for instance, the Nestor ad in *MPW* (30 July 1910), 275; and "Champion Films Make Good," *MPW* (17 September 1910), 626. Mark Dinterfass had been associated with Actophone, a reorganized version of Cameraphone, before setting up Champion; I. W. Ullman had been head of Film Importing and Trading before becoming the principal owner of Columbia—see Bowser, *The Transformation of Cinema*, 79, 157–158.

163. See the American Film Company ads in *NYDM* (5 October 1910), 31, and in *MPW* (8 October 1910), 817; and "The American Film Manufacturing Co.," *MPW* (19 November 1910), 1162. American Film was the first Independent manufacturer to be located in Chicago. All three men—Aitken, Freuler, and Hutchinson—would be involved in the formation of Mutual in early 1912. See, also, Bowser, *The Transformation of Cinema*, 79.

164. By the spring of 1911, the company was specializing in westerns alone, with its chief filmmaker, Allan Dwan—see Bowser, *The Transformation of Cinema*, 172.

165. In the conclusion of Pathé's *Gold Prospectors,* for instance, the "little son" of a miner killed by Indians gets to shoot the Indian chief in revenge—see "Reviews of New Films," *NYDM* (8 May 1909), 16.

166. See, for instance, James McQuade, "Pathé American Studio Announced by M. Berst," *FI* (9 April 1910), 1, 3; "Pathé Progress," *MPW* (9 April 1910), 557; "New Pathé Studio," *NYDM* (9 April 1910), 18; "What Pathé Is Doing," *Nick* (15 April 1910), 216; and "Pathé's American Film," *FI* (14 May 1910), 5.

167. See the review of *The Girl from Arizona* in "Reviews of Licensed Films," *NYDM* (28 May 1910), 20; and "Pathé's American Company Makes Good," *MPW* (30 July 1910), 246. Pathé itself called *The Girl from Arizona* a "sensational western drama"—see *Pathé Weekly Bulletin* (16 May 1910), n.p. In another telling sign of Pathé's capitulation to American "taste," its second film was a "remake" of *The Great Train Robbery* as *The Great Train Hold-Up:* the 35mm print of *The Great Train Hold-Up,* at the National Film/Television Archive, runs 717 feet.

168. See "Reviews of Licensed Films," *NYDM* (25 June 1910), 20, and (30 July 1910), 27. *A Cheyenne Brave* was described as "an Indian Classic . . . an intensely exciting Indian story without a white man, woman or child in it"—see the Pathé ad in *FI* (20 August 1910), 24.

169. See "Comments on the Films," *MPW* (26 November 1910), 1238. See, also, the reviews of *The Girl from Arizona, White Fawn's Devotion,* and *The Cowboy's Sweetheart and the*

Bandit, in "Comments on the Films," *MPW* (28 May 1910), 889, (2 July 1910), 24, and (6 August 1910), 296.

170. See, for instance, "Reviews of Licensed Films," *NYDM* (28 May 1910), 20, and (25 June 1910), 20; and "Comments on the Films," *MPW* (27 August 1910), 463.

171. See Spencer, "Notes on the Los Angeles Studios," *MPW* (28 February 1910), 302; and "James Young Deer," 999.

172. See "Pathé Progress," *MPW* (15 October 1910), 867.

173. See Bowser, *The Transformation of Cinema,* 176. Even the *World* published an article debunking the overproduction of "these stupid Indian and Cowboy themes," in "The Indian and the Cowboy," *MPW* (19 December 1910), 1399. Pathé may have gone on making Indian subjects because they continued to be popular (and profitable) in Europe.

174. Pathé also continued to make Indian subjects, which, as in *A Cheyenne Brave,* asked audiences to distinguish between tribes of Plains Indians rather than simply assume that Indians were undifferentiated *others;* in films such as *The Cheyenne's Bride,* Young Deer even had the audacity to cast a white actor in disguise as the villainous Indian opposite his own heroic figure.

175. See "Editorial," *MPW* (15 October 1910), 867.

AFTERWORD

1. "Notes from the Manufacturers," *MPW* (11 July 1910), 165.

2. Lux Graphicus, "On the Screen," *MPW* (22 January 1910), 90.

3. This sense of American imperialism already was widespread as early as 1895, when "the National Association of Manufacturers made overproduction the main theme of its organizational meeting" and invited William McKinley to deliver a keynote address on "access to overseas markets as the 'only promise of relief'"—see Richard Ohmann, *Selling Culture: Magazines, Markets, and Class at the Turn of the Century* (London: Verso, 1996), 55. Literary figures like William Dean Howells, however, did not shirk from such a stance, as when, in 1902, he wrote that literary exiles were the "vanguard of the great army of adventurers destined to overrun the earth from these shores, and exploit all foreign countries to our advantage"—quoted in Alex Zwerdling, "Anglo-Saxon Panic: The Turn-of-the-Century Response to 'Alien' Immigrants," *Ideas from the National Humanities Center,* 1.2 (Winter 1993), 44.

4. Thompson contends that "American producers began a systematic push into foreign markets" in early 1909, but her own chronology suggests this did not occur until late 1909 or even the spring of 1910—see Kristin Thompson, *Exporting Entertainment: America in the World Film Market, 1907–1934* (London: BFI, 1985), 28, 200.

5. It is worth noting that, for the trade press, by 1911, the "one American article of import out of which fortunes [were] being coined in every corner of the world . . . [was] the picturesque—what is bizarre, exciting, and unusual in American life, chiefly scenes of cowboys and Indians"—see "Exporting the American Film," *Motography* (August 1911), 90.

6. See the "Motion Picture Merit List Coupon" and "'Mirror' Merit List," *NYDM* (19 October 1910), 29 and 30.

7. "Merit List," *NYDM* (8 February 1911), 33–34. Problems immediately developed with this "contest," which required readers to send in a dated coupon with their list, and the *Mirror*

had to defend the disinterestedness of its process and take steps to discount any "padding"—see "Purity of Merit List," *NYDM* (9 November 1910), 30.

8. The exceptions that I have identified from 1909 are Biograph's *Pippa Passes* (81 votes), Pathé's *Drink* (38), Gaumont's *Mozart's Last Requiem* (26), and Pathé's *Rigoletto* (25).

9. The other Gaumont titles were *Fishing Smack* (37) and *Samson's Betrayal* (27); the other Pathé titles were *Love Ye One Another* (37), *Saved by Divine Providence* (31), and *Sunshine in Poverty Row* (29). Pathé fared somewhat better in an informal survey conducted by the *World* in the spring of 1911. One exhibitor recalled its 1909 *Trip through Ceylon* as the "greatest scenic" and its 1910 *Abraham Lincoln's Clemency* as the greatest "historical drama"; another still considered the *Passion Play* "the most impressive picture" ever—see "Public Opinion Controls," *MPW* (29 April 1911), 933–934.

10. Edison had twelve titles, Kalem had seven, and Essanay had six. Only Selig and Lubin had fewer, at four and three, respectively.

11. Michael Denning, *Mechanic Accents: Dime Novels and Working-Class Culture in America* (London: Verso, 1987), 201–213.

12. Charles M. Harvey, "The Dime Novel in American Life," *Atlantic*, 100 (July 1907), 37–45.

13. Denning, *Mechanic Accents*, 202.

INDEX

Italicized numbers indicate pages with illustrations.

Redemption (1910), 284n160; *Cowboy and the Squaw, The* (1910), 167; *David Garrick* (1908), 269n51; *Girl and the Fugitive, The* (1910), 275n49; *Heart of a Cowboy, The* (1909), 157, *157*; *Indian Trailer, The* (1909), 157, 166; *James Boys in Missouri, The* (1908), 154; *Mexican's Gratitude, A* (1909), 167, 281n123; *Road Agents, The* (1909), 156, 161; *Sensational Logging* (1910), 132; *Two Brothers* (1909), 269n49; *Western Chivalry* (1910), 171; *Western Maid* (1910) 171

Exhibition services: Biograph, 2, 3, 5, 7, 9; Kalatechnoscope, 3, 202n51; Kinetograph, 3; Kinodrome, 3, 5, 6, 7, 10, 26, 29, 80, 195n52; Lubin Cineograph, 5, 204n90; Lumière Cinématographe, 2, 10; Selig Polyscope, 4, 7, 27, 200n27; Shepard's Moving Pictures, 24–25, 26, 43, 113, 202n49, 207n120; Vitagraph, 3, 5, 6, 7, *9*, 12, 14, 21, 22, 24, 26, 29, 194n36, 202n49, 219n97, 233n34

Faivre, Abel, 229n9

Family vaudeville theaters: Auditorium (Cedar Rapids), 27; Bijou (Des Moines), 26, 27, 31, 33, 80; Bijou (Duluth), 23, 199n12, 205n102; Bijou (Fall River), 202n49; Bijou (Portland, Oregon), 27; Boston (Lowell), 4, 32, 202n55; Casto (Boston), 202n55; Crystal (Milwaukee), 26; Dewey (Oakland), 207n122; Dreamland (Decatur), 207n122; Edison (Seattle), 6; Electric (Waterloo), 207n122; Empire (Los Angeles), 207n122; Gem (Lynn), 4; Gem (Sioux City), 22; Grand (Milwaukee), 26; Grand (Portland, Oregon), *27*, 27–28, 33, 35, *36*, 118, 202n63; Grover's Garden (Lynn), 6, 7; La Petite (Seattle), 6; Lyric (Portland, Oregon), 23, 27; Mechanic's Hall (Lynn), 4; Novelty (Topeka), 224n154; Park (Evansville), 6; Park (Youngstown), 23; People's (Cedar Rapids), 27, 43; People's (Lowell), 4, 33, 40, 202n55; Savoy (New Bedford), 207n122; Seaside (Marblehead), 5; Star (Atlanta), 26; Star (Pittsburgh), 26; Star (Portland, Oregon), 27, 32, 202nn58, 63; Star (Saint Louis), 27; Unique (San Francisco), 10; Zoo (Toledo), 207n122

Faure, Gabriel, 116

Feminization, cultural, 11–12, 33, 41, 66–69, 117, 118–119, 123, 125, 163–164, 171–172, 256n79, 271n70, 279n101

Fielding, Raymond, 153

Film d'Art (France), 116, 127, 129

Film d'Art films: *Assassination of the Duke of Guise, The* (1908), 129, 131, 140–141, 248n47, 257n89, 258n96, 274n40; *Grande Bretèche, La* (1909), 134, *134*; *Père Milon* (1909), 131, 157; *Return of Ulysses, The* (1909), 141; *Scar, The* (1908), 131, 248n47; *Tosca, La* (1909), 116, 129; *Tower of Nestle, The* (1909), 131

Film d'Arte Italiana (Italy), 270n72

Film Index, 85, 123, 124, 126, 129, 135, 143, 145, 146, 147, 156, 160, 230n29, 235n57, 248n54, 264n8, 265n16, 275n49

Film Service Association (FSA), 84, 90, 95, 151, 152, 222n132, 231n1, 232n22, 234n48, 235n53, 241n119

Fiske, John, "Manifest Destiny" (1885), 158, 276n60

Fleckles, Morris, 99

Foucault, Michel, 198n3, 223n152

Fox, William, 30, 51, 61, 62, 64, 71, 94, 100, 221n121, 266n22

Fraser, James Earle, "End of the Trail" (1894), 168, 281n133

Frelinger, Gregg, 116–117, 248n53; *Motion Picture Piano Music* (1909), 116

French, James Bernard, 52

Freuler, John, 173, 214n29, 284n163

Fuller, Kathryn, 150, 201n47, 221n117

Fuqua, Chas. [Charles], 172

Fynes, J. Austin, 30, 61, 64, 195n53

Ganes, William, 61

Garland, Hamlin, 126

Gasnier, Louis, 173

Gates, Eleanor, 118

Gaudreault, André, 6, 212n53

Gaumont (France), 51, 57, 70, 83, 93, 106, 107, 151, 178, 198n18, 212n55, 215n42, 233n23, 234n41, 257n88, 276n55

Gaumont Chronophone, 114, 247n30

Gaumont films: *Enfant prodigue, L'* (1907), 247n40, 260n136; *Fishing Smack* (1910), 286n9; *Mozart's Last Requiem* (1909), 286n8; *Passion Play* (1906), 212n55; *Penitent of Florence, A* (1910), 248n52; *Red Man's Revenge* (1908), 151; *Samson's Betrayal* (1910), 286n9; *Story of Esther, The* (1910), 227n191; *Waters of Life, The* (1907), 212n55

Gauntier, Gene, 148

Compositor:	Impressions Book and Journal Services, Inc.
Text:	10/12 Baskerville
Display:	Baskerville
Printer and Binder:	Malloy Lithographing, Inc.